THE WASHINGTON STAR
Garden Book

by Wilbur H. Youngman
Star Garden Editor

INTRODUCTION

The Washington Star Garden Book by Wilbur H. Youngman, Garden Editor of The Washington Star, is a simplified guide designed specifically for use in the metropolitan area of Maryland, Virginia and Washington, D.C.

Most gardening enthusiasts are part time cultivators. Their limited time, and in many cases, limited space must be used to the best advantage. These requirements, and the unique conditions and special difficulties of the area, are the factors Mr. Youngman considers in the preparation of the manual.

To help you have a better garden, Mr. Youngman tests varieties offered by seed companies to determine how they fare under local conditions. He attempts to bring gardeners the best and most authoritative information available on plants, shrubs, trees, and how they grow here.

The garden book is revised every two years in order to keep the gardener up to date with changing plant varieties, new research in fertilizers and pesticides and other improvements that will benefit him. You can be sure the latest and best gardening information available is contained in this book.

A recognized gardening authority, Mr. Youngman has been Star Garden Editor since 1938 and has written The Star Garden Book since its inception in 1944.

In addition to being an accredited judge for the American Rose Society for many years, he has received many awards and is an honorary member of many gardening groups. He himself has been an active gardener for many years. Mr. Youngman's particular favorites are roses, camellias, azaleas, daylilies, Oriental poppies, and daffodils. He has a half acre garden at his home in Silver Spring, Md.

Mr. Youngman is the editor of The Star's Garden Pages published every Sunday throughout the year and, in addition, every Friday during the Spring and Fall growing seasons.

In these pages the reader will find timely suggestions, authoritative articles and news of general interest for profitable year-round gardening.

THE WASHINGTON STAR
WASHINGTON, D. C.

TABLE OF CONTENTS

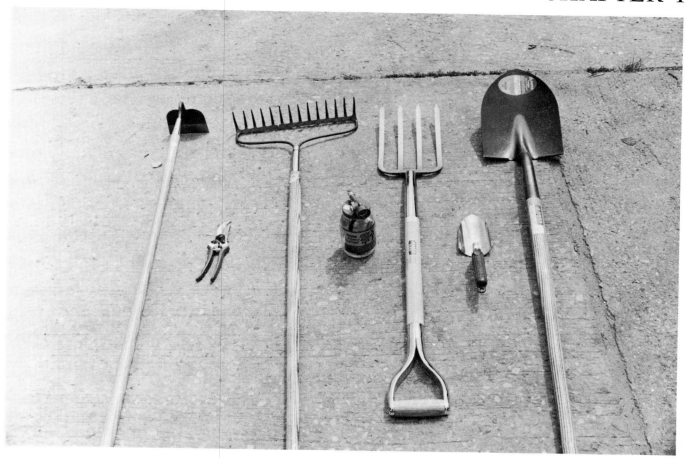

CHAPTER I

SOILS AND SOIL PREPARATION

Testing the Soil

The list of flowers and vegetables that may be grown successfully in this area contains several that do best in a "sweet" soil. What is a sweet soil? Soils range from highly acid to highly alkaline. The midpoint in the soil chemists scale, which is commonly known as the pH scale, is 7 (neutral). Less than 7 in the rating means acid; above 7, sweet or alkaline soils. The only importance of this technical point is that we may need to know the meaning of the scale if we send our soil samples to a soil-testing laboratory.

Some plants, such as azaleas, Turk's cap lilies, tomatoes and shade-loving plants, thrive in an acid soil. Most kinds of vegetables and flowers prefer a slightly acid or neutral soil. Still others, such as California poppies, pinks, onions, lettuce and spinach do best in a sweeter soil. Fortunately, most plants are tolerant and will do fairly well under the general conditions that exist in this area if the soil is fairly rich and not too dry or too wet. But to get the most out of fertilizers the soil should be at the most favorable level of acidity or sweetness for each type of plant.

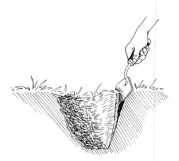

A thin slice from the vertical surface exposed by removing a spadefull of soil is ample for a soil test.

What Does pH Mean?

(Descriptive name for pH values)

	pH		pH
Extremely acid	Below 4.5	Mildly alkaline	7.4-7.8
Very strongly acid	4.5-5.0	Moderately alkaline	7.9-8.4
Strongly acid	5.1-5.5	Strongly alkaline	8.5-9.0
Medium acid	5.6-6.0	Very strongly alkaline	9.1 and
Slightly acid	6.1-6.5		higher
Neutral	6.6-7.3		

1

Since we expect our plants to make good growth, it will probably pay us to test our soils with pieces of red and blue litmus paper purchased at the drugstore. If the blue paper turns red when placed between moist pieces of soil, the soil is acid. If the red paper turns blue, the soil is sweet. If both turn purple the soil is neutral.

For the gardeners who wish to obtain more information about soil, there are testing kits of simple as well as of complicated equipment. However, it is suggested that the simplest and surest method of all is to take a sample (a tobacco can will hold all that is necessary) and send it to a soil laboratory. For residents of Maryland the Soils Department of the University of Maryland will make such tests. For non-residents the charge is $1 per sample.

In taking a sample for testing be sure to take a thin slice to a depth of 6 inches, which is the usual depth of the plant bed. To do this remove a spadeful of soil. This should expose a vertical soil section from which the thin slice is readily taken. If the garden plot is not uniform it is desirable to take several samples which are then placed in a pail or box and thoroughly mixed before drawing the sample for mailing.

A brief note giving the location and the intended use will help the soil people in giving advice as to the best treatment for improving the soil. Usually this advice will indicate the amount of lime and humus (decayed vegetable matter) needed to make it productive.

The Virginia Polytechnic Institute, Blacksburg, Va., will make tests for residents of Virginia. The United States Department of Agriculture does not test soils.

Lime? How? When?

Some gardeners add a bit of lime to their garden plot each year, perhaps as a spring ritual. This may keep their soil in the desired state of sweetness except where heavy applications of manure or humus are made. However, unguided applications of excessive quantities may be more harmful than beneficial since lime can lock up needed soil minerals. Overliming is detrimental to vegetables and to many annuals as most of them do best in a slightly acid soil.

Most soils in this area are acid. To make them suitable for garden crops they should be made neutral or only slightly acid. To accomplish this, lime may be added in the form of ground limestone, ground oystershell lime, or hydrated lime. All forms may be obtained

Use of Finely Ground Limestone to Make Soil Sweeter

Change of pH	Pounds per 1,000 sq. ft.
From 3.5 to 4.5	35
4.5 to 5.5	40
5.5 to 6.5	50

Important: Light soils (sands and loamy sands) require smaller amounts while heavier soils (clays and mucks) require more than the above amounts which are for *loams*.

locally. The hydrated lime is most active and should be avoided for most garden uses.

The two recommended — ground limestone and pulverized oystershell lime — are slow acting and will not

Use of Chemicals to Make Soil Acid

Change of pH	Sulphur	Aluminum sulphate (pounds per 100 feet)
From 8.0 to 7.0	2.0	4.5
7.5 to 7.0	1.75	3.5
7.5 to 6.5	2.0	5.0
7.5 to 6.0	3.5	7.5
7.0 to 6.5	1.5	2.5
7.0 to 6.0	2.0	5.5
6.5 to 6.0	1.5	3.0
6.5 to 5.5	2.5	6.5
6.0 to 5.5	1.5	3.5
6.0 to 5.0	3.0	7.5
5.5 to 5.0	1.5	4.0
5.5 to 4.5	2.4	8.5

It is not considered good practice to change the soil pH reaction more than 1 pH unit in one year.

injure seed or plants. However, because they are slow acting, it takes twice as much, but the benefits last longer.

Ground limestone and ground oystershell lime of equal fineness have about the same value and effect. Dolomitic ground limestone may be preferred as it provides a small amount of magnesium, an element frequently deficient in local soils.

Lime is ordinarily applied after the ground has been spaded or plowed and before harrowing or raking. An application of from 20 to 60 pounds per 1,000 square feet will be sufficient under most conditions. Twenty pounds of hydrated lime will only whiten the surface, while 60 pounds will give a distinct coating.

Four pounds of ground limestone per 100 square feet will reduce the acidity on the pH scale one degree.

Lime serves several purposes, but it is not classed as plant food. It is a soil conditioner. It makes certain plant foods accessible, which under more acid conditions are not available to plants. Lime renders heavy clays more loamy — not so compact. Lime speeds the decay of humus and thus liberates the plant food there. Beneficial soil bacteria do not live and function in the more acid soils — especially the nitrogen-gathering bacteria. Lime locks up some harmful elements such as aluminum sulphate.

Lime and manure should not be mixed or applied at the same time. Hydrated lime releases the nitrogen from the manure in the form of ammonia and it is lost. If the manure is plowed under before the lime is added, the soil can absorb the nitrogen.

Compost

While composting is an old-time garden practice, it is not practiced as freely as it should be by the city gardener. Where there are shortages of animal manures, when chemical fertilizers and peat moss are rather costly, the need for compost is likely to be acute.

The soil needs vegetable matter for several purposes: 1. To hold moisture for the growing plants—a reservoir. 2. To make the soil more friable (loose) so that the plant roots may penetrate it in search of moisture and plant food. 3. In decaying the vegetable material releases plant food and makes it available to growing plants. 4. The process of decomposition produces a weak soil acid which dissolves some of the soil minerals not soluble in water, making them available to the plants. 5. Soil bacteria cannot live and function without a certain amount of plant material (humus) being in the soil. 6. Soils rich in humus are cool soils and plant systems function better in a cool moist soil than in a hot dry one.

The above is only a partial list of the functions of humus in the soil, but they are the major ones and are indicative of its importance to the garden. Now, since not all gardeners can afford to depend upon the purchase of animal manures or peat moss, we must turn to other sources.

The saving and rotting of leaves, weeds, grass and other vegetable matter is known as composting. A pit or bin in a shady, out-of-the-way place is all that it takes in the way of equipment. While the plant material will rot down in time without any supplemental help, lime, sulphate of ammonia and water will greatly speed the process. Animal manures are also useful for this purpose. Frequent forking-over helps.

Commercial mixtures are available for adding to the plant material to aid in speeding the decomposition, but gardeners may use the ordinary garden fertilizer. Still

A compost pile is built-up of layers of plant material, soil and chemicals (lime, ammonium sulphate and superphosphate).

others prepare a mixture such as this one: 45 per cent ammonium sulphate, 40 per cent ground limestone and 15 percent superphosphate. This is used at the rate of 7 to 8 pounds per 100 pounds of dry material. For green material the rate of application is cut in half—3½ to 4 pounds per 100 pounds. When such a method of composting is practiced the resulting material is a rich plant food.

Ordinarily the compost is not ready for use the first year, since bacterial action largely ceases during the winter months. However, partially rotted compost may be mixed with the soil in the spring or used as a mulch during the summer. When well rotted, it is most useful spread on the freshly turned soil and raked into it. This helps to prevent crusting and is especially valuable when spread over the rows of seed, particularly if well sieved.

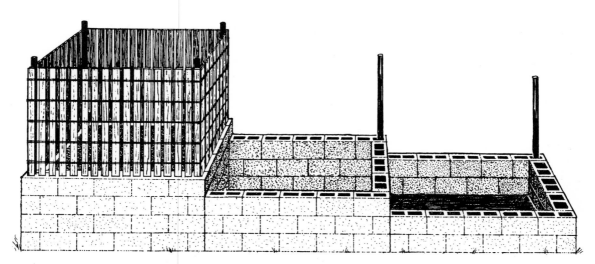

An easily constructed three section compost maker. Cement blocks and stakes or iron pipe are used in lieu of permanent construction. The large bin is for the freshly collected leaves, weeds, etc. The middle bin is less than half in size, it receives the partially rotted compost from the large bin. The third bin, the smallest, holds the finished compost until used.

Green Manures

Compost is one way of adding humus to the garden soil. Another way, one that will appeal to many gardeners who dislike to fuss with compost piles, is the planting of green manure crops. A green manure is a crop planted in the garden specifically to be plowed or spaded into the soil for its improvement.

Rye, annual ryegrass, vetch, crimson clover, soybeans, Korean lespedeza and many other crops may be used as green manures. In this area, crimson clover is one of the most effective green manures, but it should be sown in late August or early September if it is to make suitable fall growth. Since dry periods frequently occur at this season, and the soil moisture is too low to enable the clover seed to germinate, it cannot always be depended upon.

For late fall seeding—September and early October —rye and vetch are two of the most commonly planted green manures. While they may be planted separately, the usual practice is to mix them. The rye provides the bulk of the plant material. The vetch supplies nitrogen as well as plant tissue.

For spring planting, soybeans, rape, Korean lespedeza and buckwheat are well adapted to this area. However, a spring-sown crop prevents the use of soil in the spring and summer so most gardeners prefer to use those adapted to fall planting.

Crimson clover may be sown between the vegetable rows at the last cultivation. Rye and vetch are often sown the same way.

Where a legume is used as a cover crop for the first time, the seed should be inoculated to stimulate bacterial action. Inoculants may be obtained from a garden supply house or from seed dealers. Ask for the specific inoculant for the seed to be planted. The inoculant is usually diluted and then sprinkled over the seed and well mixed with it. Immediately after mixing, the seed should be planted. If there must be some delay, cover the seed to prevent drying, which kills the bacteria. The sowing of inoculated seed should be done on a cloudy day.

Green manures should be spaded or plowed under before they become tall, woody and hard to handle. To avoid delaying the planting of early spring crops, plant only a part of the garden with green manures each season, the area without the green manures being the part reserved for the early spring crops — potatoes, peas, cabbage, broccoli, etc.

Animal Manures

All animal manures that are obtainable, including poultry, should be spread and turned under with spade or plow. They will furnish nitrogen and small quanties of the other two major plant foods — phosphate and potash — as well as humus. Lacking animal manures, compost, decayed straw, weeds — in fact any kind of decayed or partly decayed plant materials — should be added to the soil. These materials, in rotting, liberate plant foods, and so should be incorporated in the soil before planting time. When merely spread on the surface of the ground, only the plant food which may be washed out of them by the rain becomes available to the growing crops.

While the animal manures add nitrogen and humus to the soil, most soils are deficient in both phosphate and potash which all plants need. These are readily available as superphosphate and muriate of potash. However, most commercial fertilizers contain reasonable quantities of both, and supplementary amounts will be needed in only a few cases.

Measuring Chemicals for Compost Heaps

(From Agriculture Department Tables)

In making compost heaps with oak leaves as the chief source of organic matter, together with some grass and other plant materials, chemical aids are needed to disintegrate the more durable parts. If, however, a considerable quantity of lawn clippings and other plant tissue is used, the weight or measure of the chemicals named below may be somewhat reduced. When manure constitutes half the organic matter, no nitrogen is required — only the phosphate and limestone. No limestone should be used if resulting compost is to be applied to blueberries, azaleas, or similar acid-loving plants.

The compost may be prepared in layers: a layer of garden soil or dark-colored surface soil out of the woods about ½ to 2 inches thick, alternating with each 6 or 12-inch layer of fresh plant material. When finished, the whole should be covered with 2 to 4 inches of soil.

Volume measures of chemicals are added separately to each bushel of plant material in making a compost pile and at specified rates per ton of material.

Chemicals	Weight Needed per ton of Material	Volume Measure Needed per Bushel of Material [1]
Method I:	Pounds	Cups
a. Either ammonium sulphate	80	1
or ammonium nitrate	50	½
b. Either ground dolomitic limestone [2]	60	⅔
or woodashes [2]	80	1½
c. Superphosphate	50	½
d. Magnesium sulfate (Epsom salts) [3]	8	1 Tbs.
Method II:		
a. Mixer fertilizer (5-10-5)	300	3 Cups
b. Ground dolomitic limestone [2]	60	⅔

[1] Packed tightly with the hands.
[2] For acid compost omit lime, limestone, and wood ashes.
[3] Epsom salts to be added only if dolomitic limestone is unavailable and ordinary limestone is used (at the same rate).

SOILS AND SOIL PREPARATION

Commercial Fertilizers

Applications of fertilizers to plants or the lawn are not always the "magic cure-all" that many envision. Plant food will not overcome poor soil preparation or correct faulty drainage. Using grass seed mixtures not adaptable to environmental conditions often results in lawn failure. An active feeding program cannot overcome this condition. Plants requiring acid soil often will not grow well or will fail in an alkaline soil. An active feeding program will not help unless the soil is made medium acid.

Plants need many minerals in addition to organic matter for growth, but we have assumed that we need only the three major minerals—nitrogen, phosphate and potassium. The commonly sold fertilizers supply these three in the usual formula of 5-10-5 or similar mixture. The three numbers printed on the tag or the package itself relate to the percentages of nitrogen (5%), phosphate (10%) and potassium (5%) in the packaged material. Few of the commercial fertilizers contain any of the minor or trace elements. Our soils may be deficient in one or more of them. It has been shown that iron is lacking in both azalea and rose plantings in this area. The foliage turns a yellowish green with the veins sharply outlined. Iron may be and often is present, but in a form that is not available to the plants. This deficiency may be corrected by increasing the acidity of the soil to release the iron or by applying iron in a form that is available to them.

Other minerals such as boron and magnesium may be deficient, but this can be demonstrated only with a test or by sending a soil sample to a soil-testing laboratory. To check, apply small amounts to a plot leaving a similar area untreated. A tablespoon or two of each per 100 square feet of area is ample. Lima beans set a much better crop of pods if boron is present; carrots are sweeter when magnesium and boron are available.

Commercial fertilizers may contain nitrogen in several forms. Sulphate of ammonia and nitrate of soda are two of the most common, but there are others, some of which are organic. Nearly all are quickly available and must be applied with care. Do not apply the standard fertilizer mixtures to plants unless the soil is moist. When spread on the turf, unless washed off by rain or hose, these soluble nitrogens will burn the foliage. This does not apply to the organic forms, one of which, bloodmeal, is quickly soluble.

We now have a new form of nitrogen that seems to fit the gardeners' needs. It is usually referred to as "slow-acting" or "nonburning." The first term is not quite accurate since "urea" is a nonburning but rather quickly available form. The newer fertilizers employ ureaform (formaldehyde-urea formulations) and similar materials which are slowly available. While more expensive than the older nitrogens, they offer so much to the home gardeners that their use seems well justified. First, they are easier to apply because they do not burn tender foliage. Secondly, they release the nitrogen slowly over a period of many weeks. The rate of growth remains fairly uniform — perhaps as long as for 2 or 3 months. Thirdly, there is practically no loss through leaching. And fourthly, the number of feedings necessary to keep lawn and garden in good growth is greatly reduced. These slow-acting, nonburning nitrogens may be obtained separately or in combinations with phosphate and potassium.

The new fertilizers should not displace the standard mixtures. There are many gardeners who, because of costs, will need to depend upon the lower priced forms of plant food. For special forcing or supplemental feeding the standard mixtures are still the ones to use.

A third type of plant feeding is finding a growing number of devotees. Foliar feeding consists of applications of special fertilizer compounds in solution to the plant foliage which take it up quickly. However, this requires frequent applications. Foliar plant foods may be applied at the same time as pesticides, a satisfactory program for some rose growers.

All plants do not need to be fed every year. In fact, feeding trees and shrubs that are growing as fast as desired or that have reached the desired height for the best landscape design effect will often result in excessive growth; the plants will then require extra pruning to keep them at the desired height. Appearance of plants is often a clue as to whether feeding is needed. Look for these hunger signs:

Leaves not normal in size
Yellow or chlorotic leaves
Sparse foliage—thinner than normal
Crown full of dead branches
Dying back of branches at tips
Short annual twig growth
Stunted growth

Some of these symptoms may also be caused by unfavorable soil environment, as well as lack of nutrients. A careful analysis should be made, considering all factors.

A word of caution should be added about using fertilizer while planting trees and shrubs. Careless handling of fertilizer may cause injury to the plant roots. To avoid the danger of fertilizer burn of the root system, do not use fertilizer for 6 to 12 months after planting or transplanting. Provide the plant with a soil high in organic matter.

Garden supply houses sell specially prepared, packaged fertilizers commonly spoken of as soluble plant food. Do not confuse them with the chemical plant foods used in soilless plant culture which are not recommended for garden use.

In addition to the soluble plant foods often referred to as starter solutions and applied as solutions, many manufacturers are now offering fertilizers that may be sprayed on the foliage of the plants. Some contain only the three major elements. Others contain, in addition, some of the trace or minor elements which are in such form that they can be absorbed through the leaves. While these are relatively more costly than other forms, they do have the advantage of being taken up quickly and safely and being of immediate use to plants.

One of the advantages of this type of fertilizer is that it can be applied through the garden hose when watering the garden by using a special syphon attachment.

A third type of fertilizer is now available for the azalea and camellia grower. The plant foods are in such a form that they increase the soil acidity, do not injure tender roots, and are slower acting than the ordinary commercial plant food. However, if properly applied, the usual garden fertilizer may be used without injury to the plants.

A gardener may mix his own soluble fertilizer by adding a tablespoonful of nitrate of soda, 3 tablespoonfuls of superphosphate, and 1 tablespoonful of muriate of potash to 1 gallon of water. This is concentrated plant food and should be diluted before using—1 part of stock solution to 3 parts of water.

FERTILIZER PROGRAM FOR ESTABLISHED PLANTS

Deciduous Shrubs—Apply 2 to 3 lbs. of a 5-10-5 fertilizer, or 1 lb. of a 10-10-10 fertilizer, to 100 sq. ft. of shrubs in early spring just as growth starts.

Needle Evergreens—Apply 2 to 3 lbs. of a 5-10-5 fertilizer, or 1 lb. of a 10-10-10 fertilizer, to 100 sq. ft. of shrubs in early spring.

Broadleaf Evergreens—At first signs of growth in the spring, apply no more than ½ to 1 lb. of ammonium sulphate to 100 sq. ft. One month later apply ¼ to ½ lb. of ammonium sulphate to 100 sq. ft. Or use fertilizer especially prepared for broadleaf evergreens available from commercial dealers.

Note—If ⅓ of nitrogen is in ammonium form, use the rates recommended by manufacturer.

Trees—For trees up to 3″ in diameter, apply 2 lbs. of 5-10-5 or 1 lb. 10-6-4 per inch of trunk diameter at 4½′. For trees over 3″ in diameter, use 5 lbs. of 5-10-5 or 3 lbs. of 10-6-4 per inch of trunk diameter at 4½′. Apply fertilizer so that not more than 1 lb. is spread over 100 sq. ft. of soil surface. Soak in the fertilizer. Organic fertilizer may be used in place of inorganic. Fertilizers may be broadcast, or injected into the soil at 18″ intervals to a depth of 8″ to 18″ for deciduous trees; and to 8″ for evergreen plants starting

2½′ from the trunk. Broadcasting is preferable for young plants.

Annuals-Perennials—During the growing season, apply dry fertilizer at the rate of ½ cup of 5-10-5 commercial fertilizer worked into the soil around each perennial. This can be done early in the spring when growth starts. If additional growth is desired, apply a complete fertilizer lightly at 2 to 4 week intervals during the growing season.

During the growing season, apply a sidedressing of a 5-10-5 fertilizer at the rate of 1 lb. per 100 sq. ft. at 2 to 4 week intervals beginning when annuals are ⅓ grown.

To be vigorous, lawn grasses require an annual feeding program. In general, lawns and similar turf areas need 4 to 6 lbs. of nitrogen, 1½ to 3 lbs. of phosphorus, and 1½ to 3 lbs. of potassium per 1,000 sq. ft. each year. Phosphorus and potash can generally be applied once annually. Soluble sources of nitrogen must be applied several times, but slowly available nitrogen can be applied twice a year.

Frequently there is need for supplemental feedings of nitrogen. It is convenient to have either nitrate of soda or sulphate of ammonia on hand. Dissolved in water and applied with a sprinkling can (1 pound per sprinkler) it is effective in supplying additional nitrogen to cabbage, lettuce and other leafy plants.

How Much Fertilizer?

Weights of Fertilizer per Acre Converted into Amounts for Smaller Areas

Acre	1000 sq. ft.	100 sq. ft.
100 lbs.	2½ pts.	½ cup
200 lbs.	5 pts.	1 cup
400 lbs.	5 quarts	1 pint
600 lbs.	7¼ quarts	1½ pints
800 lbs.	2½ gallons	2 pints
1000 lbs.	3 gallons	2½ pints
2000 lbs.	6 gallons	5 pints

The conversions in the above table are only approximate, but are close enough for practical purposes.

Tools for the Garden

A good workman likes to have good tools and enough to meet every need. Most gardens are small enough to be spaded by hand, providing the gardener is not so ambitious that he tries to do it all in one day. It is good judgment to spread strenuous work of this kind over a period of several days, and especially for those who are not used to heavy manual work.

Spading is ordinarily done with a spading fork, but a long-handled shovel or a spade may be used for this purpose. Some gardeners prefer one; some the other.

Every gardener needs some kind of a rake to remove the rocks, smooth the soil, serve as a light cultivator to break the crust or to firm the soil over newly sown seed.

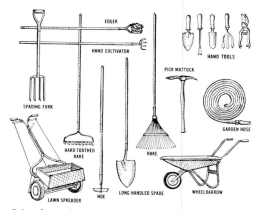

Only a few tools are essential. Keep them in good repair.

A garden hoe is a simple tool which may be bought in any one of several patterns. Each is useful and may be employed effectively for some specific job, but it is doubtful if more than a plain 5 or 6 inch bladed hoe is needed. With it a gardener can chop the weeds, open a furrow for seed, break clods and loosen the soil.

A wheel hoe is a necessity in the larger garden—the kind that some of the more experienced suburban gardeners have. The same is true of seed drills, fertilizer spreaders and the larger sprayers.

In addition to the tools listed, most gardeners will find it desirable to have a small hand duster. This inexpensive tool is especially effective if it is equipped with an extension so that the nozzle may be placed close to the ground, directing the dust toward undersides of the leaves of the plants.

The complete list of tools will include a small garden trowel for setting plants, several stout stakes and a piece of strong string. This is not an imposing list nor does it represent any substantial investment, but it will take care of the smaller gardens without taxing the gardener's pocketbook.

Quality, durability and ease of operation or use are more important than price in buying tools.

Spading the Garden

American gardeners do not as a rule take the spading of the garden—soil preparation—with a great deal of seriousness. The English gardener, on the other hand, goes to great lengths to see to the proper turning and pulverizing of the soil. Perhaps this is because we have not considered ourselves a nation of gardeners as the English have. Or it may be that we still believe our soils to be so fertile that they will produce abundantly without effort on our part.

Turning the soil is important in that it serves to pulverize the soil, enabling the plant roots to penetrate it. The more deeply it is worked the more the root area is increased. Moisture readily penetrates a well-loosened soil but runs off one that is packed. Roots need air. By loosening the soil they are able to secure it. In addition to this physical effect we may also incorporate humus into the soil as we spade it.

Some thoughtful gardeners look on turning the soil as a means of bringing a fresh supply of plant food to the surface. That is, they try to go a bit deeper each time they spade the garden to bring up some new soil. A very small quantity may be desirable. In the long run that is the way the top soil is deepened. This practice, however, can easily be overdone for the subsoil is devoid of bacteria and humus. For the immediate need, we may concentrate on carefully pulverizing the top 6 to 8 inch layer.

The main consideration, then, should be to loosen the soil thoroughly to a good depth. This may be accomplished by pushing the spading fork or shovel its full blade length into the ground. If the workman will push the blade straight down, rather than at an angle, he will in most cases dig as deeply as necessary. If the soil is heavy it is better to take a small "bite" even though the digging does not go so fast.

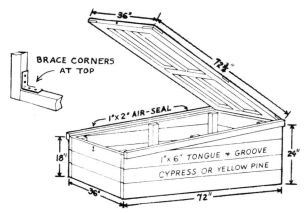

Cold frames have many uses: Starting seeds, winter storage for tender plants and year-round propagation. Build the frames in 3x6-foot sections. Use wood or cinder blocks, which should last for several years. Treat the wood with a rot-proofing. Place the frame 6 inches into the ground and mound soil up on the outside. Use 1x2-inch strips to act as an air-seal around the top. A hook and eye will help to hold the top snugly. Cover the top with reinforced plastic; or better still, cover both sides of the top with clear plastic.

The choice between a spading fork and a long-handled shovel for turning the soil is irrelevant. The important thing is not the tool but how it is used. A careful workman can accomplish the same results with either one.

In spring spading it is well to lift the "bite" and to deposit it on the top of the last row. In this way it is easy to knock the litter and weeds from the top of the "bite" into the bottom of the furrow. Then the rest of the "bite" may be pulverized with the back of the tool.

In the spring, after spading a strip 3 or 4 feet in width, it is well to take the rake and further pulverize as well as smooth the surface of the freshly turned soil. In this way tramping the freshly turned soil may be avoided. Any litter or unbroken clods are pulled into the furrow where they may be covered.

Avoid spading the ground when it is either too moist or too dry. Moist or wet soil puddles when worked. Dry soil is hard and clods are exceedingly difficult to break up.

To test soil for spading, take a handful and squeeze it firmly. Open the hand and tap the ball of earth gently. If it falls apart the soil is dry enough to work. If it retains its shape when struck it is too wet.

Fall spading is not practiced as often as it should be. Unrotted materials turned under in the fall decompose by spring and thus make plant food available. Fall-turned soil needs only to be raked in the spring to be ready for planting. Fall working of the soil turns up many grubs and other insect pests to be killed by winter weather. Soil that is turned in the fall is usually in better tilth, due to the action of frost.

Fall-spaded ground should not be pulverized, but left "rough" so that the frost may have full effect without danger of erosion.

BREAKING UP THE SOIL AND PLANTING IN THE GARDEN

A—Don't *begin digging* the soil when it is wet. If it packs or forms a sticky ball in your fist, then it isn't ready to be broken. Wait until it crumbles easily.

B—If you are starting a new garden plot, remove weeds, stumps, or bushes to prevent interference with the growth and care of the garden.

C—Dig *straight* down and make sure that you reach the soil at least 6 to 8 inches below the surface. Bring that underneath soil to the top.

D—Break the clods as you dig; leave the soil loose, fine and crumbly.

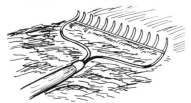

E—When your soil is turned over and broken up, smooth it with the back of a garden rake.

F—Rake your garden bed slightly higher in the center than at its border, to prevent finding your garden a huge puddle after a heavy rain.

G—Pound stakes at either end where you want each row; tie a string to the stakes as your guide in marking rows.

H—It is not necessary to *dig* furrows. You can make deep enough seed furrows with the end of your rake handle.

I—Space seeds in furrows as recommended for each variety.

J—Often one packet of seed of each variety is sufficient.

K—Unless soil is unusually damp, apply starter solution (see section on liquid fertilizers) directly to the seeds before replacing soil.

L—Use your seed envelope or a label as a marker at the end of row until crop is up.

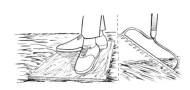

M—Firm your soil well with a plank or with the back of the rake.

N—Some sort of a border, preferably a wire or a picket fence, will greatly improve the looks of your garden and help to keep out rabbits.

CHAPTER II

SEEDS AND CUTTINGS

The early ordering of seeds is recommended since nearly every year some kinds of varieties are in short supply. Old seeds, unless stored under favorable conditions, are likely to be unsatisfactory. They should be tested and if found to be low in germination discarded.

The average-size garden does not require a great quantity of seed. A small packet of tomato or zinnia seed, for instance, should produce more than enough plants to supply the garden. The same is true of the seed packets of eggplant, pepper, cucumber, broccoli, etc., as well as many kinds of flowers. To avoid waste, packets may be divided with neighbors.

Knowing the number of feet of row to be planted, it is comparatively easy to estimate the quantities of seed needed. The table on page 163 gives the usually recommended amounts (in ounces) per 100 feet of row for the principal vegetable crops. However, they are generous allowances and can be safely reduced by 50 per cent in well-prepared soils. Most gardeners sow seed too thickly for good growth and must thin the seedling 50 per cent or more.

It is often desirable for the home gardener to procure plants rather than to attempt growing them where suitable facilities are lacking. The cost of the plants may seem high compared to the cost of a packet of seed, but this is seldom the case considering the effort and the results obtained.

Use good seed of locally adapted varieties. Those varieties listed on the following pages have been tested and proven under local conditions.

For earliest crops, seeds may be started in the cold frame or indoors, 2 to 6 weeks before it is safe to plant them out of doors.

Seed should be planted in a well-prepared seed bed if it is to germinate properly. The smaller the seed the more important it is that the soil be finely pulverized. In the early spring the soil need not be pressed firmly over the seed, but in the summer it is well to pack the soil over the seed. Spring-sown seed need not be covered as deeply as summer sown. The soil is colder in the spring and deeply planted seed do not receive the heat necessary for germination. In the summer the soil is warmer and deeper planting is necessary to insure the moisture required for sprouting.

Starting Seeds Indoors

An early garden, one that produces useful crops early in the season, should be the aim of every home gardener. Strong, healthy, sturdy plants, ready to set out in the garden as soon as the weather permits, is one way to attain this objective, but starting seeds indoors in February and early March is not easy without special equipment.

To build a hot bed for this purpose hardly seems practical considering how few plants are needed. Growing plants in the kitchen window is not as easy today as it was in grandmother's time. Our houses are too hot and too dry.

There are ways other than making arrangements with a nearby commercial grower. We may build a lean-to over the basement window or we may grow the plants under a "bell" jar in a cool room, provided there is ample sunlight.

The seed should be sown in carefully sifted soil that has been treated to prevent the "damping-off" fungus. This treatment may be as follows: (1) Mix the soil with formaldehyde dust, (2) bake it in the oven for one hour, (3) dust the seed with red copper oxide and spray the surface with a red copper oxide solution (⅓ teaspoonful to 1 quart of water) or (4) steam the soil. A few crystals of paradichlorobenzine dusted over the surface of the pot or seed flat is another aid in keeping disease under control.

A newer and very effective method of growing seedlings that seems to make them rather immune to this trouble is to sow the seeds in sphagnum moss. The moss is used in place of soil. Pulverized sphagnum moss may be purchased ready for use. Place a half-inch layer of it on some kind of filler. Pack it tightly and water. Sow the seed, covering them very lightly with some of the dust from the sphagnum moss. The moss holds moisture and a better germination may be be expected than is usually obtained with soil-filled pots. No feeding is necessary.

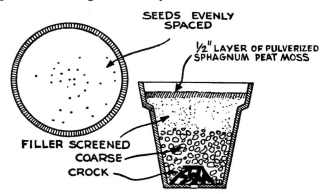

4-to-6 inch flower pots may be used to start a supply of plants for the small garden.

Another good inexpensive medium for the seed flat

is vermiculite (plant aid), usually sold under a trade name. Use a medium grade (size) and soak before sowing the seed. This absorbent material swells when moistened, hence, need not be packed or tamped when filling the flat.

If soil is used to fill the seed flat or box, it should be fairly light and should contain enough humus to facilitate germination. Usually such a mixture of ¼ sand, ¼ compost or leaf mold, and ½ garden loam. Some gardeners use very well rotted cow manure for this purpose, but that hardly seems necessary. The soil should be well mixed and screened before filling the seed flats.

In filling the seed flats or flower pots, it is wise to put the coarser material in the bottom and to cover it with the more finely pulverized soil mixture. Press firmly with a flat board or block to firm the soil.

The seed may be sown broadcast or in rows. Most gardeners prefer the rows. This may be done by pressing the edge of a stick or ruler into the soil. The seed are scattered very thinly in the little furrow and covered with sand, finely pulverized compost, sphagnum moss or vermiculite.

The flats or flower pots should be well watered after planting and then placed in the lean-to, cellar window or wherever they are to be kept. Until the seeds break through the soil they do not need sunlight. Many gardeners cover with newspapers or burlap to hold the moisture until the seedlings begin to appear.

Water should be given as needed. Preferably, the boxes or pots should be placed in a tub or large container so that the water may soak up from below. If sprinkling is necessary it should be done in the morning so that the foliage will dry before night.

Or better still, cover the seed flat with polyethylene plastic. Flower pots may be placed in polyethylene bags and the tops tied tightly. No further watering is likely to be needed until the seedlings are large enough to be transplanted.

Many seed may be started in seed beds out of doors. It is well to prepare the soil in them carefully, incorporating well-decayed compost to hold moisture. It is a desirable practice to sterilize such beds with DD before sowing the seed. A half-teaspoonful of DD (soil sterilizer) poured into holes 6 inches deep and spaced 10 inches apart will destroy disease spores, weeds and nematodes. Plug the holes with dirt, water and cover the bed with canvas or pieces of roofing paper. Remove the cover after 3 days to allow the disinfectant to escape. This should be done at least a week before the seeds are to be sown.

Transplanting the Seedlings

Seedlings usually are grown in a rather infertile soil, the plants making most of their growth from the strength stored in the seed. Thus, transplanting them to fertile fibrous soil as soon as the first pair of true leaves appear is necessary if they are to keep growing and developing.

The flats prepared for the reception of seedlings should be filled with a soil mixture containing well-rotted compost and manure or garden loam enriched with compost. If the soil is heavy, some sand should be added.

The Cornell Mix for seedlings and plants is a sterile artificial mixture free of weed seeds, nematodes, soil insects and diseases. Prepare it as follows: For one bushel use four gallons (2 pecks) of shredded peat moss, 4 gallons vermiculite (Terra-Lite No. 2), 4 level tablespoonsful of 20% superphosphate, ½ cup (8 tablespoonsful) of pulverized limestone, and one cup of 5-10-5 fertilizer. Mix thoroughly. This is an excellent mixture for potting plants except such acid soil lovers as azaleas, African violets, etc. It is not suitable for starting many kinds of seeds.

The handling of seedlings has much to do with the success of the plants after they are set out in the garden. Seedlings are delicate little plants. Unless they are lifted when ready and transplanted into specially prepared soil, their growth is seldom as desired.

Seedlings may be spaced in the flat approximately 2 inches apart each way. This provides the minimum space necessary for the development of a good root system. Closer planting encourages spindling growth and straggling root systems. Wider spacing is unnecessary, especially if the growing space is limited.

Many supply stores offer "bands," small paper pots and pressed pots for the growing of seedlings to transplanting size. These small containers enable the gardener to transplant from flat to garden without shock to the plants — an important consideration.

Seedlings, to make a desirable stocky growth, should be grown in full sunlight in fairly cool temperatures— around 60 degrees in the daytime, lower at night. Watering is best done in the morning so that the foliage is dry during the night.

No fertilizer is needed during this period if the soil has been properly prepared and mixed. The emphasis should be primarily on root growth, and the old belief that roots grow best if they have to stretch out for their food is justification enough for not feeding.

Just before moving the plants from flat to garden, it is desirable to "harden" them off. This refers to gradually adjusting them to outside temperatures. A cold frame offers the best opportunity, but since few gardeners are so equipped, a sun porch or the garage may be used. A few days with only partial protection from the cold air and finally no protection, except from the wind, is sufficient. The last step is moving them into the garden.

Transplanting is done preferably on a cloudy day. If the roots have been disturbed, the plants should be shaded with boards, berry boxes, paper or shingles for two or three days, until the roots are established.

Sowing Seed in the Garden

Seeds vary in size from large ones such as peas, marigolds and sunflowers to such tiny ones as parsley, peppers, petunias and poppies. It is only reasonable to expect that the plants coming from the smaller seeds will have difficulty in pushing through heavy soils or from a great depth. For this reason our soil should be well prepared, and the seeds covered according to their size with a soil cover that will not form a hard impervious crust.

A soil that has considerable sand in it or that contains peat moss or compost is not apt to form a hard crust. Lacking this kind of garden soil, it may be well to cover the smaller seeds with compost, sand, or even coal ashes. Germination will be much better.

The smallest seeds should not be covered with more than one-fourth inch of soil, perhaps only one-eighth inch. The larger seeds may be covered as much as two inches.

Seeds need not be covered as deeply in the spring when the soil is cold, showers are frequent and the soil is moist, as in the summer when the soil is warm and dry.

It is not necessary to press the soil about the seeds in the spring to insure germination, but in the summer this is an important practice.

Many gardeners sow radish seed in the rows of carrot seed to help break the crust and also to mark the location of the row because carrot seed are so slow to germinate.

Large seeds may be properly spaced at planting time. The smaller seeds are not so easily handled. A method used by many gardeners is to tear off the end of the envelope, pressing the edges so that the end opens up, and by rolling the packet back and forth the seed come out in a fairly steady stream. Another method is to mix sand with the smaller seeds.

New Plants From Cuttings

Propagating plants from cuttings is an age old practice that is still used by amateur and commercial plant growers. Many kinds must be propagated vegetatively if the varieties are to be kept true. Vegetative propagation includes cuttings, grafting, budding and layering. The cuttings are used wherever possible since they take less skill and can be handled in larger quantities.

There are two main types of cuttings, softwood and hardwood. The softwood cuttings are taken during the growing season while the plants are in active growth and usually of the current season's growth. Hardwood

TRANSPLANTING SEEDLINGS TO THE GARDEN

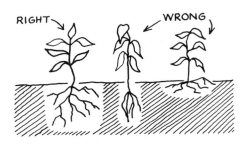

Be sure to dig the garden holes wide and deep enough to set roots in their natural position.

When you begin transplanting, dig only a few seedlings at a time and get them into the garden soil as soon as possible.

As you take the seedlings from your flats to transplant to the garden, be sure to get an ample size ball of soil with the roots.

Make hole with trowel and set in plant before removing trowel. Then add starter solution.

Then fill in with soil. Firm with your fingers but do not pack tightly.

If transplanting in July or August, it is a good idea, even though extra trouble, to put a paper bag over each plant just for a few days to protect the plants from driving wind, rain, or sun till they get started in the ground. Hold down the paper bags with a trowelful of soil.

cuttings are taken in the late fall or early winter after the wood has matured. Other types of cuttings are: leaf-cuttings, root cuttings, tuber cuttings, and bud cuttings.

The softwood cuttings usually are taken at some special time when they root most readily. The evergreen azalea cuttings should be taken between mid-July to mid-August. Cuttings taken at other seasons will root but seldom give as high a percentage of rooted-plants. Rose cuttings may be taken whenever the flower on the new shoot has faded, thus they can be taken over a much longer season than can azaleas. Some plants are extremely hard to root from cuttings; this includes the rhododendrons and the deciduous azaleas. However, the newest method of rooting cuttings—mist propagation — has shown promising results with both of these hard-to-root plants.

In taking a softwood cutting it is advisable to cut the new shoot about a ¼-inch below a node. This is the area where the largest concentration of adventitious root cells may be found on most kinds of plants, but varies greatly between the different kinds. The top cut, if one is necessary, should be about a ¼-inch above a node, and is made on a slant with a bud or node at the tip of the cut.

The use of rooting hormones (auxins) is generally helpful. A few kinds — chrysanthemum, deutzia, forsythia, pyracantha, boxweed, etc., for example — do not respond as satisfactorily. The American holly needs a stronger concentration than most other kinds. There are texts that not only tell when to take cuttings but also the kind of stimulant to use.

Softwood cuttings must have leaves present if they are to develop roots and grow. For some years it was thought advisable to reduce the leaf surface to conserve moisture but that has been disproved. Even the chrysanthemum grower does not chop off the tops of the leaves as formerly. However, the common practice is to leave all leaves on that are above the planting depth —there should be two or more nodes covered by the propagating media and two or more above the media. This is readily seen on a rose cutting but not with a boxwood cutting where the nodes are so close together this rule cannot be followed.

The size of the cutting will vary greatly between kinds of plants. The rose cutting mentioned above will need to be 6 to 8 inches long in order to have 4 or 5 nodes, while the boxwood need not be more than 2 or 3 inches. Over-sized cuttings seldom pay unless they can be grown under exceptionally favorable conditions of light, heat and humidity.

There are numerous kinds of rooting media in use today. The more commonly used are sharp sand, sphagnum moss, vermiculite, perlite and combinations of these such as sand and sphagnum, perlite and sphagnum. Others used by some specialists include such uncommon materials as fly ash, powdered styrofoam, pumice and silver sand. All have one characteristic in common—they permit air to reach the roots in spite of all the packing the gardener may give. To be effective they must be sterile and free from dirt and salt.

Some cuttings root best in a non-acid media such as the sand and perlite. Others do best in an acid media such as the sphagnum. However, there is considerable tolerance if other conditions are favorable. Geraniums seem to be the exception and best rooting results are usually obtained in clean, sharp sand.

The cuttings may be placed in a specially prepared bed, in flats, and in flower pots. The beds are best where a considerable number are to be handled at one time. Cold frames make satisfactory propagating beds in the summer. Flats are commonly used where only a few score cuttings are to be rooted. Flower pots are handy and work very well for a dozen or two cuttings.

After the cuttings are dipped in a rooting hormone (auxin) and the surplus knocked off, space them from 2 to 3 inches apart, depending upon the size of the leaves. Firm the media about the cuttings as well as possible. In well firmed sand the cuttings should take a sharp tug to pull them out.

When the cuttings are placed and the media firmed about them they should be watered with a fine mist, then covered. In beds or flats they are usually covered with newspapers which cut off the light and conserve the moisture. When the cuttings are placed in pots it is well to make certain that all excess moisture drains away. When moss is used it is wise to let the pots stand for a day or two. More cuttings fail to root when the pots are placed in a freezer bag, because of excess moisture than from almost any other cause. But the freezer bag does away with the necessity of a daily watering that is required when flats or beds are used.

The cuttings should be removed from the propagating media and potted when the roots are an inch or two in length. This is somewhat indefinite since they should not be disturbed until they are strong enough to withstand handling. If taken too early there is some likelihood of their being brushed off. At this stage the roots will be able to take up moisture and plant food, thus the potting mix might well be made of equal parts of loam, sand and peat moss with a quart of dehydrated cow manure per bushel of soil. Moisten and cover for a few days until the rooted cuttings have become established. It is not uncommon to water the newly potted cuttings with a soluble plant food, commonly referred to as a starter solution. In many cases this speeds the establishment of the cuttings.

Hardwood Cuttings

The hardwood cuttings are usually taken in late fall or early winter after the tree or shrub is fully dormant.

Sometimes the winters are mild enough that cuttings taken in late February or early March give satisfactory results. The cuttings should be of the past season's growth.

Cuttings 6 to 8 inches in length are usually satisfactory. Tie them in bundles of a dozen or more, label and place in a moist but frost free situation. A shallow trench filled with peat moss may serve, but it should be covered with a generous layer of leaves to prevent freezing should we have unusually low temperatures. The bundles should be placed "butts-up." This seems to stimulate the callousing which is necessary for root formation.

In early March or whenever the soil is workable, prepare a propagating bed where the cuttings may be lined-out about 6 inches apart in rows a foot apart. If the soil is hard a furrow might be made, but usually at that season the soil is moist enough so that the cuttings may be pushed into the ground to the desired depth. A long pencil or pointed stick may be used to punch the holes. The cuttings should have at least two nodes underground. The soil should be firmed about the cuttings whenever it is dry enough to be walked on.

It is a good practice to remove the lower buds on the hardwood cuttings. This may be done with a sharp knife by making a slight notch which removes the vital part of the bud.

The hardwood cuttings will need to be watered occasionally, whenever rainfall is inadequate. But this will vary depending upon the texture of the soil. Light sandy soils will need much more water than loams or clays.

Some gardeners dip their hardwood cuttings in a rooting hormone before planting; others wet the soil about the cuttings with such a solution.

Mulches seem to encourage rooting, perhaps because the soil is cooler, or it may be that they keep the soil moist. Undoubtedly a mulch is beneficial in that it avoids the necessity of cultivation and weed pulling which might disturb the newly forming roots.

The cuttings should remain undisturbed in the propagating bed for a year; they can remain for two years if necessary. However, if they are to be left two years they may well be spaced 8 or 10 inches apart. When planted 6 inches apart they should be lifted and replanted a foot or more apart. It is well, when lifted, to shorten the roots to encourage a bushy, compact root system. The cutting back should not be severe; only the longer ones will need to be pruned.

The tops of the cuttings of many shrubs may need to be pruned to stimulate bushy compact plants. This may be done during the growing season by pinching them or it may be left until the dormant season. The pruning of cuttings of trees should be to stimulate tall growth; thus all side branches should be removed until

they are 3 feet or more in height. This too can be done during the growing seasons or when dormant.

Root Cuttings

Some kinds of trees and shrubs may be propagated by root cuttings. They are taken in the fall after the trees are dormant. To take a root cutting, it is customary to expose the roots on one side of the tree or shrub until sufficient large roots are uncovered to supply the need. Roots approximately as large in diameter as a small lead pencil should be taken. They may be cut in 2 to 4 inch lengths with the butt end a square cut, the tip slanting. Tie in bundles and bury in peat moss or some other media that will keep them from drying out. This storage space should be frost-free. During this storage period the cuttings should callous and be ready for planting in a shallow trench in late March or early April.

The cuttings may be placed slanting or horizontal, but should be covered with about 2 inches of a friable loam. Soils that crust should be avoided. As soon as the new growth breaks through the ground the rows should be mulched.

Cuttings of the Conifers

The cuttings of the conifers—yews, pines, arborvitae, hemlock, etc. — are usually considered hardwood cuttings in that they are taken in the early winter when the plants are dormant. However, they are treated much as softwood cuttings and are kept in a moist atmosphere and in the light at all times. In root cuttings of evergreens it is desirable, where feasible, to place them where the bottoms of the propagating frame, flats, or pots can be kept warm. When bottom heat is used to speed the rooting, the maintenance of moisture in the media is likely to be a problem. Heating cables are commonly used for this purpose in a coldframe or hot bed. Flats are more difficult to handle; but flower pots in a freezer bag can be placed near a hot water pipe or radiator.

The cuttings of the conifers are commonly the short side shoots and are torn off rather than cut. The exception to this would be cuttings of an upright yew—they should be taken from the upright top growth. Cuttings torn from a branch usually have a "heel," a short angular stub. Some believe this should be left on, but such a shape makes it somewhat difficult to avoid air pockets. Hence most propagators clip them off just before treating with a rooting hormone and placing in the rooting media.

With the exception of the junipers, the conifers may be rooted satisfactorily in a sand-peatmoss mixture. The junipers do best in clean sharp sand.

In selecting plants for propagating, it is desirable to take cuttings only from those with desirable characteristics. Plants that are lacking in vigor for any reason should be avoided. Cuttings taken from such plants are unlikely to thrive and may not produce desirable plants. It is desirable to note the growth habits, the freedom of bloom, and especially the vigor. If the gardener is to give the time and attention necessary to grow new plants from cuttings, he should be assured that all new ones produced have as many of the desirable qualities as possible. This seems especially true of roses—there is a marked difference between the growth habits and flowering of a given variety to be found in our gardens. Take cuttings only from the best bushes—growing your own then becomes a worthwhile project.

NOTES

CHAPTER III

CROP CULTURE

The small garden will need to have the best use made of all available space if it is to provide the flowers and vegetables needed in the home. One way to accomplish this is through the use of supports for several of the vining and sprawling garden crops. By growing the tall kinds with suitable supports, greater returns may be had from the space occupied.

Stakes to support a dahlia or a heavily laden tomato plant should not be less than 1½ by 1½ inches by 8 feet long. A 2-by-2-inch stake is even better. The stakes should be driven into the ground at least 15 to 18 inches.

Staking begins at planting time. Tie with soft twine or strips of rags at 10 or 20 inch intervals.

If the gardener does not care to use stakes for his tomatoes, he may make supports in the form of cylinders made from woven wire, such as is used for reinforcing, or other materials. Usually such a support does not require the tying of unpruned shoots to keep them off the ground.

Garden peas, dwarf as well as tall, need support for disease prevention, and for ease of cultivation. Prunings from privet hedges are ideal for this purpose, but any kind of brush will do. If the peas are planted in double rows, the brush is placed between the two rows that are close together. Lacking the brush, one may use string and stakes such as suggested for pole beans, but on a much smaller scale. An old piece of wire fencing will serve.

Weed Control

Weed control is important in that the weeds compete with the garden plants for food, moisture and sunlight. When large, they shut off the air circulation, a condition that favors the development of diseases.

- Rake the garden thoroughly just before planting.
- Control weeds in the rows by pulling them as soon as they get started.

- Rake between the rows after every rain when weeds are just coming up.
- If weeds are 4 inches or more high, they must be pulled by hand and should be pulled from the bottom so that their roots come out with them.
- Tall weeds, a foot high, have their roots intertwined with the plant roots and cause damage if pulled from dry soil. Better to cut them with pruning shears.

The best time to kill weeds is while they are so small they can hardly be seen. At that stage they have but the tiniest roots and it takes very little disturbance to kill them. Later on, when well rooted, considerable effort and a sharp hoe are needed to bring them under control.

Frequent cultivation of the soil to provide aeration and to conserve moisture is, of course, all that should be necessary to control the weeds. If the soil is cultivated following each shower or watering, the weed problem will in most cases be solved. However, during the summer, it may be that the weeds, especially crabgrass, will get a start during prolonged periods of rainfall. When that happens a light cultivation is seldom sufficient to put a stop to the growth. A second cultivation a day or two later is often necessary.

The best tools for weed control depend upon those at hand and upon the habits of the gardener. Some gardeners do everything with the common garden hoe. It is a good tool. When sharp and well handled, it is quick and effective. However, if a start is made early in the spring and kept up, the common steel garden rake is a very good tool. It will cover much space in a short time. It does not turn the soil too deeply and tends to pull the weeds out of the soil. A third tool, known as the "victory" cultivator, has a group of five shovel-like tines. By drawing it through the soil, weeds and crust are broken up. While an easy tool for men to use, it does not always pull well-rooted weeds out of the soil.

Special type tools make cultivation easier, but when weeds get out of hand, the common hoe will be needed.

Another tool is the small, four-tined hoe. It looks like a small potato drag and is called the "speedy" cultivator. It, too, is effective only while the weeds are small. The scuffle hoe, an English tool that is pulled rather than used to chop with, is very good. Many

stores, however, do not handle it.

When weeds are once established they must be chopped out, cutting the roots off below the surface of the ground and spreading the plants out to dry in the sun. This slow and laborious method seems to be the only way to bring them under control once they get away from the gardener.

Modern research has provided several chemical weed killers that may be used effectively by the home gardener. One of these, 2,4-D, may be used to eradicate broad-leaved weeds from the lawn. It is ineffective on narrow-leaved weeds and will not kill crabgrass. However, there are chemicals on the market which will kill crabgrass.

The field of chemical weed control is being explored by many agencies and new and more effective materials are constantly being released. Some are highly selective and will kill only certain kinds of weeds; others are placed after the crop is up to kill the germinating weeds as they appear. Still others are spread over the soil before planting, which is delayed a few days, so that the chemical can kill the weeds before the crop is planted. (These developments will be described on the Garden Page of The Star as they are announced.)

Ammonium sulfamate may be used to control weeds, including poison ivy, but because it kills all plants must be used with care. Aminotriazole is especially good and safer to handle.

In using chemical weed killers, the gardener should carefully note on the labels the plants listed as affected and unaffected. These chemicals are most effective in the early summer when the plants are in active growth.

General Chemicals for Use in Controlling:

1. Weeds in Lawns.

The most effective method of weed control in lawns results from good management techniques supplemented by improved methods of weed control. Proper management and maintenance techniques include: adequate fertilization based on fertility needs as established by a soil analysis; planting turf grasses best adapted to the soil and location; mowing most turf grasses to a height of 1½ to 2½ inches; use of proper watering practices (infrequent but thorough wetting of the soil); and controlling insects and diseases. A healthy vigorous lawn is the first step in obtaining a weed-free lawn.

A. Broad-leaved Weeds.

(1) Dandelion, buckhorn, other plantains, curled dock, and many other relatively easy to kill weeds: Ester forms as well as amine salt of 2,4-D, also combinations of 2,4-D, 2-4,5-T and 2,4,5-TP— follow the instructions on the label. A pre-emergence application of siduron or DCPA of bensalide to the lawn will prevent their seeds from germinating.
(2) Wild onions, wild garlic, red sorrel, knotweeds and

some other hard-to-kill broad-leaved weeds:
Repeated sprayings with a low volatile ester of 2,4-D or an amine salt of 2,4-D plus a detergent. To control onion and garlic, spray in late fall and again in late winter or early spring each year. To control such weeds as red sorrel and knotweed, spray annually in the spring. A new material, dicamba, may be used to control them when growing in the lawns.

(3) For control of white clover, chickweed, henbit, knotweed, and many others:
Silvex is effective for control of these species. Follow dilution and timing as shown on the label.

B. Crabgrass and other grassy weeds.

Crabgrass and other annual weeds can be prevented before they grow in well-established lawns by using chemicals which kill the dormant seed. There are several on the market and new ones in the offing. They attack the dormant crabgrass seed and unless the soil is disturbed which might bring more seed into the germinating zone (½ inch), will prevent crabgrass growth. In each case follow the manufacturer's direction both as to rate of application and timing.

Crabgrass is an annual weed; it sprouts from seeds left from the plants that have died the year before. Without competition from crabgrass, desirable lawn grasses can spread and grow into a tight turf.

(1) Pre-emergence control of annual grassy weeds and many broad-leaved weeds in moist situations:
If some crabgrass has sprouted, use mixture of 2,4-D and PMA, or a mixture of DMA and 2,4-D according to directions on the label of each.

(2) Pre-emergence control of crabgrass:
Calcium arsenate—or
Dacthal—
Siduron—Follow instructions on the label.

(3) Control of perennial grasses such as orchardgrass, timothy, quackgrass, Bermuda grass, nimblewill, tall fescue and others:
Dalapon—¼ lb. in 1 gallon of water. This material will kill desirable grasses so use as spot spray only. Will usually disappear in 3 to 6 weeks in warm moist soil.

Control of Bermuda grass:

Methyl bromide, a soil fumigant, will control Bermuda grass if applied according to instructions on the label. An airtight cover is required. Apply when both soil and air temperatures are above 65. The cover can be removed 24 to 48 hours after treatment and the area can be seeded 48 to 72 hours following removal.
Dalapon applied in July at ¼ lb. per 1,000 square feet in one gallon of water has given good control of Bermuda growing in moist soils. Usually follow-up treatments in August are necessary to kill surviving plants. If there is adequate moisture and the temperatures are warm, lawn grasses can be seeded 3 to 4 weeks after the last treatment.

C. Comments and Precautions.

(1) PMA, DNBP, DMA, Chlordane, and Sodium Arsenite are poisonous to warm-blooded animals. They usually are not hazardous to man or animals after they are applied to turf. As a precautionary measure, however, keep children and animals off sprayed areas until after a rain or sprinkling.

(2) KOCN should be used with care on lawns containing bentgrasses and fescues. Avoid use of 2,4-D on bentgrass lawns at rates of more than ¼ pound per acre.

(3) Flowers, shrubs and trees may be damaged by spray drift or vapors, which may be avoided by spraying when wind velocity is nil. Use only salts or low-volatile esters of 2,4-D or MCPA.

(4) Broad-leaved weeds such as wild onion, wild garlic, dandelions, and plaintain may be killed with spot treatments of 2,4-D without spraying the entire lawn. For control of spot infestations of wild onion and wild garlic, use 5 ounces or 10 tablespoonful of an amine salt of 2,4-D in approximately 1 gallon of water. Place a rubber glove over the hand to protect it from the chemical and pull an absorbent cotton glove over the rubber glove. Apply the solution to these weeds by dipping a gloved hand into the mixture then grasping the tops of the weeds. Press hard enough to break through the waxy coating on the leaves. This will permit the chemical to penetrate into the plant and completely kill it.

(5) For spot treatment control of dandelions, plantain, and curled dock, apply the same solution used to kill wild onions. Fasten a piece of kitchen sponge to the end of a stick or broom handle. Dip the sponge into the solution and spot treat the broad-leaved weeds by pressing the moist sponge against the crown of each plant. This spot-treatment method eliminates danger of spray drift and allows the operator to kill weeds growing close to desirable flowers and shrubs.

(6) After applying spray materials to the weeds, delay mowing for 24 to 48 hours. For materials that kill upon contact with the foliage or are taken from the soil (PMA, DNBP, KOCN, and Sodium Arsenite), mowing and removal of clippings before spraying may increase the efficiency of the treatment. Rain or sprinkling shortly after treatment with some herbicides will not decrease their effectiveness, but, as a general rule, avoid sprinkling for 24 to 48 hours.

(7) Avoid spraying very young seedlings of lawn grass with herbicides. After they have begun to stool or spread by rhizomes they may be given moderate herbicide treatments.

2. Weeds in Flowers and Ornamentals.

A. Gladiolus, Dutch Iris, Narcissus.

(1) Pre-emergence control of annual grasses and broad-leaved weeds:
2,4-D (2.8 ounces/6 tblspns), or Sesone (3.5 ounces/9 tblspns) or CIPC (5.6 ounces/12 tblspns), or DNBP (5.6 ounces/12 tblspns) in one gallon of water per 1,000 square feet of area. Effective for 30 to 60 days or more. Trifluralin protects for 60 to 90 days.

(2) Post-emergence:
Sesone (3.5 ounces/9 tblspns) to one gallon of water applied per 1,000 square feet 30 to 60 days after pre-emergence treatment but before weeds begin to emerge will usually extend period of weed

control until harvest. This should be applied after irrigation or soil soaking. 2,4-D at rates up to 0.7 ounces may be used if applied before leaf blades open.

B. Established Evergreens and Deciduous Plants.

(1) For control of annual grasses and broad-leaved weeds in rows of coniferous transplants and deciduous stocks:
Sesone (3.5 ounces/9 tblspns), or CIPC (5.6 ounces/12 tblspns) in one gallon of water per 1,000 sq. ft. Should be applied as a basal directed spray. They should be applied prior to emergence of weeds—one month is the usual rule. Or trifluralin granular 10 ounces per 1,000 sq. ft.

(2) For control of annual weeds between rows:
DNPB (2.8 ounces/6 tblspns), or Sesone (3.5 ounces/9 tblspns) per one gallon of water applied to 1,000 sq. ft.

C. Comments and Precautions:

Perennial weeds are not controlled by these treatments. Use a low pressure sprayer and a hooded boom to prevent spray drift from coming into contact with nursery stock. Granular materials are easier to apply, such as trifluralin and casuron.

3. Seedbeds and Transplant Beds.

A. For control of most annual and perennial weeds:

(1) Methyl bromide at 1 pound per 100 sq. ft. applied under a plastic cover. Cover may be removed after 24 hours. Methyl bromide does not persist in soil and plantings may be safely made within 72 hours. Soil fumigants such as SMDC and DMTT are also available for application as drenches at a stated period prior to planting and do not require use of air-tight plastic covers.

4. Weeds in Small Fruits.

A. Brambles (raspberries and blackberries) and blueberries:

(1) For control of weeds in early spring in brambles grown in rows:
First application—
DNBP (12 ounces/25 tblspns), or Amine Salt of 2,4-D (0.3 ounce/2 tspns), or Sesone (2 ounces/3 tblspns) in one gallon of water per 1,000 sq. ft.
Second application—
2,4-D delay application until new canes are tall enough to permit directed basal applications.

(2) For control of winter annual grasses and broad-leaved weeds in fall or early winter:
CIPC, or Monuron.

B. Comments and Precautions:

Do not use 2,4-D in brambles during the flowering stage.

C. Grapes

Diuron—2 lbs. in 40 gals. of water per acre, one application a year in early spring.

D. Strawberries

Pre-planting—
DNBP, or CIPC, or 2,4-D, or Sesone applied 10 to 15 days before planting.
Post-planting—

14 to 21 days after planting.
Sesone (3 to 6 pounds in 10 to 40 gallons of water), per acre, after each cultivation until runner development precludes cultivation.
For fall and winter weed control when strawberries are dormant DNBP or CIPC, or Sesone.

E. Weed Control in Vegetable Crops—

Vegetable	Pre-Emergence	Post-Emergence
Asparagus	Monuron	Monuron
Beans	DNBP, CIPC, EPTC	(after cutting season)
Beets	....	....
Cole Crops	CDEC	....
(Cabbage, cauliflower, broccoli, Brussels sprouts, kale, collards, turnip greens, mustard greens, Hanover salad)		
Cantaloups, Cucumbers, Watermelons	NPA, CDEC	NPA
Carrots, Celery, Dill Parsnips, Parsley	Stoddard Solvent	Stoddard Solvent
Spinach	CIPC or CDEC	CIPC
Onions	CIPC	CIPC
Peas	DNBP	DNBP
Irish potatoes	....	EPTC, Sesone
Sweet potatoes	NPA	NPA or CIPC
Sweet corn	2,4-D, DNBP, Atrazine	....

F. Control of weeds along fence rows, roadsides, etc.

(1) Foliage sprays
  a. Woody plants—2,4,5-T, 2,4-D, Silvex, MCPA, and Ammonium sulfamate
(2) Basal Sprays during growth or dormant periods
  a. Trees and brush less than 6 inches in diameter —2,4-D, 2,4,5-T
(3) Cut surface treatment
  a. Frill applications (over-lapping axe cuts)— 2,4,5-T, 2,4-D
  b. Cup or notch application—½ ounce ammonium sulfamate in each notch. Notches not more than 6 inches apart
  c. Tree injection—2,4,5-T, 2,4-D in diesel oil— 1 tspn in each injection, 2 inches apart at base.
(4) Stumps and Stump Sprouts
2,4,5-T and ammonium sulfamate

G. Ditch bank weeds—

Broad-leaved—2,4-D.
Annual weed grasses—Dalapon, amitrol, or dinitro-fortified fuel oil, when grasses are small.
Perennial grasses—Repeated applications of dalapon, amitrol, or aromatic oil or dinitro fuel oil. Oil treatments often must be repeated every 3 or 4 weeks in 1 or 2 growing seasons. Usually, 1 or 2 applications of amitrol or 2 or 3 applications of dalapon per year.
(6) Driveways, patios, walks, etc.—Stoddard solvent, methyl bromide, and combination of dalapon or TCA with 2,4-D and 2,4,5-T.

H. Aquatic weeds in ponds and lakes

a. Submerged weeds in still water—sodium arsenite— 3 to 4 p.p.m. On shore line may require 6 to 10 p.p.m. Do not use water for 3 days after treatment.

b. For control of Parrot Feather, Waterweed, Coontail, Pondweeds, and Naiad: Dichlone—10 to 20 lbs. per surface acre.

c. For control of blue-green Algae: Dichlone—1 pound per surface acre.

d. For control of filamentous green algae: Copper sulfate (0.5 to 1.0 p.p.m.) or RADA (0.3 to 1.0 p.p.m.).

e. For control of cattails and bulrushes: 2,4-D (4 to lbs. in a 1 to 20 oil water emulsion, or dalapon, or amitrol).

(Source—Suggested Guide for Chemical Control of Weeds —ARS 22-46, U. S. Department of Agriculture, April, 1961)

The names and initials used above are the common ones and do not in any case include trade names. The rates of concentration vary greatly between containers and between manufacturers, hence the rates of application, where given, should be carefully checked against the labels before using. FOLLOW THE MANUFACTURERS DIRECTIONS CAREFULLY.

It is important to have one sprayer reserved for use with the weed killers since it is difficult to remove these chemicals by rinsing with water. It can be best done with ammonia: 3 tablespoonfuls to 3 gallons of water. Allow to stand overnight and rinse thoroughly.

Mulching materials may be used to control weeds if applied before the weeds get started and if put on thickly enough so that the weeds cannot push through. Compost, straw, grass clippings, peat, etc., may be used for this purpose, although few gardeners use them, usually because such material is not available in sufficient quantity, or if obtainable, the cost is prohibitive.

Summer Cultivation

Summer cultivation is hardly a field of activity that appeals to the gardener, but it means much to the success of the garden. Cultivation helps to control the weeds; keeps the soil loose so that rainfall easily soaks into the soil; retards moisture loss through evaporation, and enables the plant roots to obtain air. In all gardens, unless mulched, cultivation should begin early and be repeated after each shower. By keeping the soil loose at all times, the cultivation may be accomplished with a rake or speedy cultivator. Let the soil become hard and baked or weedy and the work of breaking it up with a hoe is many times greater. A light rake used within two or three days after a shower will loosen the soil easily and quickly. Beginners sometimes try to cultivate the garden while it is still too wet. This can do more damage than good. Work the soil only when it will crumble easily. The same test discussed under spading applies.

Summer cultivations are for the most part shallow. Plant roots are not far below the surface of the ground and deep cultivation is apt to injure many of them.

Deep cultivation turns up too much of the moist soil, allowing it to dry out.

Shallow cultivation, if well done, will give just as much protection against evaporation loss as a mulch.

Many garden plants will suffer if the soil is allowed to crust to the extent that they are unable to get sufficient air. Sweet corn is often badly stunted from lack of soil aeration.

Even if mulches are employed during the hotter part of the summer, the soil should be thoroughly stirred before applying the mulching material. Early application of mulches is not advisable since they tend to delay the maturity of the garden crops. It is only after the soil is thoroughly warmed that we may safely substitute mulches for cultivation.

Watering the Garden

Watering garden plants or flowers is not as simple as it may seem. Many gardeners give it little thought. The time of day and the method of applying water have much to do with the beneficial effects.

Barely moistening the surface when watering may have an injurious effect. It encourages the roots to grow toward the surface of the soil. Plant roots normally grow downward in search of moisture and thus if not watered suffer less in time of drought than those close to the soil's surface. When watering, the general recommendation is to let the sprinkler or hose run until the soil is moistened to a depth of at least 4 inches. Six inches are better. It usually takes a half hour or longer to give the soil a really good soaking. One good wetting of the soil should last a week or more.

Before watering plants, it is desirable to loosen the soil with a hoe or rake so that the water will readily penetrate into the soil rather than drain away. However, it is not safe to loosen the soil so deeply that shallow-growing roots are injured.

After the application of water to the plants and after the soil has dried sufficiently but before it has become baked, the soil should be cultivated until well pulverized. This prevents baking and tends to reduce evaporation losses.

Watering is best done in the early morning or early afternoon. Contrary to the usual practice of applying water in the late evening, based on the theory that it will soak into the soil before the sun draws it off, we take into consideration the spread of disease. Wet leaves encourage the development of disease spores and so it is recommended that the time of watering, as far as practicable, should be regulated that the foliage will dry before night.

Sprinklers are a favored method of applying water since they cover a large area. However, more and more gardeners are using methods or devices by which the water reaches the soil without wetting the foliage. This would seem desirable since it helps to protect plants from disease. Canvas or plastic hose which permits the water to soak through is one device. Removing the nozzle is a common practice; on level ground irrigation ditches is another. Regulate the flow of water so that it soaks into the soil rather than running so fast that it washes away the topsoil.

Watering is not necessary to the success of a garden. Many farm and city gardens depend entirely upon nature. But, if you do water—do it so that it is a benefit to the plants. Judicious use of water should keep the plant growing vigorously and productively.

Watering the garden with city water is sometimes prohibited during July, August and September. Of course, this does not affect gardeners who have their own wells or who save water and carry it to their plants, but for those who do not have access to water, it is well to point out again that deeply prepared seed beds and especially soils which have had liberal quantities of humus incorporated into them are fortified to withstand droughts without too great a loss. This indicates that early spring soil preparation is the first step in solving the soil moisture problem.

Mulching the Garden

As research shows us more and more values to be gained from a mulch about our plants during the growing season, it is evident that gardeners should give more heed to this practice. The supply of organic matter in the soil may be maintained fully as well, if not better, through surface applications. The problem of controlling weeds is ever present although if the mulch is applied thickly enough weeds cannot get through. Getting moisture into the soil is often a problem on the heavier soils because as the droplets of moisture strike the ground they churn the clay particles into a soup which soon seals the pores in the soil surface and subsequent moisture runs off. A mulch will prevent this by breaking the force of the drops of water permitting moisture to enter the soil in much larger volume than would otherwise take place. A direct corollary of this is the reduction or prevention of erosion.

A surface mulch by keeping the soil spaces open maintains an air supply to the roots. Plants do not thrive for long without air. A mulched soil is cooler, which is of immeasurable value to many kinds of plants whose roots apparently are unable to function in a hot soil. And, of course, everyone looks upon mulching as a means of conserving moisture.

These are the major functions of mulches. There are other values, but these should be sufficient to indicate the importance of mulching the gardens and borders during the growing season.

The kind of material used is not important. Usually, the gardener considers the appearance and seeks a material that is comparatively inconspicuous. In addition, it is desirable to avoid those materials which are so light that they blow away with the first gusts of winds. Also objectionable are those mulches which tend to cake or crust. If the areas to be mulched are large it is well to obtain whatever material may be had at the most reasonable cost.

In this area gardeners generally use one of the following materials: Peatmoss, ground corncobs, pine needles, chips from the planning mill, tanbark, compost, sawdust, chopped up brush, straw, hay or two or three light spongy materials sold under trade names.

The depth to apply these mulching materials and the quantity needed will vary with the kind. Peat moss, tanbark and the mineral mulches are usually applied to a depth of an inch, whereas straw, hay and other course materials may need to be applied to a depth of 3 or 4 inches. Compost for mulching should be rather cause. Sawdust, chopped twigs and the pulverized corncobs are usually applied to a depth of 2 or 3 inches.

If weeds start showing up in a mulched bed the thickness of the mulch can be increased to a depth where their growth is completely checked. Bermuda grass and bindweed seem to be able to push through a greater thickness of mulch than crabgrass, chickweed and other less vigorous annual weeds.

Nearly all of the plant materials used as a mulch should receive nitrogen in some form to supply the bacteria that work upon them. Some materials such as sawdust and corncobs require more nitrogen than compost and hay. Tanbark normally is very slow in breaking down and does not require the use of as much nitrogen as the others. Gardeners normally apply some fertilizer after the mulch is in place letting the rains or watering carry the plant food down to the feeding roots of the crops. If this application is increased slightly it will take care of the needs of the mulch, if there are any.

The time of application of mulches is open to some question. There are those who wait until the soil is quite warm, while others will apply it as soon as the seedlings are large enough. For perennials and shrubs this can be quite early. However, an early application keeps the soil cool and tends to delay growth. This is seldom serious except for hot-weather plants such as tomatoes, zinnias, marigolds, etc. Azaleas, rhododendrons, camellias, hollies and other broad-leaved evergreens need a mulch at all times.

There are a few plants that resent having a mulch close to their crowns. Delphiniums and painted daisies, for example, are subject to crown rot and should not have the mulch within 3 or 4 inches of their crowns. Iris plants also want to be exposed to the hot summer sun and should not have a mulch over their rhizomes.

Some gardeners think it necessary to remove the mulch in the late fall or early winter. However, this practice does not seem beneficial. If the ground is to be spaded in the fall the mulch can be mixed into the soil. However, after planting in the spring, it will need to be replaced if the new plants are to benefit.

The above refers to mulches as they benefit growing crops and save the gardeners work. There is another function of mulches which is of importance—to keep the soil from freezing, or to keep it frozen as a protection against "heaving." Heaving is the result of alternate freezing and thawing—a common experience in the Washington area.

Young plants or shallowly planted bulbs may be pushed out of the soil through frost action and for them a mulch is most beneficial if applied immediately after the ground is frozen to a depth of an inch or two. Unfortunately, in the Washington area this is often hard to determine and occasionally does not happen. Nevertheless a layer of pine boughs, compost or other materials should be scattered over such beds to prevent or at least to retard their thawing. It is well to remember that such mulches if applied too early—before the ground is *frozen*—are apt to provide a home for the field mice.

Fall-planted shrubs, particularly the evergreens, frequently are not well enough established for their roots to function properly. A thick mulch will keep the soil from freezing and permit the roots to function much later into the winter than if not given this warm insulation.

NOTES

CHAPTER IV

PROTECTING THE GARDEN

Most of the flower and vegetable crops are attacked by one or more insect pests and by diseases. Their control is just as important to the success of the garden as are cultivation and fertilization.

Sprays or dusts to be effective must be on the leaf surfaces before the bugs take a bite or the disease spores arrive. Thus, all the work we need to do to control insects and diseases is preventive. In other words, the effectiveness of any spray or dust program depends upon keeping the foliage covered. Regularity of application is of greatest importance to effective protection.

Sprays or dusts, however, should not be applied so thickly that they prevent sunlight from reaching the leaf. To cover foliage so thickly that it cannot function deprives the plant of sunshine—its source of energy. A thin layer or coating that is barely visible to the eye is, under most conditions, sufficiently effective. Thus a fine mist from a sprayer or a billowing cloud from a duster are desirable for good coverage.

The choice between a spray or a dust is largely a matter of personal convenience and preference. A good job can be done with either one; both have their faults and their advantages. Dusting is usually quicker, and a dust gun is relatively inexpensive. Sprays last longer on the foliage, but take longer to apply and a sprayer costs more than a dust gun. Dusting cannot be done on a windy day, and a 10-minute shower can completely nullify an application, but the gardener will probably use a dust gun with greater regularity than he will a sprayer because of the convenience and time saved.

There are sprays and dusts available to the gardener that give relatively effective control over the insects and diseases that are prevalent in this area. The first of these is rotenone dust. It is effective against many chewing and sucking insects and will not injure the tender foliage of such crops as beans and peaches. It is non-poisonous to warm-blooded animals. However, it has no effect on disease spores. To meet this deficiency, some manufacturers are mixing rotenone with sulphur, copper, bordeaux, or with a new type of fungicide called carbamates and are selling under trade names. All are effective agents for the destruction of disease spores. The combination of one of these with rotenone will control most insects and diseases.

Recommended Program

Because a gardener, as a rule, is not interested in chemistry, pathology or entomology, but in keeping his plants healthy and free from insect injury, the use of all-purpose dusts or sprays is recommended. There are a number on the market, some being non-toxic for use in the vegetable garden, others are for the fruits, and there are those designed for use on ornamentals. The manufacturers include many of the newer compounds which are more or less specific in combinations so that the mixture is effective against most of the pests encountered as well as the common diseases. Because of the continued developments in this field, new materials are being discovered, tested and introduced. Manufacturers are constantly revising the combinations used in the all-purpose sprays and dusts.

The gardener in selecting all-purpose combinations for his particular use should check the label to determine whether or not they contain a stomach poison for the chewing insects, a contact poison for the sucking insects and a fungicide for the diseases. The following list of commonly-used materials is divided according to field of use. The common names are shown rather than trade names because of their multiplicity.

Insecticides

For Chewing Insects	For Sucking Insects	For Scale Insects
Lead arsenate	Nicotine sulfate	Lime-sulphur
*Rotenone	*Pyrethrum	Miscible oils
*Pyrethrum	Ovatran	Malathion
Methoxychlor	DDT (Pea aphids)	Dimethoate
DDT	Thiocyanates	
Chlordane	Organic phosphates	
BHC (Benzine hexa-	(HETP, TEPP, EPN,	
chloride)	Malathion, etc.)	
Malathion	Dimethoate	
Lindane	Aramite	
*Sabadilla	Arathane	
Dieldrin	Kelthane	
Sevin	Meta-Systox R.	

* Not toxic to warm-blooded animals.

Fungicides

(For the prevention of disease)

Bordeaux mixture	Karathane
Sulphur and sulphur compounds	Captan
Copper compounds	Phygon
Organic mercury compounds	Ferbam
Cadmium compounds	Nabam
Napthoquinone	Zineb
Phaltan	Ziram
Cyprex	Manzate
Acti-Dione P.M., RZ, Thiram	Piperalin

DDT, which has proved to be wonderfully effective against certain insects, including the Japanese beetle, the Colorado potato beetle, the flea beetle and many others is now being supplanted by methoxychlor. The latter is toxic to more insects and is less toxic to human beings and does not persist in the soil for as long a period in a stable form. DDT remains in the soil for a considerable period, affecting germination and growth of some plants. Perhaps this is true of other new materials so until they are tested gardeners should avoid using them in excessive amounts. Follow the recommendations of the specialists.

Since the advent of DDT, which kills many of the natural enemies of the red spider, gardeners are having more serious infestations of that pest. However, malathion or one of the other mitacides may be included in the dust or spray to control them.

However, dimethoate, a new systemic material, now available should do much to control the red spider mite and many other sucking insects. Dimethoate is absorbed by the plant through its leaves or roots and is an effective insecticide that remains potent for several weeks, is easy to apply, and is only slightly more toxic than malathion.

Conversion Table

(VOLUME—NOT WEIGHT)

1 tablespoonful equals	3 teaspoonfuls equal	½ fluid ounce
2 tablespoonfuls equal	6 " "	1 " "
1 gill equals	½ cupful equals	4 " "
1 cupful "	½ pint "	8 " "
1 pint "	½ quart "	16 " "
1 quart "	¼ gallon "	32 " "
1 gallon		128 " "

VOLUME AND WEIGHT

(Cold water but not in general to spray liquids)

1 fluid ounce equals	1 ounce avoirdupois
1 gill "	4 ounces "
1 cupful "	8 " "
1 pint "	16 " "
1 quart "	32 " "
1 gallon "	128 " "

(Adopted from Bureau of Standards Miscellaneous Publication 39)

Protection From Four-Legged Pests

Rabbits, birds, squirrels, mice and chipmunks sometimes invade the garden and destroy some of the crops. They are not as easily controlled as are the insects and oftentimes are more destructive. Rabbits love the tender young leaves of beans, peas, cabbages, beets and carrots. Moles, fieldmice, rats, ground squirrels or chipmunks and the common squirrel can be a nuisance but they are seldom as destructive as the rabbit who often devours a whole row of plants overnight while bugs only chew holes in a few leaves at a time.

Rabbits may be controlled in several ways besides shooting them. Repellants may be sprayed on the foliage and thus protected they probably will grow to maturity. Of the repellants, nicotine sulphate is probably the most effective, but because it is volatile it will have to be applied every few days, especially if showers are frequent. Foliage covered with bordeaux is protected against both the rabbits and the diseases.

Other repellants are: Three ounces of epsom salts to one gallon of water; one teaspoonful of creolin to one gallon of water; or lime or blood-meal dusted on the foliage while it is wet.

Moles can be trapped with metal traps or poison gases such as carbon bisulphide; calcium cyanide may be injected into their tunnels. In most cases they will be either killed or driven out. This same procedure may be used against field mice and ground squirrels.

Poison bait, prepared by coating diced sweet potatoes or carrots with powdered strychnine, or oats soaked in a solution containing the strychnine may also be used to control mice and chipmunks. However, these are *deadly poisons* and *great care* must be used in their preparation, handling and use. Put these where pets and children *cannot reach them.*

Fungicides and Insecticides
Per Gallon of Spray

INSECTICIDES			FUNGICIDES		
Common Name	Form and Concentration	Quantity Per Gallon (teasp's)	Common Name	Form and Concentration	Quantity Per Gallon (teasp's)
Rotenone	4-5WP	12	Bordeaux Mixture		
DDT	50WP	5	Ferbam	76WP	5
Methoxychlor	50WP	9	Manganese carbamate		4
Lindane	25WP	3	Thiram		
Chlordane	50WP	5	Zineb	75WP	5
Aldrin	25WP	1½	Ziram	76WP	6
Dieldrin	25WP	4	Captan	50WP	3
Heptachlor	25WP	2½	Lime-sulphur (liquid)		1*
Parathion	25WP	2	Semesan		3
Malathion	25WP	6	Sulphur	WP	8
Tepp	40Emulsion	½	Karathane	25WP	1
Sulfotepp	25Emulsion	1	Phygon		
Schradon	25Emulsion	1			
Demetox (Systox)	26Emulsion	1½	Organic mercury		
Aramite	15WP	4			
Dimite (DMC)	40WP	6	Copper compounds		
Ovotran	50WP	6	Phaltan	75%	3
Chlorobenzilate	25WP	2	Cyprex	65W	1
Nicotine-Sulphate	40Emulsion	1	Maneb		6
Dimethoate	2-Emulsion	2			

WP—Wettable powder.   * 1 cup to 9 cups.

NOTES

CHAPTER V

DEPENDABLE WASHINGTON FLOWERS
Annuals

Annual flowers are those which grow, bloom, seed and die in one season. Many of the most exquisite flowers are annuals. They are attractive in the garden—some for bedding, some for borders, some for rock gardens, some for climbing or trailing and others for their foliage only. Many are invaluable for cutting. There are annual flowers for every purpose; all are lovely and, with proper selection, blooms may be had from early summer until frost. Annuals are widely grown and greatly enjoyed by all gardeners. There are many, many kinds from which the gardener should select those which best suit his needs.

Few annuals will tolerate more than light shade. They are members of a sun-loving group. Cornflower, larkspur, pansy, salvia, snapdragon and sweet alyssum are considered tolerant of shade. Of these the pansy, impatiens, snapdragon and alyssum will tolerate the most shade. This, of course, assumes that they will not be in competition with tree roots at the same time.

Most annuals are easily grown, although the seed of some kinds are so small that unless special attention is given them germination is apt to be poor. For this reason it is desirable to start the seed in flats or pots, preferably in sphagnum moss or vermiculite, to avoid trouble with the disease "damping off." This applies especially to petunia, snapdragon and pansy seed.

Annuals often make a poor showing because they are not started early enough and are not thinned properly while small. It is a waste of time to thin after the plants have grown tall and leggy.

Snapdragons, hollyhocks and pansies which are included in this chapter are normally grown as biennials, i.e., their seed are sown in July and August and the young plants transplanted to the flower borders in September. With some protection both the pansy and the snapdragon will live over winter and bloom a second season.

Most annuals benefit by heavy cutting. Being annuals, they consider their mission in life completed when they have bloomed and developed seed. By cutting the flowers for use indoors or as they fade, the formation of seed is prevented and the plants continue to grow and flower.

To produce bushy plants it is common practice among experienced gardeners to "pinch back" most kinds of annuals as they are transplanted. "Pinching back" means to remove the top of a young plant. This practice is satisfactory only when the plants are given good culture and kept growing vigorously. Frequent

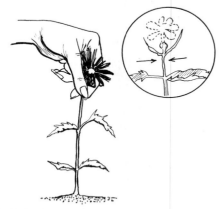

Pinch back the tops to stimulate branching and stocky growth.

cultivation of the soil, weed control, fertilization and water are needed for best results, and the results well repay the extra care in vigor and quality of bloom.

The preparation and enrichment of the soil for annuals is the same as discussed in Chapter One. Ample quantities of compost or peatmoss should be worked into the soil. Like many vegetable crops the annuals want a soil that is not too acid. Lime should be added where the acidity is lower than pH 6. Fertilizers may be added to the soil at time of preparation and additional quantities added during the growing season to keep the plants growing vigorously. The ordinary 5-10-5 commercial mixture will serve the needs of the annuals.

Annuals afford an opportunity for color harmony in mass effect. Two or more colors may be combined, but in planning such a harmony annuals with a long-blooming season, such as petunias and zinnias, should be selected.

Plant annuals among the bulbs as their foliage begins to die down. This serves to hide what might otherwise be an unsightly spot. The annuals give the dormant bulbs a certain amount of protection.

AGERATUM

(Ageratum houstonianum—Floss Flower, Tassel Flower)

Uses:	Low edging plant, rock gardens, indoor pot plant.
Blooms:	Throughout the summer.
Varieties:	Blue Boy, Blue Mink, Fairy Pink
	F Hybrids—Blue Mist, Blue Chip.

Height:	6 to 24 inches.
Seed:	Indoors early February or March. Transplant in late April or May.
Blooms:	9 to 12 weeks.
Plant:	Set plants 6 to 12 inches apart.
Soil:	Prefer a rich and moist, but well-drained soil.
Exposure:	Sun.

* * *

Ageratum is one of the most popular of edging plants. The bushy little plants produce a profusion of fluffy flowers from May to October. Thus they make excellent edging plants, but also are useful as pot plants. The taller growing varieties are excellent for cutting. They are of easy culture but do best in a rich moist soil. The ageratums are comparatively free from insect and disease problems.

The ageratum is easily grown from seed and from stem cuttings. Because of the difficulty in having plants of uniform height when grown from seed the experts like to grow plants from cuttings. This, however, is done during the winter which makes it impracticable for the small gardener.

Ageratum is often used as a mass planting to provide season long color in the border. The taller growing varieties should be selected for this purpose.

However, the main use of the ageratum has been as an edging plant or in the rock garden. That is why there are so many varieties in the 4 to 6 inch height. The blue flowered varieties are most numerous. Attention has also been given to other colors and so in addition to shades of blue we now have white and pink flowered varieties. Midget Blue (3-inch), an All America, is considered to be the best of the very dwarf varieties.

Ageratum seed should be sown indoors in February or March if the gardener is to have husky plants for transplanting to out of door beds in May. It takes about three months from time of sowing of seed until flowering. Seed sown out-of-doors (May) may not begin to flower until August.

The plants will need a certain amount of attention if they are to remain attractive throughout the growing season. The first step is to remove spent blossoms. This not only removes unattractive tops but it also diverts the plant's strength from the formation of seed to the producing of new stems and flowers.

Ageratum is comparatively free from insects and diseases, but if they should appear, they may be controlled with an all-purpose dust or spray. Usually when watering, a hard stream of water will do much to protect the plant from red spider mites and other pests.

The plant commonly called Hardy Ageratum is not an ageratum but a weedy, fall-flowering plant whose flower heads resemble the ageratum. It is known botanically as Eupatorium coelestinum. It has many common names. Mistflower is probably the most descriptive. This plant spreads both by seeds and by underground rootstems which make it objectionable in the small flower border or in the rock garden.

ALYSSUM

(Alyssum maritima—Sweet Alyssum, Sweet Alice, Heal-dog, Madwort)

Uses:	Edging, rock gardens.
Blooms:	May to October.
Varieties:	Little Gem, Violet King, Royal Carpet, Carpet of Snow.
Height:	4 to 10 inches.
Seed:	Indoors—March; Out-of-doors—Late April.
Blooms:	5-6 weeks.
Plant:	6 to 10 inches apart.
Soil:	Ordinary garden loam.
Exposure:	Full sun.

* * *

One of the most widely grown of edging plants is sweet alyssum, a dainty little free-flowering, fragrant plant of long-season blooming habit and relatively easy care. Its habit of growth is so spreading that the edging cannot be kept narrower than 6 inches. It has a comparatively uniform height of growth.

The seed may be sown indoors in March or out-of-

doors in April. Sweet alyssum requires approximately six weeks from seed sowing until blooming. The white flowered varieties may be sown out-of-doors in the fall

in the Washington area. In fact, they will often self-sow if left to seed in the border. The violet and pink varieties, however, are more tender and should not be planted in the border until the soil has begun to warm up.

Set the seedlings, or thin them, to about 6 inches apart.

For the best bloom in late summer and fall, the tops of the plants should be clipped first on one side of the row and then on the other. This causes the plants to develop new branches and gives them renewed vigor.

Cultivation and light feeding is desirable, although this little annual does not demand too much attention. If disease or insects should prove troublesome, spray or dust with an all-purpose garden mixture.

While the alyssum is usually called sweet, it is the tall variety, Alyssum maritimum (10 to 12 inches), that is fragrant. However, it is seldom grown as an edging plant because of its height, but it should be included in every fragrant border because of its long season of bloom.

Shearing the dwarf Alyssum removes spent blossoms and encourages new growth.

ASTERS, ANNUAL

(Callistephus chinensis—China aster)

Uses:	Cutflowers, bedding.
Blooms:	August until frost.
Varieties:	Wilt resistant varieties in the Queen of the Market, Giant Branching and Princesses classes; Charming, Scarlet Beauty, Radiance.
Height:	18 to 36 inches.
Seed:	Indoors—mid-March; Out-of-doors—May 1.
Blooms:	3 to 5 months.
Plant:	12 to 15 inches apart.
Soil:	Rich moist loam.
Exposure:	Full sun.

* * *

The China aster is an excellent flower for cutting during the summer and fall, coming in a wide range of colors. They are non-fading and produce an abundance of bloom when well grown. The flowers under good

growing conditions may average 3 inches across.

Formerly the China aster was an important commercial flower but diseases have made them rather difficult to grow. In this area we expect good results in one year out of three but with special care this can be improved. The soil must be free from the disease known as "fusarium wilt" and from "aster yellows."

If the gardener has not grown asters before there should be no trouble with the yellows, but many of our garden plants are subject to fusarium wilt. Asters should be planted in soil that has not been used for flowers or vegetables for some years. Wilt resistant varieties are important.

The seed should be started indoors in mid-March to insure having plants ready to be planted out of doors by early May. Even with this early start, blooms should not be expected before August.

The plants should not be pinched. Space them from 12 to 15 inches apart. The early varieties are smaller growing and need not be planted as far apart as the later blooming ones. Feed once or twice during the growing season with a general garden mixture such as 5-10-5. Keep the plants cultivated or mulched to prevent weeds and to keep the soil from crusting. The asters will need watering whenever rainfall is insufficient but take care not to wet the foliage.

The China aster seems to do best in a soil that has been limed to reduce the acidity. Ground or pulverized limestone, 2 to 3 pounds per 100 square feet of area, is generally needed. Plant in a soil that has been enriched with compost or well-rotted cow manure.

Should insects appear, they may be controlled with an all-purpose dust or spray. If disease should appear, especially the one that causes the leaves to wilt, usually on one side, do not attempt to save the plant but pull it up and burn it.

BEGONIA

(Begonia semperflorens) F₁ Hybrids

Uses:	Bedding, cutflowers.
Blooms:	June to frost.
Varieties:	Green foliage—Dwarf—6-8 inches
	Pink—Pink Pearl, Sleeping Beauty
	Red—Chrisy
	White—White Tausendschon
	Intermediate—8-10 inches
	Pink—Pink Tausendschon
	Red—Matador, Red Tausendschon
	Bronze foliage—Dwarf—6-8 inches
	Pink—Steffi

	Red—Red Comet
	Intermediate
	Pink—Luise
	White—Cappuccino
Height:	Dwarf 6-8, Intermediate 8-10 inches
Seed:	Indoors—Jan.
Blooms:	Four months—seed to blooming-sized plants
Plant:	8 inches apart
Soil:	Well supplied with peatmoss or compost
Exposure:	Sun or light shade

* * *

The waxy-leaved begonias are only now coming into their best use—bedding. The hybrids provide vigor and uniformity that makes them one of the best bedding plants requiring very little care; they are superior to the older varieties. They do well in full sun and will take light shade. The soil should be well supplied with compost or peatmoss.

They are seldom troubled by disease or insect pests.

The begonia requires little watering—they should not be watered in full sunlight; if planted in shade, they should not be watered in the evening. Too much watering and at the wrong time of day is likely to do more harm than good.

In the fall, some of the plants may be lifted and potted for indoor use.

BELLS OF IRELAND

(Molucella laevis—Bells of Ireland, Molucca balm)

Uses:	Cutflowers, dried arrangements,
Blooms:	August-September.
Varieties:	None.
Height:	2 to 3 feet.
Seed:	Indoors—March; Out-of-doors—May.
Blooms:	10 to 12 weeks.
Plant:	10 to 12 inches apart.
Soil:	Ordinary garden loam.
Exposure:	Sun or partial shade.

Bells of Ireland is an interesting and attractive, though odd, plant with large, very pale translucent, green, shell-like calyxes, each containing a little white flower. The flower drops out as they reach maturity leaving the green calyxes or bracts which are so popular especially in dried flower arrangements.

The seed should be started indoors in March or out-of-doors in May after the soil has lost its chill. Early seeding is important as the seed may take 4 weeks to germinate. The branching plants should be spaced about a foot apart. They will thrive in a moderately rich garden loam.

While they seemingly are immune to insects and diseases, the gardener should be prepared to protect them with an all-purpose dust or spray, since it is important to have them free from injury or markings.

BROWALLIA

(Browallia spps. and hybrids)

Uses:	Bedding, borders, winter pot culture in the house.
Season of bloom:	All summer outside, all winter indoors.
Varieties:	Sapphire—dark blue with small white eye.
Height:	10 to 18 inches.
Seed:	Early spring.
Plant:	Close together for early bloom—6 inches.
Soil:	Well-drained.
Exposure:	Shade.

* * *

If the bed is protected over winter, the plants may self-sow. If some plants are pinched back, they will branch and remain dwarfed, blooming later in the season, thus giving a long season of bloom.

Seed of Browallia speciosa should be planted in pots in the late summer for winter bloom. Treat it as a hanging basket plant for full display of blooms.

CALENDULA

(Calendula officinalis—Pot Marigold, Scotch Marigold)

Uses:	Cutflowers, bedding.
Blooms:	June; September-October.
Varieties:	Lemon Queen, Ball Gold, Pacific Beauty strain.
Height:	18 to 24 inches.
Seed:	Indoors—February; Out-of-doors—July.
Blooms:	2 to 3 months.
Plant:	12 to 15 inches apart.
Soil:	Well enriched loam.
Exposure:	Sun or very light shade.

* * *

The gorgeous calendula is a cool weather plant that should be started early indoors for bloom before hot weather or started in the early summer for fall bloom.

The flowers are long lasting and much desired for cutting. They are of comparatively easy culture and are not greatly troubled by insects or diseases.

The calendula is a fairly hardy annual and in some years will self-seed. Occasionally they may be fall sown, but this is not a dependable practice in the more exposed areas.

The seed should be started indoors early in February so that good sized plants will be ready for planting out of doors in April. Otherwise seed planting should be delayed until early in July. The fall flowering period is generally considered the more desirable in this area.

Space the plants a foot or more apart as they tend to sprawl. Staking is seldom practiced or needed if the plants are well grown. This means that they should be

The calendula is a universal favorite as a winter flower for cutting.

kept growing strongly during the late summer. Fertilize once or twice and water as needed. Mulching is beneficial since they seem to thrive best under cool growing conditions. If the plants can be placed so that they are protected from the mid-day and afternoon sun, they seem to do much better.

The calendula does not seem to be subject to insects or diseases in this area except perhaps a leaf-eater. An all-purpose dust or spray will protect them.

CALLIOPSIS

(Coreopsis tinctoria—Tickseed)

Uses:	Cutting, border effect, and as an edging.
Blooms:	Spring and early summer.
Varieties:	Tall, dwarf and doubles are listed; Golden Ray.
Height:	9 to 36 inches.
Seed:	Sow in fall for earliest bloom where plants are to grow; in late summer for fall bloom.
Blooms:	About 40 days.
Plant:	Thin to 8 to 12 inches apart.
Soil:	Any good garden loam.
Exposure:	Sun.

DEPENDABLE WASHINGTON FLOWERS

The calliopsis is an annual form of the Coreopsis and has much the same habit of growth. It is an excellent cut flower. It does well in the sunny border. The dwarf varieties may be used as an edging. The calliopsis is of easy culture and hardy.

The seeds should be sown in the fall where they are to grow, since they do not transplant easily. For fall bloom, they may be sown in late August or early September, but this hardly seems worthwhile. Thin the seedlings to 8 to 12 inches, the taller growing varieties need the more space.

They seem to thrive in any good garden soil and do best if in full sun. Unless the flowers are kept cut, the season of bloom is apt to end early, but with such a profusion of flowers this can hardly be avoided.

The calliopsis is best known for its yellow flowers marked with crimson, red or mahogany, although there are several named varieties on the market with solid or definite color markings. Calliopsis Golden Wave is a golden yellow with a reddish brown center. It grows to a height of 20 inches. There is a double calliopsis available in mixture. Generally, gardeners are satisfied to buy mixed colors and do not plant the named varieties. This is a satisfactory practice where the seedlings are allowed to grow.

The calliopsis is seldom troubled by insects or diseases. Should a disease appear, it is usually best handled by changing the area of seeding.

CELOSIA

(Celosia argenta (cristata, childsi, plumosa)—Cockscomb, Chinese Wool-flower)

Uses:	Cutflowers, dried flowers.
Blooms:	August—October.
Varieties:	Crested—Toreador, Fireglow, Kardinal, Improved, Feather —Fiery Feather, Golden Feather, Purple Plume, Forest Fire, Fire Glow.
Height:	10 to 36 inches.
Seed:	Indoors—March; Out-of-doors—late April.
Blooms:	About 2 months.
Plant:	12 to 18 inches apart.
Soil:	Any good garden loam.
Exposure:	Sun.

* * *

The Cockscomb is an old-time garden plant that has achieved some popularity in recent years. Probably much of the new interest comes from the development of the "feather" varieties. The early gardeners seem to

have striven for huge crested blooms that were almost grotesque. Today the emphasis is on the smaller cockscombs and plumy feathers which are much more useful in floral arrangements. The latter are excellent for dried flower arrangements.

The cockscombs thrive in any good garden loam in a sunny situation. They are comparatively easy to grow and do not require any special care.

The seed should be started indoors in March in order to have good-sized plants to put in the border in May when the soil is warm. Give the plants at least 12 inches of space between them, 15 to 18 is a better spacing. The dwarf varieties may be planted closer together. Crowding prevents the growth of good foliage.

The soil should be kept cultivated or mulched to avoid weeds and crusting. Fertilize once a month to insure good foliage using a general garden mixture (5-10-5 or similar). Water as needed.

The colors of the cockscomb type are mostly dark reds, but there are scarlet and yellow ones and a dwarf white. The plume type comes in many shades but most interest seems to center in the shades of yellow.

The celosias seem to be very free from insect and disease injury but since the foliage is so important to their appearance, it should be protected at all times with an all-purpose dust or spray.

CHRYSANTHEMUMS, ANNUAL

(Chrysanthemum carinatum—Annual Chrysanthemum)

Uses:	Cutflowers, bedding.
Blooms:	July—September.
Varieties:	Rainbow, Single mixed, Coronarium Double mixed, Polar Star.
Height:	1½ to 2 feet tall.
Seed:	Indoors—March; Out-of-Doors—late April.
Blooms:	5 to 6 months.
Plant:	8 to 10 inches apart.
Soil:	Rich, moist, garden loam.
Exposure:	Sun.

The annual chrysanthemums are free flowering, summer bloomers that seem to do best in a cool climate. They have been used successfully in this area and probably deserve more attention than they have received.

The seed should be started indoors in March so as to have husky plants for planting in the garden as soon as the soil is warm. They should be kept growing vigorously in order to produce an abundance of bloom.

Until recently only single and double flowered mixtures were available. The first named variety, Yellowstone, is a bright yellow.

Give the plants plenty of space and keep the soil mulched from the day they are transplanted to the garden. These practices are necessary to keep the plants free from disease and nematodes which are splashed onto the leaves from the soil if it has not been covered with a mulch.

CLEOME

(Cleome spinosa—Spider Flower, Rocky Mountain Bee Plant)

Uses:	Background planting, cutflowers.
Blooms:	June until frost.
Varieties:	Pink Queen, Helen Campbell, Golden Sparkler, Purple Queen, Snow Crown.
Height:	4 to 5 feet.
Seed:	Out-of-doors in May where they are to grow.
Blooms:	8 weeks.
Plant:	2 to 3 feet apart.
Soil:	Any garden soil, sandy is best.
Exposure:	Sun or very light shade.

* * *

The Cleome is a striking tall growing plant with flowers resembling small orchids. Long stamens give it a spidery appearance. However, it is the seed pods on the spent blossoms that give it the name Spider Flower. It is constantly in bloom from June until frost, and this—together with its height—makes it useful in front of shrubbery or as a background planting. The grayish green foliage is attractive, but, as the plant reaches mature size, the lower leaves thin out and hence it needs growing plants in front of it. The foliage has a rather strong but not unpleasant odor.

The Cleome is very tolerant as to soil and location. The flowers are larger and fuller if given some attention, especially watering during summer drought periods.

The seed should be sown where the plants are to grow about the time of the last killing frost—April 20, or a week or two before. Cover with ½-inch of soil and as soon as they come up, thin to 2 or 3 feet. The plants can be transplanted but not without care.

The variety Pink Queen is most generally planted because of its clear colors. Too often the seedlings have a muddy color. The white is well recommended, if the seed can be found. The experts do not consider the yellow to be worth planting.

There is one word of caution in growing the Cleome —remove the spent seed pods. Otherwise you will be swamped with seedlings. The Cleome is seldom troubled with insects or diseases.

CORNFLOWER

(Centaurea cyanus—Bachelor's Button, Ragged Robin, Basket Flower)

Uses:	Cutflowers.
Blooms:	May and June from fall-sown seed; July and August from spring sowing of seed.
Varieties:	Pinkie, Blue Boy, Snowman, Red Boy, Jubilee Gem, Double Blue.
Height:	2 to 3 feet.
Seed:	September or March where they are to grow.
Blooms:	6 to 8 weeks.
Plant:	Thin to 12 inches apart.
Soil:	Any good garden loam.
Exposure:	Sun.

* * *

The Cornflower is a widely grown, hardy annual that will self-seed if given a chance. It is easy to grow and will produce a wealth of bloom with very little care. There are a number of named varieties but most gardeners are content with the common mixture of double-flowered forms. The Cornflower is comparatively free from insects and pests. The flowers are especially long-lasting as cutflowers.

There are several forms of Centaurea. C. cyanus, the Cornflower, is the most widely cultivated. Sweet Sultan and the Basketflower, as well as the gray foliaged edging plant, are other forms that are not as commonly grown.

DEPENDABLE WASHINGTON FLOWERS

The seed of the Cornflower should be planted in the late fall or in the early spring several weeks before the last killing frost is expected. When these planting dates are observed the plants will be taller and bushier, thus making a better display in the garden as well as providing much more cutting material. However, the seed may be sown in the spring and summer and will grow and flower; but the plants will be smaller and not as productive.

The plants should be thinned to at least one foot if they are to have room to produce bushy growth.

The gray-green foliaged plants are literally covered with flowers an inch or more in diameter. Cornflower blue is a popular color. The variety of this color is Blue Boy. There are pinks, red, white and various shades in between as well as other shades of blue.

Ordinary garden care is adequate for this dependable, easily grown annual.

The Cornflower is sometimes troubled by the rust disease of the foliage but it may be controlled by dusting or spraying with an all-purpose mixture. The plants are subject to the aster yellows. Should this disease appear—yellow sickly plants—they should be pulled and burned.

COSMOS

(Cosmos bipinnatus)

Uses:	Background, cutflowers.
Blooms:	August to November.
Varieties:	Sensation varieties—Pinkie, Purity, Radiance, Sunset, Orange Flare, Orange Ruffles, Fiesta.
Height:	3 to 8 feet.
Seed:	Indoors—March; Out-of-doors—late April.
Blooms:	10 to 12 weeks.
Plant:	2 feet apart.
Soil:	Average garden loam.
Exposure:	Sun or light shade.

* * *

The older varieties of the Cosmos were tall, late flowering plants, excellent for background plantings. The foliage was light and graceful, although by pinching the plant back when less than 2 feet in height, branching was stimulated and the bean pole effect avoided. The colors were clear and attractive (white, rose, pink, red and yellow), but the lateness of flowering was disappointing to many. The Cosmos withstood light frosts, all of which indicated that they were worthwhile annuals.

However, the hybridizers produced Extra Early and Sensation types which flower in 10 weeks or less instead of the 3 to 4 months of the early forms. The new plants are not so tall, about 3 to 4 feet, and they tend to be bushier with the flowers massed all over them. There has been some change in flower form. The changes for the better have been so marked that 4 of the above named varieties received honors in the All-America Selection trials. The 5th went to mixed seed of the Sensation type.

Cosmos are tender annuals and the seed should be started indoors in March. However, the seed may be sown out of doors in late April after the soil has warmed. The plants transplant readily and should be pinched as they are being put in the garden to induce branching.

Cosmos need to be fertilized every month or six weeks to insure good growth and large showy flowers; water as needed. The taller varieties need staking to keep them from blowing over during high windstorms in late August and September.

Insects and diseases are seldom a problem with the Cosmos in the home garden although there is a stem blight disease. Infected plants should be pulled and burned. A stem borer may be a problem. The cure— slit the stem with a thin bladed knife to kill the worm. The problem is to know which of the plants, if any, have been attacked.

CUPFLOWER

(Nierembergia—Blue Cups)

Uses:	Edging, rock grarden.
Blooms:	July until frost.
Varieties:	Purple Robe
Height:	4 to 6 inches.
Seed:	Indoors—March; Out-of-doors—May.
Blooms:	About 15 weeks.
Plant	6 to 10 inches apart.
Soil:	Rich, moist.
Exposure:	Sun or light shade.

The Cupflower is an excellent edging plant, producing a wealth of cup-like flowers throughout the season. If started indoors, bloom may start in June and continue until frost. The needle-like foliage is unnoticed because of the abundance of flowers.

The Cupflowers like a rich moist soil for best growth, but they will thrive and flower during the hottest, driest part of the summer.

The varieties are described as having a dark purple color, but the color is variable and may be lavender and even almost white. Nevertheless the Cupflower is considered one of the most useful dwarf-edging plants for window boxes and in flower vases.

The seeds should be started in a warm place, either indoors or out.

The Nierembergia seem to be untroubled by insects or diseases which is an added factor in their favor.

DAHLIA

(Dahlia species)

Uses:	Cutflowers, bedding.
Blooms:	July to frost.
Varieties:	Unwins dwarf hybrids, semidouble; Coltness hybrids, single; Zulu, Sunburst, Cactus flowered mixture (large flowered).
Height:	15 to 24 inches.
Seed:	Indoors—late March; Out-of-doors—May.
Blooms:	8 to 10 weeks.
Plant:	12 inches apart.
Soil:	Rich, moist.
Exposure:	Sun.

* * *

Growing dahlias from seed is not as common a practice as it should be. The dwarf dahlias grown from seed make excellent bedding plants, which flower from June or July until frost. The flowers are useful for cutting. They are comparatively easy to grow and need only a fertile soil and plenty of moisture for best results. They are not often troubled by insects or diseases.

The seeds should be started indoors in late March so as to have strong plants ready for the border as soon as the soil is warm. The young plants should be pinched at transplanting to stimulate branching. Space them a foot apart in the bed or border.

Mulch the dahlia bed as soon as the plants are well started since they will take up all of the space as they spread out and cultivation will be difficult. Fertilize the bed at time of preparation and again just before the spreading plants make work difficult. The dahlias need lots of water, so whenever rainfall is inadequate, they should be watered.

Dahlias may be troubled by red spider mites which may be controlled by Malathion, or by a blast of cold water from the garden hose. Such other diseases and insects as may appear are best controlled with an all-purpose spray or dust.

Some gardeners in their efforts to have uniform beds of one color will save the tubers and use them instead of seed for future plantings. However, most gardeners are satisfied with the season-long display of bright colors and use the mixtures that are obtained from a packet of seed.

FORGET-ME-NOT

(Cynoglossum wallichi—Hounds Tongue)
(Cynoglossum amabile—Chinese Forget-Me-Not)

Uses:	Background, cutflowers.
Blooms:	June to frost.
Varieties:	Firmament, Blanche Burpee, Amabile Blue.
Height:	18 to 30 inches.
Seed:	Indoors—March; Out-of-doors—April.
Blooms:	8 to 10 weeks.
Plant:	6 to 10 inches.
Soil:	Any good garden loam.
Exposure:	Sun or light shade.

* * *

The Chinese Forget-me-not is a biennial treated as an annual because it will bloom the first season from seed. It is a hardy plant and probably would grow just as well from seed sown in the fall as from spring-planted seed. The modern variety, Firmament, is a low-growing (15 to 18 inches) fragrant plant with indigo blue flowers. The foliage is grayish green.

The Cynoglossum tends to self-seed, and this tendency should be kept under control since the seeds are "stick-tights" and can become widely distributed. Young plants will live over winter with little or no protection. They will thrive in sun and in light shade.

The Cynoglossum does not require any special care, although moderate care in watering and fertilizing insure longer sprays for cutting. It seems to be free from insects and diseases.

FOUR O'CLOCK

(Mirabilis jalapa—Marvel of Peru, Four O'Clock)

Uses:	Background, border display.
Blooms:	June until frost.
Varieties:	Mostly mixtures, Petticoat, Mirabilis.
Height:	About 3 feet.
Seed:	Indoors—March; Out-of-doors—April.
Blooms:	About 2 months.
Plant:	About 2 feet apart.
Soil:	Any garden loam.
Exposure:	Sun.

* * *

DEPENDABLE WASHINGTON FLOWERS

The Four O'Clocks are tender plants that should not be planted out of doors until the soil has warmed and there is little danger of a hard frost. The plants are strong growing, well branched, and need little cultural care to insure abundant bloom. If allowed to seed, there will be many volunteer seedlings the next season. They produce such a mass of color that even before the flowers open in the late afternoon, they are attractive. The usual form is yellow, but there are red and white ones in the mixtures.

The seed of the Four O'Clocks may be started indoors in March and the plants set out in early May, or the seed may be sown in the border where they are to bloom in April. They flower in about 2 months from seed.

The Four O'clock is a strong grower and will thrive in almost any soil and thus is useful in unfavorable locations. However, in this area the Japanese beetles will feed on the blossoms of the yellow and white flowered plants. Some people plant them to attract the Japanese beetles away from roses and other flowers.

The plants form tubers somewhat like those of a dahlia which may be dug and stored over winter for spring planting. There is no advantage in this practice except to keep a particularly desirable color.

Because the blossoms do not open until late afternoon, except on cloudy days, they are of little use for indoor decoration.

GAILLARDIA

(Gaillardia pulchella—Blanket Flower)

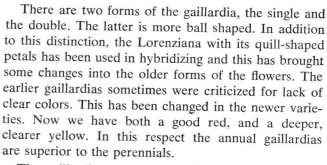

Uses:	Cutflowers, bedding.
Blooms:	June to October.
Varieties:	Double—Fiesta, Lorenziana, Sunshine. Single—Indian Chief, Pinwheel, The Warrior.
Height:	18 to 24 inches.
Seed:	Indoors—March; Out-of-doors—late April.
Blooms:	9 to 10 weeks.
Plant:	9 to 15 inches apart.
Soil:	Rich, light, well-drained.
Exposure:	Sun.

* * *

The annual gaillardias are very useful cutflowers and they make a colorful display in the border. They tend to be less sprawling than the perennial gaillardias and will thrive in the hottest part of the garden. The newer varieties are more colorful than those formerly available. They are not hardy but their long season of bloom makes them very desirable. They will self seed under favorable conditions.

The seeds should be started indoors to have them ready for a long season of bloom in the garden. Set the plants in as light a soil as possible. If necessary, add sand and partially rotted compost. The plants should be spaced 9 to 15 inches apart to allow for good branching.

There are two forms of the gaillardia, the single and the double. The latter is more ball shaped. In addition to this distinction, the Lorenziana with its quill-shaped petals has been used in hybridizing and this has brought some changes into the older forms of the flowers. The earlier gaillardias sometimes were criticized for lack of clear colors. This has been changed in the newer varieties. Now we have both a good red, and a deeper, clearer yellow. In this respect the annual gaillardias are superior to the perennials.

The gaillardias seem to thrive in the hottest, driest weather, and for this reason mulches are not suggested. Clean cultivation and fertilizer applied only at the time of soil preparation are suggested.

The gaillardias seem to be comparatively free from insect and disease. However, should the plants be attacked, they may be protected from further damage with one of the all-purpose sprays or dusts.

HOLLYHOCKS

(Althaea rosea—Hollyhock)

Uses:	Background, bedding.
Blooms:	August.
Varieties:	Indian Spring, All Colors. Mixed (double), Powder Puff (double) Mix.
Height:	4 to 5 feet.
Seed:	Indoors—February; Out-of-doors—late April.
Blooms:	5 to 6 months.
Plant:	12 to 18 inches apart.
Soil:	Rich, moist.
Exposure:	Sun.

* * *

The biennial or perennial hollyhock is well known and widely grown for its stately display of large showy flowers. The annual is just as attractive although lower growing. They make a pleasing background for a border or for a low screen.

The seeds should be started indoors in late February or early March so that large, strong-growing plants will be ready for the border by late April or early May. Seed may be sown out-of-doors in late April.

After the first bloom spike has finished flowering, it should be cut off to encourage a second blooming from side shoots which will emerge from below the point of cut. They will be smaller and not as upright, but will give a second flowering.

Hollyhocks are strong growers, but in order to get the best results from the annuals, they should be planted in a well prepared bed that has been deeply dug. Fertilizing once or twice during the growing season is helpful. Give the plants water as needed.

The hollyhocks are usually troubled with the disease called "rust". This can be controlled by dusting or spraying with an all-purpose mixture sold for use in the flower garden.

IMPATIENS

(Impatiens Holsti, I. sultani—Patience, Sultana)

Uses:	Bedding.
Blooms:	June—frost.
Varieties:	Dwarf—colors, Mixed. Tall—Holsti Mix. Tall Hybrids—Jewel series, Imp series.
Height:	6-12 inches.
Seed:	February.
Blooms:	June-frost.
Plant:	6-10 inches apart.
Soil:	High in humus, moist.
Exposure:	Shade.

* * *

For many years the Patience plant was considered a house plant, but then we learned it would bloom all season in the shade. If healthy, it would self-seed. The Impatiens is the one annual that will flower in deep shade when not in competition with shallow-growing tree roots.

The Patience plant is not commonly used as a cut flower, but it does provide color in the shady garden.

A generous supply of leafmold, compost, or peatmoss should be worked into the soil both as a reservoir of moisture for the plants and as a soil improver. They do very poorly in a heavy clay soil.

Choice plants may be lifted and potted before frost for continued bloom indoors.

LARKSPUR

(Delphinium ajacis, D. consolida—Larkspur)

Uses:	Cutflowers, border display.
Blooms:	June to September.
Varieties:	Giant Imperial Strain—Bluebell, Steeplechase strain, Salmon Supreme, Flamingo, White Swan.
Height:	2½ to 5 feet.
Seed:	Fall—October; Spring—Early March.
Blooms:	2 to 3 months.
Plant:	Space plants 8 to 12 inches apart.
Soil:	Usual garden loam.
Exposure:	Sun.

* * *

The larkspur is one of the most useful of the early flowering hardy annuals. The seeds need only be scattered on the ground in late October to produce a mass of flowers for border display and cutting. They require little care. Unless the plants are pulled as soon as they have finished blooming, they will self-seed and produce a new crop the next season. While the seedlings may not be as fine or tall growing as the new varieties, they will be quite useful. Larkspur is an annual delphinium and should be used in most gardens rather than the showy perennial which is adapted to more northern climates.

There are two main types of larkspur. The giant imperial is supposedly an improvement over the tall branching or double stock-flowered type. The early giant hyacinth-flowered is nonbranching. The newest strains, Steeplechase and Regal, are taller growing and more nearly approximate the perennial delphinium than the old common types of larkspur.

The main cultural practice to keep in mind is that the seeds must be sown either in the fall or in the very early spring so that they can germinate and start growth while the weather is *cool*. A light application or two of fertilizer during the growing season will be beneficial. Larkspur may be transplanted if it is done early in the spring and the roots are not severely disturbed.

Larkspur are seldom troubled by diseases although there are several that are known to infect them. If diseased plants should appear in a planting, they should be pulled and burned. Subsequent planting should be made in another part of the border.

LOBELIA

(Lobelia erinus—No common name)

Uses:	Edging, pot plant.
Blooms:	June until frost.
Varieties:	Cambridge Blue, Crystal Palace, Sapphire, Heavenly.
Height:	4 to 6 inches.
Seed:	Indoors—February, March.
Blooms:	About three months (the seed take 4 weeks to germinate).
Plant:	6 to 8 inches apart.
Soil:	Rich, moist.
Exposure:	Light shade, sun.

* * *

The Lobelia is a favorite edging plant in cool climates, the tiny compact plants flowering continuously until frost. They grow best without full sun in Washington's hot climate. Nevertheless they are desirable plants because of their compact branching type of growth and freedom of bloom; they are well adapted to the narrow border. Lobelias come in various shades of blue, some with a white eye.

There are two types of Lobelias. The one mentioned

above grows erect. The other spreads, and is more useful in window boxes, vases and baskets.

Lobelia seed should be started indoors very early since it takes nearly a month for the seed to germinate. It is very tiny and the seedlings also are so tiny that they seem impossible to handle. Once started, however, they grow sturdily. The plants should be grown under cool conditions.

In this area the Lobelias are most likely to give satisfactory results when grown in a cool situation, preferably in light shade. The compact habit of growth and blue flowers make them very desirable for edging in many places. Oftentimes by shearing the plants once or twice during the summer, they can be made to provide a satisfactory showing even in sun.

The Lobelias need a rich, moist soil, adequate spacing for good air circulation, and fertilization once or twice during the growing season. A mulch will help to keep the roots cool.

The Lobelias are subject to disease and to insect pests. Dusting and spraying will protect them should it be necessary. Yellowing of the lower leaves and diseased spots on the stems indicate a rot that is difficult to control. If this disease appears, the plants should be pulled and burned. Further plantings should not be made until the soil has been sterilized with bichloride of mercury or some similarly effective material.

MARIGOLD

African   Fluffy   Carnation
French Single   Crested   Double

(Tagetes erecta, T. patula, etc.—Marigold)

Uses:	Cutflowers, bedding plants, background.
Blooms:	June until frost.
Varieties:	Tagetes patula—French.
	6 in. Double—Petite strain, by colors, Mixture.
	8 in. Double—Pygmy strain (Primrose, Yellow, etc.)
	8-12 in. Double—Sparky, Harmony, Butterball, Color Magic, Spry, Sunkist.
	12-16 in. Double—Rusty Red, Tangerine.
	Single—Naughty Marietta, Red Head.
	Tagetes erecta—African.
	10-12 in. (Dwarf)—Dolly, Spun Gold, Spun Yellow.
	18-20 in. Diamond Jubilee, Golden Jubilee.
	30 in. Gold Coin series—(Double Eagle, Doubloon, Sovereign).
	24-30 in. Carnation-flowered—Crackerjack, Man-in-the-

Moon, Yellow Supreme, Super Chief.
30-36 in. Climax series—(Yellow Climax, Toreador).
18-32 in. Chrysanthemum-flowered—Glitters, Mammoth Mum, Limelight.

Height:	6 inches to 3 feet.
Seed:	Indoors—March; Out-of-doors—early May.
Blooms:	7 to 10 weeks.
Plant:	African type—12 to 18 inches; French type—12 to 20 inches.
Soil:	Any good garden loam.
Exposure:	Sun.

* * *

The marigolds are a large and complex group of annuals which, because of their popularity and ease of culture, the plant breeders have been developing and improving. Some breeders have succeeded in removing the more or less disagreeable odor of the foliage. Others have produced new forms of flowers as well as better colors. They still do not have a white. The habit of growth varies from that of the tall, bushy African groups to the dwarf, much branched Mexican. The French groups are characterized by stocky, bushy growth.

The Tall African—the word tall is misleading since they have now produced miniature African—have many forms. The old single flowered is seldom grown, but there are Chrysanthemum-flowered, Carnation flowered, Odorless, Giant Fluffy, and other strains each with a number of varieties varying from pale yellow to deep orange. Similarly, the French type has many strains with singles, doubles, and crested flowers ranging in color from yellow to deep mahogany. The latest are known as Petite which grow from 6 to 10 inches tall and make excellent edging.

In spite of the multitude of strains and varieties, the gardener seldom buys one that is not satisfactory in some situation. This is largely because they thrive under our soil and climatic conditions and produce an endless number of blooms before being cut down by frost in the late fall. They do not need heavy feeding to produce an abundance of flowers. Fertilization usually promotes foliage instead of bloom.

The seed may be started indoors in March for plants to be set out in the garden in May. Or the seed may be sown out-of-doors in late April or early May for bloom in late June or early July. The plants are easily transplanted even when in bloom. The plants of the taller growing strains should be pinched at time of planting. The French type do not need pinching, as they branch very well without it.

The marigolds need watering during summer drought periods if they are to keep growing vigorously. The taller types need to be staked in exposed situations; otherwise they are likely to topple over during some of our severe thunderstorms. Cultivation around marigolds should be shallow to avoid injury to the roots.

The Marigolds are seldom bothered by insects or diseases although the Japanese beetles feed in their flowers. If disease should appear, the best procedure is to pull and burn the infected plants.

NASTURTIUM

(Tropaeolum majus—Nasturtium, Nose Twister)

Uses:	Cutflowers, bedding.
Blooms:	June until frost.
Varieties:	Dwarf—Golden Globe, Primrose Gem, Cherry Rose, etc. Gleam—Golden Gleam, Scarlet Gleam, Orange Gleam, Moon Gleam. Climbing—Mixtures. Dwarf Gem—Mixtures.
Height:	1 to 6 feet.
Seed:	Out-of-doors—May 1.
Blooms:	6 to 8 weeks.
Plant:	Thin plants to 12 inches.
Soil:	Ordinary loam.
Exposure:	Sun.

* * *

The nasturtium is one of the old-timers that is still popular, largely because it is a prolific bloomer, will grow in poor soil, and has a rather sharp fragrance. Undoubtedly, it will take a hot bank and poor soil as well as any annual.

The dwarf Gem mixtures are recommended for planting as edgings, although they are only slightly smaller than the dwarf Gleam. The latter might well be called semi-dwarf since they do have short runners. The tall or climbing nasturtiums are noted for making a wonderful showing when trained to string or brush.

Outside of the tall or climbing nasturtiums, most of today's varieties are classified as doubles. The color range has been extended from a creamy white through yellow, rose, salmon, orange, and scarlet to maroon.

Nasturtiums do best in a sunny situation and they do not need to be fertilized! In fact to put them in a rich soil is to produce a mass of leaves and very few blooms. They do, however, need to be watered as needed because they are succulent plants. In fact so succulent that some use the tender leaves for flavoring salads. The first name given to them was by the English who called them Indian Cress. However, overwatering can be injurious, hence watering should not be started until the leaves show signs of wilting.

The free-flowering nasturtiums will cease to be free-flowering if they are allowed to set an undue amount of seed. Thus it is inadvisable to make too large a planting — one that cannot be kept reasonably clean.

The one real problem in growing nasturtiums is to keep the aphids under control. They cluster about the tem on the undersides of the leaves. Obviously, this is a difficult place to reach with a spray. One good method is to take a dishpan full of soapy water and throw it at the row in such a way that the leaves are flattened. The soapy water is an effective killer of aphids and the weight of the water turns many of the leaves so that the aphids are wet.

NICOTIANA

(Nicotiana alata, var. grandiflora—Flowering Tobacco)

Uses:	Bedding, fragrance.
Blooms:	June until frost.
Varieties:	Sensation mixed, Daylight White, Crimson Bedder, Dwarf White Bedder.
Height:	12 to 36 inches.
Seed:	Indoors—March; Out-of-doors—May.
Bloom:	12 to 14 weeks.
Plant:	10 to 15 inches apart.
Soil:	Any ordinary garden loam.
Exposure:	Sun or partial shade.

* * *

The Flowering Tobacco plant is not a particularly attractive plant during the day when the tubular flowers are limp and hanging down. It is at night when the starry flowers are open and when the fragrance drifts across the garden that they are most appreciated. They frequently self-seed, but most gardeners consider the volunteer seedlings of little value.

The Fowering Tobacco is a small seeded plant that is sometimes difficult to start indoors. Modern techniques make it much easier than formerly. Also, for those who wish to have more of a daytime showing, the Daylight Hybrids remain open during the hours when most people view their gardens. However, this new strain or type lacks the fragrance for which this annual has long been noted.

The older varieties were tall and slender, whereas the newer ones are shorter and thus the plants can be fitted into more spaces. The color range has been extended somewhat. It extends from white through red, maroon, rose, and yellow.

The Flowering Tobacco plants should not be heavily fertilized if a good display is desired, but a well prepared seed bed in a sheltered situation is needed for best results.

The Flowering Tobacco is not immune to a number of insects and diseases, although many gardeners grow it without trouble. However, should either insects or diseases appear, they can be controlled through the use of an all-purpose dust or spray.

PANSY

(Viola tricolor, var. hortensis—Pansy, Heartsease, etc.)

Uses:	Cutflowers, bedding.
Blooms:	March—June.
Strains:	Oregon Giants, Roggli Mixture, Steele's Jumbo Mix, Steele's 400.
Varieties:	Alpenglow, Coronation Gold, Thunnersee, Swiss Blue, Moon Moth, Pay Dirt, Golden Rapture, Hoehenfeuer, Glowing Orange, F₁ Hybrid—Majestic White with Blotch, Majestic Mixed.

Pansy (Continued)
Height:	8 to 12 inches.
Seed:	Mid-July to Mid-August.
Blooms:	6 to 7 months.
Plant:	10 to 12 inches apart.
Soil:	Rich, moist.
Exposure:	Sun and light shade.

*   *   *

Pansies are one of the really attractive perennials that are variously treated as biennials and annuals. However, they are cool weather plants and should be handled to take advantage of the Washington climate. This means fall planting so that they will start blooming the first warm period in March. The production of flowers during the early spring makes an exceedingly effective border or bed. They are available in a wide range of colors. They are of easy culture and inexpensive.

Most gardeners prefer to buy and use the large-flowered mixtures, although some such mixtures have too great a proportion of the darker shades when the majority wish to have those in the yellows, lighter reds, a few whites and some of the lighter lavenders. However, there are a number of varieties so that it is possible to select colors and plant any desired color combination. The new F. Hybrids seem to be better able to take our summer heat and thus flower longer.

Pansies may be planted as edgings and as solid beds. Many people wishing to have an abundance of flowers for the youngsters to pick, plant some in a warm, protected sunny situation for earliest spring bloom and some in a cool shaded place for summer bloom. In the latter situation pansies frequently bloom all summer long. In the hot dry areas they will usually succumb to summer heat by mid-June.

Pansies in the Washington area may be grown from seed started about mid-July to mid-August. It is sometimes difficult to get new crop seed before the first of August. New crop seed gives quick germination and an excellent stand whereas old seed is slow to sprout and the germination is generally poor. The seed should be started in a cool shaded situation and the seedlings transferred to a flat or pots as soon as the first true

leaves are well developed. Many growers like to transplant to a flat and then transplant to pots. This helps to develop a compact root system. The plants should go into the border in late October or early November. They should be well mulched, but the leaves must be left uncovered.

The mulch for pansies might well be a mixture of rich compost and dried cow manure. In the spring this can be supplemented with commercial garden fertilizer. A second feeding might well be made in April so as to keep the plants growing vigorously. Do not remove the mulch in the spring because pansies like a cool moist root run.

Pansies are not immune to disease or insect pests. In this area the major problem is the removal of the soil after growing pansies 3 or 4 years. There is a build-up of disease and it is necessary to replace the soil to insure health, or, if that is impracticable, to shift locations of plantings. Replacing the top 3 or 4 inches of soil is usually the easiest solution. For insect and disease problems, should they appear, use an all-purpose dust or spray.

The pansy plants may be spaced as close as 6 inches, but if they are to be planted in a good rich soil and properly fertilized, the spacing might well be increased to 10 or 12 inches.

If the plants live over until fall, it is possible to get a second season of bloom by shearing them and fertilizing. The shearing consists of cutting the stems back to 3 or 4 inches in length.

Keep the spent blooms removed from the plants to stimulate flowering. Of course, this is impracticable on large beds, but in most gardens the children will help because they love the brightly colored flowers.

PERIWINKLE

(Vinca rosea—Madagascar Periwinkle)

Uses:	Ground cover.
Blooms:	All summer and fall.
Varieties:	Bright Eyes, white with rose eye; Purity, pure white; Twinkles, blush pink with bright red eye; Rose Carpet, rose, 6-inches creeper; Coquette, Pink.
Height:	1½ to 2 feet.
Seed:	February.
Plant:	Early May.
Soil:	Ordinary garden loam.
Exposure:	Hot, dry, well-drained.

*   *   *

The periwinkle is a tender perennial that may be grown as an annual It is a good garden plant with rosy-purple flowers. Some gardeners will grow the named varieties. It is most useful as a bedding plant where its long season of bloom is most effective.

The seed sown indoors early in February will need to be transplanted several times before being ready for the garden.

PETUNIA

(Petunia hybrida—Petunia)

Uses:	Bedding, edging, window boxes.
Blooms:	June until frost.
Varieties:	Semi-dwarf-(12 inch)-Linda, White Magic, Snow Lady, Silver Medal, Red Satin, Blue Lustre, Glitters, Satellite, Crusader, Neptune, Coral Satin, Gay Paree. Bedding-(12-24 inches)-Snowstorm, Maytime, Balcony-(18 inch)-Red Cascade, White Cascade, Pink Cascade. Ruffle-Fringed—Apple Blossom, Ballerina, Fire-dance, La Paloma, Lavender Lace, Tango, Capri, Calypso, Mercury, Starfire, Red Magic, Pink Magic, Sugar Daddy, Sugar Plum, Bingo. Double—Colossal Shades of Rose, Allegro, Sonata, Caprice, Orchid Beauty, Pink Riches, Cherry Tart, Honeybunch, Think Pink, Blue Danube.
Height:	6 to 24 inches.
Seed:	Indoors—March; Out-of-doors—May.
Blooms:	2 to 3 months.
Plant:	6 to 12 inches apart.
Soil:	Average garden loam.
Exposure:	Sun or light shade.

* * *

Petunias are probably the most popular annual in America today, and no small wonder. Because of their long flowering season, their ability to take heat and drought, and their relative freedom from insects and diseases, they are especially useful. They are most prolific of bloom. Whether used as an edging, for a mass or bed, or in window boxes and pots, they provide a continuous display throughout the season. They are available in a wide range of color, all except a good deep yellow.

The growing of petunias from seed, especially the newer ruffled and double types, is more difficult than for the common strains of yesteryear. However, by using the method outlined on page 10, a reasonable chance for success is assured with even these difficult types. Petunia seed are as fine as dust and should be handled with care to prevent their drying out before their tiny roots begin to function.

The tiny seedlings should be transferred to pots as soon as the leaves are formed and before the roots become intertwined with other plants. A second transplanting is seldom necessary when the seedlings are moved from the seed flat to pots.

Transplanting to the border or to window boxes should not take place until the soil is well warmed and there is no danger of frost. Set the plants from 6 to 12 inches apart. The small mound type for edgings need the most space. The balcony type can be planted fairly close as can the bedding types.

The petunias should be planted in a soil that has been well enriched with compost, leafmold, or peatmoss. Dried cow manure might well be mixed at time of preparation as well as 2 or 3 pounds of an all-purpose commercial fertilizer per 100 sq. ft.

Feeding during the growing season is not often done, but for strong growth until frost cuts down the plants it is advisable to give them one or two additional feedings, depending upon the richness of the soil. Where the plants have grown into a solid mat this may be accomplished by using one of the soluble non-burning fertilizers, of which there are several on the market. Also, if after a summer vacation the plants look a little bit tired and worn, they may be cut back to 3 or 4 inch stems. Stir the soil and add an application of fertilizer which will insure new growth and bloom until frost.

Because of the popularity of petunias, there is an immense number of varieties and types from which to select. The new F1 Hybrid petunias are strong growers with large flowers, but there are many strains and lines which provide a bewildering array from which to choose. The varieties listed above are those recommended by the University of Maryland and local growers. However, even the experts cannot possibly keep up with all the new introductions each year.

PHLOX

(Phlox drummondi—Annual or Summer Phlox)

Uses:	Cutflowers, bedding.
Blooms:	July to October.
Varieties:	Tall Giant—Art Shades; Grandiflora; Giant Tetra—Glamour, Mixed; Starred and Fringed—Tall Mixed; Dwarf Star Mixed and Twinkle. Large Flowered—Mixed.
Height:	6 to 20 inches.
Seed:	Indoors—March; Out-of-doors—late April.
Blooms:	8 to 9 weeks.
Plant:	6 to 10 inches apart.
Soil:	Light, porous, well-drained.
Exposure:	Sun.

* * *

The annual or bedding phlox makes a colorful display from mid-summer to frost. They are only half-hardy so should not be planted out-of-doors until danger of frost is past. Gardeners should start their plants out-of-doors for late development, in order to avoid hot weather and disease. The bedding phlox makes finest showing in late summer and fall.

The colors of the annual phlox range from white to crimson and lavender, many of the flowers having dark or white eyes. Some gardeners buy single colors, but most prefer to buy the mixtures.

The seedlings should be pinched to encourage branching. This practice is also valuable in producing stockier plants that will stand up better than those that are taller and spindling. Removing spent flowers encourages new growth and prolongs the flowering season.

Phlox do not do well in a rich soil, but neither do they thrive in a poor soil. An average garden soil, one that has been lightened with sand or ashes and compost, suits them very well.

The red spider mite is fond of all types of phlox and must be kept under control either through dusting with sulphur, an occasional strong blast from the garden hose, or spraying with a material containing Malathion. The sulphur will also control mildew. Fortunately this disease is not as troublesome on the annual phlox as it is on the perennial.

PINKS

(Dianthus chinensis—Chinese Pinks)

Uses:	Cutflowers.
Bloom:	July to October.
Varieties:	Floradale—deeply fringed edges. Heddewigi varieties—one of the best, Laciniatus, Bravo, Red Monarch, Baby Doll.
Height:	10 to 15 inches.
Seed:	Indoors—March; Out-of-doors—April.
Blooms:	80 to 90 days.
Plant:	6 inches apart.
Soil:	Rich, well-drained.
Exposure:	Sun.

* * *

The annual pinks are popular, long season flowers for the cutting bed. They are available in both single and double-flowered forms, and in a moderate range of colors. However, they are all so useful that it does not make a great deal of difference which one you plant. They do not demand a great deal of care, nor are they often bothered by insects and diseases. They do best in a dry season.

The seedlings will take severe weather and fall planting is a possibility in the more protected sections of the area. Actually the Chinese pinks are short-lived perennials treated as annuals. On well drained soils the plants will live over for a second season of bloom.

The seedlings may be transplanted to the border by late April. Space them at least 6 inches apart. If a wider spacing is given, it will pay to stake the plants to keep the flower stems from sprawling in the dirt. Pine needles make an excellent mulch for the Pinks

since they are airy and let moisture through. However, any material that keeps the soil moist is likely to attract slugs and snails which like to hide under the stems. If this problem should arise, use one of the prepared slug and snail baits containing metaldehyde. (Place the bait under a board or flower pot to keep it away from children and pets.)

It is commonly stated that Pinks do best in a poor but well drained soil. This is a general statement and it is likely that most local soils will need to have both compost and pulverized limestone worked into them before the Pinks will thrive and produce good quality bloom.

POPPIES

(Papaver rhoeas, P. nudicale—Shirley, Iceland, Flanders Field)

Uses:	Cutflowers, bedding.
Blooms:	Shirley—August-September.
	Iceland—June-Steptember.
Varieties:	Shirley—Single and double (Ranunculus-flowered), Sweet Briar. Iceland—Dwarf, Gartford's Giants, single, Imperial Jewels, Pink Champagne, Red Cardinal.
Height:	Shirley—18 to 36 inches.
	Iceland—12 to 24 inches.
Seed:	Out-of-doors—October-November, or February-March.
Blooms:	8 to 10 weeks.
Plant:	Thin to 6 to 10 inches.
Soil:	Any good garden loam.
Exposure:	Sun.

* * *

The annual poppies are very satisfactory bloomers. Their dainty tissue-like texture and soft colors—pink, salmon, terra cotta, etc.—have made them favorites for many years in gardens everywhere. Today there are more colors, and the forms of the blossoms have even greater variation, including doubles. However, notwithstanding these fine qualities, many gardeners do not grow them, thinking that they are difficult. Much of this is due to sowing seed too late in the spring. If planted in the fall in a well-prepared bed and covered with grass clippings or cheese cloth, or sown on the snow in February or in early March, they make a splendid showing with no other care.

The Shirley and Opium poppies are true annuals, while the Iceland is a short-lived perennial that flowers the first year from seed and is treated as an annual. The Iceland poppy is low growing—12 to 24 inches. The others are taller, from 1½ to 3 feet, with larger flowers. The seed of the opium poppy is not offered by seedsmen.

For satisfactory use as cutflowers, poppies should be cut in the morning before the buds open. They will then last in water for several days.

Poppies do not transplant easily; hence the seed should be sown thinly where they are to grow. Whether sown in the fall or very early spring, the plants should be thinned to 6 to 10 inches apart, depending upon the richness of the soil. The dwarf Iceland poppies can be left as close as 6 inches if they are treated as annuals.

Poppies are sometimes troubled with a serious disease. It may be recognized by the black spots on stem and leaf. Pull and burn any plants showing this type of infection. Aphids may sometimes trouble poppies and they may be controlled with a blast of cold water from the hose, by spraying with Malathion, and by most of the all-purpose dusts and sprays.

PORTULACA

(Portulaca grandiflora—Rose Moss, Garden Portulaca)

Uses:	Ground cover, edgings, rock garden.
Blooms:	June to October.
Varieties:	Mostly offered as mixtures, Double rose-flowered—Alba, Coccinea, Salmon, Red Jewel (large single-flowered White Jewel), Magic Carpet.
Height:	4 to 6 inches.
Seed:	Late fall and winter.
Blooms:	6 to 8 weeks.
Plant:	Space seedlings about 4 inches apart.
Soil:	Dry, open soil.
Exposure:	Sun.

* * *

The portulaca is one of the best flowering covers for dry, sunny situations. The flowers continue to open until frost kills them. They require practically no care during the season except that competing weeds and grass should be removed. They are practically free from insect and disease problems. The flowers open only on sunny days which may be a disappointment to some.

Rose moss like a warm sunny situation in an open or porous soil. Our heavy clays can be made suitable by mixing compost and sand into the area where they are to be seeded. The Rose moss is not considered hardy by some but it must be seeded in the late fall and winter in order to obtain good germination. Spring planted seed seldom gives satisfactory results.

Sow the seed on the open ground and let the frost cover it as needed. The double flowered varieties are most popular but unfortunately only a small portion of the volunteers that come up from a planting of the doubles may be expected to be doubles. The singles, of course, produce worthwhile volunteers each season. Many gardeners have had the pleasant experience of having one seeding last for many years.

For many years the Rose moss was offered only as mixtures, but today we have a number of named varieties, mostly by color—Alba, Rosea, Coccinea, etc. There is one large flowered single variety—Jewel, a crimson.

It should be noted that the young plants of the Rose moss resemble the weed commonly called "Pusley, Pigweed, Portulaca". In fact it is of the same family and naturally has considerable resemblance until the flowers begin to open.

RUDBECKIA

(Rudbeckia species—Coneflower)

Uses:	Cutflowers, bedding.
Blooms:	July until frost.
Varieties:	Gloriosa Daisies, Pinwheel, Sullivante, Goldstorm, Sombrero.
Height:	1 to 4 feet.
Seed:	Indoors—March; Out-of-doors—late April.
Blooms:	8 to 10 weeks.
Plant:	10 to 18 inches apart.
Soil:	Ordinary garden loam.
Exposure:	Sun or shade.

* * *

Most gardeners do not give much thought to the Purple Coneflower or the Black-Eyed Susan and yet they represent a toughie that can take our climate. The Rudbeckias will withstand both heat and drought and have a long season of bloom. The modern varieties make a very pleasing show. The hybridizers have taken advantage of the toughness of the "natives" and now we have plants with pleasing bloom, a long flowering season, and few insects and diseases.

The Rudbeckia seed may be sown indoors and transplanted to the border in early May. Or the seed may be sown out of doors a week or two before the last killing frost is expected in the spring.

The Rudbeckias like sun but will take a surprising amount of shade. They make bushy plants that, depending upon variety, will grow from 1 to 3 feet tall. For best results and big plants, they should be planted in a moderately rich and moist soil.

The newest members of the Rudbeckia family are the Gloriosa daisy and Gloriosa double daisy. There are some perennials that may be treated as annuals if that should be desired and also several biennials. However, the annuals are less coarse foliaged and more likely to be in keeping with the smaller gardens.

SCABIOSA

(Scabiosa atropurpurea—Pincushion flower, Mourning-Bride, Sweet Scabious)

Uses:	Cutflowers, bedding.
Blooms:	July to October.
Varieties:	Giant Hybrids, Imperial Hybrids, Dwarf Ball-Shaped.
Height:	18 to 36 inches.
Seed:	Indoors—March; Out-of-doors—April.
Blooms:	10 to 12 weeks.
Plant:	10 to 12 inches apart.
Soil:	Good garden loam.
Exposure:	Sun.

* * *

The Pincushion flower is an old-time favorite that has been greatly improved in recent years. There are better colors as well as dwarf, medium and tall growing varieties and strains. They make good cutflowers and the medium tall are suitable for bedding. Apparently they are untroubled by disease and insect pests.

Since the seeds are slow to germinate it is better to start the seeds indoors or in a cold-frame so that strong vigorous plants can be placed in the border late in April. They should be given about a foot of spacing so that they can be cultivated during the early part of the season. One or two feedings during the season will keep them growing vigorously and provide many long-stemmed flowers for cutting.

A mulch will save cultivation during the heat of the summer as well as keep the roots cool and functioning.

The Scabiosa is not a demanding flower and will do well in the border without any special attention. However, feeding and watering will keep the flowers large and attractive. Being free from pests, they should receive more attention from gardeners who want something easy to grow.

SCARLET SAGE

(Salvia splendens, S. farinacea, etc.—Scarlet Sage, Mealy-Cup Sage, Gentian Sage, Etc.)

Uses:	Bedding, borders, cutflowers.
Blooms:	July to frost.

Salvia splendens:

Bloom begins:	June 20	July 1	July 10	July 15	Aug. 1
Height:	8-10″	12″	14-16″	18-20″	26-30″
Varieties:	Fireball	St. John's Fire	Blaze of Fire	America	Bonfire
		Pink Rouge	Cardinal	Evening Glow	Tall Splendor
		Salmon Pygmy	Violet Flame		

Salvia farinacea:

Blue Bedder 2′

Regal Purple 2′

Height:	6 to 36 inches.
Seed:	Indoors—February or early March.
Blooms:	10 to 12 weeks.
Plant:	10 to 15 inches apart.
Soil:	Rich, moist, garden loam.
Exposure:	Sun or light shade.

* * *

The Scarlet sage is one of the most common bedding plants, but because of the brilliant red color should be used with caution. The red does not blend with other colors. Recently other colors have been evolved and now there are pink, rose, salmon, wine, and white. In addition several of the blue-flowered perennial varieties may be treated as annuals. However, they have a different habit of growth and flowering. Actually, they are more useful for cutting than for bedding.

The Salvias are slow germinators so the seed should be started indoors about six weeks before the last killing frost of the spring. They are so slow in starting that it is seldom advisable to try sowing seed out of doors.

Once established, the plants grow rapidly and begin to flower profusely. They will keep on blooming until frost cuts them down. There are a number of varieties ranging from the tall (3 feet) to medium (18 to 24 inches) and dwarf bedders (6 to 12 inches).

The Salvias seems to be relatively free from disease and insect pests.

SNAPDRAGON

(Antirrhinum majus)

Uses:	Cutflowers, bedding and edgings.
Blooms:	July-September.
Varieties:	Rocket Strain, Super Jets Strain, First Ladies Strain, Torch, Hit Parade, Foral Carpet Strain, Bright Butterflies (Mix), Ginger Snaps Strain, Giant Ruffled Strain.
Height:	6 to 36 inches.
Seed:	Indoors—March; Out-of-doors—April.
Blooms:	About 4 months.
Plant:	6 to 18 inches apart.
Soil:	Rich garden soil.
Exposure:	Sun or light shade.

* * *

Snapdragons are perennials that are treated as annuals; they will flower from seed the first year even when the seed is sown out of doors. They will often survive our winters if given a little protection, especially the first year plants. Snaps were very popular with gardeners for many years until the disease known as "rust" made culture difficult. Today we have a group of rust-resisting varieties. It would be foolish to plant other than a rust-resisting variety.

The tall-growing varieties are very attractive, but will need staking to keep them from sprawling over other plants. Unless the gardener is willing to stake them, he should grow the semi-tall varieties, which are best for bedding. They are also probably the best for general garden use. The dwarf varieties are not commonly grown but may be used for a foreground planting in the rock garden or even as an edging plant.

Snapdragon seed should be started indoors in February or early March. The seed are very small and the seedlings are susceptible to the disease known as "damping-off"; hence to avoid trouble, they should be sown in sphagnum moss, vermiculite, perlite, or sterilized soil. By using these materials to start the seed, there will be little danger of trouble with this disease. Transplant the seedlings to a soil mixture when the first true leaves are well developed, not later than the second pair of true leaves.

When the soil out-of-doors has been prepared, the seedlings may be transplanted to the border, setting them 12 to 18 inches apart. At the time of planting, they should have the top inch pinched off to encourage branching. This is necessary if several long stems for cutting are to be had from each plant.

The snapdragons like a rich, well-prepared garden loam for good growth. On the heavier soils they should be mulched with compost, grass clippings, sawdust, peatmoss, or some similar material to keep the soil from crusting. The plants should be fertilized once a month to keep them growing vigorously. Watering is needed whenever rainfall is insufficient to keep the soil moist.

Other than the disease called rust, the snapdragons are comparatively free from insect and disease troubles. Should the plants be troubled, an all-purpose dust or spray may be used to protect them. It should be mentioned here that some of the so-called rust-resistant varieties are not so rust-resistant, and should you obtain one, it may be kept growing by spraying or dusting with a material known as "fermate". This material is good for the control of disease but it gives the foliage a sooty appearance. It may be easily wiped off of the stems cut for use indoors.

The F. Hybrid—Rockets (6 colors) should be superior to the above listed varieties if breeding counts. However, the F2 Panarama strains and the Giant Ruffled tetraploid will find many backers.

STRAWFLOWERS

(Helichrysum bracteatum-Strawflower, Dust Catcher, Everlasting, Gomphrena-Globe Amaranth)

Uses:	Border, dried flowers.
Blooms:	July to October.
Varieties:	In separate colors or in mixture; Helichrysum—Giant Flowered, Dwarf Mixed, Roggli Mixed. Gomphrena—Buddy, Rubra.
Height:	1 to 3 feet.
Seed:	Indoors—March; Out-of-doors—May.
Blooms:	12 or 15 weeks.
Plant:	12 to 15 inches apart.
Soil:	Any good garden loam.
Exposure:	Sun.

* * *

The Strawflowers are considered to be the best for drying, although they make an excellent showing in the border. The large showy flowers are available both in single and double forms. They are easy to grow and normally reach a height of two feet or more. They will tolerate our hot dry summers exceptionally well. Also, they are one  of easiest of the garden flowers to dry for winter bouquets.

Some gardeners insist that it is better to sow where the plants are to grow, but the experts recommend transplanting two or three times. The main emphasis on planting is that they be spaced not less than 12 inches apart. Gomphrena makes an excellent Strawflower; two varieties are outstanding—Buddy and Rubra (tall).

The Strawflowers are not demanding as to soil, but for good growth they should be put in a soil that is moderately rich and moist.

For drying, the Strawflowers should be cut just as the flowers begin to unfold. The leaves should be stripped and the bunches hung with the heads down in a dry airy place. The white Strawflowers do not make an acceptable dried flower for winter arrangements.

SUMMER CYPRESS

(Kochia scoparia, var. tricophila—Summer Cypress, Burning Bush)

Uses:	Low hedge.
Blooms:	Inconspicuous.
Varieties:	Childsii.
Height:	2 to 3 feet.
Seed:	Late April.
Blooms:	....
Plant:	18 to 24 inches apart.
Soil:	Good garden loam.
Exposure:	Sun.

* *

The Summer Cypress is a useful finely-leaved bushy plant that resembles a small evergreen. They are commonly used as a low background or to mark drives. They are

fairly rapid growers and relatively free from insects and diseases.

The seed should be soaked overnight before sowing in a prepared bed or where they are to grow. If a very early planting is desired, the seeds may be started indoors and transplanted to the garden about mid-April. The Summer Cypress should be given a wide spacing so that they may develop into symmetrically shaped plants. The fall coloring gives them their second common name, Burning Bush.

The plants should be cut down and removed before the seeds fall to the ground, otherwise they may become a nuisance.

SUNFLOWER ANNUAL

(Helianthus—Sunflower)

Uses:	Background, cutflowers.
Blooms:	June until frost.
Varieties:	Sutton's Red, Excelsior Hybrids, Red and Gold Hybrid, Sun Gold, Italian White, Teddy Bear, Chrysanthem Flowered.
Height:	1½ to 6 feet.
Seed:	Out-of-doors—late April.
Blooms:	10 weeks.
Plant:	24 to 48 inches apart.
Soil:	Any good garden loam.
Exposure:	Sun.

* * *

The annual sunflowers are commonly neglected by the home gardener; he thinks of sunflowers in terms of the seed producer, with its huge coarse leaves and stem, and with a flower head a foot or more in diameter. However, there are a number of annual varieties whose flowers are much more in keeping with the ornamental border. Not only do they thrive in hot dry situations, but they have a very long flowering season. They seem to be free from insects and diseases.

The seeds should be sown out-of-doors as soon as the danger of frost is past. While they withstand transplanting, the seeds sown where they are to grow seem to reach flowering more quickly; there is no advantage in starting them indoors.

Give the plants plenty of space since they branch and produce many side flowers. They should be planted in a soil that was enriched with both fertilizer and compost at the time of preparation. Do not mulch the plants, but keep the soil cultivated and free from grass and weeds. Water as needed.

SUNFLOWER, MEXICAN

(Tithonia rotundifolia (speciosa)—Mexican Sunflower, Golden Flower of the Incas)

Uses:	Background, cutflowers.
Blooms:	June-October.
Varieties:	Torch, Avalons, Speciosa.
Height:	4 to 10 feet.
Seed:	Indoors—March; Out-of-doors—May.
Blooms:	3 to 4 months.
Plant:	2 to 3 feet apart.
Soil:	Ordinary garden loam.
Exposure:	Sun.

* * *

The Mexican sunflower is a tall growing and somewhat coarse foliaged plant, but the long stemmed flowers are most attractive. They are like small lacquer-red sunflowers. The plant grows too strongly if given a rich moist situation unless considerable height is desired for use as a background or screen.

For the earliest bloom, the seed may be started indoors in pots or berry baskets for transplanting to the garden in early May.

The Mexican sunflower is of easy culture and undemanding, and also free from insect and disease problems. At least none have been reported locally. The species and the variety Torch seldom flower before the first of August. The strain Avalons Earliest is reported to flower by the end of June.

TORENIA

(Torenia fournieri)

Uses:	Rock garden, shady border.
Blooms:	June until frost.
Varieties:	T. fournieri, light blue with deep blue blotch.
Height:	12 inches.
Seed:	Indoors, late March.
Plant:	6 to 8 inches.
Soil:	Moist, rich.
Exposure:	Half shade.

* * *

The Torenia is not showy but will add interest and charm to a border, window box or rock garden. The plants resemble small snapdragons and are tender, so sould not be set out until all danger of frost is past.

VERBENA

(Verbena species—Verbena)

Uses:	Bedding, edging, cutflowers.
Blooms:	July to frost.
Varieties:	Tall varieties—Spectrum Red, Amethyst, Calypso, Sutton's Blue, Miss Susie. Dwarf varieties—Firelight, Crystal, Dazzle, Sparkle, Early Dwarf Rainbow Mixed, Delight, Splendor.
Height:	6 to 18 inches.
Seed:	Indoors—March; Out-of-doors—May.
Blooms:	8 to 10 weeks.

VERBENA—Continued

Plant:	10 to 18 inches apart.
Soil:	Fertile sandy loam.
Exposure:	Sun or light shade.

*   *   *

Verbenas are old-time favorites that are not widely planted today except in window boxes. They make one of the most colorful low plantings for the home garden. The trailing branches are very attractive in low bowls for indoor decoration.

The new large-flowered tall growing mixtures are excellent for cutflowers; while the small compact plants may serve as edgings or for mass planting in the foreground. The dark green foliage makes an effective background for the solid colors of the flower heads which rise several inches above the leaves. The flower heads vary from 2 to 3 inches or more in diameter.

The seedlings should be twice transplanted if they are to have a large fibrous root system when set out of doors. The tips of the young plants should be pinched to stimulate branching.

The spent flower heads should be removed to encourage the plants to continue blooming.

Mildew is the principal disease; it may be controlled by an all-purpose dust that contains sulphur or the new fungicide Phaltan. These mixtures are also useful should insects infest the plantings.

ZINNIA

(Zinnia elegans, Z. angustifolia—Zinnia, Poorhouse Flower, Old Faithful, Cut and Come Again, etc.)

Uses:	Edging, bedding, background, cutflowers.	**Blooms:**	6 to 8 weeks.
Blooms:	June to October.	**Plant:**	6 to 18 inches apart depending on type.
Height:	6 to 36 inches.	**Soil:**	Well-enriched, moist soil.
Seed:	Indoors—late March; Out-of-doors—April.	**Exposure:**	Sun.

*   *   *

Height (inches)	6″	12″	18-24″	24-30″	30-36″
Variety & Type	Thumbelina (by colors)	*Cupids*	*Lilliputs* (by colors) (Gem)	*Merry-Go-Round* (by colors)	*Dahlia Flowered* Canary Bird Polar Bear Exquisite Royal Purple
		Buttons Pink Buttons Red Buttons	Cut & Come *Again* Elegans pumila Polynesian (by colors)		*Mammoth* Envy Golden Dawn Purity
		Sprite *Mixture*		*Pumila* (by colors) Peppermint Stick	
		Tom Thumb (Mixture)			*State Fair Series* (Giant Tetra) (by colors)
				Miss Universe (mixed)	Fantasy Series (by colors)
	Miscellaneous Pinwheel Mixed Red Lady—Scabiosa flowered —Gaillardia flowered Persian Carpet* { Linearis Haageana Mexicana Old Mexico*		*Burpeeana* (Art Shades) Empress Red Man Snow Man	*Giant Cactus* Lilac Time Blaze Riverside Beauty	
				Zenith Yellow Zenith Princess Firecracker Bonanza	*Ortho Polka* (Mixtures)

* Resistant to mildew

Zinnias are one of the most popular of the annuals since they take relatively little care, are colorful, and have a long season of bloom. They last well as cut-flowers and in the border retain their color for a long period of time. They have strong stems and heavy foliage so that they present their colors in an effective setting.

There are so many types, strains, and varieties of zinnias now available that the average gardener is bewildered by the number. There are several types of the giant flowered. The Dahlia flowered is favored by some over the older flat or shallow flowers. The Fantasy type with its quilled petals is very attractive to many gardeners. The David Burpee type is also quilled, but does not have the open center of the fantasy. Many prefer it for its excellent color combinations or shadings.

The smaller flowered zinnias—variously known as lilliput, pompon, baby, or cupid zinnias—are as attractive and useful as their larger-flowered relatives. They are excellent cut flowers for the smaller arrangements. In addition to those just mentioned, there are the Linearis and Mexicana zinnias with somewhat different foliage and petals. They are well worth growing and are increasing in popularity.

Still other forms are the crested and double crested zinnias, which are interesting and useful variations.

Not only are the forms interesting, but the colors are too. Today zinnias have clearer colors, without the fulvous overcast or lack of brilliance and depth that formerly was so common. In addition we have striped and mottled petals (Ortho Polka and Peppermint Stick).

Zinnias benefit by rich soil and adequate supplies of moisture. They are rapid, strong growers that need plenty of food and water if they are to do their best. This means that they should be watered when needed, and they should be fed three or four times during the growing season. Some gardeners incorporate liberal quantities of manure in the bed at the time of soil preparation. However, a liberal supply of compost together with 2 or 3 pounds of the usual commercial fertilizer mixture per 100 square feet will serve the same purpose. This will keep the plants growing strongly for the first month; then a supplemental feeding in July, August, and again in September will insure good growth and flowering.

Zinnias are susceptible to several insect pests and diseases. Mildew is the most common disease. It may be controlled with dusting sulphur or the new material known as Phaltan. However, an all-purpose dust or spray applied regularly should give all of the protection needed in most gardens. Persian Carpet and old Mexico varieties as well as the Zenith series are reportedly mildew resistant.

Annual Vines

CANARY BIRD VINE

(Tropaeolum peregrinum—Canary Bird Vine)

Uses:	Screen.
Blooms:	Late June until frost.
Varieties:	Only species.
Height:	10 feet.
Seed:	Indoors—late March; Out-of-doors—late April.
Blooms:	July through summer.
Plant:	12 to 18 inches apart.
Soil:	Dry, porous.
Exposure:	Sun.

* *

The Canary Bird vine is a member of the Nasturtium group. The leaves are deeply lobed. The flowers have an interesting form from which the vine derives the common name. The flowers are not especially showy individually, but the mass of yellow bloom gives a pleasing effect.

The Canary Bird vine should be started indoors about a month before the outdoor planting date for nasturtiums. This vine requires a sunny situation. It is noted for its tolerance of dry situations.

The same aphids that trouble the Nasturtiums may be expected on the Canary Bird vine, although they should be much easier to control. A malathion spray should be most effective.

CARDINAL CLIMBER

(Quamoclit sloteri hybrida—Cardinal Climber, Starglory)

Uses:	Screen, shade.
Blooms:	July through summer.
Varieties:	None.
Height:	10 to 20 feet.
Seed:	Out-of-doors—May.
Blooms:	About 3 months.
Plant:	6 inches apart.
Soil:	Light, sandy soil.
Exposure:	Sun.

* *

The Cardinal vine has an attractive, finely divided foliage and cardinal-red, morning-glory like flowers. The foliage is so light that the shade from the Cardinal vine is not of much protection from the hot afternoon sun.

The Cardinal climber is a twiner and needs only to

be started up a string or wire. Under favorable growing conditions it may reach a height of 15 to 25 feet.

The seed should be notched and then soaked over night in hot water before planting.

Seed of the Cardinal climber are frequently listed as a form of the Morning-glory (Ipomoeas).

CUP AND SAUCER VINE

(Cobaea scandens—Cup and Saucer Vine, Cathedral Bells)

Uses:	Screen, shade.
Blooms:	Mid-summer until frost.
Varieties:	Blue, white and mixed.
Height:	20 to 30 feet.
Seed:	Indoors—Late February; Out-of-doors—late April.
Blooms:	4 to 5 months.
Plant:	18 to 24 inches apart.
Soil:	Good garden loam, moist.
Exposure:	Sun or partial shade.

* * *

The Cup and Saucer vine is a tender perennial that is treated as an annual. It is a rank grower; under favorable conditions it reaches a height of 40 to 50 feet. The large cup-shaped flowers appear late in the summer and are followed by plum-shaped fruits.

The Cup and Saucer vine should be started in late February indoors and the seedling transplanted to pots—first a 2 or 2½-inch and then to a large pot. Then the husky plants will be ready to go into the garden in mid-May.

The large flat seeds should be planted on edge, otherwise germination may be very poor.

The vines climb by means of tendrils so that they may be trained on any rough surface or wire frame.

CYPRESS VINE

(Quamoclit pinnata—Cypress vine, Starglory)

Uses:	Screen.
Blooms:	July until Fall.
Varieties:	Scarlet, white.
Height:	10 to 20 feet.
Seed:	May.
Blooms:	About three months.
Plant:	6 inches apart.
Soil:	Ordinary garden loam.
Exposure:	Sun.

* * *

The Cypress vine—which is closely related to the Cardinal climber—has fine, fernlike, dark green foliage. Thus it is more ornamental than shade affording. The attractive star shaped flowers, 1 to 1½ inches in diameter, have long tubes somewhat resembling the Flowering Tobacco.

The Cypress vine is available occasionally in other than the common scarlet and white colors.

The seed of the Cypress vine should be notched and soaked in hot water for a day before planting.

JAPANESE HOP VINE

(Humulus japonicus—Japanese Hop Vine)

Uses:	Shade.
Blooms:	Bloom inconspicuous.
Varieties:	Green or variegated foliage.
Height:	20 to 35 feet.
Seed:	May.
Blooms:	....
Plant:	12 inches apart.
Soil:	Rich garden loam.
Exposure:	Sun or shade.

* * *

The Japanese Hop vine is considered the best for covering trellises and large arbors; the foliage is much more attractive than the common Hop. The flowers are so inconspicuous that the Japanese Hop is grown only for its luxuriant foliage. It is one of the few annuals that does well in moderate to light shade.

The seed should be sown in the light rich soil at the base of the trellis or arbor that it is to cover. The planting should be done in May after the soil has warmed.

The Japanese Hop vine seems to withstand both drought and heat without injury; it is free from insect pests.

The leaves are large, broad or toothed. The plant produces rather dense shade. There is also a variegated form—the leaves streaked and blotched with white.

MOONVINE

(Calonyction aculeatum—Moonflower)

Uses:	Flowers, screen.
Blooms:	July through summer.
Varieties:	Giant Pink, Giant White, Bona Nox.
Height:	10 to 20 feet.
Seed:	May.
Blooms:	Approximately three months.
Plant:	18 inches apart.
Soil:	Rich, moist.
Exposure:	Sun.

* * *

The Moonflower is a fragrant, night-blooming perennial from the tropics that is treated as an annual in the north. The large trumpet-shaped flowers unfold in the evening and close the following morning (by noon). The Moonvine makes a showy combination with the Morning-glory, although other than the combination of bloom, it would appear to be only exotic.

The Moonflower seed are hard-coated and should be notched and soaked in warm water before planting so that germination will not be delayed.

The Moonflower is attractive in foliage, but this depends upon the richness of the soil and the moisture provided. The heart shaped leaves form a pleasing background for the large saucer-shaped flowers.

MORNING-GLORIES

(Ipomoea purpurea—Morning-glory)

Uses:	Screen, shade, ground cover.
Blooms:	June until frost.
Varieties:	Climber—Heavenly Blue, Scarlet O'Hara, Pearly Gates, Candy Pink, Double Rose Marie, Tinkerbell's Petticoat (Double). Dwarf Bush Type—Crimson-Monarch, Rose, Royal Ensign.
Height:	10 to 15 feet.
Seed:	Out-of-doors—late April.
Blooms:	About 3 months.
Plant:	18 inches.
Soil:	Rich, moist.
Exposure:	Sun.

* * *

The morning-glories are among the most popular climbers grown in the garden. They not only produce a wealth of bloom, but their rich, dark green foliage is most useful as a screen and as a background for the large, brightly-colored trumpet-shaped flowers. The morning-glory is often used to cover a low trellis or pergola—as well as fences—because of its rapid growth. They are not often troubled by insects or diseases.

The morning-glory is a natural climber and only needs help to start in the right direction. They are twiners, so they must have something small enough for them to wrap around. Scarlet O'Hara is rated as the best variety for climbing; but all will climb 8 feet or more in a season, depending upon the soil and the moisture.

The morning-glories are aptly named because their flowers open in the very early morning and close about mid-day. Thus to be fully enjoyed, they should be where they can be observed in the morning. This also applies to the dwarf or bush form.

Morning-glory seed is very hard; to speed the germination it should be soaked overnight in water or the coat should be notched with a file. Since the plants cannot be transplanted, the seeds should be sown where they are to grow. Occasionally, plants are started in pots or baskets and successfully transplanted. This is of value only in that it assures bloom earlier in the season. Otherwise, bloom should not be expected before late July.

SCARLET RUNNER BEAN

(Phaseolus coccineus—Scarlet Runner)

Uses:	Shade, ornamental, edible pods.
Blooms:	June until late fall.
Height:	10 to 20 feet.
Seed:	Late April.
Blooms:	8 to 10 weeks.
Varieties:	None.
Plant:	8 to 12 inches apart.
Soil:	Ordinary garden soil.
Exposure:	Sun.

* * *

The Scarlet Runner Bean is ordinarily grown for flowers which are rather attractive for a member of the bean family. However, in England it is an important food crop since the pods are edible. There are a number of named varieties. The leaves are rather large for a bean and, of course, are rough. It is sometimes troubled by the red spider mite.

The Scarlet Runner Bean is an easy vine to grow. The seeds should be sown where they are to grow in late April or early May. String or poles should be provided for the vine to climb on. It is a twiner and does best on strings strung from the ground to the eaves or wherever shade is wanted.

The Scarlet Runner Bean does not want a rich soil. The leaves would be too coarse. The flowers are partially hidden by the foilage.

If the pods are to be used for cooking, it is important that they be harvested while young and tender.

Perennials

Perennials are plants which live for more than two years, in contrast to annuals and biennials. They are important to the garden because they provide a varying picture of bloom from season to season, and do not have to be replaced each season or year. Perennials offer a wider range in plant material than annuals.

The perennial border, being more or less permanent, should be well prepared before planting so that the plants will thrive and provide an attractive, healthy-appearing display for many years. The incorporation of quantities of humus, bone meal, and well-rotted manure is desirable wherever possible. Good drainage should be provided where necessary. If the soil is a heavy clay, sand or ashes will be needed to lighten it.

The list of perennials for this area is long and there are many types and varieties of most of them from which to choose. Those that are specifically adapted to this area should be given first consideration. There are many that thrive in the North, such as delphinium, canterbury bells, etc., that are exceedingly difficult to grow in this area. There are many attractive ones that grow here with much less coddling.

Perennials may be started from seed, although there are only a few that will bloom the first year. Many kinds come true only from divisions and cuttings. For such kinds it is better to buy a few plants and let them become established. From such plants others can be grown to expand the planting. Most perennials, to be effective, should be planted in groups of several of a kind.

The sowing of seed of perennials has for a long time been a midsummer job, although it is more or less difficult because of the hot, dry weather. However, if the seed are sown in a protected bed that can receive attention as needed, this should not be difficult. If this is not desirable, the seeds may be sown in March or April and the seedlings transplanted to a growing bed where they will continue their development until planting time in September. Seeds of those which germinate in a relatively short time, many be sown in the early fall, but they should not be transplanted until March or April.

Division of established clumps will in most cases take place in the spring for the fall bloomers and in the early fall for the spring bloomers. Some, such as iris and primroses, may be divided immediately after the flowering season. Poppies are handled only during the dormant period.

Cuttings may be taken in the spring when the new shoots are 6 to 8 inches long. Some will do better if taken in the late summer. This will differ with the various kinds. Unless unusual care is given, good results cannot be obtained at other seasons.

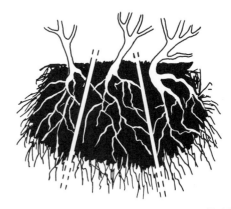

Some plants such as perennial alyssum may be divided by cutting the mass of roots into sections.

Most of the perennials are relatively free from diseases, although they are known to be subject to them under unfavorable conditions. Thus the first step in keeping plants healthy is to keep them growing vigorously—well cultivated, fed and watered. Where diseases do appear, the infected plants should be removed and the others sprayed with either bordeaux or sulphur.

Insect pests are apt to be common. Since this area seems to be the meeting ground of the bugs from the North and the South, we have the insect pests common to both areas. However, any good insecticide applied regularly will keep them under control.

Most perennials benefit by a shallow but frequent cultivation. Primroses seem to resent it, preferring a light mulch. If the border is properly laid out, this will not be difficult. Plants that are properly spaced have room enough about them to permit the workman to use a hoe or larger tool.

Most perennials make a rather vigorous growth and flower freely. This requires considerable moisture, so provision should be made to supply the perennial border with such moisture as may be necessary.

Only a few of the perennials require a sweet soil. Flax and dianthus are two of them. Most of the others will thrive in a soil that is slightly acid. The shade-loving plants, however, seem to need a distinctly acid soil for best results. These requirements should be observed in selecting plants for the garden.

DEPENDABLE WASHINGTON FLOWERS

ARTEMISIA

(Artemisia albula)

Uses:	Foliage, cutting and background.
Height:	2-3 feet.
Blooms:	Inconspicuous.
Propagate:	Division—April; Cutting—May.
Plant:	April-May.
Distance:	18-24 inches.
Soil:	Ordinary garden loam.
Exposure:	Sun.
Varieties:	Silver King, Silver Mound (dwarf).

* * *

Artemisia, Silver King, is a useful perennial for the hardy border. The silvery foliage is effective in the border because it adds contrast to the green foliage of other plants and at the same time helps to harmonize the many colors of surrounding flowers. Because its finely cut foliage does not wilt readily, it is excellent for bouquets.

Artemisia is easily propagated by dividing the roots in the spring or by cuttings which root readily if taken in May.

This perennial sends out strong underground shoots and soon develops into a large clump that unless kept within bounds may become a nuisance. Apparently the Artemisia is seldom troubled by insects and diseases.

HARDY ASTER

(Aster novae-angliae)—(Aster novi-belgi)

Uses:	Cutting, background, foreground.
Height:	10-48 inches.
Blooms:	September-October.
Propagate:	Division in April or May.
Plant:	April-May.
Distance:	2-3 feet.
Soil:	Average garden loam, moist.
Exposure:	Sun, partial shade.
Varieties:	Barr's Pink, pink (4-5 ft.); Harrington Pink (4 ft.); Mount Everest (4 ft.); The Cardinal, red (3 ft.); Persian Rose (12-15 in.); Twilight (12-15 in.); Rosana (12-15 in.); Snowball (12-15 in.); Constance, pink (10-12 in.); Lilac Times, blue (10-12 in.); Niobe, white (10-12 in.); Little Red Boy (10-12 in.); Eventide, blue (10-12 in.); Red Sunset (10-12.); Twinkle; Pacific Amaranthus.

* * *

For fall bloom, the hardy asters are a dependable perennial. They have been much improved over the native wildings from which many of them have descended. They withstand drought very well—neglecting to water them only makes the flowers smaller. With reasonably good cul-

ture, they produce a mass of nearly solid bloom that is very effective in the perennial border. The tall forms make good background material. The dwarf ones are excellent in the front of the border.

Divide and replant at least every other spring, enriching the soil while doing so. Stake the taller varieties.

Two other asters should be listed. Aster Frikarti (2-2½ ft.) is an old favorite. Plant it in sun or light shade. It blooms from July until frost. Two new asters, Aster Farreri Berggarten (18-24 in.); and Aster Yunnanensis Napsbury (25 in.), which bloom from July to August, are good blues.

The hardy asters are relatively free from insect and disease troubles. Mildew and such other leaf diseases as may appear are easily controlled with a good all-purpose dust.

BABY'S BREATH

(Gypsophila paniculata)

Uses:	Cut flowers, border.
Height:	24-36 inches.
Blooms:	June-September.
Plant:	Seed, division, cuttings—in early spring or fall.
Distance:	April or September.
Propagate:	4 feet.
Soil:	Dry, rather poor soil.
Exposure:	Sun.
Varieties:	Bristol Fairy, Ehrlie, Repens (6 in.), Pacifica (rose), Perfecta (24 in.); Flamingo (15-17 in.); Pink Fairy.

* * *

Gypsophila is a popular cut flower, especially useful in bouquets with other flowers. The small, dainty foliage and tiny single or double flowers are most effective. Because of its ease of culture and long season of bloom, most gardens should have one or more plants from which sprays may be cut as needed.

The hardy gypsophila thrives in a rather poor dry soil that is loose; thus cultivation is important. The plants may be divided or set out in the early spring or in September.

There are some very attractive double forms of the gypsophila, but they may be propagated only by grafting. The single-flowered forms may be grown from seed; or the old plants may be divided; or cuttings may be taken in August and rooted in peatmoss.

Repens, a 6-inch dwarf, is excellent for the rock garden, where its dainty white flowers in June and July make a pleasing display.

There is a new creeping form with pale pink flowers, Rosy Veil, which blooms in the early summer. It is a good ground cover in sunny places.

BALLOON FLOWER

(Platycodon grandiflorum)—(Chinese bellflower)

Uses:	Cut flowers, border, rockery.
Height:	12-36 inches.
Blooms:	June-October.
Propagates:	Seed—March, August.
Plant:	April, September.

BALLOON FLOWER

Distance:	8-12 inches.
Soil:	Medium, well-drained, sandy loam.
Exposure:	Sun, part shade.
Varieties:	G. caeruleum, 3 ft., lavender-blue. G. Mariesi, 18 in., violet-blue. G. Mariesi album, 18 in., white; Shell-Pink, 18 in., pale pink; Double White, 18-24 in.; Double Blue, 18 in., deep violet-blue.

* * *

The balloon flowers are an excellent substitute for the bell flowers in this area. These hardy perennials may be grown from seed sown in early March and will flower the first season. The species P. grandiflorum is blue flowered, but there is a white form as well as a double. P. g. mariesi is dwarf and suited to the rock garden.

The balloon flower makes strong bushy plants which seldom need staking. If well grown, they are a most attractive plant in the hardy border.

A deep, rich, sandy soil that is well drained suits them best. They are grown most easily from seed as the fleshy roots are difficult to divide. The crown should be about an inch below the surface of the soil. Because it is close to the surface, care should be used in removing the dead bloom stalks in the fall to avoid injury to the crown.

CANDYTUFT

(Iberis corifolia)—(I. sempervirens)

Uses:	Edging, rockery, bedding.
Height:	6-12 inches.
Blooms:	April-June.
Propagate:	Cutings—September; Division—September; Seed—August.
Plant:	September-April.
Distance:	15-24 inches.
Soil:	Moist, moderately rich.
Exposure:	Sun.
Varieties:	Besides the species sempervirens, Snowflake, Purity, (the latter is dwarf) and Autumn Snow (summer and fall), Pygmy and Dwarf.

* * *

The perennial candytuft, one of the best of the edging plants, is really a small shrub. It is very useful in a rock garden. It is of easy culture and may be grown from seed, divisions or cuttings. It takes two years to produce compact plants from seed.

The plants form a dense mat of foliage and when once established should not be disturbed. They are all relatively low-growing. There are a few named varieties on the market that are more dwarf than the species.

Because it is evergreen, the candytuft is especially useful in the rock garden, where its rich green foliage shows up well during the winter. Purity is a free bloomer and compact. Snowflake probably has the best foliage for winter effect.

CHRYSANTHEMUM

(C. indicum, C. morifolium, C. sibiricum)

Uses:	Cutflowers, bedding.
Height:	August-November.
Blooms:	1 to 5 feet.
Propagate:	Division, cuttings—April to June.
Plant:	April to July 15.
Distance:	12 to 18 inches.
Soil:	Rich, moist, garden loam.
Exposure:	Sun.

Garden Hardies

Name	Color	Type	Height	Bloom Date
Gianna D'Angelo	Yellow	Spoon	Medium	Mid October
Ruby Breithaupt	Yellow	Reflex	Low	Mid October
King's Ransom	Yellow	Decorative	Medium	Mid October
Happiness	Yellow	Single	Tall	Late October
Gold Coast	Yellow	Pompon	Tall	Late October
Jessamine Williams	White	Spoon	Medium	Early October
Larry	White	Decorative	Medium	Early October
Blizzard	White	Pompon	Tall	Mid October
Ostosa	White	Decorative	Low	Early October
Ruth Lehman	White	Large Dec.	Tall	Mid October
Raspberry Ice	Fuschia Pink	Decorative	Medium	Mid October
Purple Waters	Purple	Decorative	Low	Early October
Elizabeth Kover	Pink	Decorative	Tall	Late Sept.
Pink Nificent	Pink	Spoon-Spider	Medium	Mid October
Pink Dot	Pink	Pompon	Medium	Late October
Dolli-ette	Bronze	Spoon	Medium	Early October
Remembrance	Red	Pompon	Medium	Early October

Cushions

Name	Color	Type	Height	Bloom Date
Ann Ladygo	Pale pink	Anemone	Low	Mid October
Mango	Dark pink	Anemone	Low	Mid October
Taffy	Bronze	Anemone	Low	Mid October
Spunky	Bronze	Button	Low	Early October
Marbletop	White	Anemone	Low	Mid October
Lyric	White	Single	Low	Early October
Corsage Cushion	White	Carnation Flowered	Low	Mid October
Red Mischief	Red	Single	Low	Mid October
Ruby Mound	Red	Decorative	Low	Early October
Pathfinder	Yellow	Carnation Flowered	Low	Early October
Newgo Yellow	Yellow	Anemone	Low	Early to Mid October
Supreme	Yellow	Decorative	Low	Early October
Cameo	Pink	Decorative	Very Low	August to Frost

DEPENDABLE WASHINGTON FLOWERS

CHRYSANTHEMUM

Disbuds

Mrs. Kidder	Yellow	Incurve	Medium	Oct. 20-25
Gold Lode	Yellow	Reflex	Low	Oct. 22-27
Butterball	Yellow	Incurve	Medium	Oct. 15-25
Luyona	Yellow	Spider	Tall	Oct. 25-30
Albatross	White	Incurve	Medium	Oct. 25-30
Silver Sheen	White	Incurve	Medium	Oct. 25-30
Silver Strand	White	Spider	Medium	Oct. 25-30
Major Bowes	Pink	Incurve	Medium	Oct. 20-27
Pink Chief	Pink	Incurve	Medium	Oct. 15-23
Quarterback	Pink	Incurve	Low	Sept. 25 to frost
Stadium Queen	Bronze	Incurve	Medium	Sept. 25 to frost
Symbol	Orange	Reflex	Tall	Oct 27-30
Sandra Gail	Red	Spider	Medium	Oct. 25-30
Cloudbank	White	Anemone	Tall	Oct. 25-30
Honey	Bronze	Spoon	Medium	Oct. 25-30

Harvest Giants
These may be grown as disbuds or garden hardies

Bronze Song	Bronze	Incurve	Medium	Sept. 15
September Song	Incurve	Pink	Medium	Sept. 15
Silver Song	Incurve	White	Medium	Sept. 15
Indian Summer	Incurve	Red	Tall	Oct. 20
Pumpkin	Incurve	Bronze	Short	Sept. 20
Redskin		Red	Tall	Oct. 25
Autumn Leaves	Incurve	Orange	Tall	Sept. 25
Touchdown	Reflex	Pink	Tall	Oct. 15
Full Moon	Incurve	White	Tall	Oct. 15
Yellow Moon	Incurve	Yellow	Tall	Oct. 15

* * *

The chrysanthemums have long been the mainstay of the fall perennial border. In recent years hybridizers have brought us many early-blooming varieties in many types and colors which escape the first frost. The flowering season for this area is divided into early (Sept. 5 to Oct. 5), midseason (Oct. 5 to 25), and late (Oct. 25 to Nov. 5). The color range varies from pure white through the yellows, pinks, bronze, purple and reds. We have low-growing chrysanthemums, medium height and tall.

The chrysanthemum fanciers now speak of the different varieties according to the bloom structure. The two visible characteristics are identified by a difference in the outer petals and center or disk petals. Some of the major classes of the modern chrysanthemum are singles, anemones, pompons, incurves, reflexes, decorative reflexes, spoons, quills, threads and spiders.

Most gardeners use the bush-type plants listed above for mass effect in landscaping. If these varieties are grown to single blooms, they are very small. Those gardeners interested in exhibition blooms may grow the large standards or disbuds. Disbuds suggested as proven varieties for this area are Silver Sheen, Apricot Queen, Major Bowes, William Turner, Ambassador Watanabe, Gaiety, Albatross, Ben Leighton, Bess Witt, Bunbu, Peggy Ann Hoover, Rayonante Group, Nightingale, Giant Betsy Ross, Luna, Zylon, Queen of Pinks, Albert Witt, Sunnyslope Splendor, Luyona, and Sandra Gail.

Chrysanthemums may be propagated by division of the clumps each year in the spring. A still better method involves rooting cuttings taken from the top 3 inches of the new shoots when they are at least 8 inches high. Placed in a moist mixture of sand and peat moss, they will root in about two weeks. When the plants have roots ¼ to ½ inch in length, they are ready for transplanting into pots or beds.

The cultural requirement for the growing of the chrysanthemum can be condensed to three points: (1) Mulch to keep the roots cool and functioning, to conserve moisture, to avoid laborious cultivating, and to keep nematodes from splashing up from the soil to the foliage; (2) Keep the plants growing continuously by watering as needed and feeding lightly every 2 to 3 weeks until the buds begin to show color, and (3) use an all-purpose dust or spray to keep the foliage free of disease and to control the insects. A mixture containing malathion and DDT will control most of the insects, while ferbam, captan, or zineb will protect the plant from most diseases and fungus.

For good bushy growth of the hardy garden types, the young plants should be pinched when established and again about every two weeks until about the 15th of August. Remove only the tip. Do not pinch the cushion mums. The standards or exhibition varieties should be grown to not more than 3 stems by removing all side shoots after the first pinch. Since the latter type will grow tall, it is suggested they be supported. However, they are only expected to produce 2 to 4 flowers per plant, whereas the hardy garden types are expected to produce several spray and many blooms per plant. Staking is desirable for all except the cushions.

Chrysanthemums bloom according to the length of the night. That is why the greenhouse gardener with his shading cloth (black sateen) and electric light can produce blooming plants any time of the year. Twelve to 14 hours of shading per day are necessary to start the budding process in controlled blooming.

Cushion mums, those early blooming mounds of color mentioned above, make an excellent edging for the later blooming decoratives and pompons. They seemingly need only to be well watered and fed to produce a mass of bloom from late August to October. Because of their habit of growth, they do not need pinching to produce a mass of branches well coated with blooms.

When chrysanthemums have finished blooming, cut the plants off 4 to 6 inches from the ground and destroy the cut off tops. Mulch them with a loose airy material such as straw after the ground is frozen to prevent repeated freezing and thawing. If the plants do not have good drainage, lift them with a large clump of dirt, set on ground in a well drained location, and mulch them. Loosen mulch if snow packs it around the plants. A cold frame that is kept cool and well ventilated is a fine place to over-winter favorite varieties. Spray with an insecticide and a fungicide in March. As the weather becomes warm in March and April, side dress the plants with fertilizer and gradually remove the mulch to assure healthy shoots for propagation.

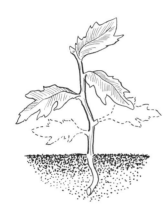

A chrysanthemum shoot stripped for rooting.

COLUMBINE

(Aquilegia)

Uses:	Cut flowers, border.
Height:	12-36 inches.
Blooms:	April-June.
Propagate:	Seed—June; Division—September.
Plant:	Early spring, September.
Distance:	9-18 inches
Soil:	Light, warm, moist.
Exposure:	Light shade, sun.
Varieties:	Crimson Star, Dobbies Imperial hybrids, Mrs. Scott Elliott hybrids, Rose Queen, Chrysantha, McKana's Giant, Longissinia hybrids.

* * *

The columbine is a lovely, dainty perennial for the early spring border. The newer types with their long spurred flowers are attractive and now available in a wide range of colors suitable both for cutting and border display. They need protection from the hot midday sun.

The native species all do well here and add interest to the border. Canadensis (18 inches) with reddish orange flowers, Longissima (18 inches), pale yellow flowers with exceedingly long spurs, and caerulea (2

feet), the famous Rocky Mountain blue columbine are all native species.

With the exception of the named varieties, columbines are usually propagated from seed which should be sown either in the early spring or late summer. They will not grow well during the heat of summer. Established plants of desirable color may be lifted and divided in the early fall.

Columbines are frequently troubled by leaf miner, which is not serious except for disfiguring the foliage and is easily controlled with dimethoate. Crown rot is troublesome on the heavier soils. Frequent lifting and dividing may avoid this difficulty. Most gardeners sow seed each spring or in August, thus insuring young plants for flowering the following spring.

COREOPSIS

(C. grandiflora)

Uses:	Cutting, bedding.
Height:	1-3 feet.
Blooms:	June-October.
Propagate:	Seed—March or July; Division—April-May.
Plant:	April-May.
Distance:	12-18 inches.
Soil:	Rich, moist.
Exposure:	Sun.
Varieties:	Golden Giant, Perry's Double, Golden Shower.

* * *

The coreopsis, or tick-seed, is one of the most dependable yellow flowered perennials. With a relatively long season of bloom, they make a colorful spot in the flower border as well as a useful cut flower. They are of easy culture, being grown either from seed or from division—the doubles only by division. If the seed are sown in the early spring, the plants will flower the first season.

A new variety, Baden Gold, has very large flowers on stiff wiry stems, 18 to 24 inches tall. It bears pleasing golden yellow blossoms from May to July.

There is also a dainty species, Auriculata nana (15 inches), which blooms all summer.

The large single flowers seem to be more popular than the doubles which have recently become available.

The coreopsis is occasionally troubled by a beetle which may be controlled by spraying.

SHASTA DAISY

(Chrysanthemum maximum)

Uses:	Cut flowers, bedding.
Height:	12-24 inches.
Blooms:	June-August.
Propagate:	Division—April, September.
Plant:	April-May.
Distance:	12-18 inches.
Soil:	Deep, rich, moist.
Exposure:	Sun.
Varieties:	Double—Chiffon, Esther Reed, Mt. Shasta, Marconi, Aglayia, Wirral Supreme. Single—Supreme, Majestic, Alaska.

* * *

Shasta daisies are a popular garden flower, a member of the chrysanthemum family. Their large flowers on long stems make them ideal for cutting. The single-flowered varieties are more vigorous growers than the double-flowered. Some of the newer varieties flower nearly all summer. However, Marconi seedlings are the most dependable.

Shasta daisies need a well-prepared soil. They should be lifted and reset every other year. If neglected, they tend to run out and become weak and unattractive.

The various varieties have different flowering seasons, so for a long period of cutting, several varieties should be planted. Keeping the plants watered and fed and the spent flowers removed will also help to prolong the flowering season.

Occasionally the Shasta daisy is troubled with leaf blotch. This disease may be controlled by spraying with bordeaux. Removal of dead leaves and stems in the early spring will help to keep the planting free of disease.

DAYLILIES

(Hemerocallis)

Uses:	Border and bedding.
Height:	1½-4 feet.
Blooms:	May-September.
Propagate:	Seed—November; Division—April and immediately after flowering.
Plant:	April thru September.
Distance:	2-5 feet.
Soil:	Average garden loam.
Exposure:	Sun or light shade.
Varieties:	Frances Fay, cantalope, 2 ft., midseason, reblooms. George Cunningham, apricot, 3 ft., midseason. Cartwheels, gold, 30″, midseason. Luxury Lace, Lavender, 30″, midseason. Puritan Maid, cream, 20″, midseason. Fairy Wings, pastel blend, 38″, midseason. Jack Frost, light yellow, 3 ft., midseason. Jake Russell, greenish gold, 30″, midseason. Rare China, pastel blend, 30″, midseason. Quincy, eyed variety, 30″, midseason. McPick, small flowered orange, 3′, midseason. Full Reward, light yellow, 30″, midseason. Mary Lawrence, melon, 30″, midseason. Curls, miniature pastel melon, 18″, midseason. Lucky Strike, pink, 24″, midseason. Tinker Bell, miniature gold, 20″, midseason. Shreveport Belle, good orange, 38″, midseason. Parade Rest, gold, 38″, very late. Queen of Gonzales, orange, 30″, very early. Tanya, tan and yellow, 24″, very early and very late, longest blooming season of all. Bess Ross, red, 3′, midseason. Shooting Star, light yellow, late midseason, 3′. Congo Magic, 30″, large dark red, midseason. Pink Imperial, 30″, pink, midseason.

(National Capital Daylily Club)

* * *

The daylilies are one of the most dependable lily-like flowers of all perennials. They are hardy, tolerant, free blooming, and immune to most insects and disease. They require little in the way of culture, and little or no fertilizer. By a careful selection of varieties, flowers may be had from May until September.

Some varieties are rather dwarf, while others are tall—up to 4 feet. They do best in light shade or sun. They will not flower in heavy shade.

The colors, until the last few years, have been mostly shades of yellow. Now pinks and reds are being offered, but as yet no whites. Before selecting varieties, it is well to see them in flower; especially those having red in them, for they may have a fulvous overcast which makes them less attractive to most buyers.

GAILLARDIA

(G. aristata)—(Blanketflower)

Uses:	Cutting, bedding.
Height:	18-24 inches.
Blooms:	June-October.
Propagate:	Seed—July; Division—April; Stem cuttings—August-September; root cuttings—October.
Plant:	April-May or September.
Distance:	12-18 inches.
Soil:	Sandy garden loam.
Exposure:	Sun.
Varieties:	Burgundy, Dazzler, Goblin, Sunset Tangerine, Attraction.

* * *

The gaillardia is a very satisfactory perennial with a long season of bloom. It is not too particular in its requirements although it repays good culture. It is useful for cutting, and makes a colorful showing in the perennial border. It is relatively free from insects and diseases.

Burgundy is the reddest gaillardia, with shining wine red petals tipped with yellow. Dazzler has bright golden yellow petals with a maroon center. Sunset and Tangerine are more nearly yellow than are most varieties. The Portola hybrids are bronzy scarlet tipped with yellow.

The gaillardia my be readily propagated by division and by cutting, as well as grown from seed. The named varieties can be reproduced only by division and cutting. For this reason many gardeners prefer to buy a mixture and propagate by division those colors which they desire. Occasionally an old clump grows well but does not flower. This usually can be corrected by lifting and dividing in the early spring.

The gaillardia does best in full sun in a soil that is not too heavy. They tend to sprawl over nearby plants. This may be prevented by staking, by pruning, or by growing the so-called upright strains of which there are several on the market. The upright forms are not as tall growing and probably will be found more satisfactory in the smaller borders.

For use indoors, the flowers should be cut before they are fully opened, i.e., while flowers are still cup-shaped.

IRIS

(I. Germanica)—(Bearded Iris)

Uses:	Cut flowers, bedding, edging.
Height:	4 to 48 inches.
Blooms:	April-June.
Propagate:	Division—after flowering.
Plant:	June-August.
Distance:	6 to 15 inches.
Soil:	Moderately rich, well-drained.
Exposure:	Sun.
Varieties:	Tall-bearded—Argus Pheasant, golden brown; Blue Rhythm, medium blue; Cliffs of Dover, ruffled white; Golden Sunshine; Happy Birthday, pink; Lynn Hall, deep pink, May Hall, light pink; Pierre Menard, blue; Port Wine, red purple and white plicata; Solid Mahogany, mahogany red; Sable Night, red black; Starshine, cream white; Temple Bells, apricot yellow; Tranquility, milk white; Truly Yours, white and yellow, Violet Harmony, violet; Zantha, golden yellow.

(Mr. and Mrs. Ivan Richmond, American Iris Society)

* * *

Iris breeders have provided gardeners with a wonderful selection of the "Rainbow" flower from which to choose almost any color, height, or flowering season. The bearded iris begins its blooming season with the dwarfs, in April, followed by the intermediates, and then the tall-bearded varieties which extend the season into early June.

In the culture of bearded iris, there are two important requirements, namely sunshine and good drainage. The first is easily arranged, except in gardens that are shaded. If an open area is not available, the plants should be set where they will receive sunshine for one-half day. The second presents little or no difficulty in light soils, but in heavy loam and clay, drainage must be considered. If the soil is in good tilth, as found in a good garden, adequate drainage may be provided by raising the bed a few inches. A heavy loam or clay soil may be lightened by adding organic matter such as decayed leaves, rotted manure, or composted materials. Blue chip, kelp (Sea-Born), bonemeal, cottonseed meal, or pulverized phosphate rock may be added. All material should be thoroughly mixed with the soil and allowed to settle before planting begins.

For good growth, avoid using fertilizers high in nitrogen content, and do not over-fertilize. Lush growth may be produced, which renders the rhizome more susceptible to rot by organisms ever present in the soil. Dolomite, a calcium magnesium carbonate, may be used to neutralize excess acidity caused by decaying organic matter. The fertilizer may be worked into the soil either at the time the bed is prepared or shortly before planting.

The best time to plant iris is late June and early August, which will allow time for the plants to become fully established, thus preventing heaving during the winter months. Later plantings may be made, but precaution should be taken to prevent heaving by use of a mulch of coarse materials such as pine boughs or salt hay put in the bed after the ground is frozen.

The plants should be set with the rhizome slightly exposed or barely covered with soil (see illustration). The slender roots should be spread out and downward and the soil firmed about them. Do not plant deeply. The plants may be set 8 to 24 inches apart. If a more immediate effect is desired, plant more closely or in groups of three or more plants 4 inches apart. Thin or move iris when they become crowded. It is preferable to remake the bed about every three years. Newly set plants should be watered if the ground is dry, and a thorough watering should be given in dry weather.

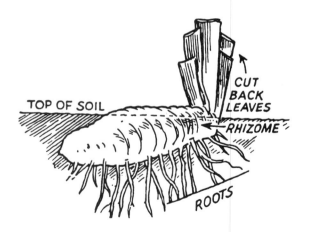

For bearded iris, prepare entire bed, then plant singly in holes ample enough to permit proper spread of roots. Leave top of rhizome exposed.

The cultivation of iris should be shallow to avoid disturbing the roots. Keep the beds free from weeds and do not permit encroachment by other plants. Remove outer leaves should they turn brown. At all times, keep old iris leaves, grasses, etc., away from the rhizomes. Clean cultivation is a good preventive for rhizome rots.

If rot should appear, scrape out all affected tissue and expose to the sun for several days, after which the rhizome may be dusted with a copper compound, such as Bordeaux mixture, and reset.

The iris borer is a pest, but there are effective sprays and dusts available which protect the plants when used according to directions on the package. A homemade mixture of DDT and a good sticker and spreader sprayed on the foliage every two weeks, beginning as soon as possible after growth begins and continuing until mid-June, will give good control. A fungicide might be added to the DDT if iris leaf spot is present. Borer control is most important since rhizome rot usually follows its entry. The system dimetheoate is reported an effective borer control.

Consideration of the many other kinds of iris such as beardless and oriental is omitted because of space limitations.

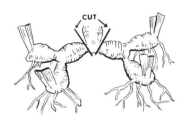

Don't make the iris divisions too small—it delays blooming a year.

PAINTED DAISY—PYRETHRUM

(Chrysanthemum coccineum)

Uses:	Cut flowers.
Height:	18 to 24 inches.
Blooms:	May-June.
Plant:	Division, seed.
Propagate:	April, September.
Distance:	12 inches.
Soil:	Rich garden loam.
Exposure:	Sun, light shade.
Varieties:	Crimson Giant—scarlet. Eileen May Robinson—pink, single. Many other varieties are offered, but most of them are less dependable than those listed here.

* * *

The painted daisy, or pyrethrum, is a spring-flowering chrysanthemum that is a garden favorite with many because it is such an excellent cut flower in May and June. The long-stemmed flowers, pink and red, have excellent keeping qualities when cut, and finely cut, neat, attractive foliage is of value after the flowers are gone.

Painted daisies are not demanding in their cultural requirements, although they do best in a well-enriched, loamy soil. Drainage is important to their health and summer moisture seems to injure them. Very little summer watering is needed; avoid wetting foliage. They can withstand severe drought. If the tops are sheared immediately after flowering, a second crop of blooms may be expected in late summer.

Propagation is by division or seed. The clumps may be divided in early spring (April) and in the fall (September). This should be done every second or third year to maintain health and vigor. Plants grown from seed are likely to contain some undesirable colors but, of course, they can be discarded. The doubles do not come true from seed, and, if named varieties are wanted, they must be obtained from a plant grower. However, many gardeners are satisfied to buy seed of a good mixture from which plants may be grown, selecting those which are most desirable for propagating.

The painted daisy is subject to about the same pests and disease as is the hardy chrysanthemum and the treatments are the same. Most gardeners consider them to be remarkably free from troubles when well-fed and in a properly prepared bed.

PENSTEMON

(P. torreyi)—(Beardtongue)

Uses:	Border plants.
Height:	2-4 feet.
Blooms:	June-August.
Propagate:	Seed—March; Division—September; Cuttings—September.
Plant:	Early spring.
Distance:	1 foot.
Soil:	Light, well-drained garden loam.
Exposure:	Light shade.
Varieties:	Pink Beauty, Garnet, Fire Bird, Ruby King, Rose Elf.

* * *

The penstemon is an easily grown, long-season perennial for the hardy border. It is free flowering with attractive dark green foliage. It will do best in light shade in a well-drained but not-too-dry loam. The addition of sand and compost is necessary if it is to thrive in a clay soil.

They are comparatively easily grown from seed, oftentimes blooming the first season from early-sown seeds. Divisions may be made in the fall.

There are a number of species of the perennial penstemons but barbatus, torreyi, digitalis and grandiflorus are most commonly grown.

PEONIES

(Paeonia officinalis)

Uses:	Cut flowers, border, bedding.
Height:	18-36 inches.
Blooms:	May-June.
Propagate:	Division—August-September.
Plant:	September.
Distance:	3 feet.
Soil:	Heavy well-fertilized loam.
Exposure:	Sun.
Varieties:	Double—Festiva Maxima, Frances Willard, Baroness Schroeder, Martha Bullock, M. Jules Elie, Karl Rosenfeld, Richard Carvel, Georgiana Shaylor, Reine Hortense, Therese, Walter Faxon, Blanche King, Avalanche, Mrs. Edward Harding, Primavere.
	Single—L'Etincelante, Rosy Dawn, Mrs. F. G. Hemmrick.

(Recommended by Leland Cole—Takoma Hort. Club.)

* * *

Peonies are one of the oldest, most widely planted of the spring flowering perennials. They thrive in the border where their huge blooms make a splendid showing. They are popular as a cutflower, although their blooms are rather large for most uses.

Peonies last for many years, hence the planting site should be deeply and well prepared before they are set out. Set the roots with the eye not over 1 to 2 inches below the ground level. Planting deeper than this is apt to result in failure to bloom.

Peonies need supplemental feeding and clean culture for best results. Bonemeal and well-decayed manure worked into the soil around the crown in the late summer will aid materially in keeping them vigorous. The larger flowered varieties should be staked.

Peonies are not greatly troubled by insects or diseases. A bud-rot may appear but this may be controlled by keeping aphids and ants off, and by removing and burning the old foilage in the fall.

There are a number of types of peonies besides the commonly planted "bomb." The single, Japanese, semi-double, crown, and rose are other attractive and useful types. Especially is this true from home decoration where the "bombs" are apt to be too large and heavy.

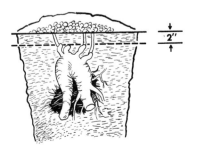

Plant peony roots with the eyes only an inch or two below the surface or they may fail to bloom.

Early maturing varieties and species are most likely to prove satisfactory in the Washington area.

Tree peonies, unlike the herbaceous just discussed, need light shade, and may be safely planted 4 to 6 inches deep. Both types must have good drainage to thrive. The tree peonies retain their above grown stems which are brittle and easily broken, thus protection may be needed. The National Arboretum has an excellent collection which might well be used to select varieties.

PHLOX

(Phlox decussata, divaricata suffruticosa, subulata)

Uses:	Cut flowers, bedding, edging, rock garden.
Height:	Subulata—creeper.
	Suffruticosa—20-36 inches.
	Decussata—20-40 inches.
Blooms:	Subulata—May-June; Suffruticosa and Decussata—June-September.
Propagate:	Division, cuttings.
Plant:	April, September.
Distance:	10-18 inches.
Soil:	Well drained, rich.
Exposure:	Sun, light shade.
Varieties:	Divaricata stolonifera—Blue Ridge.
	Subulata—
	Fairy—pale blue, lilac eye.
	Rosea—rose-pink.
	Alba—white.
	Alexander's surprise—salmon-pink.
	Lilicina—pale blue.
	Vivid—bright pink, dark pink eye.
	Maysnow—white.
	Nivalis Camla—salmon pink, late (English hybrid).
	Suffruticosa—
	Miss Lingard, 2½ ft., white.
	Decussata—
	Blue boy, 2 ft., deep violet.
	Charles Curtis, 2½ ft., sunset red.
	Purple Heart, 2 ft., blue purple.
	Harvest Fire, 2½ ft., salmon orange.
	Leo Schlageter, 2½ ft., chalk white.
	Marie Louise, 2½ ft., chalk white.
	Starfire, 2-3 ft., bright red.
	Painted Lady, 2½ ft., silvery pale rose.
	White Admiral, 2½ ft., pure white.
	Progress, 2½ ft., salmon-pink, white eye.
	Salmon Beauty, 2 ft., salmon-pink, white eye.
	Sir John Falstaff, 2 ft., pink.
	San Antonio, 2 ft., blood red.
	Thunderbolt, 2 ft., tangerine scarlet.

*   *   *

A well-grown planting of the hardy garden phlox is a thrilling sight, especially in late summer when there

are so few perennials in bloom. The large trusses of brightly colored flowers make a commanding sight. However, the early spring blooming phlox subulata or moss pink is a welcome sight, for, if planted on a sunny slope or in the rock graden, it puts on a showy display in early April.

Plant breeders have produced a large number of varieties. The color range includes: pure white, whites having variously colored eyes, pinks and reds, and shades of violet and purple. The heights range from 2 to 4 feet. The varieties may be subdivided according to season of bloom—early, mid, and late season.

The gardener may decide on the colors, height, and season of bloom before examining a plant catalog. The above list contains highly rated varieties, but is intended only to give an indication of the range of varieties available to the home gardener. No one nurseryman, even though he may sell 50 or more varieties, could be expected to have all of those listed here.

The new Phlox Stolonifera Blue Ridge, a dwarf dark blue, is excellent for light shade and will tolerate sun.

The moss pink is of the easiest culture. It will grow into a large "mat" if the soil is well drained and the plants enjoy full sun throughout the summer. The new English variety, Nivalis Camla, is similar to subulata but less rampant. The hardy garden phlox, as distinguished from the annual phlox drummondi, is a summer bloomer. In the North where the cooler moist growing conditions enable it to thrive without unusual attention, it is the mainstay of the garden. In this area, while we want its marvelous display, we must be prepared to meet certain requirements.

Phlox require a deeply prepared soil—one in which quantities of compost or rotted manure have been incorporated. This provides the cool root-run needed as well as the plant food essential for the vigorous growth desired. The plants should be well spaced so that air circulation is good—one step in the control of mildew and the red spider. A light airy mulch is needed to keep the roots cool if the ground is not fully shaded by the foliage. Ground corn cobs make a better mulch than does peatmoss which is highly acid. Coarse compost is good.

The plants should be lifted and divided at least every third year and replanted in well-enriched soil. Each spring the weaker shoots should be removed before the flowering season. It may also pay to thin out the remaining stems to insure the production of larger, even though fewer, blooms. As soon as the florets have faded, the bloom head should be removed. This is to prevent the growth of seedlings which are seldom worth having, and to retain the plant's strength for the formation of more bloom.

Disease and insect control can easily be accomplished with an all-purpose dust or spray provided regular applications are given. The red spider mite, rust, and mildew are the ones to watch for since they are nearly always encountered wherever phlox are grown. However, vigorous growing plants seem to be less difficult to protect than are plants struggling under a cultural handicap.

PHYSOSTEGIA

(P. virginiana)—(Obedient Plant)

Uses:	Cut flowers, bedding.
Height:	18-60 inches.
Blooms:	August-September.
Plant:	April-May.
Distance:	8-15 inches apart.
Soil:	Rich, moist.
Exposure:	Sun or light shade.
Varieties:	Vivid, Rosy Spire, Summer Glow, Summer Snow.

* * *

Physostegia, sometimes called false-dragon-head or obedient plant, is a little-appreciated hardy perennial. It is easily grown, but more importantly a later summer bloomer. The taller varieties flower in August. The dwarf P. virginiana and its variety Vivid (vivid pink) bloom in September and October.

The physostegia should be lifted and reset in good soil each spring for best results. They are such strong growers that they soon exhaust the soil. If unthinned they grow too thickly and the blooms lack quality. This is especially true of P. virginiana and its variety, Vivid.

PINKS

(Dianthus)

Uses:	Cut flowers, border, bedding.
Height:	6-18 inches.
Blooms:	May-September.
Propagate:	Seed—April; Division—April; Cuttings—June; Layers—Summer.
Plant:	April, September.
Distance:	9-12 inches.
Soil:	Warm, moderately rich garden loam. Sweet.
Exposure:	Sun.
	Allwoodi—A hybrid resembling a carnation. D. plumarius—grass pink, 18 inches. D. Caesius—Cheddar pink, 4-10 inches. D. arenarius—sand pink, 6-15 inches. D. deltoides—Maiden pink, creeper. D. alpinus—Alpine pink, 4 inches.
Varieties:	Evangeline, 12-15 in., Persian rose, double.
	Cheerfulness, 12-15 in., white and crimson, semi-double.
	Lucia, 15-18 in., salmon scarlet, double.
	Salmon Unique, 12-15 in., salmon, double.
	Serena, 12-15 in., ivory white, double.
	Wallace Red, 8-12 in., crimson red, semi-double.
	Apple Blossom, 10 in., soft pink.
	Bobby, 8-12 in., deep rose, crimson ring, single.

* * *

The Dianthus, or pink family, is a large and complex one, with many desirable hardy species and numerous varieties; some of which closely resemble a hardy carnation. It includes low-growing, prostrate plants and tall, stately ones, most of which are fragrant.

The pinks like a warm loose soil well supplied with lime. A soil that tends to become wet causes the prostrate stems to rot. Whenever the clumps become large and crowded they should be lifted and divided.

There are a number of diseases and insects affecting this group of plants, although if planted in a suitable situation little trouble may be expected. Where "slugs" abound they cause considerable damage. By scattering sharp cinders under and around the plants, this trouble may be eliminated.

PLANTAINLILY

(Hosta)

Uses:	Edging, border, specimen planting.
Height:	10 to 30 inches.
Blooms:	July-September.
Propagate:	Seed—April; Division—September; Cuttings—September.
Plant:	March-April.
Distance:	9-24 inches.
Soil:	Medium rich, moist, but well drained.
Exposure:	Shade, tolerates sun.
Varieties:	H. plantaginea, 2 ft., white flowers, August.
	H. caerulea, 2½ ft., blue flowers, July.
	H. lancifolia, 2 ft., pale lilac flowers, September.
	H. sieboldiana, 2½ ft., white flowers, July.
	Thomas Hogg, 8 in., silver-edged foliage, lavender flowers, September.
	Honeybells, 3 ft., lavender-blue, July-August.

* * *

The plantainlilies, sometimes called Funkia, are frequently grown for their foliage effects although all have attractive flowers. The summer-blooming H. plantaginea is noteworthy in that it flowers during a period when few perennials are in bloom; it has large ribbed, glossy leaves that are most attractive. The plantainlilies are of easy culture and thrive in shady situations. Some tolerate sun and can be used in the perennial border. The best of these is the new variety Royal Standard.

When the plantainlilies are used in foundation plantings and other unfavorable plant locations, the soil should be carefully and deeply prepared. Quantities of manure or compost should be worked into a subsoil to increase the water-holding capacity of the soil.

The plantainlilies may be grown from seed, but most gardeners depend upon division.

In poorly drained soils, crown-rot may ruin a planting. When this occurs, the plants should be lifted and destroyed and the soil sterilized with a corrosive sublimate solution.

PLUMBAGO

(Ceratostigma plumbaginoides)

Uses:	Ground cover.
Height:	6-12 inches.
Blooms:	August-October.
Propagate:	Division—April-May.
Plant:	April-May.
Distance:	12 inches apart.
Soil:	Any good garden loam.
Exposure:	Sun.

* * *

The plumbago or leadwort is a desirable late season flower for the rock garden or border in a well-drained situation. Because the blue flowers persist until freezing weather, it is especially valuable for the sunny rock garden and as a sunny place ground cover.

The plumbago is not fussy as to soil so long as it is well drained. It starts into growth so late in the spring that it may be injured if left unmarked.

POPPY

(Papaver orientale)

Uses:	Border, cutting.
Height:	18-36 inches.
Blooms:	May-June.
Propagate:	Division—August-September; Root cutings—August-September.
Plant:	August-September.
Distance:	18-36 inches.
Soil:	Moderately rich, deep, well drained.
Exposure:	Sun.
Varieties:	Indian Chief, Barr's White, Mrs. Perry, Beauty of Livermore, Crimson Pompon (double), Watermelon, Carnival, May Curtis, Helen Elizabeth, Warlord.

* * *

The Oriental poppy is one of the most vividly colored perennials that can be grown in the spring flower garden. Their huge flowers and striking colors command attention. They are easily grown and handled if taken at the right season of the year—August and September.

The Oriental poppies start into growth in the early fall and retain their leaves during much of the winter. In spring they make rapid growth and throw up many flower stems which bear huge cup-like flowers in May and June.

The plants die down in July and August; it is wise to fill the holes left by the dying stems with dirt to avoid water standing around the dormant root.

The Oriental poppies may be lifted and divided in August or September. One method is to cut the roots with a spade and lift the clump out, leaving the cut roots in place. Fill the hole with soil and a season later there will be a number of well-started plants to be lifted and reset; each piece of root left in the ground will become a new plant.

The Oriental poppies seem to be relatively free from pests and disease in this area, although there are a number known to attack them. The bacterial blight cannot be prevented by spraying, and so infected plants should be destroyed. The aphids may be controlled with nicotine sulphate.

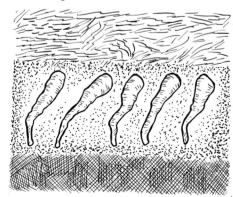

Increase poppies by root cutting—plant them right side up (August). Cover the row of cuttings with an inch or two of mulch.

PRIMROSE

(Primula—Cowslip)

Uses:	Edging, bedding, cutting.
Height:	4-12 inches.
Blooms:	April-June.
Propagate:	Division—September; Seed—March or August.
Plant:	April, September.
Distance:	6-9 inches.
Soil:	Moist, rich, well drained.
Exposure:	Medium shade.
Varieties:	P. vulgaris—Common or English Primrose. P. veris—Cowslip. P. elatior—Oxlip. P. polyantha—Polyanthus, and Pacific Hybrids.

* * *

Primroses are colorful perennials for use along shady paths, for shady nooks in the woods or near the house. They are distinctly shade loving, but more important, they require considerable moisture and a cool growing situation. Too often the shady  spot selected for them is also dry because of tree roots. If being grown under a tree, it is essential to incorporate quantities of compost or peat moss into the soil to insure sufficient supplies of moisture for them.

Formerly, primroses were available principally as strains, such as the Pacific Hybrids. Today we have a considerable number of named varieties on the market. Acaulis-Blue, Auricula-Giant hybrids, Julias-Edestein, Julias-Wanda, and Veris-Colossus are varieties now listed in perennial catalogues.

Primroses are best started from seed in a coldframe in March or out of doors in April or May. Some gardeners wait until July, but they are apt to run into difficulties because of the hot weather. Divide established plants in the spring immediately after flowering. The early fall is even more satisfactory.

Primroses are troubled by red spider and the primrose flea beetle. The red spider may be controlled with dimethoate. It is usually necessary to use lead arsenate for the beetle or a combination of DDT and HETP may be used.

In a favorable situation, there are a number of other primrose species that are hardy, but more exacting in their requirements.

SCABIOSA

(Scabiosa caucasica—Pincushion-Flower, Mourning Bride, Blue Bonnet)

Uses:	Cutting, border.
Height:	24-36 inches.
Blooms:	June-September.
Propagation:	Seed, division.
Plant:	Spring, mid-summer.
Distance:	10-12 inches.
Soil:	Well-drained, sweet.
Exposure:	Sun.
Varieties:	House Mixture, Caucasica.

The scabiosa is an easily grown, although short-lived, sun-loving perennial. There have been a number of named varieties introduced, but they have been largely displaced by the (Isaac) House Mixture.

The seed may be started in the early spring or in July. The latter date is pre-ferred since spring sown plants may not bloom the first season.

The seedlings should be pinched to produce well-branched plants. They are sun lovers and do best in a sweet soil (6.5-7.0 pH).

In cutting the flowers of the perennial scabiosa, it is good practice to leave the foliage—this is the opposite of the cutting practice for the annual scabiosa. The plants are at their best for three years.

SPURGE (JAPANESE)

(Pachysandra terminalis)

Uses:	Ground cover.
Height:	6-8 inches.
Blooms:	Inconspicuous.
Propagate:	Division—April, September; Cuttings—July-August.
Plant:	April, September.
Distance:	12 inches apart.
Soil:	Well-drained garden loam.
Exposure:	Shade.

* * *

The Japanese spurge is one of the more important shade-loving ground covers. It will thrive in even less favorable situations than periwinkle and English Ivy. Spurge may also be used in partial shade or where it receives only the morning sun.

The rooted cuttings may be planted 12 inches apart, but for a quicker effect may be as close as 6 inches. The soil should be carefully prepared with considerable compost or well-rotted manure incorporated before planting. A top-dressing with compost should be made after planting to keep the soil cool.

The cuttings may be pinched back the following season (a year after planting) to force new growth to spring from the roots.

Pachysandra is not often troubled by disease, although there is a disease of the leaves which may occur. If discovered, remove all diseased plants and spray with bordeaux. Feeding to increase the vigor of the plants following such an attack is desirable. Some scale insects attack pachysandra and should be controlled with a dormant spray, such as used on evergreens, but this requires care.

SUNFLOWERS (Perennial)

(Helianthus decapetalus, orgyalis, mollis, etc.)
(Heliopsis helianthoides, scabra)

Uses:	Cut flowers, background.
Height:	2 to 5 feet.
Blooms:	June-September.
Propagate:	Seed, division, cuttings.
Plant:	Seed in March, plants—April.
Distance:	18 to 24 inches.
Soil:	Ordinary garden loam.
Exposure:	Sun.

Varieties:	Height	Type	Bloom Season	Color
Helianthus Multiflorus fl.-pl.	4'	D	June-July	Clear yellow

DEPENDABLE WASHINGTON FLOWERS

Heliopsis Varieties				
Gold-Greenheart	4'	D	June-Aug.	Buttercup yellow
Scabia incomparabilis	3'	S-D	July-Oct.	Golden yellow

The perennial sunflowers are valuable plants for the sunny border, producing a long season of bloom and making a pleasing display in the garden over much of the summer. The flowers are useful for cutting. There are both single and double varieties that are long-lasting. The perennial sunflower undoubtedly is seldom considered for the flower border, perhaps because it is normal to imagine a relationship between the perennial and the huge annual (Helianthus annuus) which is commonly grown for chicken feed. The names are the same but the performance is far different. The perennial is a much lower growing plant, from 2 to 4 feet in height. The garden varieties are much branched and the flowers seldom exceed 3 inches in diameter.

The perennial sunflower is of the easiest culture, requiring only a sunny border. It may be safely transplanted with a ball of soil about its roots at almost any season. Only a few insects and diseases trouble the perennial sunflower. A fungicide may be desirable to control rust in the summer and mildew in the fall.

Some varieties of the perennial sunflower, those arising from Heliopsis helianthoides, have leaves that are quite smooth. Those developed from Heliopsis scabra have rougher foliage. Some varieties of Helianthus tend to spread and need more space than others without this habit of growth.

VERONICA

(Speedwell)
(V. maritima, spicata, incana, teucrium, latifolia)

Uses:	Cut flowers, border.
Height:	18-24 inches.
Blooms:	June-August.
Propagate:	Division—April; Seed—March or August.
Plant:	April, September.
Distance:	6-12 inches.
Soil:	Moderately rich garden loam.
Exposure:	Sun or light shade.

Varieties:	Blue Champion, 2-3 ft., late summer.
	Blue Peter, 18 in., deep blue, June-September.
	Blue Spire, 18-24 in., deep blue, June-September.
	Incana, 12 in., June.
	Incana Rosea, 12 in., June.
	Longifolia (martima) subsessilis, 18-24 in., July-Sept.
	Rupestrist, creeper, May.
	True Blue, 12 in., May-June.
	Icile, 18-24 in., white, July-September.
	Minuet, 15-18 in., rose-pink, July-August.

* * *

The veronica family has a number of very useful garden subjects. Their clear blue flowers and dark green foliage are a desirable addition to the hardy border. The taller growing species (maritima) are good for cutting. Longifolia subsessils is one of the best for this area.

Veronicas prefer a moist soil for best results, although it should have good drainage. They may be planted in the early spring or early fall, and are not demanding. They are seldom troubled by insects or diseases.

The veronicas may be propagated by seed or division. They are easily divided, either in the spring or late summer.

VINCA MINOR

(V. minor, Periwinkle, Running Myrtle)

Uses:	Ground cover.
Height:	6-8 inches.
Blooms:	April-May.
Propagate:	Division, cuttings—in April or September.
Plant:	April or September.
Distance:	12 inches.
Soil:	Ordinary garden loam.
Exposure:	Shade or sun.
Varieties:	Species is violet-blue; Bowles—deeper blue; Minor alba—white, Miss Jeykel's—white.

* * *

Vinca minor is one of the most useful of the ground covers. It is evergreen and the stems root so that it is a useful plant for shady slopes. It will tolerate sun but is slower growing under such conditions.

The flowers make a colorful showing in early spring. Vinca major has both larger leaves and flowers, but is not as hardy. The white-flowered form is not as commonly grown as the blue one.

The plants may be set out in the early spring or in early fall. Spaced a foot apart, they will in the course of 2 or 3 years form a solid mat that will last for years. When used for an evergreen edging, the runners should be pinned into place and unneeded shoots kept trimmed off.

Layering is an easy safe method of propagating many plants.

CHAPTER VI

PLANTS FOR THE INDOOR GARDEN

The indoor culture of plants is an age old practice; the only changes are the substitution of flowering and foliage plants for those which were grown for flowering and herbs. The more rigorous the winter the greater the urge, it seems, to have something green or in flower during the winter months. The promotional specialists know full well that plants and flowers have a major eye appeal. They use them throughout the homes and interiors they advertise.

The choice of plants for indoor use is currently engulfed with an amazing variety of new kinds as well as improved forms of the old standbys. However, the wealth of new plant material should not blind the gardener to the importance of selecting those best adapted to the light, heat and humidity of the situation where they are to grow.

As a general rule, few plants will flower in situations away from direct sunlight. There are a number of foliage plants which can tolerate such conditions and because of their variations in texture and color can and should provide plant interest. The more light that is available the wider the choice of plants.

Heat is not so much a factor today as it used to be. The florists and plant growers now provide an amazing array of plants that can withstand the usual house temperatures. The air humidity, however, is still a major problem in all except the most modern homes. Humidifiers are still in the early stages of development; at least most homes lack effective ones. It is this area where the growing of house plants still requires a bit of skill and ingenuity on the part of the indoor gardener. There is no one general rule that can be given to guide the indoor gardener in the proper watering of house plants. The amount that should be given a pot will vary between rooms, between seasons, and even between plants in the same window. Consequently, the best rule to follow is one based on plant behavior. Adequate watering should give the foliage a fullness that is in keeping with the particular kind of plant. Overwatering is likely to result in yellowing of the foliage—occasionally in wilting of the leaves. Keeping the pots in saucers or jardinieres with water touching the bottoms of the pots usually results in water-logged soil and often brings root rot.

Some of the problems in watering stem from the soil mixtures used. As a general rule, the soil should be light enough so that surplus water drains away quickly. The soil mixture, however, should contain sufficient humus materials to absorb and hold moisture for the plant where the roots can get to it.

The soil mixtures for the house plant vary markedly between the many kinds. The following mixtures will meet most of these requirements:

Potting Mixture No. 1—A standard mixture for general use.

2 parts of good garden loam
1 part peatmoss or leafmold
1 part sharp sand
or
3 parts of screened soil from the compost pile
½ part sharp sand
½ part peatmoss

Potting Mixture No. 2—For cactus and succulents
To the standard mixture add:
¼ by volume of crushed mortar, gravel mixture, or similar materials, plus 1 quart of ground limestone per bushel.

Potting Mixture No. 3—Begonias, ferns, African violets, etc.
To the standard mixture add:
¼ by volume of peatmoss, compost, or leaf mold.

Potting Mixture No. 4—Azaleas and other acid-soil loving plants.
To the standard mixture add ¼ by volume of oak leafmold or oak leaf compost.

Any of the above mixtures may be enriched through the addition of two quarts of pulverized cow manure per bushel of mixture. Ground bonemeal may be added as a source of phosphate—1 quart per bushel to each of the mixtures except No. 3 and No. 4.

GENERAL RULES

1. Most plants should be watered thoroughly from below until moisture appears on the surface of the soil. An occasional watering from the top is needed to flush out the salt accumulation left by evaporation. Pour off any excess water in the saucer after an hour or two. Do not water again until the surface of the soil becomes almost dry to the touch. Syringe the leaves of glossy-foliage plants. Even African violets may be gently syringed with tepid water to remove the dust but care must be taken to see that the leaves are dry before moving the plants into sunlight.

2. Give the plants fresh air but avoid draughts.

3. Fertilizing once a month is a general rule. Sometimes as the plants are forming flower buds, it is wise to feed even as often as once a week. During the dormant period (mid-winter) no feeding should be the rule. Regardless of the plants needs for fertilizer, the manufacturer's directions should be followed.

4. Keep the plants free from insect pests and diseases. There are several general purpose mixtures now available for use on house plants, some of which are in aerosols. Often a thorough syringing will remedy the ill.

5. A brief session in the shower bath is another method of thoroughly soaking the soil in the pots. In addition, the shower helps to flush out accumulated salts, remove sucking insects (a cold shower is most effective), and of course, removes accumulated dust from the foliage. African violets, gloxinias, and the velvet plant, however, will not tolerate a cold shower— they enjoy one that is tepid in temperature.

6. Many house plants may be set outside during the summer months. Sink the pots up to their rims in a sunny or shaded spot in the garden according to the need of each plant. Water and feed as necessary. In the fall, bring them into their accustomed places in the house in a gradual manner allowing them to slowly adjust to the change in air and humidity. This should be done early enough so that the transition is completed before the windows are closed for the season. Before bringing the plants indoors, they should be thoroughly sprayed three times at weekly intervals to remove all insects. Repotting should as far as practical be taken care of at the time the plants are moved out-of-doors, rather than in the fall when they are being brought indoors.

A—Flowering Plants
Popular House Plants and their Requirements

AFRICAN VIOLET

(Saintpaulia ionantha)

Exposure:	East or west window, partial sun.
Temperature:	65° nights, 70° F. day.
Soil:	Mixture No. 3.
Water:	Keep soil moist, never waterlogged.
Propagate:	Leaf cuttings, especially in March.
Colors:	White, pink, blue, lavender, purple.
Enemies:	Cyclamen mites, mealy bug, crown rot.
Varieties:	

FOREVER WHITE—Best Single white

DELFT IMPERIAL—Ruffled blue double, white edge
SNOW BALLET—Double, white tailored foliage
BLUE ADORA—Large, single medium blue, prolific
ANN SPENCER—Giant single pink, white edge
RENE EDMUNDSON—Light blue double, bronze foliage
PINK GOLIATH—Excellent, single pink, tailored foliage
JANNY—Bright lavender, pink star, white edge
CORTEZ—Double, purple
VELVET POM POM—Double, dark purple
CHANTICLEER—Light pink double, lovely foliage
MARINER BLUE—Dark blue, white-edged single
IVORY FASHION—Large, single, ivory-pink, dark leaves
POLAR QUEEN—Creamy white, double
LILIAN JARETT—Pink double, variegated foliage
TOMMY LOU—Double white, dark foliage edged in white
SHADES O' WINE—Huge, single, bi-colored lavender, green
   edge
CLOVER GLOW—Large, white edged, double pink
PLUM ROYAL—Velvety double plum
ATOMIC BLAZE—Best single, glowing fuchsia red
MOLTEN FIRE—Double, dark red
WHITE PERFECTION—Giant, white, double
STEPHY—Profuse double, shell-pink
INCA MAID—Single red, girl foliage
POWDER BLUE—Semi-double, light blue
MY MARYLAND—Outstanding double blue
WASHINGTON STAR—Very good. Double brilliant cerise-
   red, compact growth

(Recommended by Mrs. Albert Behnke)

* * *

African violets can be grown in almost any location. Provided the light is sufficient, a north or east window seems best. Place the plant as near the window pane as possible without actual contact with the pane. Early morning sun is not harmful but some protection is needed in the summer after 10 a.m. An African violet will bloom well in full sunshine, but foliage will be bleached, detracting from the beauty of the plant.

Top or bottom watering is a matter of choice; a thorough watering is desirable, but do not let pot stand in a saucer full of water for more than an hour or two.

Feed monthly with balanced food, according to directions on label.

When plants become pot bound, repot into next larger size of pot. Use a light, porous soil mixture, preferably one that has been sterilized. Do not disturb the root ball when repotting.

Remove spent blossoms, dead leaves, etc., for sanitary reasons. Turn plant ¼ every 2 or 3 days to keep growth symmetrical.

During cold weather protect plant from chill of window with shade, Venetian blind, or newspaper. The African violet thrives in a daytime temperature of 70 or 75° and a nighttime temperature of 65° but is likely to be injured by 60°.

A weekly spraying with warm water will keep the foliage free of dust, but allow foliage to dry before placing in sun. Humidity is necessary for good blooming. This is why they do so well on the kitchen window sill. Spray as needed with an all-purpose mixture containing malathion to control sucking insects, perhaps dimethoate can take the place of such mixtures.

AMARYLLIS

(Hippeastrum)

Exposure:	South window, full sun.
Temperature:	65° to 70° F.
Soil:	Mixture No. 1.
Water:	Sparingly until new growth is well started, then copiously.
Fertilize:	Every two weeks; ½ cup of weak liquid manure, or soluble fertilizers.
Propagate:	Old bulbs develop offsets. Separate when large enough.
Colors:	White, pink, white and pink, red, red striped.
Varieties:	Single—Queen Elizabeth; Double—Helen Hull.

* * *

An amaryllis will not bloom if it has been planted too deeply or in too large a pot. Use pots only 1 or 2 inches larger in diameter than the bulb. In planting the bulb, only the lower one-half to two-thirds of the bulb should be covered by the soil.

After flowering, the bulb should be kept watered and fertilized until warm weather permits the pot to be plunged into the border for continued growth. In the fall when cool weather is approaching, the pot should be lifted—the bulbs dried and stored. A rest period is essential to the flowering of many bulbs (but not all hybrids).

BEGONIAS (WAX)

(Begonia semperflorens)

Exposure:	South window, sun.
Temperature:	60°-65° F.
Soil:	Mixture No. 3.
Water:	Regularly, but allow to dry out between drinks.
Fertilize:	Sparingly.
Propagate:	Seed, cuttings.
Colors:	White, pink, red.
Varieties:	Single—white, pink, and red Pearl.
	Double with flowers like small roses.

* * *

The wax begonias are one of the most popular and easily grown of the common house plants. Almost untroubled with insects or diseases, they require only sun for good growth. Watering is an easy task because they need to dry out occasionally. Feeding is moderate, an occasional application. The wax begonia may be pinched back whenever it becomes leggy so that it seldom needs to be tossed out as an overgrown plant. In summer give them a partially shaded spot in the border.

BEGONIAS (ANGEL-WING)

(Begonia; B. Orange rubra, B. Coccinea, B. Veitch's Carmin

Exposure:	South east window.
Temperature:	60° to 70° F.
Soil:	Mixture No. 3.
Water:	Moderately, allow to dry a bit between waterings.
Fertilize:	Moderately.
Propagate:	Cuttings.
Colors:	Deep pink.
Varieties:	Not named as such.

* * *

The B. coccinea has large flowered, pendant clusters of deep pink. Plants grow fairly large—to 24 inches in height. Leaves are broad at the base, long, and pointed. It blooms continuously.

The name Angel-Wing is given to forms of three species—B. coccinea seems the most logical.

BOUVARDIA

(Bouvardia humboldti)

Exposure:	Sunny window.
Temperature:	55°-65° F.
Soil:	Mixture No. 3.
Water:	Freely—after flowering reduce.
Fertilize:	Regularly.
Propagate:	Cuttings—after flowering.
Colors:	White (also yellow and red).
Varieties:	

* * *

The Bouvardia is unique with its four white waxy petals. Grow the plant in a cool but sunny window. Syringe the leaves weekly for plant health as well as to control the red spider mite. The cuttings should be potted as soon as rooted and the pots sunk to the rim in the garden in a partially shaded situation.

CACTI AND SUCCULENTS

Exposure:	Sunny window.
Temperature:	65° to 70° F.
Soil:	Mixture No. 2.
Water:	Syringe until a period of new growth, then sparingly.
Fertilize:	While in active growth, once a month.
Propagate:	Division or cuttings.
Varieties:	**Cacti—**

Astrophytums	Opuntias
Echinopses	Christmas (Zygocactus)
Mamillarias	Orchid (Epiphyllums)

Succulents—

Agaves	Haworthias
Aloes	Sedums
Ceropegia	Sempervivums
Crassula arborescens	Stapelias
Echeverias	Kalanchoe cocchinea
Gasterias	

The Christmas cactus prefers only partial sun. The temperature should be slightly lower (60-70 degrees) and soil mixture No. 3 is better than that given above for cacti and succulents. For good bloom, begin watering in September. Continue every other day with daily syringing of the foliage to supplement the pot watering. The plants need long nights beginning in early October for flower bud formation. As soon as the buds form, curtail watering. During the summer the pot may be placed in a lightly shaded situation in the garden where the rainfall is likely to provide sufficient moisture.

The Kalanchoe, like the other kinds named under cacti and succulents, needs full sun but with a somewhat lower temperature—(55-65 degrees). The plants should be watered moderately until bloom is past, then curtail until the pot is sunk in the garden in a sunny situation. The feeding of the Kalanchoe is limited to the fall or until buds show color. There are several species and a number of varieties of this attractive house plant. The gray-green scalloped leaves have red edges.

CLIVIA

(Clivia miniata, Kafir lily)

Exposure:	East or west windows.
Temperature:	60°-70° F.
Soil:	Mixture No. 1.
Water:	Very little during rest period.
Fertilize:	Once a year.
Propagate:	Side shoots (suckers).
Colors:	Orange.
Varieties:	Hybrids.

This is an easy one especially during the rest period when they can be stored anyplace that is frost-free. As the flower stalks begin to emerge between the thick glossy, strap-like leaves, they will benefit from watering and a warmer situation.

The commonly-grown clivia is the species but there are interesting hybrids which may be of interest.

The clivias develop a massive root system and, unless repotted every 3 or 4 years, may burst the pot. They resent disturbing the roots but when a side-shoot develops, it becomes necessary to cut enough of the roots to permit separation. During the summer they may be parked in a shady situation.

COLEUS

(Coleum)

Exposure:	Sun or partial sun.
Temperature:	70° F.
Soil:	Mixture No. 1.
Water:	Freely; will grow in water.
Fertilize:	Moderately.
Propagate:	Cuttings.
Colors:	Infinite variety of coloring in leaves.

* * *

Coleus are normally used for bedding purposes in the summer, but are fully as useful in the indoor garden. There are an endless variety of markings and shadings to be selected from. The best color is obtained from plants in a sunny window in a warm room. Cuttings may be taken at any time and rooted in water—there is no point in keeping an old gangling or unsightly plant. Mealy bugs are often a problem but can be controlled easily with an all-purpose aerosol. Flowering shoots should be pinched.

FERNS

(Various species)

Exposure:	Shade—north or west window.
Temperature:	55°-65° F.
Soil:	Mixture No. 3.
Water:	Daily; must have excellent drainage.
Fertilize:	None.
Propagate:	Division.
Varieties:	Boston or Sword (Whitmani, Verona).
	Holly.
	Rabbit Foot.
	Bird's-nest.
	Pteris or Table (P. cretica).

* * *

The ferns of yesteryear are generally too large for the present-day house. There are a number of very excellent smaller varieties which add green to the modern room. They require high humidity and perfect cleanliness. The ferns do not need to be in sunlight but

they do want filtered light such as from a north window. Ferns benefit by repotting each spring just before they are moved to their summer home in the garden.

FLOWERING MAPLE

(Abutilon hybridum, A. megapotamicum)

Exposure:	Sun.
Temperature:	60°-70° F.
Soils:	No. 1.
Fertilize:	Monthly.
Propagate:	Cuttings, seeds.
Colors:	White, pink, yellow, red.

* * *

The flowering maple is a dependable grower with a long season of bloom. While called the flowering maple, it more nearly resembles a hollyhock. It is a large (3 ft.) pot plant.

The flowering maple tends to be leggy unless pinched while young to force branching. New ones should be grown from cuttings as replacements for the leggy plants.

Keep the plants somewhat pot-bound for the best flowering.

FUCHSIA

(Fuchsia hybrids)

Exposure:	Partial sun—east or west windows.
Temperature:	50°-65° F.
Soil:	Mixture No. 1.
Water:	Lightly until good growth, then plentifully while in bloom.
Fertilize:	Sparingly.
Propagate:	Cuttings—new growth after rest period.
Varieties:	Hybrids are numerous; many have been named.
Colors:	White through blush pink, deep cerise, red-purple to violet.

* * *

Fuchsias which bloomed during the summer will not bloom the following winter. They require a long rest period. Buy new plants in the fall or grow them from cuttings taken from the new growth following a rest period. Resting consists of putting the plants in a cool, dry place and withholding water except enough to prevent drying. Start watering and feeding in December and by February there should be new shoots long enough for cutting. White fly is usually a serious pest of the fuchsia.

GERANIUMS

(Pelargoniums)

Exposure:	Sun.
Temperature:	45°-65° F.
Soil:	Mixture No. 1, keep potbound.
Water:	Keep on dry side.
Fertilize:	Liquid once a week.
Propagate:	Cuttings—rooted in slightly damp sand.
Colors:	White, pink, red.
Varieties:	Zonal (Olympic, Improved Richard, Beaute Poitevine, etc.)
	Lady Washington.
	Ivy.
	Nutmeg.
	Rose, etc.

* * *

Geraniums for indoor bloom should be young plants—not old plants that have exhausted themselves through summer blooming in the garden. They like to be kept on the dry side. Do not water until the soil feels dry to the touch. For symmetrical growth, the pots should be turned frequently. Discard overgrown plants, replacing with young plants grown from cuttings (at any season).

PATIENCE PLANT

(Impatiens sultani)

Exposure:	East window, partial sun.
Temperature:	60°-65° F.
Soil:	Mixture No. 1.
Water:	Keep well-watered, syringe weekly.
Fertilize:	Sparingly.
Propagate:	Cuttings (slightly moist sand), seed.
Colors:	White, pale pink, rose salmon, nasturtium red.
Varieties:	A-go-go, Tangerine, double.

* * *

The "patience" plant is one of the most obliging year-round bloomers if given plenty of moisture. This plant will wilt more quickly from lack of moisture than any other house plant. Overgrown plants may be severely pruned and still make a good display in the summer garden. The cuttings should be rooted in only slightly damp sand or in water.

SPATHYPHYLLUM

(Spathyphyllum hybrids)

Exposure:	Light shade summer, sun in winter.
Temperature:	60°-70° F.
Soil:	Light humus No. 3.
Fertilize:	Monthly.
Propagate:	Division.
Colors:	Creamy white.
Varieties:	Mauna Loa.

* * *

The spathyphyllum is well adapted to the home, has a long flowering season, and is much easier to grow than its relation the anthuriums.

The free flowering species, S. floribundum, has much

less attractive foliage than the hybrid, Mauna Loa.

The spathyphyllum likes daily watering, likes moisture in the saucer and if freely fed, is very free blooming. However it grows rapidly and has to be divided or shifted into a larger-sized pot each year.

A large plant—24 inches—it is best kept in a jardiniere or in a deep saucer so as to obtain the maximum moisture. Some use a jardiniere on a three legged stand to make handling easier; this helps to keep it from dominating a window.

B–Foliage Plants

Foliage plants have gained a great deal of attention since the advent of planter boxes in modern homes. Every plantsman is searching for new forms or species to enrich and increase the gardener's interest in such plants. Many are put on the market before there is time to study their needs as to light and temperature. However, because most of them are from the tropics, it may be assumed that they need a well drained soil that is enriched with compost, peat moss, or leaf mold.

Most of these foliage plants are of interest because they will grow without direct sunlight and in areas where few, if any, flowering plants will thrive. Many of them will grow in parts of rooms far from the windows. However, there are a few such foliage plants which will provide flowers as well as attractive foliage and, unfortunately, most of these must have sunlight in order to flower. Such plants should be rotated if possible between sunny windows and light shade.

Most of the foliage plants need a soil that is rich in humus (No. 3 or 4)—which is easy to understand since most of them are from the tropics. However, the Saxifraga, Sansevieria, and Pandanus require a soil that is only slightly acid or neutral.

Most of these plants are shade lovers, and for easy reference are listed here according to their relative light requirements:

Least Light—Aglaonema (Chinese Evergreen), Aracucaria (Norfolk Island Pine), Aspidistra (Cast Iron Plant), Aucuba (Gold Dust Plant), Dieffenbachia (Dumb Cane), Dracaena (Corn Plant), Philodendron, Sansevieria (Snake Plant), Schefflera, and Syngonium.

Moderate Light—Peperomia (Watermelon begonia), Pothos (Gold Dust Plant), and many of the first group will thrive better in this light.

Moderate Shade—Fatshedra, Ficus (Fig, Rubberplant), Hedera helix (the Ivy), Pothos var. Marble Queen, and many others.

The **moisture** requirements of the Foliage Plants vary greatly between the species. Most of the tropicals want a moist but not water-logged soil. This is best supplied by incorporating sufficient sand in the loam, together with coarse compost or leaf mold. During the dormant season, usually the winter, watering should be reduced: when new growth begins in the spring, watering should be increased. However, an occasional drying out between waterings is helpful to most kinds.

Anything that can be done to improve the humidity about the plants generally contributes to their vigor. Syringing the foliage of plants is probably the easiest method, but gravel-filled pans on which the pots rest is more lasting. Do not let the bottoms of the pots sit in water.

Temperatures. Most of the plants listed below thrive with a daytime temperature of 70 to 75 degrees; the nighttime reading should be 5 to 10 degrees lower. A few are indicated to need a warm situation and they will prefer a warm, sunny window; most of those listed will thrive, other factors being equal, at the usual thermostat setting in the home. A few plants such as the Poinsettia and the Crotons cannot withstand chilling, and like a warmer situation than is ordinarily available.

Sanitation. All house plants need to have their foliage washed free of dust occasionally. However, a good forceful syringing with cold water once every week or two will not only remove the dust but will also tend to curb the sucking insects that tend to plague the plants. This is a more practical approach than trying to spray the plants with an insecticide.

The foliage plants, to be effective, need to be kept clean and in vigorous growth (at least in appearance), although some will grow out of bounds quickly if fertilized liberally. The Philodendrons in particular should be starved for the desirable short nodes (spaces between leaves). In fact, it is good practice to keep most of the foliage plants "pot-bound" and when repotting to use the next larger size of pot. Even with this practice the Pandanus, Chinese evergreen, and Dumb-cane will soon outgrow their usefulness in the average-sized room.

AGLAONEMA

(Chinese evergreen)

An attractive shade lover that has the minimum requirements for care. It is a hardy, long-lived house plant that requires no direct sunlight. It is one of the few plants that cannot be overwatered—in fact it will live for months in a vase of water. The Chinese Evergreen seems to thrive best if pot-bound. If too tall for the situation, the top may be cut off and new shoots will form.

APHELANDRA

(No common name)

A sun-loving warm room plant. The handsome leaves, 4 to 6 inches long, are prominently veined. In the fall or early winter the Aphelandra produces showy, terminal, orange-colored flower-spikes, oftentimes topping brightly colored bracts. However, most interest is in the attractive foliage. This plant may be cut back if too tall, preferably following a rest period.

ACALYPHA HISPIDA

(Chenille plant)

An ornamental with heart-shaped leaves and bright flowers that look like long red tails. It likes a moderately warm situation with a 55° temperature at night. The chenille plant likes a sunny situation in the winter but through spring and summer it needs light shade.

AUCUBA JAPONICA

(Gold Dust tree)

A widely grown, attractive, shade loving shrub, that may well be used indoors where its interesting leaf coloring will add color to the shady situation. There are many variations in leaf coloring from bright green to soft green splotched with yellow. If both male and female plants are grown together, the females often produce scarlet fruits. The Aucuba is very tolerant of temperatures, but best growth is obtained at moderate temperatures of 60° to 65°.

ASPIDISTRA

(Cast Iron plant)

This well known house plant is distinguished because of its toughness and ability to withstand almost any condition. However, if well grown, the foliage is useful in flower arrangements. While the Aspidistra will withstand dim light and desert-like dry air, it will grow vigorously, even flower under more favorable conditions. Well grown plants soon fill their pots and need dividing every two or three years.

BEGONIA, REX

(Begonia assamica)

There are many, many varieties of the Rex begonia, all grown for their colorful foliage. Merry Christmas is one of the more widely grown varieties. The Iron Cross variety is commonly associated with the Rex but properly should be B. masoniana. Both have comparatively inconspicuous blooms.

These two begonias thrive under the same conditions as the African violets, perhaps requiring a bit more humidity and less light. Some varieties of the Rex begonia need a rest period. Do not overwater.

CRASSULA ARGENTEA

(Jade plant)

The Jade plant is grown for its interesting thick fleshy leaves, although they do flower under favorable conditions. Give them a sunny situation and a sandy

soil. While in active growth they need an abundance of water, but not while resting. There is a large number of species of the Crassula, the differences being mostly in the shape of the leaves and the color of the flowers. It seldom flowers indoors. The Jade plant is quite tolerant of indoor conditions so long as it is in a sunny situation.

DIFFENBACHIA

(Dumbcane)

The Dumbcanes like a warm, moist situation. They have a more limited usefulness than many other foliage plants. However, they are very attractive with their large variously colored leaves which in some species may be two feet long. The Dumbcane is a shade lover. Where temperatures are favorable (70°-80°) and moist air is abundant, they make an excellent showing. Another point in their favor is that some species do not exceed 4 feet in height, whereas most large leaved tropicals soon outgrow their situation.

(Dumbcane)

DRACAENA

(Cornplant)

Two species of the Cornplant are well adapted to household conditions—D. fragrans and D. godseffiana. The experimentally inclined may want to grow some of

the others for their unusual foliage. The Cornplant thrives in rather dimly lighted situations and withstands household conditions very well. Both of the species named have many variations in leaf marking, striping, margins and splotching. When a Cornplant becomes "leggy" the top may be taken as cuttings and new plants started.

FATSIA JAPONICA

A large plant with glossy, tropical-appearing foliage. It is much used out-of-doors in the deep south and in southern California. The large nearly round leaves (9 to 15 inches) are deeply lobed.

FATSHEDRA LIZEI

This is another interesting strong growing foliage plant, although it takes more light than the Chinese evergreen, Cornplant, etc. It will thrive under about the same light conditions as the Pothos.

FICUS SPECIES

(Rubber plant—Fig)

The common Rubberplant is looked upon as being too strong a grower and not being particularly attrac-

tive. However, there are a number of species and varieties that bear little resemblance to the plant commonly associated with that name. And they are just as tolerant to dimly lit situations, household air, and humidity. The creeping Fig, F. pumila, is interesting because of its small leaves and its ability to grow on wall and posts. It is also useful as a hanging vine. The F. lyrata, sometimes called the Fiddle-leaved Fig because of the shape of its leaves, is a strong growing plant. The F. parcelli is a bushy plant with thin light green leaves, marbled with creamy-white. The F. decora has very attractive foliage. Give these plants only moderate light and ample water during the growing season but very little moisture during the winter season when they are practically dormant.

FITTONIA ARGYRONEURA

(Silvernerve)

This is an attractive low-growing plant that thrives in a moist soil. A second species, F. verschaffelti, has dark green, heart-shaped leaves with conspicuous red veining on the undersides. Both may be used as a ground cover in the planter box. The Fittonias like a well drained but moist soil, one that is prepared with equal parts of sand, loam, and leaf mold. Light shade and a moderate temperature serve them very well.

CUPHEA HYSSOPIFOLIA

This species is much more attractive than the better known Cigarflower (C. platycentra). Conspicuous by its continuous bloom, this compact little shrub is a sun lover which thrives in a soil that is half loam and half leaf mold. C. hyssopifolia has violet-white flowers. There is also a variety, Firefly, with deep, rosy-scarlet flowers.

JACOBINIA PAUCIFLORA

(Brazilian Plume)

The Brazilian Plume, an unusual plant, likes a moderately cool situation (55°-60°), light shade in the summer, full sun in the fall, and a loose soil that provides good drainage. The bright plumes, scarlet tipped with yellow, are borne over a long season.

MARANTA LEUCONEURA

(Prayer plant)

A foliage plant with interesting markings on the leaves, which at night fold as if in prayer. They are

shade lovers and want a moderately warm (65°-75°) situation. Several named varieties are being offered. Ample moisture is needed during the growing season. A loose humus laden soil is needed to supply moisture to the roots.

NORFOLK ISLAND PINE

(Araucaria excelsa)

The Norfolk Island Pine is an excellent house plant for use away from the windows. It resembles a small Christmas tree with good evergreen foliage.

This plant is undemanding and is best kept on a minimum feeding schedule—if well-fed it will outgrow its usefulness. Allow the soil to dry between waterings. Insect and disease problems are few, although it may be troubled by the mealy bug and scale insects.

PANDANUS VEITCHI

(Screwpine)

The Screwpine requires little or no sun and withstands the conditions in the modern home. The long, interesting foilage, which is sometimes variegated makes the Pandanus a popular houseplant. While the plants tend to grow out of the pot with age, the offsets may be rooted to form new plants. Water freely while in active growth.

PEPEROMIA SANDERSI

(Watermelon begonia)

The Peperomias are tropical plants of widely varying characteristics. Only two are in general cultivation; one is P. sandersi var. Argyeria, commonly called the Watermelon Begonia. The second, P. obtusifolia, has thick green leaves. Now we have such interesting varieties as Green Ripples, Silver Heart, and Hederifolia. The latter is so named because of the slight resemblance to an ivy leaf. The Peperomias like a moderate temperature, plenty of moisture, and frequent applications of fertilizer. A soil mixture of equal parts of sand, leaf mold, and loam suits them. These plants have leaves that are small for a tropical, hence are best used in the foreground of the planter box. Give them a nighttime temperature of 60°.

PHILODENDRON SPECIES AND VARIETIES

The well-known shade-loving Philodendron is hard to associate with the many new species and forms that are now available for indoor use. The familiar P. cordatum must compete with P. hastatum, P. panduriforme, P. pertusum, P. dubium, and P. sodiroi. These are all climbers with interestingly shaped leaves. The P. sodiroi has beautiful silvery leaves. The P.˙panduri-

forme has green fiddle-shaped leaves. The P. hastatum has narrow green arrow-shaped leaves. The P. dubium leaves are dark green and are deeply lobed. All of the climbing species require some kind of support although many people like to have them as trailers from shelves and other situations. The P. pertusum is more correctly known as Monstera delicosa and is far too large for indoor use. In addition to the climbers there are a number of bushy plants, commonly called self-heading, although most of them are too large leaved for use indoors. The P. wendlandi is an ideal house plant with broad spatula-shaped leaves.

The Philodendrons require an acid soil, limited fertilization, and abundant water in a humid, shady situation. A night temperature of 60° to 65° suits them very well. The soil should be prepared from equal parts of sand, loam, leaf mold, and compost or pulverized bark.

SCINDAPSUS AUREUS

(Devil's Ivy Pothos)

The Pothos are climbers quite similar to the Philodendrons and have the same cultural requirements. Pothos aureus is sometimes called the Gold Dust Plant because of the marking on the leaves. The P. nitens has shiny green heart-shaped leaves. Because of their smaller size, many gardeners prefer the Pothos to the larger growing Philodendrons. However, the Pothos needs much less moisture—grow on the dry side.

RHOEO DISCOLOR VITATA

(Moses-on-a-Raft, Oyster Flower, Purple-leaved Spiderwort)

The Rhoeo is an interesting tropical with the flowers blended with the leaves and borne in an umbel surrounded by two bracts—appearing as though in a cup. The under sides of the leaves are purple and the upper surface silvery-green striped with yellow. It is often grown out-of-doors in Florida, here as a house plant. The leaves are about 12 inches long. They like a potting mixture of equal parts of sand, loam, leaf mold plus a bit of dried cow manure and bone meal. The Rhoeo needs very little light.

SANSEVIERA SPECIES

(Snake plant—Bow String hemp—Leopard lily)

The toughie of the house plants, the Sanseviera, will grow in sun or in dimly lighted places; it requires little attention as to feeding or watering, and will grow in relatively cooler situations than most house plants. There are many variations in striping and banding. Most of the leaves are flat, some are concave, and one has round leaves. The Snake plant will flower if grown in a sunny window.

SAXIFRAGA SARMENTOSA

(Strawberry begonia—Aaron's Beard)

Most of the Saxifragas are grown out-of-doors but the Strawberry Begonia is a favorite of many house plant growers. It likes a sunny situation although it will tolerate light shade. A favorite for hanging baskets where the long runners make a pleasing display of greenery. For flowers, the Strawberry Begonia must have a sunny situation; the flowers are white. Magic Carpet is one of the newest varieties of this plant. The leaves are splotched or margined with white. It thrives best in a gritty soil with lime and compost.

SCHEFFLERA ACTINOPHYLLA

(No common name)

The Schefflera is a large leaved foliage plant for dimly lighted situations. In large planter boxes it is useful to give variation in foliage texture, rather than because of coloring. The Schefflera likes a soil enriched with humus.

SYNGONIUM XANTHOPHYLLUM

(No common name)

This little known house plant has gained interest as a shade lover that is suitable for table use in dimly lighted situations. Named varieties are beginning to appear. One called Green Gold, has wide stripes down the mid-ribs of the arrow-shaped leaves. In dish gardens, where the humidity is high, it thrives very well. Use a soil well enriched with humus, also some dried cow manure.

CHAPTER VII

BULBS FOR THE WASHINGTON GARDEN

When bulbs are mentioned, most gardeners think of tulips and daffodils, but there are a host of other so-called bulbous plants which have their places in the garden too. From the early spring-flowering snow-drops to the summer-flowering gladiolus and dahlias, bulbs contribute to the beauty and interest of the garden. Many produce excellent flowers for cutting.

Bulbs are undoubtedly the easiest of flowering plants to grow. This is owing, in large measure, to the fact that the spring-flowering bulbs contain an ample food supply to maintain the plant until a root system develops. Some, such as the Autumn-flowering crocus (Colchicum), need only favorable temperatures to flower. Others, such as the hyacinth, daffodil, and amaryllis, need a supply of moisture before they will bloom. These are true bulbs having, when mature, an embryo flower bud surrounded by a food supply and need only favorable conditions to bloom.

The term "bulbs" generally is used in a broad sense, referring to plants having bulbs, corms, tubers, or rhizomes which contain the necessary food supply for new growth.

True bulbs consist of layers or scales surrounding the bud. The onion is a true bulb, so is the tulip, the lily, and the daffodil. Bulbs increase in size with age,

although they may eventually divide to make new bulbs.

Corms are solid bodies without division or layer, which contain one or more buds and the food supply. A corm lasts only one year. Most cormous plants develop a new corm on top of the old one. Crocus and gladiolus are examples of this type.

Tubers are enlargements of the stem or of the root. Some have eyes on the enlargement, such as the potato, which is an enlarged modified stem. Others, the dahlia and sweet potato, are enlargements of the roots and have eyes only on the neck. These fleshly tubers provide nourishment for the new plants until roots develop.

A rhizome is a thick fleshy root rather than an enlargement of a root as just mentioned. Rhizomes usually last for several years while tubers are often absorbed in the growth process. The German iris and the canna are examples of the rhizomes.

Tulips and daffodils are more widely grown than most other kinds of bulbs, largely because of their ability to grow successfully in almost any kind of soil, except one that is water-logged. Many of the small, early-flowering bulbs are as easily grown, but they have less conspicuous flowers. The crocus, English bluebell, and snowdrop, to mention a few, while somewhat less showy, are well suited to the home garden.

This is not to say that bulbs will grow well in all kinds of soil, or that they do not respond to care, but rather that it takes less skill on the part of the gardener to grow them. Most kinds of bulbs have less difficulty in growing and flowering than has the usual collection of perennials. Containing their own food supply, they need only to be planted at the proper season. They do not require much in the way of skill or previous soil preparation.

Bulbs may be divided into "hardy" and "tender" groups. The hardy ones are planted in the fall—September to December. Among the hardy ones, several kinds do not keep well out of the ground unless protected from drying. To dry out is to lose a part of their vitality. Large plump bulbs have the most vitality and produce the finest flowers.

Most gardeners in this area do not think seriously of planting the hardy bulbs until October and are not too concerned if they do not get around to it until in November. Experienced gardeners begin in August with the Madonna lily; try to get daffodils into the ground in September, and plant the rest of the bulbs as rapidly as they are received. Planting the bulbous iris and tulips, however, may be delayed until mid-December to prevent top growth, which is injured by freezing. Bulbs should be gotten into the ground at the proper season so that they will have ample time in which to develop their root systems before the ground becomes too cold for plant functioning.

Hardy bulbs for the most part may be left in the ground for several years, or until they become crowded or have exhausted the plant food in the soil. They should be lifted after the foliage has matured. When the soil has been reworked, they may be replanted. Most kinds keep in well-drained soil better than in a musty basement. In replanting, it is sound practice to move the bulbs to a new location in order to avoid disease and insect pests.

Tender bulbs should not be planted until the soil has begun to warm up and danger of frost has passed. This too is a general rule. Many gardeners will begin putting gladiolus corms into the ground in late April. The cormels (primary corm) may be planted in late March or early April since they are very slow in developing. If planted early, they will flower the first season.

Tender bulbs normally are lifted in the fall after the first killing frost. However, gladiolus and Peruvian daffodils may be lifted before frost, the bulbs dried off and stored for the winter. Dahlias do not mature until the weather is rather cool. If dug early and placed in storage, they may not keep well.

Guide to Proper Bulb Planting

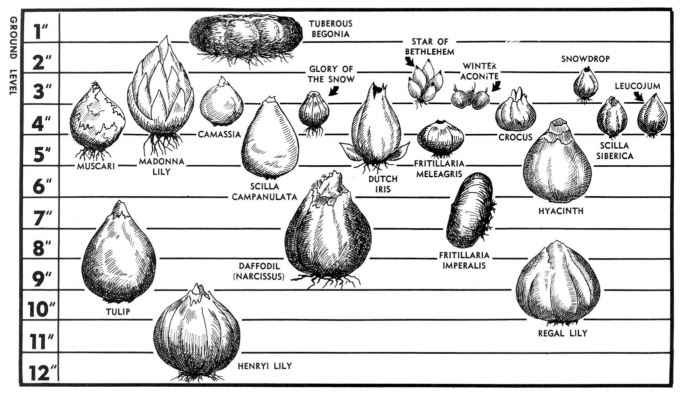

BULBS FOR THE WASHINGTON GARDEN

Bulbs do not require heavy feeding. Manure, unless very old and well rotted, should not come into contact with a bulb. Bone meal and compost are the two best ingredients for enriching a bed before planting bulbs. Most gardeners believe bulbs should go into the ground rather deeply, but when it comes to spading in plant food, they often dig it into the top six inches of the bed rather than down where the roots can reach it. Tulips, daffodils, and lilies usually are planted from 6 to 12 inches deep. For such bulbs the bone meal and compost should be mixed into the soil to a depth of 12 to 18 inches.

Beds of hardy bulbs are not often mulched in this area, although they benefit from such protection. This is not to keep the bed warm and the soil from freezing. Such mulches are put on after the soil is frozen and are kept there until early spring. The purpose is to prevent alternate thawing and freezing which may, and too often does, heave the bulbs, breaking their roots, occasionally pushing them out of the ground.

It has been mentioned that hardy bulbs are lifted only after the foliage has matured. This is to permit the bulb to complete its growth. Disturbance before growth is completed prevents the plant from fully developing and thus reduces the vitality of the bulb for its next flowering period. If it is necessary to move bulbous plants before the foliage is mature, they should be lifted with a ball of earth and planted in a trench where the growth process can be completed. Otherwise it is desirable to discard the bulbs and obtain new, plump, large-sized bulbs for planting the following fall.

Several kinds of bulbs are more or less troubled with basal rot, a serious disease which is not commonly recognized since the affected bulbs rot without the gardener having the opportunity of knowing why. Basal rot affects many varieties of daffodils, hyacinths, lilies, and others.

The prevention of basal rot has not been easy, although Mersolite has been used successfully in treating daffodil bulbs. Recently it was reported that lily bulbs planted on a thin layer of sphagnum moss were free of this disease. Gardeners might well try this inexpensive material as a means of preventing basal rot.

CROCUS

Uses:	Bedding, naturalizing and forcing.
Height:	4-6 inches.
Blooms:	March-April; October-November.
Plant:	Spring-flowering—October-November. Fall-flowering—August-September.
Distance:	3-6 inches apart.
Depth:	3-4 inches.
Soil:	Ordinary garden loam.
Exposure:	Sun or shade.
Varieties:	Spring-flowering—Excelsior, Remembrance, Golden Goblet, Queen of the Blues, Purpurea Grandiflora, Mammoth Yellow, Imperati, Cloth of Gold (C. susianus), C. vernus, C. moesiacus. Autumn-flowering—Saffron, C. sativus, C. speciosus, C. zonatus.

Crocuses, showiest of early-bloomers.

Crocuses are the most showy of the early springflowering bulbs. They appear very early in protected sunny situations and while they will do well in a shaded spot, they are generally planted so as to provide earliest spring bloom. The many species and varieties are divided into two groups—spring-flowering and autumn-flowering. This latter group should not be confused with the autumn-flowering Colchicum, a member of the lily family whose bloom resembles the crocus.

Crocuses are widely used as a border in front of shubbery, as an edging to a perennial border, and for naturalizing. In reasonably well drained soil the corms last for many years, although they tend to become crowded and need to be lifted and divided. While many gardeners like to have crocuses growing in their lawns, they dislike having to leave the grass uncut until the crocus foliage is matured. However, this is necessary if the corms are to maintain their strength and vitality. Some gardeners get around this problem by replanting with new corms each fall, since they are comparatively inexpensive.

Crocus corms are a favorite food of squirrels so it may be necessary to protect the corms. One way is to cover the corms with ¼-inch hardware cloth. When this system is used, the soil is excavated to a depth of 4 inches, the corms placed in position, and covered with a sheet of hardware cloth. The remaining soil is then spread over the bed and if desired, grass seed may be sown. The wire will prevent the squirrels from reaching the corms and they will last for years.

Fall-flowering crocus corms may sometimes be obtained in July, although more commonly they are not received until August. The earlier the bulbs arrive and go into the ground, the better. Sometimes late shipments are in bloom when they arrive. Fall-flowering corms produce only flower stalks in the fall. In the spring they produce foliage the same as the spring-flowering species and varieties. This dies down after growth is completed.

Crocuses make the most delightful display when planted in masses. A group of 25 corms planted 3 or 4 inches apart may not be as showy as anticipated the first spring, but if well planted, they will multiply and give a very satisfactory display the following years. This spacing is preferable to a closer planting which may be more showy the first spring but will soon exhaust the soil.

Crocus varieties are available in many colors and shades, although the yellows, purples, and lavenders seem most popular. Besides the named varieties there are some 40 species to choose from. Most gardeners buy mixed colors and do not bother with named varieties. However, to produce definite color patterns or to have a specific or a uniform color in the border, it is necessary to purchase named varieties having the desired colors. Some producers offer mixtures containing a limited number of colors, such as blue and white. Flowers of the species are generally smaller and daintier than those of named varieties.

Crocuses are not free from diseases and insect pests although they are seldom troubled. There is a disease of the flower which causes streaking similar to "tulip breaking." In poorly drained soils the corms may be destroyed by a disease called fusarium rot.

DAFFODILS

(Narcissus species and varieties)

Uses:	Border, naturalizing, cutting, and forcing.
Height:	4-24 inches.
Bloom:	March to May.
Plant:	September-October.
Distance:	8-10 inches apart.
Depth:	6-8 inches.
Soil:	Well-drained garden loam.
Exposure:	Sun or shade.

Varieties:

Inexpensive but good quality.
1. **Trumpets—**
   a. Lord Nelson, Garron, Mulatto.
   b. Content, Effective, Music Hall.
   c. Mt. Hood, Beersheba, Broughshane.
   d. Spellbinder.
2. **Large-cupped—**
   a. Fortune, Aranjuez, St. Egwin, Carlton, Rustom Pasha.
   b. Brunswick, Polindra, Tunis, Kilworth, Selma Logerlof, Cannes, Mabel Taylor, Mrs. R. O. Backhouse.
   c. Carnlough, Silver Bugle, Truth, Niphethos.
   d. Binkie.
3. **Small-cupped—**
   a. Mangosteen, Market Merry, Therm, Chungking.
   b. Kansas, Hardy, Limerick, Blarney.
   c. Polar Ice, Cushlake, Samaria, Cushendall.
4. **Double—**Cheerfulness, Yellow Cheerfulness, Mary Copeland, Daphne.
5. **Triandrus hybrids—**Thalia, Moonshine, Tresamble.
6. **Cyclamineus hybrids—**
   a. February Gold, Peeping Tom.
   b. Beryl.
7. **Jonquil hybrids—**
   a. Golden Sceptre.
   b. Golden Perfection, Trevithian, Cheyenne.
8. **Tazetta hybrids—**Martha Washington, Geranium, Orange Wonder, Cragford, Silver Chimes.
9. **Poeticus—**Actaea, Red Rim, Cantabile.
10. **Species—**jonquilla, cyclamineus, triandrus albus.
11. **Miscellaneous.**

New and somewhat more expensive varieties.
1. **Trumpets—**
   a. Golddigger, Kingscourt, Gold Court, Grapefruit.
   b. Foresight, Trousseau.
   c. Silver Wedding, Tain.
2. **Large-cupped—**
   a. Tinker, Galway, Ceylon, Armada.

b. Coverack Perfection, Gren Island, Fermoy.
   c. Dew Pond, Ave.
3. **Small-cupped—**
   a. Ardour, Dinkie.
   b. Mahmoud, Snow Gem.
   c. Chinese White, Foggy Dew.

a.—Yellow, b.—bicolor, c.—white.
(Recommended by Washington Daffodil Society)

The classification given above is the one used in daffodil shows and in the trade, and all registered varieties are officially classified. This will interest beginners chiefly as a help in planning bulb purchases to take advantage of the wide range in form and color available in modern daffodil varieties.

* * *

The choice of varieties for the home garden is not simple as there are hundreds to choose from. One of the easiest approaches is to visit a local daffodil show and obtain the names of those varieties which appeal to you. Those given above are fairly typical. Some are old varieties but all are of high quality. They were selected by our local growers. All will do well in this area.

Beginners are often confused by the names Narcissus, Daffodil, and Jonquil. There need be no confusion between Narcissus and Daffodil if it is remembered that Narcissus is the scientific or Latin name, and Daffodil is the common or English name. Either may be applied to all varieties and types in the genus. Jonquil, however, although widely used in the South to apply to yellow trumpets, is correctly used only for the species, Narcissus jonquilla. This species has several small fragrant florets on a slender stem; the leaves are slender and reed-like also.

Daffodils are showy, early spring-flowering bulbs that are widely planted since they are not too fussy as to soil or situation. They nearly all require a well-drained soil. Planting under deciduous trees and among the shrubbery is satisfactory since they flower and the foliage is well on its way to maturity by the time the leaves of the woody plants take over. However, only a few kinds may be successfully naturalized in the lawns, principally the poeticus varieties. Some of the older varieties do reasonable well and are employed for this purpose in order to give a longer flowering period. In a wooded area, most species and varieties thrive in naturalized planting, but the larger, more highly bred varieties do best in the flower border or in beds in full sun and without root competition from trees and shrubs. The poets, while late-flowering as a rule, do not have a long season of bloom. The usually available daffodil mixtures consist largely of the older varieties and bulbs of the newer varieties that have become mixed. For small gardens it is better to plant varieties in separate clumps or drifts, each of a single variety.

BULBS FOR THE WASHINGTON GARDEN

Deep planting of daffodils is desirable for two reasons. First the bulbs do not multiply so rapidly, hence do not need lifting and thinnning so frequently. Secondly, deeply planted bulbs do not interfere with the planting and cultivation of annuals if these flowers occupy the ground after the daffodils die down. There should be 4 to 6 inches of earth above the bulbs—in lighter soils even more. In addition they should have a like amount of well dug soil below them.

Daffodils are not seriously troubled by insect pests and diseases, although such are not unknown. The best safeguard is to buy bulbs from a reliable dealer—one who makes an effort to sell sound, disease-free bulbs. The second step is to watch them during the growing season, removing and burning all that are stricken with disease. The most common sign of the mosaic disease is a streaking of the foliage. Occasionally the trumpet varieties are troubled with a basal rot, especially in poorly drained soils. Sound bulbs planted in newly prepared soil are seldom troubled. The narcissus bulb fly is fairly common in this area as over most of the United States. The adults resemble a small bumblebee. Eggs are laid on the foliage near the ground and the hatching larvae eat their way into the basal plate of the bulb. Purchased or newly dug bulbs should be examined for signs of softness, an indication of infestation or of disease.

1. Dust the bulbs with 6-percent chlordane before planting. Dust them again before covering with soil.

2. Dig established plantings, destroy infested bulbs, and treat bulbs with chlordane dust before planting again.

3. In the spring apply chlordane dust in foliage of established narcissus. Try to get the dust into soil cracks around plants and between leaves, to destroy larvae that are attempting to descend to the bulbs.

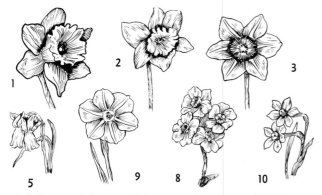

Daffodil types. 1. Trumpet. 2. Large cup. 3. Small cup. 5. Triandrus.
9. Poeticus. 8. Tazetta hydrid. 10. Species (Jonquilla).
(Numbered according to classification.)

Daffodil bulbs may be fertilized in the spring before growth appears by applying 3 to 4 pounds of standard commercial fertilizer per 100 square feet of bed. A similar application may well be applied to old plantings in late September when the roots become active. In preparing beds for daffodils, it is well to incorporate liberal quantities of bone meal—4 to 6 pounds per 100 square feet of bed.

Equally as important as fertilization is the protection of the foliage until it has yellowed, usually late in June or early July. Some gardeners who wish to keep their grounds neat and orderly tie up the foliage when it begins to sprawl on the ground. While this takes some time and effort, it does help to keep the borders neat.

DUTCH IRIS

(Iris xiphium hybrids)

Uses:	Cutting, border.
Height:	12-18 inches.
Blooms:	May-June.
Plant:	November-December.
Distance:	6 inches apart.
Depth:	4-6 inches.
Soil:	Well-drained, loamy.
Exposure:	Sun.
Varieties:	Yellow Queen, White Excelsior, Poggenbeek, Jacob De-Wet, Wedgewood and others.

* * *

The colorful Dutch iris, hybrids of the Xiphium group and of I. tingitana, are becoming increasingly popular in the florist trade and in the home garden. The Dutch iris, because of its sparse foliage, has very little landscape value and so is commonly grown in the cutting garden rather than in the flower border. However, by planting the bulbs among foliage plants the color effect is very acceptable.

The florists make extensive use of Dutch Iris. The bulbs are so inexpensive and easily grown that there is no reason why the home gardener should not also make use of them in the garden to produce an abundance of flowers for cutting. The colors range from white to yellow to blue and bronze. There are many varieties to choose from. Those given above are popular among local gardeners.

Dutch iris do best in a light sandy soil, although they can be and are planted in the heavier loams and clays of the Washington area. There is more likelihood of bulb rot in the heavier moister soils. Perhaps the English iris will do better in such soils. However, planted carefully and given ordinary culture, the Dutch iris will do very well.

Late fall planting has much to do with their successful culture. If planted too early, the bulbs will not only become well rooted but will send their tops above the surface of the ground. Subsequent winter freezes will injure the foliage and prevent normal growth of the bulbs. Late fall planting—November and early December—will give the bulbs ample time in which to become well-rooted but they will not have time enough to make top growth. Dutch iris are hardy enough. It is their quick response to warm weather that we must overcome.

The bulbs should be lifted after the foliage has matured and then stored in a cool, dry, airy situation until planting time. A number of local gardeners prefer to cut most of the foliage with the flower. They know that this results in poor bulbs but they prefer to buy new ones each season.

GLORY-OF-THE-SNOW

(Chionodoxa species)

Uses:	Border, naturalizing.
Height:	4-6 inches.
Bloom:	March-April.
Plant:	September-October.
Distance:	3-4 inches apart.
Depth:	2-3 inches.
Soil:	Fertile, well-drained.
Exposure:	Sun or shade.
Species:	C. gigantea, 5 inches—lavender blue.
	C. lucilae, 4 inches—blue and white.
	C. sardensis, 4 inches—gentian with white eye.
	C. tmolusi, 6 inches—blue and white flowers.

* * *

Glory-of-the-Snow is the second earliest of the early spring-flowering bulbs. Its bright blue color seems to make spring come early. Of easy culture, it deserves to be a part of every sunny border or rock garden planting.

The bulbs should be obtained as early in the fall as possible and planted without delay as they lose vitality when not properly stored. Like other members of the lily family they need good drainage if they are to thrive and multiply. In a fertile soil they make a much more showy display than in poor soils. Many gardeners lift the bulbs every 3 or 4 years, reworking and enriching the soil before replanting. It takes a dozen or more bulbs to a planting to make a showing.

The species listed above are the most commonly planted in local gardens. There are a few named varieties as well as other species for the hobbyist.

Mice are fond of the bulbs. Wherever moles abound mice will get to the bulbs and eat them. Control of the moles is essential to the protection of the bulbs.

For naturalizing, the bulbs should be planted in an area where the foliage may be allowed to fully mature before the grass is cut.

GRAPE HYACINTH

(Muscari botryoides, etc.)

Uses:	Border, naturalizing, cutting.
Height:	4-6 inches.
Bloom:	March-May.
Plant:	September-November.
Distance:	3-4 inches apart.
Depth:	3-4 inches.
Soil:	Loamy.
Exposure:	Sun or shade.
Varieties:	Heavenly Blue, album, Blue Bird, plumosum, armeniacum.

* * *

The Grape Hyancith is a popular early spring-flowering bulb. The tiny little bell-shaped flowers are clustered tightly together in a hyacinth-like spike, hence its name. Of easy culture, the grape hyacinth naturalizes easily, and in favorable situations will persist even under complete neglect.

While the grape hyacinth prefers a light loamy soil, it does well in almost any garden soil. The bulbs should be planted as soon as received so that they will not dry out and lose their vitality. Planted in drifts in the lawn, or in masses of 25 or more in the border, they make a very pleasing showing.

Grape Hyancinth will naturalize under favorable conditions.

While the species M. botryoides, with dark blue bead-like flowers, is a very useful bulb, the named varieties which derive from it are more showy. Album is white; caeruleum has blue flowers; Heavenly Blue is the largest flowered variety. M. armeniacum has cobalt-blue flowers and M. plumosum has feathery, violet, plume-like flowers. There are a number of other useful species but local gardeners depend mainly upon the varieties listed.

HYACINTH

(Hyacinth orientalis)

Uses:	Bedding, forcing.
Height:	10-12 inches.
Blooms:	May.
Plant:	September-October.
Distance:	6-10 inches apart.
Depth:	4-6 inches.
Soil:	Fertile, well drained.
Exposure:	Sun.
Varieties:	Grande Maitre, King of the Blues, L'Innocence, Yellow Hammer, Queen of the Pinks.

* * *

The hyacinth is a popular and widely planted spring-flowering bulbous plant. The large massive flower heads are especially showy, especially if produced by the "exhibition-sized" bulbs. However, for out-of-door culture, the bedding size, a smaller-sized bulb, is better adapted. While the blooms are smaller

and not so showy, they are less likely to be blown over by spring winds and rain. The French and Roman hyacinths, which are forms of the "Dutch" hyacinth, are still smaller sized and are favored both for bedding purposes and for potting. They usually produce two or more flower spikes to the bulb. While some claim they are not as hardy as the Dutch hyacinth, they often persist in the Washington area for several years. Certainly they are less subject to "basal" rot.

Hyacinths are available in colors ranging from white to blue and purple, with a few yellows. The smaller sized bulbs (bedding, French, and Roman) are sold by colors, but the exhibition-size bulbs usually are listed by varieties.

A paper cone will "pull" a hyacinth bloom up out of the foliage.

Hyacinths need a rich soil, one that has been deeply prepared and well drained. Even in a well-drained soil *it* is better to dig the bulbs after the foliage has matured and to cure them before storing in a cool, dry, airy situation. The bulbs are so frequently lost in our heavy soils that this extra chore is well justified. Even with this care, it is not uncommon for the bulbs to decrease in size from one year to the next, necessitating the purchase of new bulbs if exhibition-size flowers are to be produced.

The hyacinths are subject to a number of diseases and insect pests. The planting of healthy bulbs in a well-drained situation is the best safeguard. Bulbs in a moist soil are likely to be affected by sclerotinia rot, by

a bacterial slimy rot, or by a fusarium basal rot. Where any one of these appear, the sound bulbs should be disinfected with sulphur or bordeaux and moved to a new location, and the infected bulbs burned.

There is a leaf disease, Hyacinth yellows, which is contagious. Remove and burn all bulbs if the foliage shows water-soaked streaks. This is the first visible evidence of the disease. It is followed by yellowing and shrinking of both stem and foliage.

Hyacinths are generally grown in a well enriched soil in order to produce large flower heads. This may be one of the reasons that the bulbs are so subject to disease. However, only compost and bone meal should be used in preparing the soil. Plant the bulbs as early as possible so that they may become well-rooted before cold weather. The Dutch hyacinths do not need mulching except in an exposed situation. The less hardy French and Roman hyacinths need winter protection.

LILIES

Uses:	Border, Accent.
Height:	18 inches to 8 feet.
Blooms:	May to September.
Plant:	September, October, November.
Distance:	Varies as to species.
Soil:	Fertile. Perfect drainage.
Exposure:	According to variety. Sun or part shade.
Species:	Regale (white or yellow trumpet, June blooming, 3 to 5 feet).
	Speciosum (white or pink reflexed blooms, July-Aug., 4 to 6 feet).
	Henryi (apricot reflexed, August, 5 to 8 feet).
Hybrids:	Golden Chalice (yellow, upfacing, June, 2½ to 4 feet).
	Enchantment (geranium red, July, 3 to 5 feet).
	Olympic Hybrids white or pink trumpet, July, 5 to 7 feet).
	Aurelians (Class of hybrids that includes shapes varying from trumpet to flat, colors are white, pink, yellow, apricot and orange. July blooming, 5 to 7 feet).
	Fiesta hybrids (reflexed yellow, orange, red, July, 4 to 5 feet).
	Hybrids developed at Beltsville's Agricultural Station: Potomac hybrids (white and pink, August, 4 to 6 feet), Mega (Canary yellow, June, 3 feet), Mountaineer (Red, June, 3 to 4 feet).
	(Recommended by The Potomac Lily Society)

* * *

The lily is one of the showiest and most fragrant of all perennials, and although some species are difficult, there are many varieties that can be grown with great success in the Washington area. In recent years, the development of magnificent hybrids of a wide range of

forms, colors, and sizes has enabled the amateur gardener to achieve truly spectacular garden effects by meeting a few basic requirements.

The first and most important of these requirements is perfect drainage, for the lily will not tolerate wet feet. Prepare the bed deeply, incorporating plenty of compost or leafmold into the soil and fertilizing with bone meal. To further insure good drainage, many growers raise their lily beds somewhat if the soil tends to be too heavy.

Although most lilies will thrive in full sun, they appreciate the protection of a groundcover to keep the surface of the soil cool. Some lilies, such as the lovely speciosums and speciosum-auratum crosses, as well as delicately colored pink lilies and the species, Henryi, thrive in part shade.

Since growers dig their bulbs in the fall, September through November are the best months for planting; when properly stored, bulbs may also be planted in the spring. It there is danger of hard freezing before the bulbs arrive, the beds should be prepared beforehand and mulched until the bulbs can be planted.

The most common lily diseases are mosaic and botrytis Mosaic manifests itself by a characteristic mottling or striping of the leaves or blossoms into light and dark areas, and since there is no known cure for the disease, all infected plants should be dug and burned to prevent further spread of the disease. Keep aphids out of the garden, for they carry mosaic to the lilies. Do not plant old-fashioned tiger lilies or so-called parrot tulips near your lilies for they are notorious mosaic carriers.

Black or brown patches on the foliage indicate botrytis, a disease which responds to applications of Bordeaux around and on the lilies, particularly in the spring and during wet weather. When cutting lilies, leave at least two thirds of the stem, since strength returns from the stems into the bulbs in the fall thus insuring vigor for next year's growth.

Lilies may be divided into two classes, the stem-rooting and the basal-rooting. The first group, to which the Regal lily belongs, must be planted deeply so that the roots which grow from the stem above the bulb will have plenty of soil in which to feed. The basal roots of this class need food too, so the soil should be deeply prepared. The basal-rooting lilies, such as the Madonna, have roots only at the base of the bulb. They are generally planted rather close to the surface of the ground.

The Regal lilies are more or less immune to diseases. However, it pays to buy lily bulbs from reputable growers who handle disease-free stock. And, because the Regal and the old-fashioned Tiger can carry diseases which do not affect them, but which they can

give to other kinds, it is essential that all bulbs purchased be from dependable sources.

Large bulbs produce the finest flower displays. However, bulbs which are large because of forcing should be avoided. They are more susceptible to disease. Medium-size bulbs generally are the more economical to buy.

Lily bulbs can be produced from seed if the gardener is willing to give the care necessary and has the patience to wait. It takes from three to five years to produce a flowering size bulb.

SIBERIAN SQUILLS

(Scilla siberica)

Uses:	Border, naturalizing.
Height:	4-6 inches.
Blooms:	March-April.
Plant:	September-November.
Distance:	3-4 inches apart.
Depth:	4-5 inches.
Soil:	Ordinary loam.
Exposure:	Sun or shade.
Species:	Alba, atrocoerulea, azurea, taurica.

* * *

The Squill or Bluebell as it is called in some parts is a dainty little early spring-flowering bulbous plant. It is quite at home in the border or in the rock garden and will naturalize readily in suitable soils. The bright blue flowers make a very attractive showing wherever they are planted. For earliest spring bloom the squills need a protection situation.

The culture of these early spring bloomers is very simple. They prefer a soil that is not too heavy and cold. They will do well under shrubbery or in a grassy turf.

The bulbs should be planted in the fall. Drifts or clumps of 12 to 25 are desirable for a good display the first year. The bulbs are inexpensive. If well situated, they will multiply and make a striking display. Supplemental feeding in the very early spring increases their size and vigor.

They are relatively free from insects and diseases.

BULBS FOR THE WASHINGTON GARDEN

SNOWDROPS

(Galanthus species)

Uses:	Border, naturalizing.
Height:	6-12 inches.
Bloom:	January-March.
Plant:	September-November.
Distance:	3-6 inches apart.
Depth:	3-4 inches.
Soil:	Light garden loam.
Exposure:	Sun or shade.
Varieties:	G. Elwesi—Cassaba, Clawpetal, Erithrae, Glob Snowcup. G. Nivalis—Corcyrensis (Nov.), Flavescens (Yellow), Maximus, Octobrensis (Oct.), Reflexus.

* * *

The snowdrops are a most cheerful, hardy group—one that most gardeners will not wish to omit from

their plantings. The snowdrops are the very first of the early spring-flowering plants, often opening their curious little cups in January and remaining in bloom until late March. In a sheltered situation they often will begin flowering by New Year's and in spite of snow and subsequent cold weather they will open up each warm day.

They are of easy culture but resent disturbance when once established. The drooping bell-like flowers with flaring petals are a greenish white, borne on stems from 6 to 12 inches in height. The two species, elwesi and nivalis, have numerous varieties. G. elwesi is the taller and more showy of the two. Two varieties of G. nivalis are fall bloomers, although few care to grow them except in the rock garden.

A well-drained soil is desirable as a protection against the bulb rots. Some feeding and the use of bone meal in the soil before planting is desirable. Well-rotted manure may be used as a top dressing for beds and naturalized plantings.

TROUTLILIES

(Erythronium species—Dogtooth violets)

Uses:	Naturalizing.
Height:	10-15 inches.
Blooms:	May.
Plant:	September-October.
Distance:	4-6 inches apart.
Depth:	3-4 inches.
Soil:	Enriched with compost or leaf mold.
Exposure:	Shade.
Species and Varieties:	Californicum, Revoltum, Citrinum, Pink Beauty, White Beauty.

* * *

The Eastern flower lover speaks of the Dogtooth violets and is not enthusiastic about them. The Western gardener speaks of Troutlilies, Fawnlilies, and Adderstongue lilies and is usually enthusiastic about these free-blooming, showy flowers. Strangely enough the Troutlilies of the West are free-blooming compared to the native Easterner and they are usually easier to grow.

The Erythroniums are a large family, principally American, which deserve to be more widely grown in shady gardens. The principal reason why they are not better known and enjoyed is that it is difficult to propagate the bulbs, so the major portion of the commercial stocks are collected bulbs. Nevertheless, the Western species and the named varieties are hardy, long lasting, and early spring-flowering. They make excellent plants for the shady garden. In combination with Virginia Bluebells they are most effective.

The bulbs, normally available in a wide selection from the Western bulb firms, should be ordered early in the summer for shipment in the early fall. They should be planted as soon as received since they do not keep well out of the ground.

A soil that is well supplied with compost or leafmold is best for them. In nature they are often found in the sandier soils, but apparently this is not necessary for they are growing locally on some of our heavier soils. An annual mulching with leaves is all that is necessary to keep them well fed and vigorous.

The species and varieties listed above are easier to establish in this area than others which are not listed. As experience is gained in their culture, the more difficult ones may be obtained. Certainly, a collection of troutlilies would be as fascinating a collection as any other kind of plant.

TULIPS

Tulips are one of the best known and loved of the early spring blooming flowers. They are of easy culture, hardy and colorful—characteristics that should insure their culture by flower lovers anywhere. The practical Dutch, by meticulous care in the production and marketing of their bulbs, provide us with healthy dependable bulbs that are certain to bloom under almost any condition.

The long and varied culture of tulips has resulted in many varieties which have been grouped into classes. The major classes listed above are the most widely planted. The Bizarre, Ideal, Rembrandt, Triumph, Bybloem, Multiflowering, etc., are for the tulip fancier.

TULIPS

Most gardeners are satisfied with a good color selection from the scores of Darwin varieties available.

The earliest to bloom are the Single and Double Early varieties. Probably the best known of the Single Early's is Keiserskroon, a bright red and yellow striped flower on 12-16 inch stems. Some gardeners do not care for these early varieties because of their short stems, but they are excellent for forcing.

(Tulipa varieties)

Uses:	Cutting, bedding, forcing.
Height:	6-30 inches.
Blooms:	April and May.
Plant:	October-December.
Distance:	6-10 inches apart.
Depth:	6-8 inches.
Soil:	Ordinary garden loam.
Exposure:	Sun, light shade.

Single Early
(12-16 in.)
Albion
Bellona
DeWet
General Joffre
Olympiade
Pink Beauty

Cottage/Mayflowering
(20-30 in.)
Elizabeth Arden
Advance
Mrs. John T. Scheepers
Mrs. Moon
Red Matador
Rose Neyron
Smiling Queen

Parrot
(20-30 in.)
Black Parrot
Blue Parrot
Fantasy
Fire Bird
Parrot Wonder

Double Early
(12-16 in.)
Azalea
Bonanza
Couronne d'Or
Peach Blossom
Scarlet Cardinal
Willemsoord

Darwin
(24-32 in.)
City of Haarlem
Gudoshnik
Helen Eakin
Princess Elizabeth
Queen of Bartigon
Apeldoorn
General Eisenhower
Pride of Haarlem
Pride of Zwannenburg
Radio City
Royal Delight

Triumph/Mendel
(18-24 in.)
Bruno Walter
Crown Imperial
Elmus
Golden Wonder
Kantara
Merry Widow

Breeder
(20-30 in.)
Chattaqua
Cheyenne
Delaware
Crusader
Navaho
Pontiac

(Mrs. A. Kyle Goodman—Tulip Society of America)

* * *

The next classes to bloom are the Triumph and Mendel, which are crosses between the Earlys and the Cottage and Darwins. These are followed by the showy large-flowered Darwins, Cottage and Breeders, which are long-stemmed and very colorful. The Darwins are mostly solid colored flowers, ranging from pure white to blackish red and deep purple. Recently a good yellow, Yellow Giant, has been added. The Cottage group is supposedly the earlier to flower but the average gardener will note very little difference in the time of flowering of these three classes. The Cottage varieties are not as stiff stemmed as the Breeders, and the Darwins rank in-between in this respect. The Breeders carry shades and tones that the others do not. Louis XIV, a bronze and the purple edged with brown, is an excellent variety, although the cup is a bit small considering the length of stem.

It would be a distinct oversight not to mention a few of the tulip species. Tulipa clusiana, the Lady or Candystick Tulip, is a dainty, graceful variety. The outerpetals are cherry-rose while the inner ones are white. Tulipa sylvestris has small golden yellow flowers on slender graceful stems. Tulipa kaufmanniana and its varieties are showy short-stemmed tulips for the rockgarden. Commonly known as the Water-lily tulip, T. kaufmanniana, has a combination of colors that is hard to describe—white and yellow with pink on the outside. Perhaps it is better to say various color combinations in which yellow and red predominate. Red Emperor, a variety of T. fosteriana, Fusilier, a variety of T. praestans, and Eichleri, a large crimson-scarlet, have gained in popularity in recent years. All are early, bright red, and huge. These are the more commonly grown of the 40 or 50 species. They are relatively long-lived.

DUTCH TULIP PLANTING GUIDE*

*Heights of flowers and time of bloom will vary depending upon variety planted, location in the garden, section of the country and climate.

BULBS FOR THE WASHINGTON GARDEN

Tulips, as mentioned above, are of easy culture—yet good soil preparation is rewarded with finer flowers. Prepare the soil to a depth of 12 to 18 inches, incorporating bonemeal and well rotted compost in the bottom 6 to 10 inches. This seems unnecessary work, but if the bulbs are planted at the recommended depth, the roots will reach into this layer for food and moisture. Deep planting is recommended for two reasons: 1. To put the bulbs down where the soil is cool and moist—conditions favorable to good growth and 2. Deeply planted bulbs do not multiply (divide) as freely as do shallowly planted bulbs.

November planting is recommended to give the bulbs ample time in which to get well-rooted before cold weather. Overfeeding is to be avoided, especially with nitrogenous fertilizers. They stimulate bulb division. Bone meal and compost will provide all the plant food needed.

Large bulbs give the best flowers and last relatively longer than do smaller bulbs. Except in cool moist summers, bulbs of most varieties diminish in size, resulting in smaller blooms the following season. Picotee, Faust, Louis XIV, Zwanenburg and Keizerskroon are longer lasting than most of the other varieties.

To dig or not to dig is a standard question among tulip growers. Generally it is better in this area, where the soil becomes almost hot during the summer, to dig and store the bulbs after the foliage has matured, replanting in the fall. This results in less loss of bulbs from rotting and it helps to have a more uniform planting, that is, if the bulbs are sorted by sizes and uniform-sized bulbs are planted together.

Tulips are subject to diseases. "Breaking" seems to be more prevalent than other diseases. While at first it seems to give new interest to a variety, the disease soon weakens the bulb and after a few years it disappears. The disease, which is spread by aphids, is easily noticed by the streaking of the colors in the flowers. The other diseases of the tulip are "fire" and gray rot of bulbs. If healthy bulbs are planted in well-drained situations, there will be practically no trouble from them. If a diseased plant should be found in the bed, lift and destroy it before aphids can spread the disease to other plants.

WOOD HYACINTH

(Scilla (campanulata) nonscripta) (English bluebell)
(Scilla (campanulata) hispanica) (Spanish Squill)

Uses:	Border, cutting.
Height:	10-12 inches.
Blooms:	April-May.
Plant:	September-November.
Distance:	6-8 inches apart.
Depth:	5-6 inches.
Soil:	Well-drained loam.
Exposure:	Sun and shade.
Varieties:	S. nonscripta—Alba, Caerulea, Cernua, Blush Queen, Rubra, Rosea.
	S. hispanica—Blue Queen, Rose Queen, Excelsior, Coerulea, Rosalind.

* * *

The Scillas are interesting and useful spring flowering bulbs, resembling loose-flowered hyacinths. They are easily grown and the bulbs multiply rapidly. Adapted to light shade, they also do well in the sunny border and are occasionally successfully naturalized. They come in white, pink, and shades of blue. Sometimes the pink is not as clear a color as might be desired.

Scilla nonscripta, formerly known as campanulata and nutans, is sometimes called the English bluebell, also the Scotch bluebell. It is not as showy as the larger flowered Spanish bluebells. Both are of easy culture.

The Scillas do best in a soil that is faily well enriched with compost and preferably on the lighter side. They seem to withstand moisture better than most bulbs, but for satisfactory growth should be in a well-drained soil. They are relatively permanent, needing only to be lifted every 4 or 5 years so that the soil may be enriched and the bulbs thinned out. They increase rapidly by offsets and from seedlings. When naturalized, the bed should be enriched in the spring by a top-dressing of well rotted manure.

CANNA

(Canna generalis)—(Common garden Canna)

Uses:	Bedding.
Height:	4-6 feet.
Blooms:	July-October.
Plant:	Indoors—February-March; out-of-doors—May.
Distance:	18-24 inches apart.
Depth:	3-4 inches.
Soil:	Moist, rich.
Exposure:	Sun.
Varieties:	The President, red.
	Yellow King Humbert, yellow.
	City of Portland, rose-pink.
	Dwarfs—shell pink, Chinese coral, primrose yellow.

* * *

One of the showiest bedding plants is the Canna, a tender plant from the tropics. The wild species bear little relation to this modern plant which has been so skillfully developed by the plant breeder. Today we have cannas ranging in color from ivory and yellow to rose, salmon, and scarlet. None of them are hardy in this area, so the rhizomes must be lifted in the fall before the ground freezes and stored over winter in frost free storage.

The modern cannas normally are started indoors in February or March so that by the time the soil is warm and danger of frost has passed the plants are a foot or more in height. If we wait until May to plant the dormant rhizomes out-of-doors, they may not flower until late July or August. By starting them indoors we may have bloom by late June or early July which will continue until cold weather.

The dormant rhizomes may be started in any warm sunny situation where the temperature is above 70°. They may be started in soil, in peat moss or in sand. Most gardeners prefer to make a complete soil mixture —sand, garden loam and well-rotted manure. Excessive moisture at starting time may encourage disease. For this reason avoid heavy watering until the new shoots are 2-4 inches high.

As soon as the danger of frost is past, the young plants may be transplanted to a prepared bed. Give them plenty of space—18 inches or more between plants.

The bed should be well prepared. Incorporate liberal quantities of manure or compost to a good depth. Cannas are strong growers that need plenty of food and moisture to make the showing of which they are capable.

Of the many varieties of cannas available to the gardener there is one that seems to be outstanding—The President, a bright scarlet flowered plant. Yellow King Humbert's flowers are yellow dotted with orange; while King Humbert has an orange-scarlet flower. City of Portland, a rose-pink, is another that seems to be more popular than the general run of varieties. However, the hybridizers have not overlooked the cannas and there are a number of new series on the market. In general they offer new colors and the flowers are larger than in many of the older varieties. Among these newer and as yet not widely tested are Aida, old rose; La Boheme, peach-red; La Traviata, old rose; Mignon, peach-rose; Mme. Butterfly, yellow and pink, and Rigoletto, canary-yellow.

In choosing a variety, note whether or not the foliage is green or bronze. Some gardeners dislike the bronze foliage, thinking that it does not make a desirable background for the flowers. Others prefer it. Most catalogue descriptions give the color of the foliage along with that of the flower.

After the first killing frost in the fall, the tops should be removed and the rhizomes lifted and stored in a moderately cool cellar. Allowing them to mature for a few days after the tops have been removed and before digging is believed to improve the storing quality. Most gardeners do not attempt to remove the soil before

storing in sand or peat moss. Excessive dryness or moisture are the principal causes of loss during winter storage. It is quite likely that the polyethylene bags will be more satisfactory in preventing dry rot in the modern basement. However, the rhizomes must be well dried before packaging to avoid rot. Frequent checking, whether in sand, peatmoss or polyethylene sacks, is advisable if they are to be kept in good condition, plump and healthy.

In spring the clumps are pulled apart and the rhizomes divided into sections, each with 3 to 5 buds, although this division may be delayed until they have begun to sprout in the propagating bed. Starting indoors or in a hotbed is desirable for early bloom. Plants a foot or more in height are often desirable for planting in beds after the removal of the early spring-flowering bulbs.

The Japanese beetles like the soft juicy flower petals and Methoxychlor or DDT dusted on the petals are effective preventatives of damage.

If the wilted flowers are cut from the plants every few days during the flowering season the formation of seed will be prevented and the plants will continue to look fresh.

DAHLIA

(Dahlia hybrids)

Uses:	Exhibition, cutting, border.
Height:	3 to 7 ft.
Blooms:	July to frost.
Plant:	May-June.
Distance:	18-36 inches.
Depth:	4-6 inches.
Soil:	Rich, moist, well-drained.
Exposure:	Sun.
Types:	1. Formal Decorative. 2. Informal Decorative. 3. Cactus (incurved or straight). 4. Semi-Cactus. 5. Miniature (Formal, Informal, Cactus and Semi-Cactus). 6. Pompon. 7. Ball. 8. Single. 9. Peony Flowering. 10. Orchid Flowering. 11. Anemone Flowering. 12. Colarette. 13. Dwarf.

* * *

Varieties:

White—A—Lula Pattie (ID)
B—Sterling Silver (FD), Michigan White (SC)
BB—Cottonpatch (FD)
M—Geneva Crystal White (SC)
Pom—Teena
Ball—Pat 'n Dee

Yellow—A—My Doris R (ID)
B—First Lady (FD)
BB—Midas (SC), Desert Gold (C)
M—Yellow Bird (FD), Belle (C)
Pom—Py
Ball—Butterball
Orchid flowering—Imp

Orange—A—Orange Majesty (ID)
B—House of Orange (FD)
BB—Ambassador van Kleffens (FD), Joey K (SC), Helen Britt (C)
M—Jescot Tangerine (FD), Boots (SC)
Pom—Master Michael
Ball—Orange Glow
Coll—Orangeade
Sing—School Days

Pink—A—Ecstasy (FD), Surprise (SC), Danny (C)
B—Jersey's Beauty (FD), Pape's Pink (SC)
BB—Gerrie Hoek FD, Miss Rose Fletcher (SC), Kathleen (C)

BULBS FOR THE WASHINGTON GARDEN

M—Silver Spring (FD), Chasamy (C)
Pom—Betty Anne

Dark Pink—B—Clariam Luray (FD) Aileen M (C)
BB—Grace (C)
M—Little Diamond (SC)
Pom—Hallmark

Red—A—Eileen Lucy (FD)
B—Barbarossa (FD), Nicky K (SC)
BB—Hillcrest Brilliant (C)
M—Ruby Charm (C)
Pom—Ila
Sing—Temptation
Pe—Bishop of Llandaff

Dark Red—A—Pop Harris (FD)
B—David George (FD), Juanita (C)
BB—Doris Day (C)
M—Buddy (FD)
Pom—Little Matthew
Col—Woody Woodpecker
An—Comet

Lavender—A—Lavender Perfection (FD), Lavengro (ID)
B—Crystal (FD)
BB—Lawrence Welk (FD)
M—Nellie Webb (FD), Rebel (SC)
Pom—Margaret Williams

Purple—A—Jacqueline Kennedy (FD)
B—Orfeo (C)
M—Emma (FD), Kathryn Bevan (SC)
Pom—Miss Marjorie
Col—Cottontail

Light Blend—A—Shirley Jane (F)
B—Orchid Lace (C)
BB—Peach Blend (FD), Michelle Gunn (C)
M—Timmie (FD)
Pom—Janice Gough
Ball—Rosy Dawn
Sing—Crest
Min Ball—Jeep

Bronze—A—Barbara Schell (FD), Croydon Masterpiece
(ID) Brown Bomber (C)
B—Golden Treasure (FD)
BB—Chamoisette (SC)
M—Bo Bo (FD), I Believe (SC)
Pom—Gold Dust
Ball—Charlotte Caldwell
An—Vera Higgins

Flame—A—Arthur Godfrey (FD)
B—Golden Heart (SC)
BB—Pari Taha Sunrise (SC)
M—Decoy (FD). Sandra Broomley (C)
Pom—Little Edith

Dark Blend—A—John Butterworth (ID)
B—Sellwood Glory, (FD)
BB—Lady Esther (FD), Cha Cha (SC)
M—Ginny Johnston (C)
Pom—Golf Ball
Ball—Dottie D

Variegated—A—Dixie's Winedot (ID)
B—Nita (C)
BB Gypsy Girl (FD), Moya Marce (SC)
M—Beatrice (FD)
Col—Needles

Bicolor—A—Jane Lausche (SC)
B—Duet (FD), Parade (SC), Iva Jean (C)
BB—Lemon Ice (ID), Cheerio (C)
M—Johnnie Casey (FD), Raewyn Leslie (SC)
Pom—Betty Malone
Ball—Clara Clemens
Sing—Jersey Maid

The above is a list of dahlias which grow well in this vicinity and have won frequently on the show table. Practically all are suitable for the beginner. Those identified by the letter "A" are large dahlias with blooms that can be grown over 8 inches in diameter. The plants of A dahlias grow from about 4 to 7 feet. The dahlias above identified by the letter "B" normally produce blooms between 6 and 8 inches in diameter; heights of the plants are similar to those of A dahlias. "BB" dahlias produce blooms 4½ to 6 inches in diameter, and Miniature dahlia blooms are under 4½ inches in diameter. The plants of BB's usually grown between 3 and 6 feet, and of Miniatures between 1½ and 4 feet. Collarettes, singles, anemone flowering, and orchid flowering are usually under 4½ inches in diameter, and pompons are preferred an inch or less in diameter. The Ball dahlias vary rather broadly in size. In all cases, the more sunlight the plant receives, the shorter it will grow, and vice versa.

The dahlia is a popular summer-flowering tuberous—rooted plant, available in so many different types and colors that it will appeal to most gardeners. It has become so popular in this area that Washington for the past several years has had one of the largest dahlia shows in the country. These sun-loving plants can be grown (1) from seed, (2) from cuttings and (3) from tubers. Novices usually start with tubers or with plants grown from cuttings since seeds do not come true to type. They require full sunlight for at least 6 hours a day. They will grow in any type of garden soil but do best in a sandy loam that offers good drainage.

The amount of culture required in growing dahlias depends upon their size. It requires a considerable amount of skill and attention to grow exhibition dahlias measuring from 8 to 14 inches in diameter, whereas the low-growing miniature and dwarf varieties which are used by the ladies in their artistic arrangements

Modern Dahlia types: 1. Cactus. 2. Single. 3. Pompon. 4. Formal Decorative. 5. Informal Decorative. 6. Collarette. 7. Anenone-flowered. 8. Peony-flowered.

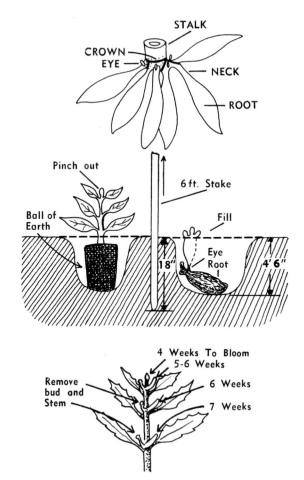

Proper method for dividing, planting and pinching dahlias.

require no staking, no fertilizing, and do not even require digging in the fall.

In growing large-flowering dahlias the soil should be turned over several weeks before planting time (May 15 to June 15) and a fertilizer, such as bonemeal alone or mixed with cattle manure, should be broadcast with a spread of 3 to 5 pounds for every 10 hills. The first step in planting is to drive 6' stakes 3' apart, if the dahlias are to be planted 1 to a stake, or 4' apart if planted 2 to a stake, with the rows preferably 4' apart. Holes are then dug close to the stakes. If watering is possible the tubers or plants can be planted as shallow as 4" but if it is not possible to water they should be planted 6" deep always about 3" from the stakes (see sketch). As soon as from 3 to 4 pairs of leaves develop the tops of the plants should be broken off (pinched out). See sketch. This forces 6 to 8 branches to grow. For the largest flowers all but the 4 best branches should be removed. For medium-flowering varieties from 6 to 8 branches can be left. All side buds appearing on these branches should be removed since each branch should bear only 1 flower.

In the absence of rain the plants should be well watered once a week and cultivated frequently up until about August 1st. They should be tied to the stakes at intervals of 12-16". A midsummer application of 5-10-5 or 4-8-12 is beneficial at a rate of 1 or 2 tablespoonfuls per plant spread 2" away from the plant. Spraying or dusting with an insecticide recommended to kill thrip, leaf hoppers, aphids and red spider should be done about once a week. By about August 1st it is advantageous to apply a mulch since cultivation must be stopped to prevent injury to feeder roots.

By this time flower clusters (usually 3 buds) are likely to appear at the ends of the branches. Since such early buds do not usually produce the best blooms, it is desirable to "time" the blooms as indicated in the accompanying sketch. The center flower bud, when the size of a pea, will bloom within about 4 weeks. Usually a leaf bud is present in the flower cluster and, if the other two buds are removed this will produce a pair of leaves and another flower cluster, the central bud of which will bloom in 5-6 weeks. One of the leaf buds adjacent to the first pair of leaves (down the stem) will produce a bloom in about 6 weeks and one still further down will produce one within about 7 weeks, the upper part of the stem and opposite bud being removed as indicated. In timing for a dahlia show the central flower bud in each cluster (about the size of a pea) should be left and the other two buds removed 4-5 weeks before show time. About this time, for the largest blooms, watering should be stepped up to twice a week and 4-8-12 should be applied at the rate of 2-3 tablespoonful per plant once a week. To harden the stems potash (muriate or sulfate) can be substituted for the 4-8-12 from 2-3 weeks before show time but this should be applied at the rate of only about **2 teaspoonful** per plant. When the flower buds open, prize blooms can be covered with bushel baskets to bring out their best color and protect them from insects. Frequent dustings with 10-25% DDT will also prevent insect damage.

The culture of medium-flowering dahlias is the same as above except that from 6 to 8 branches are grown per plant and the amount of fertilizing is reduced to about half, or less of that specified for the large-flowering varieties.

Dahlias should be cut with a slanting cut and kept in cold water for at least 3 hours before being transported. If the stems are cut under water or if the ends are treated in water just below the boiling point for about a minute they will keep longer.

Promptly after the first killing frost the dahlia stalks should be cut off close to the ground. Within 2-3 weeks the clumps should be dug and stored preferably in a root cellar or in the coldest part of the cellar in boxes or baskets covered to prevent drying out. Openings must be left for ventilation, otherwise the clumps will rot. Water can be sprinkled on the clumps once a week if they start to shrivel. In the spring the clumps should be divided into roots, each root being joined to an eye on the crown. See sketch.

The small flowering varieties of dahlias should not be fertilized since the smaller the blooms, the better. They should not be disbudded unless they are to be exhibited and then only at the time they are picked. Low-growing varieties can be planted 4 to 6 inches deep without staking in the perennial border and allowed to grow naturally with only the average attention (spraying and cultivation) given other perennials. In the fall the stalks can be cut off close to the ground and the clumps left in the ground to winter. It is best to dust the ends of the stalks with a mixture of sulphur and Bordeaux to prevent rotting. Then cover the ends with a jar top or plastic bag to prevent water from entering, finally covering over with a mound of earth or leaves. During the past several winters it has been found that about 3 out of 4 clumps of varieties making good roots can be wintered successfully by this method.

GLADIOLUS

(Gladiolus—Glads)

Uses:	Cut flowers.
Height:	36-72 inches.
Blooms:	65-95 days after planting.
Plant:	April-June.
Distance:	4-6 inches.
Depth:	4-6 inches.
Soil:	Rich, moist.
Exposure:	Sun.

SELECTED LIST OF GLADIOLUS VARIETIES BY SIZE AND COLOR

Color	Giant	Large	Medium	Small
White	Prof. Goudrian	Glacier	Rainier	Polar Cub
Cream	Landmark Lorelei	—	Fresh	Domino
Green	—	Green Ice	Green Woodpecker	Widget

Yellow	—	Prospector	—	Towhead
Buff	A. B. Coutts	Yellow Spire	—	—
	—	Patrol	—	—
Orange	Regina	Fire Opal	Cronus	Saucy
Salmon	Salmon Queen	Thunderbird	—	Parfait
Scarlet	Firecracker	San Souci	—	Atom
Pink	Pink Pride	Temptress	Gem State	Camelot
	—	Pink Prospector		
Red	Harrisburger	Band Wagon	Negus	Red Ribbon
	Oscar	Happiness	—	
Rose	Beauty Rose	Director	Ben Hur	—
	—	Pink Diamond	—	
Lavender	Cattleya	Lohengrin	Lavaesque	Pint Size
Purple	King David		Sable	
Violet	China Blue	Violet Charm	—	—
Smoky	Blue Smoke	Tan Glo	Old South	—
Tan or	—	Comanche		
Brown	Damascus	Chief		Abacadabra

(Selections by Eldon Shaw and Ken Schaible for National Gladiolus Society)

In most catalogues each gladiolus variety description has a 3-figure number and the number of days. This is part of the classification system used in describing them. 300—75 days).

The first figure in the number relates to the size of flower. It is based on the following size classification:

100—Miniature—florets under 2½ inches in width
200—Small—florets 2½ up to 3½
300—Medium—florets 3½ up to 4½
400—Large—florets 4½ up to 5½
500—Giant—florets 5 inches and larger

The last two figures indicate the color class as follows:

00	White, without C.M.	42	Pink (Medium)
01	White, with C.M.	46	Red (Light)
04	Green	50	Rose (Light)
10	Cream	60	Lavender (Light)
16	Yellow (Deep)	66	Purple
20	Buff	70	Violet (Light)
24	Orange (Light)	80	Light Rose and Violet Smoky
30	Salmon (Light)	90	Tan
36	Scarlet	96	Brown
40	Pink (Light), without C.M.		

* C.M. stands for Conspicuous Marking.

In addition to the size and color number, the catalogues may, and usually do, tell how many days the variety takes from planting until flowering; the range is 65 to 110 days. This is of interest to the gardener both for planning his supply of cutflowers and for the exhibitor who must calculate the planting date for each variety he intends to exhibit. For this area varieties are apt to flower a few days earlier than in the more northerly sections.

Gladiolus culture was not widespread or popular in the Washington area for some years because about 1930 the gladiolus thrips began ruining the opening flowers in most gardens. However, research soon developed effective measures for its control that do not involve undue effort on the part of the gardener. As a result "glad" culture has expanded in recent years. "Glads" are one of the most satisfactory of the summer flowering bulbs. As a cutflower they are hard to beat.

They are of comparatively easy culture, and by succession planting will provide cutflowers almost as the gardener wants them. When brought indoors the tall stalks, with as many as 25 buds opening gradually, insure a good display for a week or more.

Gladiolus corms may be planted from early April to mid-June, preferably in successive plantings so as to insure a continuous supply of material for cutting. The spacing and depth of planting have much to do with the quality of flowers. Shallow plantings are not recommended because the corms tend to divide or multiply. Also, shallow-planted corms tend to fall over under the weight of heavy flower spikes. Ample spacing is needed to produce large showy exhibition spikes.

Gladiolus will grow and thrive in any good soil without appreciable fertilization. However, like most plants, they benefit from generous feeding. It is good practice to work superphosphate, 2 pounds to a 50 foot row, into the soil at planting time. Lacking superphosphate, 5-10-5 or a similar fertilizer may be worked into the bottom of the planting trench, but it should be mixed into the soil and then be spread with an inch of soil free from the fertilizer over the bottom of the trench before planting so that the corms do not come into contact with the fertilizer. Maximum bloom size can be encouraged by applying a side dressing of a complete commercial fertilizer, such as the 5-10-5 or similar mixture (2 pounds per 50 foot row) as soon as the bloom spike can be felt. Contact of the fertilizer with the foliage should be avoided. Excessive fertilization may increase the likelihood of scab and other bulb diseases. Avoid high nitrogen fertilizers, the 5-10-5 or similar analysis is adequate for this area.

Watering is most important whenever rainfall is inadequate and should be applied promptly. Otherwise the spikes will crook and nothing can be done to straighten them. In this area, where bloom is wanted for summer flower shows watering is imperative to produce quality blooms of good size. Mulching is likely to be beneficial both to conserve moisture and to keep the soil cool as well as to control weeds.

Clean shallow culture is desirable both to keep down weeds and to conserve moisture. It must be shallow or the feeding roots will be injured.

Some growers stake their flowers or place strong cord on stakes on either side of the rows to keep the plant upright and to facilitate cultivation. The corms may be planted in single or double rows 6 to 8 inches apart. The space between the double rows should be 24 to 30 inches or more for convenience in harvesting the bloom and cultivation.

Gladiolus are attacked by several diseases and "thrips." The thrips may be controlled through sanitation and by spraying or dusting. The corms should be dusted before planting with DDT to take care of thrips which may have lived over winter on them. Secondly, in digging it is important to remove the tops immediately which tends to prevent the thrips from migrating from foliage to corms. After cleaning, the corms should be dusted lightly with DDT. This is a much more direct and simple operation than dusting or spraying the gladiolus plants in the garden. For spraying in the garden use 1 ounce of 50% wettable DDT to 3 gallons of water.

The diseases are rather difficult to eradicate through dipping. It is best to purchase good healthy corms. Destroy any corms that show signs of disease at the time of digging, cleaning, or planting. In the long run this will save much trouble and also will eliminate those varieties most susceptible to disease.

Another method is to dust the bulbs with Arasan, a chemical that can be obtained at most seed stores. The corms may be dusted with a duster. A small quantity may be placed in a sack with a dozen or more corms and shaken vigorously. This is a spring treatment just before planting. The treatment commonly recommended at digging time (after the corms are cleaned) is to dust them with 5% Spergon or with Spergon and DDT just before storage.

In cutting "glads" it is desirable to harvest the spike just as the first florets open. Cut only a minimum of foliage so that the corms will continue to grow and store up vitality for next season's growth. Most growers prefer to leave 4 leaves. If this is not practical the corms might well be abandoned and new ones brought for planting.

The corms may be dug 4 to 5 weeks after the flowering season is past. In this way there is less danger of diseases developing on the corms. Late-planted glads may not be ripe enough for digging until after frost. The corms are best dug by loosening the soil on both sides of the row so that the corms may be lifted without breaking away from the foliage. Remove the tops at once, leaving little if any stub. Spread the corms to dry in open containers, preferably with screen bottoms to provide for maximum air circulation. Some like to dry them in the sun for one day and then in a dry airy situation before taking to the basement for cleaning and final storage. All during the curing process there should be a free circulation of air over and under the bulbs. An occasional stirring of the bulbs in damp weather hastens the curing. An electric fan directed on the bulbs will help to dry them rapidly and thus tend to prevent disease.

When thoroughly dried the old corms and the dirt are removed. It is considered desirable to remove the lower outer husks in order to determine the health of the corms. This task can be quite a chore if attempted before the drying is complete.

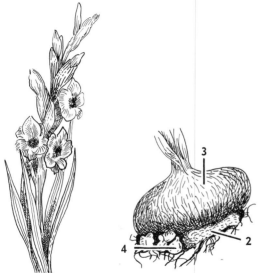

Glads: 1. Proper stage for cutting. 2. Old corm (discard). 3. New corm and 4. Cormels.

The cormels, if planted early in April will sometimes produce small flowers the first season. Some recommend soaking them before planting, and for a limited number of cormels, notching the hard, almost impervious coating may be practiced. In a well-drained soil, fall planting with a heavy mulch is satisfactory.

Ordinary purchases of "glads" might be limited to small and medium sized corms. The large sized (over 2 ins.) corms are preferred for exhibition blooms, although some maintain that summer care and feeding are more important than the size of the corm. Large flat corms generally are considered less desirable than the smaller high-crowned ones.

The list of recommended varieties is extensive. New varieties appear by the score each season. Any list of recommended varieties is soon obsolete. However, for the beginner, some of the newer and a few of the old standbys are given above.

The All-American Gladiolus Selections have brought into prominence some very choice new varieties at what might be considered reasonable prices considering their high rating.

PERUVIAN DAFFODIL

(Hymenocallis calathina—Ismene lily)

Uses:	Cutting, forcing, bedding.
Height:	18-30 inches.
Blooms:	10-15 days after planting.
Plant:	May-July.
Distance:	8-12 inches apart.
Depth:	6-8 inches.
Soil:	Moist, rich.
Exposure:	Sun or light shade.

* * *

The Peruvian daffodil is not a widely planted summer-flowering bulb, although it is easily grown and produces an interesting showy lily-shaped flower. The foliage is effective in bed or border. Because of its rapid growth, the Peruvian daffodil may be used in beds after early spring flowering bulbs, such as tulips, have been dug.

The white flowers are conspicuous with their fringed edges and rather interesting green stripes down the mid-rib of each petal. They are borne on tall naked stems before the leaves appear, somewhat like an amaryllis. A bed of the daffodils is ragged in appearance while in flower, but the foliage sion gives it a luxuriant look.

The bulbs may be planted at any time after danger of frost is past. Clean culture and ample moisture are essential for good growth, although cultivation becomes difficult as the leaves are long and drooping.

The bulbs should be dug before cold weather, although frosted foliage does not appear to injure their vitality or storing qualities. Some gardeners do not remove the foliage until after it has dried; others cut it off as soon as digging is finished. The bulbs are dried and stored in a warm place (near the furnace). They do not need to be boxed or wrapped except in a very dry basement. Do not remove the thick fleshy roots at any time.

For forcing, the bulbs may be potted at any time using a pot only slightly larger than the bulb. Bring into heat and light as soon as potted. The blooms should open in 10 days to 2 weeks. After flowering, the bulbs should be kept growing until the weather is warm enough to plant out-of-doors.

The small off-sets or side bulbs may be removed when they are no longer firmly attached to the parent bulb. If planted in the garden and given good culture, they will reach flowering size in one or two seasons. The larger the bulbs, the larger the flower and the greater the number that will be produced by each bulb.

Apparently the Peruvian daffodils are free from insects and disease troubles.

CHAPTER VIII

LANDSCAPING THE HOME GROUNDS

A planting of shrubs and trees around the home is necessary if the house is to be "tied" to the ground, and if a setting that is both attractive and homelike is to be provided. A house without any planting about it looks barren and stark.

In order to tie a house to the ground, trees, shrubs, and flowers are planted in such a way as to make them appear a part of the setting.

In the first place, the planting breaks the line between building and ground. Secondly, the taller shrubs at corners and entrance soften the vertical lines. Trees should be used to frame the house and to give it a background even though the owner may want them primarily for shade.

The size of the lot, the size and type of the building, the architectural design, and the character of the surroundings all have a bearing upon the extent and kind of plantings for the proper landscaping.

As a general rule the landscaping should more or less conform to or blend with that of the neighborhood, although the desires of the owner should also be taken into consideration.

Some builders and owners have very little interest beyond that of properly placing the house and enhanc-

ing its appearance. Others desire more extensive plantings because they like shrubs, trees, and flowers. Nevertheless, it is desirable from the community standpoint to conform as far as practicable with the general pattern.

Because these many factors have a bearing on the choice, extent, and types of plantings to be used, there are few rules that can apply to all plans. Thus the landscaping of each piece of property can be said to be a new problem.

But in spite of the lack of specific guides for plantings, we should keep in mind the basic objectives, and thus avoid doing those things which are likely to prove unsatisfactory. This latter point is most important because as we make plantings of small trees and shrubs it is hard to visualize the effect they will create when they reach an appreciable size, or at maturity.

It's Best to Make a Plan

One way to study the needs of the grounds is to make a plan; in fact several should be made until the right combination of shrubs and trees can be determined.

Cross-section paper with 10 lines to the inch is an

inexpensive but useful tool in preparing the plans. Adopt a scale that is large enough to permit a reasonably accurate placing of the important features of the lot.

With these in place on the drawing, it is then ready to have each planting tested to see the effect. Such a plan becomes of major importance when selecting the nursery stock for planting. You will need to know something of the desired size of each plant at maturity, and its requisites of soil, moisture, and exposure. Thus each plant will be bought to do a job under certain specific conditions.

Keep the Plan Informal

Very few homes in the Washington area lend themselves to strictly formal plantings which follow straight lines that tie-in to those of the house. Such plantings are normally kept neatly trimmed to straight lines and as such they seem more suitable to a public park or grounds about an institution rather than to a home.

The area between the house and the street is considered, however, more or less public and with this in mind, it should be planted in much the same pattern as other properties in the neighborhood.

If possible the front lawn should be kept open to give the appearance of spaciousness. Even the sidewalk has the visual effect of pulling the house closer to the street. If border plantings can be avoided in the front yard, it will further accentuate the appearance of large areas.

As a rule, the tree plantings, with the exception of those in the front yard, should be irregularly spaced.

Plantings of shrubbery and flower borders should follow curving lines. If space does not permit this, then the shrubs or flowers should be planted in groups which avoid to a considerable extent the appearance of straight lines.

Use Restraint

The usual landscape planting is generally overdone in an effort to get an immediate effect. Perhaps it also goes back to the days of high foundations which most property owners tried to hide.

Today, with little or no foundation showing, there is no need for heavy or dense foundation plantings. Certainly there is no point in following the old rule of "planting thick and removing twice as quick."

Simple planting of good taste require certain repetition of plants in the foundation and border plantings to carry the relationship of one part to another. Collections of varieties are interesting only to the hobbyist, not to the passerby.

Shrubbery and flowers need open lawn areas to "set them off". While this may seem at first to make the plantings appear thin or skimpy, as the plants gain in size this reaction will disappear.

The Lawn

A good lawn is important to the entire effect of the landscape plan. It is the setting for each tree and shrub. It gives tone to the entire picture. For this reason the soil should be well prepared and only adapted lawn grasses used to insure the best lawn possible.

Obviously this entails proper feeding, mowing, and weed control if the desired results are to be attained.

The lawn area should be kept free from flower beds, shrubs, fixtures, etc., so far as possible. This is particularly important to the smaller lot which should be made to appear as large as possible.

Any planting that breaks the lawn up into small areas reduces the appearance of spaciousness. This point, however, must be modified to some extent in the side and back portions of the yard if they are to serve the many functions desired. This is because there must be localized areas: A playground for the children, workroom of the hobbyist, and needed service areas for laundry yard, trash burner, etc. The fewer there are of these functional areas the more spacious the lawn will appear.

Shade Trees

Shade trees are a necessity in almost every yard because of the summer heat. However, those in the front yard should be so placed as to "frame the house" from the street.

To accomplish this they should be placed far enough to the sides of the house so that when they reach some size they will not obscure the house from the passerby. It is also desirable to so place the trees at the rear of the house that they provide a background against

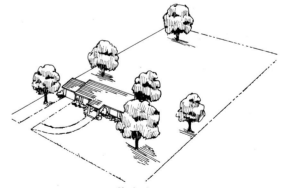

Shade trees.

which the house may be viewed. This planting will also be so placed as to provide the desired shade from the summer sun.

The selection of trees for the property should be guided as far as possible by the style and size of the dwelling. Tall-growing trees tend to "push" a one-story house into the ground. Similarly, small or medium-sized trees produce the opposite appearance for a two-story or taller dwelling.

Ramblers need trees with a habit of growth (arrangement of limbs) that blends with the lines of the building.

The size of the lot will have a considerable bearing upon the kind of trees and the number that may be used in landscaping. The smaller the lot, the smaller and fewer the number of trees to be planted.

In selecting trees for the property, it is desirable to avoid those with shallow-root systems which render the growing of grass, flowers, and shrubbery difficult—perhaps impossible.

Trees that are subject to diseases and insect pests are far less desirable than those which are relatively free of such troubles. The sweet gum for instance (Liquidambar styraciflua), a native with many desirable characteristics, is no longer recommended because if a disease now prevalent in this area.

In addition to the shade trees it is usually desirable to use several of the smaller flowering trees, such as the dogwood (Cornus floridus), flowering crab apples (Malus varieties), flowering cherries (Prunus serrulata varieties), Virginia fringetree (Chionanthus virginica), magnolia (Magnolia soulangeana, M. stellata), the hawthorn (Crataegus oxycantha, phaenopyrum, etc.), as well as a number of others. Several of these are shade-loving and may be planted beneath the shade trees.

However, overplanting of trees should be avoided since they will quickly suffer from lack of food and moisture and consequently will not thrive. Sickly, undernourished trees, or those that stretch upwards for a bit of sunlight, do not have much landscape value.

Foundation Planting

The shrubs planted close to the house are usually referred to as the foundation plantings. They tie the house to the ground. A careful selection of plants is needed to create the desired effect.

Shrubs that are too conspicuous, shrubs that grow too large, or those that by coarseness or color detract from the over-all picture should be avoided. The foundation planting is hardly the place to grow a hobbyist's collection of varieties of some shrub or flower.

Too often the foundation planting is made up of baby forest trees which soon outgrow their usefulness.

This is particularly true of the plantings around some of the new ramblers. The one-story house with little or no distance between the first floor and the ground line needs low spreading shrubs. They should be plants that are very slow growing and whose ultimate height is less than 3 feet.

Undoubtedly, many of the taller-growing evergreens can be kept low through regular pruning. All too often that chore is neglected until too late and then the job destroys their natural beauty.

The pruning of the evergreens should be done so as to retain their natural beauty. Shearing to a geometrical form is to take from them any resemblance of informality and substitutes in its place a collection of pyramids, squares, and triangles.

Good pruning shortens the branches or twigs which encourages the retention of the foliage at the center, and induces branching so that the shrubs remain compact and youthful in appearance. Much of the value of a foundation planting comes from the pleasing shadows which the plants cast on the house.

Boundary Plantings

Boundary plantings can serve several functions and those should be decided on before selecting the shrubs and trees.

If unsightly views are to be screened, then taller trees and shrubs will be needed than if there is a pleasing view to be preserved.

Sometimes the boundary planting should deaden noises and cut down on the dust from passing traffic. Heavier plantings are needed for this function. Evergreens may be the answer.

Strong prevailing winds can be tempered through the use of small trees and tall shrubs.

If only a border marker is needed, then lowgrowing, attractive flowering shrubs may be the answer, or perhaps a wire or picket fence covered with an everblooming climbing rose.

Perhaps the fence or shrub border is to be the background for a flower bed. If this is the case, avoid those kinds with shallow roots that might rob the flowers of food and moisture.

If dogs and children are to be kept out and a wire fence is not desired, then some of the thorny, compact-growing shrubs will do the job. The Juliana barberry is a good one and the fire-thorn and the trifoliate orange can be clipped to almost any height.

The choice of shrubs for the boundary plantings should take into consideration the amount of trimming and care needed to keep them in good condition. The California privet is a good example of a shrub that needs many prunings each season to keep it within bounds. There are kinds of shrubs that will serve the purpose with only one or two prunings each season.

The common barberry makes a fine low hedge, although disease occasionally invades and ruins a planting.

Scale insects formerly precluded the use of the euonymus—a moderate size evergreen that is suitable for sun or shade.

Selecting Plant Material

With the plan completed, the job becomes one of finding the right plant for each place.

LANDSCAPING THE HOME GROUNDS

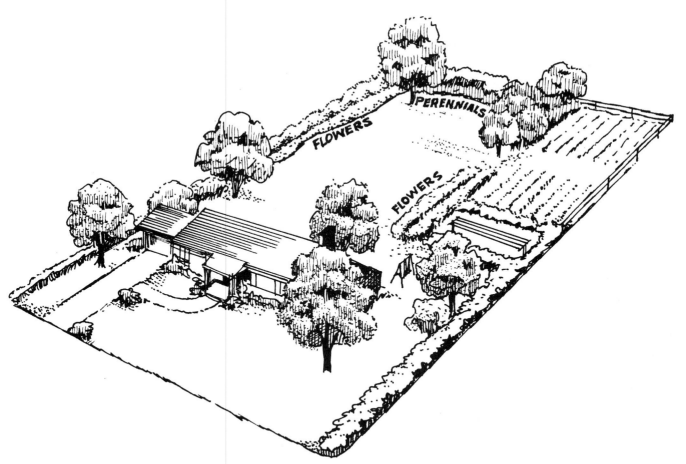

There is an infinite number of kinds of plants available to the Washington gardener. The problem is to find the right one which has the desired habit of growth and height at maturity; one that will take the sun, wind and moisture conditions, etc., found on your particular lot.

Since few know the various kinds of trees and shrubs that will grow in the Washington area, and there is no one place where they can be seen all nicely labeled so that one can tell whether or not he likes them, the only alternative is to go to a nurseryman and ask for his suggestions.

Most nurserymen are glad to give this advice, particularly if a buyer can show them a planting plan. Of course, there are horticultural books that describe the plants but they do not tell the important point—how such a plant will do on your lot.

Disease and insect pests that plague specific plant material should be ascertained before buying. No one wants to lose a tree or shrub about the time it becomes useful in the landscape. Nor does he want to spend a considerable amount of time spraying to protect them.

The root pattern may be important. Shallow-rooted trees sometimes preclude growing shrubs, roses, and other flowers. A few kinds make the growing of grass next to impossible. Obviously, if shrubs and flowers are wanted, such trees must be avoided.

From the standpoint of design, especially in the front yard, the important things are height, foliage color, and texture. The importance of height has already been mentioned. For harmony and a pleasing picture avoid those plants with coarse foliage and those with foliage of off shades or discordant colors. Try to present a picture by planting suitable shrubbery.

Maintenance

There are no "ideal" shrubs or trees. The best that are available must be given some attention in the way of pruning and, perhaps, controlling of insect pests and diseases. But they are the ones that we should select for the landscaping of our lots.

The emphasis should be placed on selecting those best fitted for the jobs they are supposed to do. Then prune, feed, and take care of them so that they will appear healthy and vigorous for years to come.

The pruning of the shrubbery is important if the plants are to give the desired effect. Many books have been written on this subject. Space does not permit discussion here. But, all shrubs need pruning.

Fertilization of the shrubbery border is a much debated subject. In the usual yard it is important that the shrubs do not overgrow or smother it. While young they should be fertilized once or twice a year preferably in the spring so that the new growth is completed and matured before cold weather in the fall.

After the shrubs have reached a modest size, further feeding is not recommended. Rather, pruning should take its place in maintaining vigor and good growth.

Many of our shrubs are too shallow-rooted for cultivation. Mulching might well take the place of cultivation; although in some cases the mulch will need nitrogen to prevent bacteria from robbing the shrubs. Nevertheless, mulching is the desired practice.

Flower and Rose Beds

The use of flowers and roses in the planting design is to be desired if it is to serve the interests of all concerned. The location should be determined in the early stages of planning, taking into consideration the sunlight needed, the nearness of trees, and the effect upon the over-all design. Sometimes a section of the border is reserved for the flowers.

Occasionally it is possible to do this with the roses. They may be worked into a border in front of the shrubbery, or a section may be fenced off with shrubs for a rose garden.

These points should be considered early in the planning stage, along with the location of service areas and the vegetable garden. Maybe there is not room for all of them on the lot; then it becomes necessary to decide which will be retained and which will be left out.

In selecting locations for flower beds and the rose gardens, it is important to have full sun at least a part of the day. Some perennials will take shade, but most annuals will not.

Roses need about 6 hours of sunshine a day. Morning sun is best. Midday and early afternoon sun are hardest on plants in this area. Some trees give a soft, filtered light that seems beneficial to most plants. Others cast such a dense shade that even grass will not thrive under them. As mentioned elsewhere, roots of shrubs and trees should be considered in determining the location of beds and borders.

Moisture is another problem that confronts the rose grower as well as the flower lover. Hot, dry slopes are not conducive to top-notch results. Try to place the beds and borders where there is a reasonable amount of moisture for the plants.

However, since the lot is small and it is necessary to make the best of what is available, it may be necessary to put these beds in somewhat unfavorable areas in order that they may have the essential sunlight.

Small beds and borders can be developed, in spite of moisture or the lack of it, through drainage or the addition of humus and other materials which retain moisture.

In planting the flower border, try to carry the general outline by planting the taller-growing perennials in the background. Fill the bed with plants whose heights will grade down from the taller plants in the background to the edging in the front.

Group the plants in sufficient numbers to give a strong effect. Planting one or two of each in a spot will usually create a less striking effect.

No landscape plan is final. We may plant it today, but tomorrow some new plant or tree may seem to offer a better effect in this place or that.

Actually every homeowner desires to improve the plantings from time to time. There are plants which have outlived their usefulness and must be discarded or a new situation may have arisen which necessitates a change.

Thus we should not consider that the home, once planted, is done. It is a changing picture, one that we should try to improve as we learn more about the plants with which we paint our landscape picture.

CHAPTER IX

LAWNS FOR THE WASHINGTON AREA

A good lawn is a mark of distinction—something that every home owner strives to have, but few seem to achieve. Part of this difficulty is owing to the lack of adapted grasses. Practically all of the grasses planted in this area are primarily adapted to cooler climates. Usually, however, it is the lack of proper care and feeding that have much to do with the lack of vigor and the presence of weeds.

Kentucky Bluegrass, creeping red fescue, redtop, ryegrass, and others thrive in cool climates. Still it must be admitted that when properly planted and fed they do not do too badly in this area. In other words, if a lawn is prepared as carefully as a farmer's crop land, the grasses will, without a doubt, give much better results. Too often the seed or sod is laid on sterile subsoil from the basement excavation. It may have an inch layer of so-called top soil spread first, but under such conditions, no one should expect a lawn to thrive.

Not only does the grass frequently starve for lack of plant food, but in addition the compacted soils prevent air reaching the roots. Plant roots cannot thrive without a certain amount of air; the usual lawn is rolled and trod upon until the soil is so packed that air cannot possibly reach the roots in sufficient volume to maintain normal functioning. Modern grass technique is directed towards methods of aerating the soil. Equipment for this purpose has only recently become available and as of now is not widely used on home grounds, but is standard on golf courses.

The grass in our lawns is expected to grow vigorously from early spring until late fall or early winter. This lush growth requires generous applications of plant food and this is best accomplished by a regular program of fertilizing. The modern turf specialists advise fertilizing in the early fall, again in October, and a light feeding in March. This is a reversal from earlier practices and came about because of the increasing number of disease problems in some sections of the Metropolitan area.

Their thinking is that heavy applications of plant food in the spring coupled with weather conditions favoring the spread of diseases justify the lighter feeding at that season.

Because of the many fertilizers available with formulas ranging from the familiar 5-10-5 (5% nitrogen, 10% phosphate, 5% potash) to a 20-10-10, the best basis of comparing or telling which will supply the needed plant food, is on the basis of the nitrogen content. Nitrogen is the basic grass food and should be supplied in the ratio of two parts of nitrogen to one each of phosphate and potash. Thus we find "turf" fertilizers with such formulas as 10-6-4, 10-5-5, 16-8-8, 20-10-10. Since the first figure is the nitrogen it is easy enough to compute the nitrogen content in pounds.

Close clipping may harm the lawn. Leave clippings for mulch and apply plant food in spring and fall.

The usual Kentucky bluegrass-fescue lawn needs from 4 to 5 pounds of nitrogen per 1,000 square feet per year. A Merion bluegrass lawn has a higher requirement—5 to 6 pounds. The Bermuda needs even more, 6 to 8 pounds of nitrogen per season.

These amounts are usually divided into 2 or 3 applications. The first and perhaps the largest feeding is given in late summer, the second in October, with a light feeding in March.

Not only are there many different fertilizer formulas but they may be made up from a number of different kinds of materials. The more commonly used fertilizers depend to a considerable extent upon water soluble sources of nitrogen, including sulphate of ammonia and ammonium nitrate. Such materials largely release the nitrogen shortly after application and the grass grows rampantly for a few weeks until it is used up.

The newer turf mixtures contain some portion of their nitrogen in slow-acting, non-burning materials, sometimes referred to as "urea-form". This is a synthetic which depends upon bacteria action for its release. In the spring when the soils are cold and bacteria action is limited, the amount released to the grass is small. For this reason some of the turf foods include some water soluble forms of nitrogen to speed spring growth.

However, the main feature of the newer forms of nitrogen is their slow release so that the turf may grow at a fairly constant rate over a large portion of the growing season. The non-burning feature will also appeal to many gardeners since it is not supposed to burn the grass when applied. The urea-form nitrogen will not burn when directions on the bag are followed, but the other forms of nitrogen may. Hence it is still advisable to apply fertilizer during the heat of the day when the grass blades are dry.

Lime is not a plant food. It is needed to correct soil acidity and to lock-up certain harmful elements. Many gardeners make an annual application somewhat on the basis that it costs very little and besides it might help the grass. Actually, when kept off the evergreens, and especially if ground limestone is used, it is beneficial. The basic plant foods—nitrogen, phosphate and potash—are readily available to the grass and several harmful soil chemicals are rendered harmless when the soil is kept approximately neutral. On the soil chemist's scale —6.5 to 7.0 pH. A soil test is the only accurate means of determining the quantity of lime needed to bring the soil to the desired level of acidity—alkalinity.

Overliming is more beneficial to some kinds of weeds than it is to the grasses which are very tolerant and will grow fairly well in an acid soil.

The Japanese beetle and other grubs which feed on the grass roots during the fall, winter, and spring months have much to do with the weakening of the grass plants. In severe infestations the roots may be practically wiped out. Under such conditions it is hardly reasonable to expect the grass to thrive. A treatment to control the grubs, using either chlordane or the milky spore disease, will curtail the damage. Chlordane produces the quickest kill but does not last more than 3 to 5 years. The milky spore disease does not reach its maximum effectiveness under three to five years but then gives permanent control of the Japanese beetle grubs.

Chlordane also gives good control of ants which often injure grass areas either by establishing too much drainage or by injuring the plants. Another benefit—moles soon leave a lawn where their food (insects) has been destroyed with the chemical chlordane. Use six to eight ounces of chlordane per 1,000 square feet of area.

During periods of dry weather it is a temptation to give the lawn a good soaking once every week or 10 days. Daily sprinklings are injurious to the permanent grasses and beneficial only to the owner, who gets some exercise from the chore, and to the crabgrass. To benefit the grass roots, the soil must be moistened to a depth of 4 to 6 inches. However, research has not demonstrated the value of watering a lawn.

Some grasses withstand close clipping while others are injured by such a practice. Experiments have shown conclusively that the length of roots on Kentucky bluegrass plants is correlated directly to the height of the grass blades. The shorter the blades, the shorter the roots. It follows then that if a close-clipped lawn is wanted, those kinds of grasses which withstand close cutting should be used. Unless a lawn that resembles a putting green is wanted, set the cutting bar to cut at 1½ inches in spring and fall, 2 inches during the summer. Conversely, some kinds which thrive under close clipping suffer if allowed to grow too high.

Considerable thought is being given to the regular use of fungicides to prevent diseases. There are several "broad-spectrum" materials available for this purpose.

The agronomists are working to provide gardeners in this area with more suitable grasses, grasses that will grow and thrive under the climatic and soil conditions, as well as the methods of lawn management which seem to be preferred by the majority of home gardeners. A bluegrass that will grow under higher temperatures, i.e., longer into the summer, has been selected and is now being multiplied. It will not withstand close clipping but will continue in active growth longer. The Japanese lawn grass, Zoysia-Meyer, and Emerald, which will crowd out weeds and withstand close clipping, are being widely planted in this area. They thrive during the heat of the summer. Several fine-stemmed Bermuda grasses noted for their growth during the heat of the summer are available to those who want to buy stolons and plant them. These grasses, if more widely used, will mean better lawns in the Washington area during the summer.

In seeding a new lawn one or two pounds of high-quality seed per 1,000 square feet of area will provide a sufficient density of plants. One pound of seed will be adequate for reseeding an old lawn.

Compost, peat moss, and green manures are good sources of humus with which to improve the soil. Coarse sand will help to correct the physical structure of heavy clay soils but it takes many tons to do the job.

KENTUCKY BLUEGRASS

(Poa pratensis)

Soils:	Moderate acidity, pH 6.0-7.0, well drained and fertile. Nitrogen and phosphate needed.
Cut:	Over 2 inches best. Not lower than 1½ inches.
Disadvantages:	Dormant during the heat of summer. Susceptible to leaf-spot. Becomes sod-bound. Can be corrected by aeration. Nitrogen feeding will help.
Advantages:	Good color in the spring and fall; heals quickly.
Rate of Seeding:	1 pound per 1,000 square feet.
Time of Seeding:	Late summer.
Method:	Firm seed bed, seed firmed into soil. Use nitrogen and phosphate at time of seeding. Two applications a year is minimum—early spring and late summer.
Fertilizer:	Apply 4 to 6 pounds of nitrogen per season.
Lime:	As needed according to test, usually 25 pounds per 1,000 square feet every 3 to 5 years. Use ground limestone.
Mixtures:	Kentucky blue Kentucky blue Kentucky blue Red fescue Alta fescue Bermuda

* * *

TALL FESCUE

(Festuca elatior var. arundinacea)

Soils:	Tolerant. Does well on poor soils and responds to fertilization.
Height of Cut:	1 inch in good soils but allow weed invasion at this height. At 3 inches or higher forms an excellent weed-free turf.
Uses:	Most standard uses. Wears well.
Disadvantages:	Rather broad-leaved in comparison to most lawn grasses. Must be clipped and fed regularly to maintain best appearance and to avoid clumpiness.
Advantages:	Tolerant of many conditions ordinarily unfavorable, excellent wear resistance, competes successfully with weeds; has good year-round color. Fewer disease problems.
Time of Seeding:	Spring.
Rate of Seeding:	5-6 lbs. per 1,000 square feet of lawn.
Method of Seeding:	Firm seed bed and covered not more than ½ inch.
Fertilization:	Two applications per year—spring and fall. 5-10-5 at 20 lbs. or 10 lbs. 10-6-4 per 1,000 square feet per application.
Lime:	As needed to maintain pH 6.0-6.5.
Mixtures:	Tall fescue Tall fescue Kentucky bluegrass Kentucky bluegrass Red fescue

* * *

DANISH BLUEGRASS

(Poa trivialis)

Soils:	Moist, shady.
Height of Cut:	1½ inches or over, becomes weedy and thin if kept lower.
Uses:	Lawns.
Disadvantages:	Summer dormancy, susceptible to leafspot.
Advantages:	Good color spring and fall.
Rate of Seeding:	1 pound per 1,000 square feet.
Time of Seeding:	Late summer.
Method of Seeding:	Firm seed bed; firm into soil.
Fertilization:	2 applications per year: Spring 5-10-5—20 lbs. per 1,000 square feet. Fall, 10-6-4—same rate.
Lime:	As needed to maintain pH of 6.0.
Mixtures:	Usually sown alone, if soil is only slightly moist may be desirable to use both Kentucky blue and Chewing fescue with the Danish Blue.

* * *

RED FESCUE

(Festuca rubra)

Creeping Red Fescue and Chewings Fescue are types of Red Fescue. Ilahee, Ranier, and Pennlawn are improved varieties.

Soils:	Prefers well-drained soils, thrives on poor sandy soil and is tolerant of shade and acid soils.
Height of Cut:	Excellent at 2 inches and above, if cut lower than ½ inches does not resist crabgrass during the summer months.
Uses:	Used chiefly in mixture with Kentucky bluegrass. Has good wear resistance.
Disadvantages:	Does not last in poorly drained soils; dormant in midsummer; susceptible to diseases; inclined to bunch.
Advantages:	Shade tolerant; does well on poor acid soils; has good fall and spring color; fine leaved; tough. Does not require frequent mowing.
Rate of Seeding:	Alone—2½ lbs. per 1,000 square feet. In mixture—½ this amount.
Time of Seeding:	Late summer.
Method of Seeding:	Firm seed bed; cover ¼ inch.
Fertilization:	2 applications—March and September. 2-3 lbs. nitrogen per 1,000 square feet each application.
Lime:	Maintain pH above 6.0.
Mixtures:	Red Fescue, Kentucky bluegrass.

* * *

BENTGRASS

(Agrostis spps.)

(Colonial bents: Astoria, Rhode Island, Highland)

Soils:	Fertile, moist. Tolerant of acid but better on neutral.
Height of Cut:	Withstands very close mowing—3/16-1 inch.
Uses:	Heavy duty lawns. Often mixed with Kentucky blue.
Advantages:	Rapid grower, heals rapidly, withstands extremely close mowing.
Disadvantages:	Susceptible to disease, especially if not kept closely mown. Requires a great deal of care. Bermuda is being substituted for bents because of the expense of fighting diseases.
Time of Seeding:	Early spring, late summer.
Rate of Seeding:	Alone—2½ lbs. per 1,000 square feet. In mixture —10%.
Method of Seeding:	Firm seed bed. Cover ⅛ to ¼ inch.
Fertilization:	2 or more applications per year. 2 lbs. nitrogen per 1,000 square feet per application.
Lime:	As needed, does best in pH range of 6.0-6.5.
Mixtures:	Not more than 10% Colonial bent with Kentucky bluegrass. May be used with Bermuda and Zoysias (summer growers) to provide year-round color.
Notes:	Creeping bents: Several varieties, primarily for putting greens.

* * *

WHITE CLOVER

(Trifolium repens)

Soils:	Tolerant, does well on poor soils.
Height of Cut:	Withstands clipping of ¼-inch or more.
Uses:	Most standard uses. Can be trampled out.
Disadvantages:	Some objection to foliage in lawn.
Advantages:	Tolerant of wide range of soil conditions. Improves soil and provides green to lawn composed of grasses that are dormant during mid-summer. Shades out crabgrass seedlings.
Time of Seeding:	Early Spring.
Rate of Seeding:	2 ozs. per 3,000 square feet (1-2 lbs. per acre).
Method of Seeding:	Firm seed bed and covered ¼ inch.
Fertilization:	Phosphate and potash needed if the 5-10-5 or 10-6-4 are not used.
Lime:	Tolerant of soil acidity—lime for other grasses in mixtures.
Mixtures:	White clover is usually seeded in mixture with the lawn grasses.

* * *

ANNUAL RYEGRASS

(Lolium multiflorum (Italica)—Italian, Common Ryegrass)

Soils:	Tolerant to wide range of soils.
Height of Cut:	1 inch or higher.
Uses:	Temporary lawns; also as green manure crop.
Advantages:	Excellent color, strong winter grower, tolerant of soil and moisture conditions. Sprouts quickly.
Disadvantages:	Adopted to cooler climates; is an annual; tends to crowd out seedlings of permanent grasses when used as a nurse crop if sown too thickly.
Time of Seeding:	Fall.
Rate of Seeding:	Alone—3.5 lbs. 1,000 square feet. In Mixture—1 lb. per 1,000 square feet.
Method of Seeding:	Firm seed bed, cover ¼ inch.
Fertilization:	20-25 lbs. per 1,000 square feet.
Lime:	pH of 6.5-7.0 optimum.
Mixtures:	Not needed in mixture.

* * *

PERENNIAL RYEGRASS

(Lolium perenne—English Ryegrass)

Soils:	Tolerant to wide range of soils.

Height of Cut:	1 inch or more.
Uses:	Large areas.
Advantages:	Quickly established, good color.
Disadvantages:	Tends to be clumpy, coarse and recovers from drought very slowly, hence, is not satisfactory for our high summer temperatures.
Time of Seeding:	Spring and fall.
Rate of Seeding:	3-5 lbs. per 1,000 square feet.
Method of Seeding:	Firm seed bed, cover ¼ inch.
Fertilization:	Two applications a year, for spring—10-6-4—20 lbs. per 1,000 square feet; for fall—5-10-5—20 lbs. per 1,000 square feet.
Lime:	Sufficient to maintain pH 6.5-7.0.
Mixtures:	Not recommended in Kentucky bluegrass mixture.

* * *

MEYER ZOYSIA

(Zoysia Japonica—Japanese lawn grass)

Soils:	Tolerant to wide range, but not well adapted to sands.
Height of Cut:	Withstands ½ inch but is best as a lawn grass at ½ to ¾ inch.
Uses:	Lawns, etc.
Advantages:	Low-growing, dense, tough, wear-resistant and tolerates light shade.
Disadvantages:	Must be planted vegetatively; slow to become established; dormant in winter.
Method of Planting:	2- to 4-inch plugs or sprigs.
Time of Planting:	Mid-May to Mid-September.
Fertilization:	Responds to heavy nitrogen feeding but persists under low fertility. After it is established one feeding per year adequate.
Lime:	As necessary to maintain pH of 6.0-6.5.
Mixtures:	Kentucky bluegrass persists for only a year or two after the Zoysia is well established.

Note: Seed of Japanese Zoysia is available but lacks the hardiness and fine texture of Meyer Zoysia.

BERMUDA GRASS

(Cynodon dactylon—Tufcote)

Soils:	Widely adapted. Becomes thin and weedy on infertile soils.
Height of Cut:	3/16 to 1½ inches. Good turf at ½ inch.
Uses:	Lawns, especially those subject to heavy wear.
Advantages:	Rapid growth; heals quickly; easy to establish; wears well; withstands close mowing; fine leaved; resistant to diseases, weeds, and insects.
Disadvantages:	Encroaches in flower beds; dormant in winter months and becomes sod-bound unless properly managed.
Rate of Seeding:	1 lb per 1,000 square feet. (Improved variety, U-3, not available and must be propagated by stolons.)
Time of Seeding:	Early summer.
Method of Seeding:	Firm seed bed; cover not more than ¼ inch.
Fertilization:	3 applications—May, July, September. 2 lbs. of nitrogen per 1,000 square feet per application.
Lime:	As needed to maintain pH at 6.0 to 7.5.
Mixtures:	Usually not mixed but Kentucky bluegrass or some other good winter grower needed for season-round color.

Research is constantly adding new varieties of lawn grasses. Most of the promising new grasses are strains or varieties of the cool weather grasses that seem more tolerant of summer heat. Meyer Zoysia—described above—has fully demonstrated its usefulness in this area as a superior hot-weather grass. Emerald Zoysia, a finer-leaved grass, appears promising.

Pennsylvania has two hybrids in production. One, Pennlawn, which will probably replace Penn State Chewings fescue, is reported the best variety for dry, shady situations. The other, a bent called Penn Cross, is of more interest to the golf course superintendents than to the gardener. Illahee and Rainier creeping red fescues are still being multiplied for the sunny lawn. These fescues have the same susceptibility as the common fescues to the disease, Helminthosporium, which ruins the Kentucky bluegrass during our hot, muggy summer.

Merion, Windsor and several other varieties of Kentucky bluegrass are receiving much attention, but so far they have not demonstrated much, if any, superiority to the common Kentucky bluegrass for this area. All go dormant in the summer. Common Kentucky bluegrass and all of it's named varieties, except Merion and Windsor, suffer from the leafspot disease. Merion and Windsor are resistant to leaf spot but are subject to rust and stripe smut. Windsor appears to be more heat tolerant than the Merion.

Tufcote Bermuda, a new variety, appears to be winter hardy and most likely to be suitable for this area.

CHAPTER X

FLOWERING SHRUBS

The selection of flowering shrubs for the home grounds, foundation plantings, shrub borders, background, and specimen planting is normally made from catalogue descriptions. The viewing of a shrub with a critical eye to determine its usefulness in a particular situation from the standpoints of soil, exposure, moisture, height, season of bloom, and the many other factors is seldom employed. Is the shrub subject to numerous insects and diseases? Can it be transplanted easily? Does it have good landscape value in addition to a short season of bloom? What value does it have in the winter? These are examples of the questions that the gardener seeking to improve the appearance of his grounds should ask about each plant under consideration.

There are hundreds of shrubs from which to make selections. In the Washington area a great many northern as well as southern shrubs can be grown with a limited degree of success. This is the southern limit for the lilac, the northern limit for the crapemyrtle and the House Hydrangea. Some kinds are classed as tender in this area, but if grown under favorable conditions will survive our winters without difficulty.

The 26 shrubs described herein are those generally planted. Each garden has its particular problems and the owner should consider how well a species or variety meets them. The information listed and the brief comments are, of necessity, in general terms. Most nurserymen are more than willing to answer more specific details than can be given within the scope of this book.

ABELIA

(Bush Arbutus—Abelia grandiflora)

Uses:	Shrub border, specimen, hedge.
Plant:	Spring/September.
Distance:	3-6 feet.
Soil:	Rich, moist.
Exposure:	Sun/light shade.
Prune:	Spring.
Species:	A. grandiflora—Glossy Abelia, 6', pink, June-Nov., semi-evergreen. Anama, 3, pink, semi-evergreen, June-July.
	A. grandiflora—var. Edward Goucher, 18-24 in., June-Nov., semi-evergreen.
	A. grandiflora—var. Sherwood, 24-30 inches, June-Nov., semi-evergreen.

The abelias are one of the most useful of the ornamental shrubs. They may be used as specimen plants in deciduous or evergreen shrub borders and they may be used as a clipped hedge. They are, however, subject to winter kill when planted in a "too-protected" situation.

FLOWERING SHRUBS

Unlike most evergreens they do not require a highly acid soil, but will do fairly well in a sweet soil, and are tolerant of light shade. If supplied with a medium amount of moisture and plant food, they will provide abundant bloom and good foliage.

The improved variety, Edward Goucher, is a dwarf growing abelia useful as a facing shrub in front of evergreens.

Propagation is by cuttings and seed. In warm climates they may be layered. Cuttings, either hardwood or softwood, taken in October may be rooted in a hotbed or propagating frame protected from freezing. Young plants will need protection the following winter from freezing cold.

The abelia is comparatively free from attack by insect or disease.

AZALEA

(Rhododendron species and hybrids)

Uses:	Floral effect, foreground, foundation, and specimen plantings.
Plant:	Spring/Fall.
Distance:	2-6 feet.
Soil:	Enriched with leafmold, acid, not too dry.
Exposure:	Shade/tolerate sun.
Prune:	After flowering.

Species and Representative Varieties:

R. arborescens, Sweet azalea, 7-9', white, deciduous.
R. calendulaceum, Flame azalea, 6-8', yellow-orange-red, deciduous.
R. molle, Chinese (mollis), 4-6', yellow, deciduous.
  Chevalier de Reali—pale yellow
  Directeur Moerlands—golden yellow
  Koningin Wilhelmina—salmon orange
  Nicolaas Beets—orange yellow
  Hugo Koster—reddish orange
  Hugo Hardijzer—orange-red
R. mucronulatum, Korean, 6', rose-lavender, deciduous (Rhodo.)
R. japonicum, Japanese, 6', orange, apricot or yellow, deciduous.
R. nudiflorum, Pinxter, var. Roseum, 6-8', deciduous.
R. kaempferi, Torch azaleas, 4-5', salmon-rose, semi-evergreen.
  Carmen   Cleopatra
  Fedora   Louise
  Othello
R. kurume hybrids, 2-3', semi-evergreen.
  Bridesmaid   Benigiri
  Christmas Cheer   Hatsugiri
  Coral Bells   (Pink Pearl) Azuma
  Salmon Beauty   Hinodegiri
  Snow   Hinomayo
R. roseum, Rose Shell, Mayflower, 6-9', bright pink, deciduous.
R. vaseyi, Pink Shell azalea, 5-6', soft pink, deciduous.
R. yedoense var. poukhanense, Korean Yodogawa, 1-3', rose-purple, deciduous.
R. (indica alba) mucronatum, Snow azalea, 6-8', white, semi-evergreen.
R. gandavense (Ghent hybrids), Ghent, 2-6', white, red, orange, yellow, deciduous.
  Daviesi—pale yellow to white (fragrant)
  Palias—orange red
  Narcissiflora—yellow (double)
  Coccinia speciosa—red
Knaphill Hybrids (incl. Exbury's) 2-8', white, yellow, pink-red, deciduous
  Gibraltar—orange   Daybreak—orange-yellow
  Exbury White—white Klondyke—orange-yellow
  Cecile—pink   Barry Rose—Rose-pink
  Golden Sunset—yellow Strawberry Ice—Deep rose

  Mephistopheles—red   Harvest Moon—Yellow
Indica type (Macrantha) 3-7', orange, pink, white, semi-evergreen.
  J. T. Lovett—orange-red
  Warai-Jishi—semi-double pink
Glenn Dale Hybrids, 2-10', white, orange-red, lavender, semi-evergreen.
  Cavalier—orange-red
  Copperman—red
  Crinoline—tyrian-rose
  Gaiety—rose-pink
  Geisha—white with blotch
  Glacier—white
  Roselight—pink
Gable Hybrids, 15 in.-6', purple, pink, white, red, evergreen.
  Boudoir—purple
  Corsage—purple
  James Gable—rose-opel
  Louise Gable—pink
  Rose Greeley—white
  Rosebud—Violet-rose
  Stewartstonian—red

The azalea is probably one of the most widely planted shrubs in the Washington area. Our climate and soils seem to suit them very well, and everyone enjoys their brilliant display of color in the spring. For the most part, they are spring-flowering shrubs with a wide range in growth habits, as well as in form and color of flower.

The azalea properly belongs to the rhododendron family, and some botanists would like to have us call them rhododendrons; but most gardeners know them as azaleas. In addition to several native species, we have hundreds of varieties of many different types from which to choose. Probably 90 per cent of the plants put out in the garden are of the Kurume group, and a very large proportion of these are of the Hinodegiri variety, a bright red but sometimes with a magenta overtone.

This restriction of planting to a single type and, in most cases, a single variety fails to put into the garden the long flowering season and variety of colors and forms of bloom possible in this area. In the National Arboretum there are some 1,200 species and varieties of azaleas. It might be assumed that Washington area gardeners have not begun to scratch the surface of this colorful shrub.

Hinodegiri is only one of a sizable list of Kurume varieties, which include such colorful and interesting plants as the white variety, Snow, Coral Bells, Salmon Beauty, Lavender Queen, Bridesmaid, and Hinomayo. These are all moderate-sized plants that produce a mass of bloom each spring. Similar to the Kurume hybrids are the Chisolm-Merritt hybrids, which were developed some years ago in this area. Others have worked with this particular groups, and so there are also many other varieties of similar habit and growth. Usually, they are listed according to the breeder or breeders who produced them, and thus are distinct from those mentioned above, which were imported from Japan.

The next major group is commonly known as the Glenn Dale azaleas.

This group was produced by the former director of the National Arboretum, the late B. Y. Morrison. More than 400 varieties of this group have been introduced into commerce. They have much larger foliage than do the Kurumes; the flowers are larger and the habit of growth is quite variable. Some of them will reach a height of 6, 8 or 10 feet at maturity.

The range of colors is quite wide—from white to deep purple. The flowering season of the Glenn Dale hybrids is usually later and lasts much longer than that of the Kurumes. The Macrantha azaleas are of interest for their late flowering season and also for some of

Name	Class 1/	Type 2/	Color	Size of Flower	Height	Season of Bloom
1. Shades of Pure Light Pink						
Cameo	Gable	Double	pale pink	1-1½"	low	midseason
Coral Bells	Kurume	H & H	light pink	1"	low	early
2. Shades of Rose Pink						
Gaiety	G.D.	Single	pale rose pink with rose red blotch	2-3"	tall	early May
3. Shades of Salmon Pink						
Hinomayo	Kurume	Single	tyrian rose	1¼"	tall	midseason
Louise Gable	Gable	Double	light salmon	3"	medium	early-mid.
Sagittarius	G.D.	Single	med. salmon	3"	dwarf	late
Guy Yerkes	Yerkes	Single	dark salmon	3½"	low	early
4. Shades of Lavendar and Lilac						
Corsage	Gable	Single	lavender	2½"	medium	mid.
Lilac Time	Kaempferi	Single	pure lilac			
Violetta	G.D.	Single	mallow purple	2-2¼"	medium	early
Yodogawa	Korean	Double	cyclamen purple	2"	medium	early
5. Shades of Purple						
Boudoir	Gable	Single	Violet red	1½"	medium	early
Herbert	Gable	Semi-Double	rose purple	2"	low	early
Purple Splendor	Gable	H & H	reddish violet	2"	low	early
Sherwoodi	Sherwood	Single	reddish violet	2"	medium	early-mid.
Templar	G.D.	Single	light mallow purple	2¾-3"	medium	early
Zulu	G.D.	Single	deep purple	3½"	medium	early
6. Shades of Red-Orange-Red, Rose Red						
Balsamina-flora	Indica	Double	orange-red	1½"	low	late
Beni-Kirishima	Satsuki	Double	orange-red	2"	medium	
Copperman	G.D.	Single	orange-red	2¾-3"	medium	late
Hexe	Sander	H & H	violet-red	1¾"	low	late-mid.
Hino-Crimson	Kurume	Single	red	1½"	medium	early-mid.
Hinodegiri	Kurume	Single	china rose	1½"	medium	early-mid.
Sherwood Red	Sherwood	Single	orange-red	1¾"	low	
Stewarts-tonian	Gable	Single	clear red			
7. Pure Whites						
Delaware Valley White	Mucro-natum	Single	white	3"	medium	early-mid.
Glacier	G.D.	Single	white	2½"	med.-tall	midseason
Gumpo (White)	Satsuki	Single	white	3"	low	late
Treasure	G.D.	Single	white	3½-4½"	medium	midseason
8. White With Other Color Markings						
Rose Greeley	Gable	H & H	white, chartreuse blotch	2½"	low	early-mid.
Palestrina	Vuyk	Single	white, chartruese blotch	2¼"	medium	midseason

1/Class—G.D.-Glenn Dale, Yerkes-U.S.D.A., Yerkes Group, Gable-Gable Hybrids, Kurume Hybrids, Sherwood-Kurume Hybrids, Vuyk-Kaempferi Hybrid, Satsuki-Indicum Hybrids.

2/Type of flower—H & H-hose-in-hose.

their flower forms. For example, Laciniatum (Kinsai) has narrow strap-like petals. However, most of the Macranthas are commonly referred to as Indicas, which are the show flowers of the Deep South and most of them are not hardy in this area.

The Kaempferi, or torch azalea, is another of the evergreen type. It is moderately tall (4 to 5 feet) and is of interest because of its orange-red colors. Examples of this type are Carmen, Cleopatra, Fedora, Louise and Othello.

The Royal azalea (R. schlippenbachi) and some of its hybrids are considered by many to be exceptionally fine. However, some of the newer introductions, such as the Gable hybrids, the Chugai, among others, offer modern competition to the older varieties.

All of the above refer to the evergreen azaleas. Most of them are hardy in this area and are dependable bloomers.

There are native deciduous species such as the Pinxter (R. nudiflorum), the swamp azalea (R. viscosum), a fragrant late-flowering white, and the flame azalea (R. calendulaceum), which may be found in shades of pale yellow to flame red. They are all of more than passing interest. The European species, usually referred to as Mollis and sometimes called Chinese, include a number of excellent named varieties. They also include a yellow. The Exbury is considered by many as outstanding and is very hardy.

Within the past few years the Department of Agriculture has released several dwarf azaleas to the nurserymen. They grow about a foot high and include several colors.

From the above it is easy to see that many persons are engaged in hybridizing the azalea. Many of them have combined the hardy American species with the tender Japanese and southern species to produce outstanding garden and florist varieties.

It is very difficult to prepare a list of recommended varieties for this area since very few people have the opportunity to grow more than a dozen varieties. However, recommendations for this area given in the Azalea Book by Frederic P. Lee, the National Arboretum, Col. C. M. Merriman of Silver Spring, the Ten Oaks Nursery of Clarksville, Maryland, and a number of local nurseries were all drawn upon to obtain opinions as to the best varieties based upon hardiness, vigor, bloom, color purity, growth habit, season of bloom, and in the case of evergreens, winter foliage values in this area. Unless a variety appeared on three or more of these lists, it was not included. The evergreen varieties are grouped according to color.

Azaleas thrive in sun or shade; although their flowering season is longer in partial shade. They do not withstand the compition of shallow-rooted trees, and they do not thrive in hot dry situations. Given a moist situation in a soil that is well supplied with peatmoss or oak-leaf compost, they may be counted upon to provide abundant color. Mulching in the spring with oak leaves gives adequate protection, and the decaying leaves provide needed plant food and keep the root systems moist and cool during the summer. Azaleas may be given a light fertilizer application if needed before or after blooming but not beyond the first of June. Most gardeners purchase a fertilizer prepared especially for azaleas.

Azaleas thrive best in a relatively acid soil, one in which the pH is below 6.0. If the planting hole was not well supplied with peatmoss, especially in foundation plantings, it may be necessary to increase the acidity with *flowers of sulphur*. Scatter this inexpensive material on the ground about the bushes and let the soil moisture dissolve and carry it down into the soil.

However, if the azalea foliage continues to show the chlorotic condition—yellowish green with the veins darker colored—it usually means that there is an iron deficiency which should be supplied in a form that is available to the plants.

There are several forms of iron available for this purpose—"Chelated," micronized, sulphate of iron, etc., are usually sold under trade names. The chelated iron should not be used as a spray but applied to the soil. One manufacturer offers vermiculite with chelated iron. The iron sulphate may be sprayed on the foliage to correct the chlorotic condition within a few hours. It is usually available only at drug stores.

The azalea is not immune to either insects or diseases. However, most gardeners experience little trouble with such pests. The lacebug and the red spider mite are the most common. A contact spray, such as malathion or Meta-Systox R, has given effective control trol when applied twice after blooming and again in August. If a combination of malathion and tedion is used, better control may be expected. A new material, dimethoate, gives season-long control with a single application and is easier to apply.

The known diseases are largely controlled with a carbamate dust applied as the buds form. Acti-dione R.Z. is the best material for combating the azalea petal blight.

Although most commercially available azaleas are hardy in the Washington area, winter injury or death may occasionally occur. Low temperatures may split the bark. Cold, drying winds, especially after a sharp temperature drop, may cause evergreen plants to dry out and wilt; this hazard is greatly increased if there has been a late summer or fall drought and the plant was not kept watered. Buds are sometimes damaged and the bloom lost due to rapid variations in warm and cold spells. The best insurance against winter injury is a healthy, well-planted bush, given adequate moisture during periods of drought. This will minimize damage caused by extremes of winter weather.

Propagation of deciduous azaleas is by budding, grafting, or layering. The evergreen and semi-evergreen species and varieties are easily propagated from cuttings taken in mid-summer when the new growth is half-ripened. Place in a shady situation in a mixture of peatmoss and sand. When rooted, transplant to pots or bed filled with a mixture of leafmold, peatmoss, and sand. The first winter they will need the protection of an oak-leaf mulch.

Azalea Progress: 1. Well-rooted 1-year-old plant. 2. Pinched-back stocky plant. 3. Bushy 2-year-old. 4. 3-year-old in bloom.

BARBERRY

(Berberis thunbergi and species)

Uses:	Hedges, specimens
Plant:	Spring, fall
Distance:	2-4 feet
Soil:	Ordinary garden loam
Exposure:	Sun, light shade
Prune:	Spring

Species and Varieties:

B. thunbergi—Japanese barberry, 4-5 feet, red fruited, deciduous

B. thunbergi var. astropurpurea, Purple leaved Jap., 4-5 ft., red fruited, deciduous

B. thunbergi var. maximowiczi—Box, 2-3 feet, red fruited, deciduous

B. Julianae—winter-green, 5 feet, bluish-black, evergreen.

B. Julianae var. nana, Dwarf wintergreen, 2 feet, bluish-black, evergreen.

B. sargentiana—Sargent, 6 feet, bluish-black, evergreen.

B. triacanthophora—Threespine, 4 feet, blue-black, evergreen.

B. verruculosa—Warty, 2 feet, violet-black, evergreen.

B. vernae—Verna, 5 feet, salmon-red, evergreen.

B. buxifolia—Magellan, 6 feet, purple, thornless, evergreen.

B. buxifolia nana—dwarf Magellan, 2 ft., purple, evergreen.

B. mentoriensis—Mentor, 6 feet, evergreen.

The barberries are a rather useful group of plants, although local gardeners for the most part employ only the Japanese barberry. It is the cheapest and most easily obtainable. However, it is a useful plant either as a specimen or as a hedge. The sharp spines can be put to other uses, such as protection of evergreens from dogs. The evergreen barberries, Julianae, Threespine, Warty, Magellan, and Mentor, are attractive evergreens and well adapted to a wider use. The foliage, habit of growth, and abundant crops of colorful fruits give them high landscape values.

The Japanese barberry, an easily propagated shrub, may be trimmed to almost any form desired. Frequent shearing makes it so compact that it will turn a dog. The small leaves and twiggy growth give the Japanese barberry landscape value as a "transitional" shrub to stand between evergreens and deciduous shrubs.

All of the barberries listed above are hardy in this area and are relatively immune to the wheatstem rust, a disease for which many barberries are an intermediate host. There are many more species and varieties which have high value as ornamentals but because they are hosts to this destructive disease should not be grown in wheat producing areas.

Barberries do not need any special care or soil, but like most plants, they will make better growth, produce more abundant crops of fruits, and attain greater vigor if fed and cared for. However, gardeners seldom have need for plants that soon outgrow their situation and for this reason heavy feeding after the first year or two is unnecessary.

Insects and diseases on the barberry are comparatively rare in the Washington area. Most people look upon them as being "foolproof."

Two types of barberry: Upright, suitable for hedge; spreading, typical of Japanese barberry.

FLOWERING SHRUBS

BEAUTYBERRY

(Callicarpa americana)

Uses:	Berried shrub for border.
Plant:	Spring/fall.
Height:	3-6 feet.
Blooms:	Inconspicuous.
Fruit:	Violet.
Distance:	4-6 feet.
Soil:	Ordinary well-drained garden soil.
Exposure:	Sun/light shade.
Prune:	Spring, removing winter-killed twigs.
Species:	C. americana—Beautyberry, French Mulberry, 6 ft., reddish violet. C. dichotoma (purpurea)—Purple beautyberry, 4 ft., lilac-violet. C. japonica—Japanese beautyberry, 5 ft., violet. C. bodinieri, var. giraldi—Girald (Chinese) beautyberry, 10 ft., violet.

The beautyberries are grown primarily for their excellent fruit display during the fall and early winter. Ordinarily the fruits, which are produced in clusters along the slender branches, are retained well into the winter.

While some gardeners will call them too tender for this area because of winter-kill, this is not a disadvantage since the beautyberry should be pruned rather severely in the early spring to promote new growth. The fruits are produced upon the new wood which heavy pruning and feeding stimulates and which is needed for the best winter display of fruits.

The American Beautyberry, a native of the South Atlantic States, is the kind most widely grown.

The beautyberries are relatively free from insects and diseases and are undemanding as to soil and exposure. Generally, they are given too much protection and suffer winter injury. In less protected situations the wood matures earlier and suffers less injury.

BUTTERFLY BUSH

(Buddleia davidi and hybrids)

Uses:	Shrub border, specimen, cutflowers.
Plant:	March-April.
Height:	4-10 feet.
Blooms:	June-September.
Fruits:	None.
Distance:	4-10 feet.
Soil:	Rich, moist.
Exposure:	Sun/light shade.
Prune:	Spring, cut back Davidi varieties severely.
Species:	Magnifica—Oxeye, 4 ft., violet-purple, July-September. Davidi Var. Superba, 5 ft., violet purple, July, September. Davidi Var. Veitchiana—Veitch, 5-6 ft., bright mauve, June-September. Davidi Var. Royal Purple, 6 ft., deep purple, July-September. Davidi Var. Black Knight, 4-5′, Royal blue, July-Sept. Davidi Var. Daybreak, lavender-pink, July-September. Davidi Var. Empire Blue, deep blue, July-September. Davidi Var. Orchid Beauty, 4 ft., orchid, July-August. Davidi Var. White Cloud, 4-5 ft., white, yellow eyes, July-August. Davidi Var. Fascination, 5 ft., rosy-pink, July-August. Davidi Var. Charming, 5 ft., lavender pink, July-September.

The buddleias, or summer lilacs, are useful summer bloomers in the shrub border or as specimen plants for the lawn. The species are stronger growers than the newer improved varieties. All are good as cutflowers, the long, pointed, terminal spikes lasting quite well indoors.

The buddleias do quite well in full sun, and if tree competition is not too severe, will grow in light shade. They do best in a rich, moist soil but seem to thrive in ordinary garden loam.

They should be cut back severely in the spring to keep them from becoming tall and leggy. The pruning also stimulates branching which most of them need, otherwise they become too tall for the smaller yard. The newer varieties are for the most part low growing, and when well branched make attractive shrubs.

Spent blooms should be removed to maintain flowering during the late summer and early fall months. Also, it helps to avoid the numerous seedlings which spring up where seed is allowed to mature. Seedlings are seldom as useful as the named varieties.

Propagation of named varieties is by cuttings taken in the early fall and protected from freeze injury during the first winter.

The butterfly bushes, so named because they attract swarms of butterfiles, are relatively free from insect pests and diseases.

CAMELLIA

(C. Japonica, Sasanqua and varieties)

Uses:	Shrub border, foundation planting, specimen, cut-flowers.
Plant:	March (container plants to late June).
Height:	3 to 10 feet.
Blooms:	According to variety—fall, winter and spring.
Fruit:	Not common.
Distance:	3 to 6 feet.
Soil:	Enriched with leafmold, compost or peatmoss. Sandy.
Exposure:	Light shade.
Prune:	As size is attained; clip after flowering.
Varieties:	BAKER'S DOZEN DEPENDABLE CAMELLIA VARIETIES **Berenice Boddy**—Light pink with deep pink under petals. MSD. Vigorous upright growth. M. This variety makes a good espalier. **Dr. Tinsley**—Very pale pink at base shading to deeper pink at the edge with reverse side flesh pink. MSD. Compact upright growth. M. **Donckelarii**—Red marbled white in varying degrees. LSD. Slow bushy growth. M. The above names all appear to apply to the same plant differing only in degrees of variegation. Other forms: Eugene Bolen—solid red form. Ville de Nantes—Dark red blotched white. LSD with upright fimbriated petals. ML. **Finlandia**—White. MSD with swirled and fluted petals. Medium compact growth. EM. Other forms: Finlandia Red—Salmon red. Finlandia Variegated—(Margaret Jack, Aurora Borealis, Speckels) White streaked crimson. King Lear—Cherry red marbled white. **Governor Mouton**—Oriental red, sometimes blotched white. MSD to loose peony form. Vigorous upright growth. **Kumasaka**—Rose pink. Medium rose form double to peony form. Vigorous compact upright growth. ML. Kumasaka Variegated—(Deacon Dodd, Gay Boy) Rose pink blotched white. **Lady Clare**—Deep pink. LSD. Vigorous, loosely branched growth. EM. Other forms: Oniji—Deep pink marbled white. Destiny—White streaked deep pink. Grandiflora Rosea is frequently mistaken for Lady Clare but has crinkled petals and blooms later.

Lady Vansittart—White striped rose pink. MSD with broad wavy petals. Slow bushy growth with holly-like foliage. ML. Other forms: Lady Vansittart Pink—(Lady Vansittart Red) Deep pink to red form. Frances McLanahan—Light pink sport. Yours Truly—(Lady Vansittart Shell) Pink streaked deep pink or red, edged white.

Magnoliaeflora—Blush pink. MSD. Medium compact growth. M. Another form: Peach Blossom—(Magnoliaeflora England, Fleur de Peche) Light pink.

Mathotiana—Crimson with purple cast. Large to very large rose form to formal double. Vigorous compact upright growth. ML. Other forms: Flowerwood—(Mathotiana Fimbriata) Crimson with fimbriated petals, also variegated form crimson blotched white. Mathotiana Supreme—(Mima-Mae) Very large SD to loose peony form with irregular petals interspersed with stamens. Mathotiana Variegated—(Paulina, Julia Drayton Var.) Scarlet blotched white. Rosea Superba—(Ada Wilson, Laura Dasher) Rose pink sport.

Pink Perfection—Shell pink, small formal double. Vigorous upright growth. EL. Another form: Pink Pearl—(Burgdorf Beauty, Badgen's Beauty) Light pink sport with high pointed ivory center.

Tricolor (SIEBOLD)—Waxy white streaked carmine. MSD of slightly cupped form. Vigorous compact upright growth. M. Other forms: Leucantha—(Wakanoura, Tricolor (Siebold) White, Shiro Wakanoura). White sport. Fred Sander—(Fimbriata Superba) Crimson with curled fimbriated petals. Lady de Saumarez—(Tricolor (Siebold) Folki, Pride of Portland) Bright red spotted white. Tricolor Red (Siebold)—(Red Douglas, Robin Hood, Wakanoura Red) Solid red form.

White Queen—White. LSD with somewhat small petals pointed at the tips. Vigorous compact upright growth. ML. MSD and LSD indicate medium or large semi-double blooms. Blooming time is indicated by an E when before January, an M for January to March, and an L for April or later. Preferred names are in capitals while names in ( ) are synonyms.

(Recommended by The Camellia Society of the Potomac Valley)

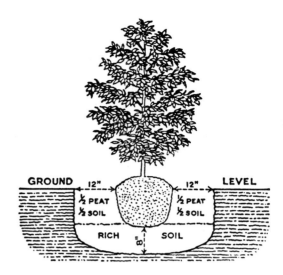

No doubt there are many who think Washington too far north for the culture of camellias out of doors. There are many plants growing in the Washington area that have been here for several decades. It is only during the past few years that gardeners have begun to use them in their yards in the fashion that gardeners do in the South.

And it is proper that they do so, for the camellia japonica, properly cared for, will live and thrive here. No doubt there will be winters when the combination of warm spells and freezing temperatures will destroy the flower buds, but that happens to plants which are far more common.

The camellia needs to make its growth early in the season in order that the new wood will have ample time to mature before cold weather. For this reason, feeding should be done early in the season, particularly if organic fertilizers are used. Quickly available chemical fertilizers may be safely applied up to the first of June, perhaps July, but that will depend upon the location.

The camellia japonica does not generally withstand full sun in winter or summer; it thrives best in partial shade, such as provided by sparse plantings or from large trees whose branches have been removed to a height of about 20 feet. Morning sun is most harmful since during the winter it thaws out the camellias to quickly. The afternoon sun is better. Planting camellias on the northwest side of the house is preferable provided there is also wind protection.

Other winter protection need be nothing more than a good thick mulch over the root area, obtained by adding more compost or pine needles to the summer mulch. Protection from strong winds such as given by a burlap screen or a few pine boughs is desirable.

Undoubtedly the beginning camellia grower has more trouble with planting than any other phase of culture. The camellia is very sensitive to deep planting, so the old saying that "one inch to deep will make them sulk and two inches too deep will cause them to die" is a good rule to keep in mind Experienced growers prepare the planting holes several weeks in advance, filling them with a mixture of equal parts of sand, loam and peatmoss so the soil will be settled by planting time. In planting they place the root ball so that it extends at least an inch or two above the ground level, filling in and around with the same soil mixture.

Where hard-pan or other factors cause poor drainage, many growers prepare a raised planting bed, placing the root ball on the surface of the ground and surrounding it with the recommended soil mixture up to within two inches of the top of the root ball and extending at least three feet on all sides, edged with bricks or stones.

Once planted, the whole area is deeply mulched with coarse materials such as partially rotted leafmold, compost, or pine needles. Such a mulch should be maintained at all times. In the winter pieces of brush may be used to hold fallen leaves and to keep them from matting. Mulches that crust or shed water should be avoided.

The camellias seem to be more tolerant of soil acidity than the azalea—it need not be quite as acid. Because the camellia is very sensitive to soil moisture they must have good drainage; but on the other hand they cannot withstand drought, thus requiring more care as to watering.

Insect and disease injury so far has not proved a problem in this area, but undoubtedly sooner or later the camellia scale and some disease will appear. It should not be difficult to control them with some of the newer, potent materials now on the market. Probably the red spider mite will attack those plants in corners lacking good air circulation. Dimethoate is probably as good a control as any. A strong blast of cold water from the hose is also very effective.

In selecting varieties for the home garden it is well to note that some have a much more spreading habit of growth than others. Some are very slow growing and will take many years to outgrow a spot in the foundation planting. The varieties listed above are currently considered the most dependable, but there are about a hundred others which have proved to be satisfactory in the more protected areas.

In addition to the C. japonica discussed above, a number of gardeners are growing C. sasanqua, a fall bloomer which makes an attractive shrub or hedge plant for the sunnier areas. While a free bloomer, the sasanqua is only for garden display, as the flowers fall quickly if cut. The culture of the sasanqua, with the exception of shade—some tolerate full sun—is the same as for the japonica varieties, although they are not quite as hardy.

CORALBERRY—SNOWBERRY

(Symphoricarpos species)

Uses:	Bank cover, winter value of fruits.
Plant:	Spring/fall.
Height:	3-6 feet.
Blooms:	Inconspicuous.
Fruits:	Coralberry—dark red.
	Snowberry—snow white.
Distance:	2-3 feet.
Soil:	Ordinary garden loam.
Exposure:	Shade/sun.
Prune:	Spring.
Species:	S. albus (racemosus)—Snowberry, 5-6 feet, large white berries. White hedge, 5 ft.
	S. albus var. pauciflorus—Dwarf Common Snowberry, 3½ ft., white.
	S. orbiculatus (vulgaris)—Coralberry, 4-6 ft., dark red berries.
	S. chenaulti—Chenault Coralberry, 6-8 ft., pink-spotted white.

The common coralberry is the most widely grown member of this group of ornamentals, although both the foliage and the fruits are rather dull. The snowberry, particularly the Chenault snowberry, has the most useful growth habit and the berries are interesting.

The common coralberry has such a spreading habit of growth that it is best restricted to banks where it is an excellent soil holder, or to the wild-flower area where its taking ways are not so disconcerting. The strong growing suckers reach out and take root unless removed.

This group of plants thrives in shade or sun and is tolerant of soil and moisture conditions. If properly used it is a most valuable shrub, otherwise it may become a nuisance and a weed.

Occasionally anthracnose attacks the plants and spoils the display of fruits. A dormant limesulphur spray, if applied in the early spring, will control this disease. It also controls the scale insects which may occasionally trouble them. Propagation is by division, rooted suckers, cuttings, and seed.

COTONEASTER

(Rockspray—Cotoneaster species)

Uses:	Border, rockgarden, walls and specimens shrubs.
Plant:	Spring (deciduous also in fall).
Height:	1-10 feet.
Blooms:	Mostly inconspicuous—spring.
Fruits:	Red, black—showy.
Distance:	2-8 feet.
Soil:	Ordinary well-drained garden loam.
Exposure:	Sun/light shade.
Prune:	Spring.
Species:	C. horzontalis—Rock C., 2-3 feet, red, rock garden—semi-evergreen.
	C. adpresso—Creeping C., 1-2 ft., red, rockgarden—semi-evergreen.
	C. apiculata, Cranberry C., 3 feet, red, rockgarden, semi-evergreen.
	C. dielsiana—Diels C., 10 ft., scarlet—deciduous.
	C. divaricata—Spreading C., 5-6 ft., red—deciduous.
	C. franchetti, 4-5 ft., red, semi-evergreen.
	C. hupehensis—Hupeh C., 6 ft., red, evergreen, white flowers, deciduous.
	C. racemiflora—Redbeard, 6 ft., scarlet, deciduous, white flowers.

C. salicifola var. floccosa—Willowleaf, 10 ft., red, evergreen.

C. Microphylla—Rockspray, 3 ft., scarlet, semi-evergreen.

* * *

The cotoneasters are useful shrubs in many situations. Their small glossy foliage, which attains attractive fall colors, and the snowy fruits make them desirable. Most kinds of cotoneasters have a graceful habit of growth and several are evergreen or semi-evergreen in the Washington area. Only two or three have conspicuous flowers in May or June.

With few exceptions the creeping cotoneasters are the most commonly grown in the Washington area. A few, such as the Spreading and Diels, are to be found in public plantings. Most cotoneasters are planted in full sun although they will tolerate light shade.

Given average garden soil they do better than in one that is so rich that it stimulates excessive growth. In the case of C. horizontalis rich soil is dangerous, since the soft succulent growth produced is susceptible to "fire blight," a destructive disease.

The bountiful supply of berries, one of the most attractive features of the cotoneasters, is enjoyed by squirrels who cut off the branches and carry them to a safe perch where the berries are eaten at leisure.

In pruning the early spring flowering shrubs, remove from ¼ to ⅓ of the oldest canes at ground.

Scale insects occasionally attack the cotoneasters and must be controlled with a dormant spray. The "fire blight" mentioned above is very infrequent in its attacks. It causes the foliage and terminal twigs to turn black. Remove the infected branches, cutting 3 or 4 inches below the visible infection being careful to dip the shears in a sterilizing solution between cuts and to burn the infected pieces.

Propagation is by cuttings, layers, and seeds.

Pot grown plants are transplanted most sucessfully, although carefully grown nursery specimens balled and burlap (B&B) is the accepted practice for specimens too large for pots.

DEUTZIA

(Deutzia species and hybrids)

Uses:	Shrub border, background, cut flowers.
Plant:	Fall/spring.
Height:	3-10 feet.
Blooms:	May-June.
Fruits:	None.
Distance:	2-8 feet.
Soil:	Well-drained loam.
Exposure:	Sun/light shade.
Prune:	Spring (after flowering).
Species:	D. gracilis—Slender, 3 ft., May, white.
	D. roseas—Rosepanicle, 4 ft., May, pink.
	D. lemoinei, Lemoine, 4-5 ft., May, white.
	Boule de Neige, 4 ft., May, white.
	D. scabia—Fuzzy, 9-10 ft., May, white.
	Pride of Rochester, 9-10 ft., May, double white, tinged pink.

* * *

The deutzias are well known to most gardeners and are of easy culture, although they do not thrive in dry soils. A good garden loam is best for them. Normally they are grown in full sun but do best in partial shade. The dwarfer growing deutzias have the greatest landscape value since the taller ones tend to be leggy and have dull foliage, hence have little landscape interest beyond their spring flowers.

The slender deutzia tends to be short-lived under neglect. The old wood should be pruned out each year —remove a fourth of the oldest canes each spring. A highly acid soil does not produce the best growth and an occasional application of ground limestone in the spring is recommended.

The deutzias are subject to two leaf-spot diseases which, should they appear, may be controlled with Bordeaux or a metallic copper fungicide.

Propagation is by softwood and hardwood cuttings and by layering. The slender deutzia may be divided.

The Lemoine hybrids are most suitable for the smaller shrub border. There are several named varieties to choose from varying somewhat in height, habit of growth and color. Foliage and habit of growth are especially important to landscape value.

FLOWERING SHRUBS

FIRETHORN

(Pyracantha coccinea lalandi)

Uses:	Specimens, hedge, shrub border.
Plant:	Spring.
Height:	6-20 feet.
Blooms:	May—inconspicuous.
Fruits:	Orange-red fruits.
Distance:	3-6 feet.
Soil:	Well-drained, neutral.
Exposure:	Sun/light shade.
Prune:	Spring.
Species:	P. coccinea, var. lalandi—Laland, 9-12 ft., orange-red berries; Bakeri (red), Rosedale (red), Graberi (red).
	P. atalantoides (Gibbsi)—Gibbs, 10 ft., large red berries.
	P. crenulata—Nepal, 20 ft., orange-red berries.
	P. crenato-serrata (yunansis)—Chinese, 10 ft., small red berries.
	P. koidzumi—Sensation, free fruiting, compact scarlet-red.

* * *

The firethorns are one of our really attractive evergreen shrubs. They are useful in the shrub border, for training against a wall, or clipped to form a hedge. Their evergreen foliage, brilliant fruits, and thorns make them especially useful. The small flowers borne in the spring are sometimes nipped by late frosts destroying their fruits for that year. A good display of fruits is especially showy and catches the eye of the gardener seeking attractive, interesting shrubs long before he notes the foliage or habit of growth.

The firethorns should not be given a too-protected situation, one in which the wood fails to ripen early in the fall and hence subject to freeze injury. The variety Laland, long considered the most hardy, is commonly available as pot plants from the nurseries. Kasan, a new, upright-growing orange-scarlet fruited variety, is rated hardier. However, there are other species which may be used in this area. The berries of all varieties usually persist late into the winter.

Because of the interest in red fruits there are a number of named varieties available. St. Joseph, a variety with large red fruits, is somewhat tender and should not be used in the more exposed situations.

Occasionally the firethorn is attacked by the fireblight, mentioned under cotoneasters (p.109). The treatment is the same. The lacebug, which is common on azaleas, also attacks the firethorn and control is the same.

Propagation is by cuttings, layering and grafting.

FLOWERING QUINCE

(Chaenomeles (cydonia)—Japonica, Firebush)

Uses:	Shrub border, hedge, fruits.
Plant:	Oct.-Dec./March-April.
Height:	3-10 feet.
Blooms:	March-April.
Fruits:	Greenish-yellow, large.
Distance:	4-6 feet.
Soil:	Ordinary garden loam, deep but not rich.
Exposure:	Sun/light shade.
Prune:	Spring (after flowering).
Species:	C. lagenaria—Common flowering quince, 4-6 ft., March-May, scarlet.
	C. japonica—Japanese flowering quince, 3 ft., March-May, brick red.
	C. sinensis—Chinese flowering quince, 8-20 ft., May.
Varieties:	Columbia, bright red; Grandiflora, deep rose; Macrocarpa, orange-red; Marmorata, soft rose White (superba), with white flowers, cameo-apricot-pink, double, and Falconet Charlot, rose-pink, double.

* * *

The flowering quince or Japonica is a popular, early spring-flowering shrub. It will often flower in late February or early March during periods of unseasonably warm weather. The attractive foliage, low growth, and freedom of bloom, as well as ease of division, have contributed much to the popularity of this hardy shrub.

There are scores of varieties listed, mainly because of the colors which range from pure white to brick red. Some varieties are lower growing than others.

The quince is of easy culture, thriving in ordinary garden loam, especially if moist. They spread by suckers which come up from the shallow growing roots and will need to be thinned and controlled if the bush is to be kept within bounds.

Both scale and fire blight attack the quince. The scale is easily controlled with a dormant spray—lime-sulphur. The remedy for fire blight is the same as given under cotoneasters.

Propagation is by root cuttings, the lifting of suckers, and hardwood cuttings. Seedlings are easily produced from the large fruits but may vary widely from the parent plant. Named varieties may be grafted.

The fruits are generally very fragrant and while hardly edible may be used in the making of quince jelly or the flavoring of other jellies.

FORSYTHIA

(Forsythia species—Goldenbells)

Uses:	Shrub, border, banks.
Plant:	Spring/fall.
Height:	4-10 feet.
Blooms:	March-April.
Fruits:	None.
Distance:	5-6 feet.
Soil:	Garden loam.
Exposure:	Sun.
Prune:	After flowering.

Species: F. intermedia—Border, 6-8 ft., April-May.
F. Suspensa—Weeping, 4-6 ft., March-April.
F. viridissima—Greenstem, 7-8 ft., April-May.

Varieties: Showy (specabilis), 6-8 ft., April-May, Fortune Weeping, 7-8 ft., April-May. Clustered, 7-8 ft., April-May. Lynwood Gold, 5-7 ft., Apr.-May. Spring Glory, 5-7 ft., Apr.-May. Beatrix Farrand, vigorous, Apr.-May; Arnold's Dwarf, 3-4 ft., Apr.-May; Karl Sax, early, Dwarf.

* * *

The forsythias probably are as widely planted as any of the early spring-flowering plants. They are one of the earliest of the spring bloomers and are cherished as evidence of returning spring. They are of comparatively easy culture, flourishing in almost all types of soil, thriving in full sun or partial shade, and for the most part untroubled by insects or diseases. Their habit of growth as well as the landscape value of the foliage is good.

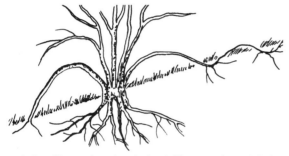

Many plants will reproduce by simply striking root from their branches. Tips may be dug into the ground, or a branch "layered" at several points. Root buds along the branch will strike root, and can then be cut and re-planted. Here is a forsythia bush with its rootings.

While some may say they are too commonplace, it would be difficult to find a better early spring bloomer. The foliage persists late into the fall, oftentimes turning purplish in color. They are easy to transplant.

The forsythia should not be heavily fertilized at any time since heavy feeding stimulates rank growth and the bloom is more widely spaced producing a thinner floral display.

Propagation is by cutting—either softwood or hardwood. F. suspensa and its varieties root at the tips of the branches when they come in contact with the ground.

HOLLY

(Ilex crenata, opaca, etc.)

Uses:	Specimen, border, hedge, foundation planting.
Plant:	Spring/Aug.-Sept.
Height:	3-50 feet.
Blooms:	Inconspicuous.
Fruits:	Yellow, red, orange, black.
Distance:	3-20 feet.
Soil:	Acid, enriched with leafmold or compost, moist.
Exposure:	Shade/sun.
Prune:	As needed at Christmas or early spring.
Species:	I. opaca—American, 45-50 ft., red berries, evergreen, sun-shade.
	I. cornuta—Chinese, 10-15 ft., red, evergreen, shade.
	I. crenata—Japanese, 3-10 ft., black, evergreen, sun/light shade.
	I. glabra—Inkberry, 5-6 feet, black, evergreen, sun/light shade.
	I. verticillata—Winterberry, 8 ft., red, deciduous, shade, moist.
	I. aquifolium—English, 40-50 ft., red, evergreen, light shade.

* * *

Named varieties of the above suitable for use in this area:

American holly (Ilex opaca)—Farage, Miss Helens/Hedgeholly, Cumberland, Old Heavyberry, St. Ann, St. Mary, Salem Compacta, Christmas Hedge, Felton's Selection, Griscom, Judge Brown, Canary, Jersey Knight (male).

Japanese holly (I. crenata)—Convexa, Microphylla, Rotundifolia, Helleri, Stokes, Kingsville, Green Cushion, Hetzi, Compacta.

English holly (I. aquifolium) Camelliaefolia, Hodgins, Louise, Rederly, Dumbarton Oaks, Lewis, Escort (male), Big Bull (male), Angustifolia, Silvary, Pinto, Yellow Beam, Teufel's Hybrid, Lilygold, Earlygold.

Chinese holly (I. cornuta)—Burfordi, Dwarf Burford, Rotunda, Shiuy-ing, Grandview (male), D'Or.

Holly hybrids—Nellie R. Stevens, Edward J. Stevens (male), Lydia Morris, John T. Morris (male), Brilliant, Aquipernyi (male), Foster #2.

Miscellaneous species—I. glabra compacta, I. glabra leucocarpa, I. pernyi, I. ciliospinosa, I. latifolia, I. verticillata, I. serrata, I. decidua, and I. pedunculosa.—National Arboretum.

The hollies offer an almost unexpected field to the average gardener. He knows the American holly but thinks of it as a tree although it makes an excellent hedge plant. The dwarf forms of the Japanese holly are useful in a foundation planting. Lightly trimmed, it becomes an effective hedge plant, adapted to sun or shade. The Chinese holly has excellent foliage and makes a splendid small specimen in the protected garden. The Convexleaf variety of the Japanese holly has a much better foliage value than does the species.

In recent years a number of the hollies have been selected because of superior foliage, fruiting habit, or for some other characteristic and have been propagated as named varieties. Usually, they are much more useful in the landscape planting than the species even though they cost somewhat more. This is particularly true of the American holly which often lacks luster and certainly seldom has an outstanding display of berries.

Hollies do best in a soil that has been well supplied with peatmoss, leafmold, or acid compost. They resent lime and inorganic fertilizers but thrive in rich leafmold that is moist and cool.

The Winterberry, a deciduous shrub often cultivated for its berries, is adapted to the moister situations. Lacking winter foliage it is not especially useful as a landscape plant.

Hollies are dioecious, that is the berries are borne by the female tree, if the blossoms are fertilized by a non-berry bearing male. For this reason gardeners desiring holly berries should purchase female plants and one male for each species (incl. species varieties). This is important since they flower at different seasons. A male tree within a block or so may serve. Otherwise it may be necessary to graft a male branch into one of the females, or during the flowering season a few branches from a male tree may be hung (in bottles of water) in the trees whose blossoms are to be fertilized.

Also, the flowers of the Chinese may be sprayed at the proper time with a hormone.

The holly trees are not easy to transplant unless they have been root-pruned. Even then it is well to strip part or most of the leaves. They should be planted so that moisture drains into the planting hole rather than away.

The hollies are not immune to disease or insect pest. The holly-leaf miner disfigures the foliage of the American holly but it may be controlled by spraying with malathion during the spring and early summer or a spring application of dimethoate (never use on the Chinese hollies). A leaf spot may attack a planting, but if detected in time, can be controlled by removing and burning infected leaves. Spraying or dusting with fermate will prevent the leaf-spot spores from entering the foliage. It will not kill spores that are already in the leaf.

Propagation is by cutting, seeds, and grafting. The new superior named varieties are raised from cuttings or are grafted on seedlings.

HONEYSUCKLE
(Lonicera species and varieties)

Uses:	Border, background, hedge, vine.
Plant:	Spring/fall.
Height:	4-12 feet.
Blooms:	Apr.-June.
Fruits:	Red, yellow, blackish-purple.
Distance:	2-10 feet.
Soil:	Ordinary garden loam.
Exposure:	Sun/light shade.
Prune:	Spring (after flowering).
Species:	L. morrowi—Morrow, 7-8 ft., May-June, white-yellow, red.
	L. morrowi Var. Xanthocarpa, 7-8 ft., May-June, white-yellow, yellow.
	L. tartarica—Tartarian, 10-12 ft., May-June, white-rose, red.
	L. bella (albida)—var. White Belle, 8-9 ft., May-June, white, red.
	L. korolkowi—Blue Leaf, 10-12 ft., May, rose, red.
	L. maacki—Amur, 10-15 ft., May, white, red.
	L. nitida—Box, 4-6 ft., May, inconspicuous, blue purple, evergreen.

The honeysuckles are a strong-growing group of shrubs that are not well adapted to the smaller yard. Most of them are free flowering and fragrant and produce abundant crops of berries which ripen in may and June. The berries remain on the bushes for a comparatively short time as they seem to be a favorite food for several kinds of birds.

The list of honeysuckle species is a long one and in addition there are a considerable number of named varieties which differ from the species in one or more ways. The common Tartarian honeysuckle, a strong growing bush with pink and white flowers, is represented by a dozen or more varieties named because they were more dwarf (low); have yellow flowers etc.

The honeysuckles thrive in the ordinary garden loam, in full sun, or partial shade, and are tolerant of moisture conditions. They seem to be relatively free of insects and diseases. With the exception of the Box honeysuckle (L. nitida) those listed above are hardy in this area. The Box honeysuckle is hardy unless grown in a too protected situation or where the soil is rather moist. In a poor soil and with moderate supplies of moisture it is fairly hardy.

The honeysuckles are mostly propagated by hardwood cuttings although softwood cuttings will be successful for some kinds. Many kinds are commercially propagated by seed.

The Japanese honeysuckle (Lonicera japonica) is not listed above because of it's rampant invasive growth. It should be considered a **dangerous nuisance.** It will smother plants, shrubs, and small trees. Even if kept under control, the birds scatter the seeds far and wide.

HYDRANGEA
(Hydrangea, arborescens, paniculata, etc.)

Uses:	Specimen, shrub border, hedge.
Plant:	Spring/fall.
Height:	3-10 feet.
Blooms:	June-Aug.
Fruits:	None.
Distance:	4-6 feet.
Soil:	Rich, moist.
Exposure:	Sun/light shade.

Prune: H. macrophylla after flowering, all other in spring.
Species: H. macrophylla—House H., 3-6 ft., June-July, pink/blue.
Domotoi, 2-3 ft., double deep pink, June.
H. arborescens—Smooth H., 6 ft., June, white.
H. arborescens grandiflora—Hills of Snow, 4-5 ft., June, white.
H. quercifolia—Oakleaf H., 3-5 ft., June, white/purple.
H. paniculata var. Peegee—Panicle, 8-9 ft., Aug., white/pink.

* * *

The hydrangeas are popular, widely planted, shrubs although their foliage is rather too coarse and dull to score very highly as landscape material. The large flowered Peegee Hydrangea which flowers in August, produces huge terminal clusters which carry on into the winter. It seems to achieve its distinction because of size rather than usefulness in the shrub border. The House hydrangea, also called Shiny-leaved, Florists. and French Hydrangea, is commonly found throughout this area, although this is the northern limit for its use in the garden. North of here it is grown as a tub plant. There is a hardy variety—Nikko Blue, also a red-flowering variety, Red clackamas. The Oak-leaf hydrangea is a native to the South. It is hardy and of interesting leaf-form, but is not widely used although it will tolerate more shade than either the Pee-gee or A.G.

Hydrangeas thrive best in a rich, moist soil since they flower on new wood and need to make strong growth each spring after pruning. The House hydrangea will not thrive and produce flowers without an adequate supply of moisture. The House hydrangea requires an acid soil if the blue flowers are desired and a sweet one for pink flowers. The acidity can be increased, consequently the depth of blueness, by adding peatmoss to the soil, cultivating flowers of sulphur into the soil, or watering with a solution of aluminum sulphate. The acidity is easily neutralized with ground limestone.

The hydrangeas are subject to attack by a number of diseases and insect pests, none of which seem to be serious in this area. However, the leaf spot may be controlled by Bordeaux, the insects with DDT or malathion.

Hydrangeas, with the exception of the House hydrangeas, should be cut back in early spring to stimulate strong growth and larger flowers. The House hydrangea is also pruned in the spring, but the pruning consists of removing the dead and weak shoots and the thinning of the remaining canes. Shortening the canes is to cut off the flowerbuds which form at the end of last season's growth. When the terminal buds are injured by freezing or removed by pruning, the season's bloom is lost.

Hydrangeas may be propagated by cuttings, division, layering, and grafting. The named varieties, of which there are a considerable number, are usually propagated by softwood cuttings.

JETBEAD

(Rhodotypos (kerrioides) scandens)

Uses:	Shrub border, specimen.
Plant:	Fall/spring.
Height:	4-6 feet.
Blooms:	May-June.
Fruits:	Black fruits.
Distance:	4-6 feet.
Soil:	Clay.
Exposure:	Sun/shade.
Prune:	Spring.
Species:	R. scandens.

* * *

The Jetbead is a useful moderate sized shrub bearing large single white flowers in late spring which are followed by shiny black fruits that persist well into the winter. This 4-5 foot shrub has excellent foliage and is bushy, hence it is good in the foreground of the shrub border. While often called White Kerria, it has stiffer, darker green canes.

The Jetbead is tolerant of soil and exposure which would seem to justify more general use. However, it seems to be a bit difficult to transplant, and so should be severely cutback at planting time to insure survival. Heavy pruning is usually needed to keep the bushes compact and vigorous.

Propagation is by seeds, softwood, and hardwood cuttings.

LILACS

(Syringa species and hybrids)

Uses:	Hedge, background, cut flowers.
Plant:	Spring.
Height:	3-10 feet.
Blooms:	April-June.
Fruits:	None.
Distance:	3-6 feet.
Soil:	Well-drained, sweet to slightly acid garden loam.
Exposure:	Sun/light shade.
Prune:	Remove part of suckers, dead wood, oldest canes.
Species:	S. chinensis (rothomagensis)—Chinese, 8-9 ft., reddish-violet, fragrant.
	S. microphylla superba, 5 ft., fragrant.
	S. persica—Persian, 8-10 ft., pale lilac, spicy fragrance.
	S. pubescens—Hairy, 10 ft., pale lilac, fragrant.
	S. villosa—Late lilac, 7-8 ft., rosy-lilac, fragrant.
	S. josikaea—Hungarian, 9-10 ft., violet, fragrant.
	S. palebinina—Dwarf Korean, 4 ft., fragrant.
Varieties:	White—single: Vestale, Jan Van Tol.
	Double: Edith Cavell, Ellen Willmott.
	Violet—single: De Mireilla, Cavour.
	Double: Marechal Lannes.
	Blue—single: Maurice Barres, President Lincoln.
	Double: Olivier de Serres, Emile Gentil, Pres. Grevy.
	Lilac—single; Marengo, Jacques Callot.
	Double: Katherine Havemeyer, Victor Lemoine.
	Pinkish—single: Lucie Ballet, Esther Staley.
	Double: Mme. A. Buchner Michael Buchner.
	Reddish—single: Marechal Foch, Chas. Jolly.
	Double: Paul Thirion, Paul Deschanel.
	Purple—single: S. Monge, Ludwig Spaeth.
	Double: Paul Hariot, Congo.

* * *

Lilac growing reaches nearly to its southern limit in the Washington area, although there are comparatively few gardens that do not contain one or more varieties. There is something about a lilac bush in the springtime that makes it somewhat of a must. In spite of our location there are many varieties and species that may be grown here. The late Dr. E. A Merritt grew many fine varieties and species, some of which are quite rare. The common lilac, Syringa vulgaris, is probably more often grown than any other species or single variety although it has less to offer the gardener. The Persian lilac which resembles the common in appearance is less stiff, flowers at a much younger age, and has more and daintier blooms.

Most lilac varieties and species are rather stiff bare-legged plants, tolerated for their bloom which is so fragrant. Because of this habit of growth, numerous suckers spring from the roots which draws somewhat upon the plant's ability to flower. Some of the suckers should be permitted to live since they may be needed to replace one or more canes should the lilac borer get in its work.

Lilacs thrive best in a neutral or sweet soil. An occasional application of ground limestone worked into the soil about the plant is needed to reduce the acidity of the soil. Wood ashes are excellent for this purpose. An annual application of compost made with limestone is another beneficial practice.

There are numerous species of lilacs which may be grown in local gardens. The Persian and the Chinese

What garden would be without a lilac bush.

are the more desirable. Of the more than 700 named varieties listed, only a few are adapted to this area. And

few gardens can accommodate or needs more than a very few. The list of varieties given here was prepared by a group of lilac specialists and includes most of those which are considered distinctive and desirable.

Lilacs are troubled with mildew in the early fall when the nights turn cool, but few consider it injurious since the foliage matures very early. However, it can be controlled with a sulphur dust or Karathane. Other diseases may appear but they are seldom encountered in local gardens. The oystershell and San Jose scales are common enemies of lilac bushes and must be controlled with a dormant spray.

Lilacs may be propagated by softwood and hardwood cuttings, although they root rather poorly. Layers are sometimes used, but budding and grafting are the more common methods. Grafting is commercially practiced on privet. It is because of this latter practice that the general recommendation is for planting varieties deeper than they grew in the nursery. In this way the plants are encouraged to develop their own roots. Shallow planting encourages the privet to develop its own top and to starve out the lilac graft.

Pruning of lilac bushes generally is limited to a thinning of the suckers, to the removal of dead wood, and where only a few bushes are grown, to the removal of the spent blooms. Renewal pruning is recommended for lilacs. Each season remove one or more of the oldest canes, depending upon the size and number of canes.

MOCKORANGE

(Philadelphus species and hybrids)

Uses:	Shrub border, cut flowers.
Plant:	Spring/fall.
Height:	4-10 feet.
Bloom:	May-August.
Fruits:	None.
Distances:	5-8 feet.
Soil:	Fertile loam, neutral.
Exposure:	Sun/light shade.
Prune:	After flowering.
Varieties:	Avalance, 4-5 feet, May-June, single, white, fragrant.
	Bouquet Blanc, 4-5 ft., June, semi-double, white, slightly fragrant.
	Boule d'Argent, 4-5 ft., June, double, white, fragrant.
	Bicolor, 6 ft., June, single, white, purple center, slightly fragrant.
	Candelabra, 4-5 ft., May-June, single, white, fragrant.
	Glacier, 4-5 ft., June, double, creamy white, slightly fragrant.
	Mount Blanc, 5 ft., May-June, single, white, fragrant.
	Snowflake, 8-10 ft., May-Aug. double, fragrant.
	Virginal, 8-10 ft., May-August, double, white, fragrant.
	P. coronarius, 9-10 ft., May-June, single, white, sweet.

* * *

The mockorange is an old popular shrub that is a favorite with many gardeners because of its excellent floral display in the spring and its delightful fragrance. Virginal is easily the best long-season variety where but one bush may be used. The flowers, largely white, are borne in clusters along the branches and the main difficulty seems to be to prune in such a way as to keep them well distributed from bottom to top of the bushes. Most gardeners neglect to prune the mockorange and the shrubs soon become barelegged. The renewal system of pruning is needed for this reason.

The mockorange is not fussy as to soil so long as it is reasonably fertile and is not too wet. They thrive in sun or light shade.

By pruning after the flowering season, new growth is encouraged from the base of the plant before the formation of new buds for the following season's bloom.

The mockorange seems to be immune to most insects and diseases, although the aphids are frequently injurious to them. They are easily controlled with nicotine sulphate or pyrethrum. The leaf miner is sometimes present and may be controlled with malathion or dimethoate spray; the latter also controls aphids.

Propagation is by softwood and hardwood cuttings. Some varieties sucker freely. The seed of the species is not difficult to start.

Mockorange blooms, single or double, bring fragrance to shrub borders in the spring.

PEARLBUSH

(Exochorda racemosa (grandiflora)

Uses:	Specimen, shrub border.
Plant:	Fall/spring.
Height:	8-10 feet.
Blooms:	April-May.
Fruits:	3-winged capsule.
Distance:	4-6 feet.
Soil:	Light, acid.
Exposure:	Sun.
Prune:	After flowering.
Species:	E. giraldi Var. Wilsoni, 10 feet.
	E. macrantha, 15 ft.

* * *

The Pearlbush is an attractive shrub when young and in full bloom. Because it is difficult to transplant, except balled and burlaped, and because it has a strong tendency to become leggy with age, it is looked upon with disfavor by many. However, the bush does have considerable landscape value if properly pruned. This should start with the young plant. The floral dis-

play is well worth the extra pruning required. An annual pruning which removes from ¼ to ⅓ of the canes at the ground is all that is needed. The Pearlbush requires a sandy, acid soil for best growth, and does not tolerate shade.

The Pearlbush is comparatively free from insect pests and diseases.

Propagation is slow although the following methods may be used: Seed, grafting, layers, and cuttings.

PRIVET

(Ligustrum species)

Uses:	Hedge, tall background.
Plant:	Fall/spring.
Height:	5-15 feet.
Blooms:	July-Sept.
Fruits:	Black, bluish-purple.
Distance:	1-3 feet.
Soil:	Ordinary garden loam.
Exposure:	Sun/light shade.
Prune:	When needed.
Species:	L. vulgare—European privet, 15 ft., black berries.
	L. ovalifolium—California, 15 ft.
	L. ibolium—Ibolium, 8-10 ft., black berries.
	L. amurense—Amur, 15 ft., black berries.
	L. quihoui—Quihou, 6 ft., black berries.
	L. obtusifolium regelianum—Regal, 5-6 ft., black berries.
	L. lucidium—Glossy, 8-12 ft., black berries.

* * *

The privets are a group of evergreen or semi-evergreen shrubs widely used for hedges, tall screens, and background plantings. They withstand unfavorable soil, shade, and city conditions better than most other similar types of shrubs. Some, such as the California privet,

How to Plant a Hedge.

may be pruned to a narrow hedge. Most of the privets hold their foliage well into the winter in this area and seldom suffer freeze injury. Even though injured, they need only be cut back to live wood.

The privets are easily transplanted either in spring or fall. For quick recovery it is well to cut them back almost to the ground.

Most of the privets produce small racemes of white flowers during the summer, which are followed in the fall by black or bluish-black fruits. The flowers are objectionable to some because of their odor, which is unknown to most of us because clipped hedges do not produce blooms.

The Regal privet is a useful large shrub where space

Care in planting and pruning has much to do with the future appearance of a hedge.

permits its use. The Glossy, Japanese, and Quihou are considered to have exceptional landscape values. The Glossy (Ligustrum) cannot withstand winter winds in suburban areas.

The privets are sometimes attacked by fungus diseases and scale insets. Both, however, are normally controlled with a dormant strength limesulphur spray during the winter months after the foliage has fallen.

The privets are easily propagated by cuttings, the hardwood cuttings rooting without difficulty.

RHODODENDRONS

(R. species and hybrids)

Uses:	Shrub border, foundation planting, specimen, cut flowers.
Plant:	Spring.
Height:	1-20 feet.
Blooms:	March-June.
Fruits:	None.
Distance:	3-6 feet.
Soil:	Enriched with leafmold, compost or peatmoss.
Exposure:	Shade-sun.
Prune:	Cutting the flowers usually sufficient.
Species:	R. carolinianum—Carolina, 4-6 ft., pink, sun, light/shade.
	R. catawbiense—Catawba, 6-9 ft., rosy-lavender, sun/shade.
	R. keiskei—Keisk—2 ft.-3 ft., yellow.
	R. minus—Piedmont, 6-20 ft., lilac-purple, shade.
	R. racemosum—Mayflower, 1 ft., light rose, shade.
	R. smirnowi—Smirnow, 6 ft., rosy-lilac, shade.
	R. mucronulatum—Korean, 4-5 ft., lilac-rose, sun/shade.

Hardiness Rating	Variety	Color	Habit of Growth
	Varieties		
	Top Dozen		
H-1	Album Elegans	White	T
H-1	America	Dark red	M
H-2	Blue Peter	Lavender-blue	L
H-1	Catawbiense Album	White	M
H-2	Everestianum	Rosy, lilac	M
H-2	Gomer Waterer	White	M
H-1	Ignatius Sargent	Deep pink	M
H-2	Mars	Deep red	M
H-1	Nova Zembla	Dark red	M
H-2	Purple Splendor	Dark purple	M
H-1	Roseum Elegans	Soft rose	M
H-3	Vulcan	Bright red	M
	Also Good		
H-2	Mme. Masson	White, yellow blotch	M
H-1	English Roseum	Pink	
H-1	Parson's Gloriosum	Orchid pink	M
H-2	Lee's Dark Purple	Purple	M
H-1	Caractacus	Purplish red	M
H-2	Dr. V. H. Rutgers	Aniline red	M
H-1	E. S. Rand	Red, yellow eye	L
H-2	Pink Perfection	True pink	M
	Dwarfs		
H-3	Blue Tit	Bright blue	
H-2	Impeditum	Purple blue	
H-2	Ocean Lake	Deep blue	

Hardiness Rating	Height
H-1—Hardy to 25° below zero	L—3-4 feet
H-2—Hardy to 15° below zero	M—4-6 feet
H-3—Hardy to 5° below zero	T—over 6 feet
H-4—Hardy to 5° above zero	

(Recommended by Dr. Henry Skinner, Fred Coe, Albert Behnke and others.)

* * *

There are some 850 known species of rhododendrons and 2,000 varieties to choose from. Those listed here have been given ratings by the rhododendron groups of England and our Pacific Northwest. However, they did not have this area in mind when rating the various species and varieties. No doubt they have selected those with the best floral characteristics and foliage values, and for that reason we can use their ratings. Many more kinds which they consider lacking in hardiness may be adapted to this area.

Rhododendrons as a group like some shade. A few cannot withstand direct sunlight. This is true of the one most commonly planted, the Rosebay, which is native to the Alleghanies where it thrives in deep shade in moist soils. The Catawba and the Carolina rhododendrons and their hybrids can withstand considerable direct sun although they are likely to be at their best in partial or light shade. A moist yet well drained soil freely supplied with leaf-mold, compost, or peat moss is needed for good growth. Avoid planting in heavy Washington clay soil unless the whole area has been so extensively or deeply dug that water cannot remain standing about the plant roots. Rhododendrons are shallow-rooted and must be planted practically on top of the soil. Protection from strong winds is desirable.

A winter mulching with oak leaves or pine needles is beneficial. The mulch should remain during the summer months to keep the soil cool. An oak leaf mulch helps to maintain the soil acidity needed for good growth, but may need supplementing with an inexpensive grade of sulphur.

If these ideal cultural conditions are observed—shade, moisture, protection from injurious wind, and a generous mulch—there is little danger of diseases attacking the planting. Lacking in this care, there is some likelihood of disease and insect attack. The lace-bug is the most common and is controlled by spraying or dusting with malathion in the late spring and early summer, or with dimethoate in May.

Propagation is not easy without special equipment. Grafting, layering, and the rooting of cuttings are the methods employed by commercial growers.

ROSE OF SHARON

(Hibiscus syriacus—Shrub althea)

Uses:	Shrub border, hedge, specimen.
Plant:	Spring/fall.
Height:	10-12 feet.
Blooms:	August.
Fruits:	———
Distance:	2-6 feet.
Soil:	Ordinary moist garden loam.
Exposure:	Sun/shade.
Prune:	Early spring.
Varieties:	Blue Bird—Single blue.
	W. R. Smith, single white.
	Jeanne d'Arc (Flore alba plena), double white.
	Bicolor, white, dark center, semi-double.
	Coelestis, single, violet-blue.
	Boule de Feu, single, violet pink.
	Peony, semi-double, light pink with red center.
	Woodbridge, deep pink.
	Hamabo, white with red eye.

* * *

The Rose of Sharon is a tall, upright-growing shrub that will tolerate almost any kind of situation, although it thrives best in a moist, loamy soil. It may be used as a specimen bush, as a hedge, or in the shrub border where its late summer bloom is often useful. There are many named varieties available in single, semi-double, and double forms.

The Rose of Sharon is untroubled by disease. The Japanese beetle delights in eating the flower petals, so a protective spray or dust may be needed to curb them.

The Rose of Sharon should be pruned in the early spring to whatever form is needed. Heavy pruning stimulates new growth and better flowers.

Propagation is by cuttings, although seeds germinate readily. Most seedlings, however, are lacking in form and clearness of colors.

SPIREA

(Spirea species and hybrids)

Uses:	Shrub border, foundation planting, hedge, specimen.
Plant:	Spring/fall.
Height:	3-9 feet.
Blooms:	Mar.-Aug.
Fruits:	None.
Distance:	3-6 feet.
Soil:	Good garden loam.
Exposure:	Sun.
Prune:	Spring flowering—after flowering.
	Summer flowering—spring.
Species:	S. thunbergi—Thunberg's, 4-5 ft., Mar.-Apr., white.
	S. arguta—Garland, 5-6 ft., Mar.-Apr., white.
	S. prunifolia—Bridalwreath, 5-7 ft., May, white.
	S. van houtti—Van Houtte, 6-9 ft., May, white.
	S. bumalda var. Anthony Waterer, 3 ft., Crispa 2-2½ ft., June-Aug., rosy-crimson, var. Coccinea, 3 ft., June-Aug.
	S. billardi—Billard's, 5-6 ft., June-Sept., rose.
	S. trilobata, Swan Lake, 3-4 ft., white, May.
	S. japonica alpina—Daphne 1 ft., May, pink.
	S. nipponica—Snow Mound, 3-4 ft., June, white.

* * *

The spireas comprise a large and varied group of deciduous shrubs that are widely used for landscape planting. They are mostly spring bloomers although there are several which flower throughout the summer. Most spireas are tolerant of soil and exposure, although they do best in full sun in a good garden loam.

While a number of hybrids have been produced, for the most part they are listed as species. Most of them seem to be adapted to the Washington area. The most commonly grown species, Van Houtte's spirea, is a graceful spreading bush that needs considerable space. The dwarf Anthony Waterer is very compact and useful in the foreground. The upright grower, Billard's spirea, is a vigorous grower producing rosy pink, fuzzy blooms intermittently throughout the summer. The double flowered Bridalwreath with gracefully drooping branches is still a favorite with many.

Thunbergi is the first to flower in the spring. In fact, it will flower in February during periods of mild weather. Arguta is an improved hybrid of thunbergi.

The spireas are easily transplanted as well as propagated. Hardwood cuttings taken in August root readily. Division of Anthony Waterer, Billard, and Bridalwreath are comparatively easy.

Diseases and insect pests are not troublesome, except for the aphids which congregate on the tender young tips in the spring.

SWEETSHRUB

(Calycanthus floridus—Sweet scented shrub)
(Carolina Allspice)

Uses:	Shrub border.
Plant:	Spring/fall.
Height:	4-5 feet.
Blooms:	May-June.
Fruits:	Interesting capsules.
Distance:	4-6 feet.
Soil:	Moist, medium garden loam.
Exposure:	Partial shade.
Prune:	Spring.
Species:	C. floridus—Sweet shrub, fragrant, purplish-brown flowers.
	C. fertilis (glaucus)—Pale, purplish-brown, not as fragrant.
	C. occidentalis—Calif. Sweetshrub, not reliably hardy.

*   *   *

The Sweetshrub, an ornamental shrub of good landscape value, is grown largely for sentimental value. Its spicy fragrance is its chief charm since the chocolate-colored flowers are hardly beautiful.

The Sweetshrub is easily grown in the average garden, although it does best in light shade and in not too dry a situation. There are some strains which are lacking in fragrance and should be avoided. This, of course, is not easily done since the bush must be in bloom to determine its fragrance.

The other species listed, Pale and California, are less desirable in that they are not reliably hardy here and if anything lack the spiceness of the Sweetshrub.

Propagation is by division, softwood cuttings, root-cuttings which root rather freely, and by seed. Mound layering is also practicable.

The Sweetshrub seems to be comparatively free of insect pests and diseases.

VIBURNUMS

(Viburnum species and hybrids)

Uses:	Background, shrub border, specimens.
Plant:	Fall/spring.
Height:	1-30 feet.
Blooms:	Mar.-June.
Fruits:	Red, black, blue, yellow.
Distance:	4-8, 15 feet.
Soil:	Moist, enriched with humus, sandy loam, pH 5.5-6.5.
Exposure:	Shade/sun.
Prune:	Spring.
Species:	V. trilobum-American Cranberry bush, 8-12 ft., white blossoms, May, red fruit, sun/shade.
	V. opulus Nanum-Dwarf Cranberry bush, 2-3 ft., white, May, no fruit, sun/shade.
	V. opulus Compactum, 2-3 ft., creamy-white, May, red fruit, sun/shade.
	V. dentatum-Arrow-wood, 10-12 ft., white, June, blue-black, sun/shade.
	V. rhytidophyllum-Leatherleaf, 6-15 ft., white, May, red/black, shade.
	V. sieboldi-Siebold, 8-30 ft., white, May, red-black, sun.
	V. sargenti-Sargeant, 12 ft., white, May, red, sun/shade.
	V. carlesi-Korean spice (Fragrant), 4-6 ft., pink, April, blue-black, sun/shade.
	V. plicatum tomentosum-Double-file, 6-12 ft., white, May, blue-black, sun.
	V. plicatum tomentosum—Mariesi, 6-12 ft., white, May, red, sun.
	V. cassinoides—Withe-rod, 5-6 ft., white, June, yellowish-green, sun.
	V. burkwoodi—Burkwood, 4-6 ft., pinkish-white, Apr., blue-black, shade.
	V. acerifolium—Dockmackie, 3-6 ft., yellowish-white, June, black, shade-dry.
	V. plicatum (tomentosum sterile)—Jap. snowball, 10 ft., white, May, sun.
	V. carlcephalum, 6-7 ft., creamy-white, Apr., black, sun/shade.
	V. wrighti-4-6 ft., white, May, red, sun/shade.
	V. bodnantense—Bodnant, 10 ft., pale pink, Mar.-April, black, sun/shade.
	V. opulus Xanthocarpum, Yellow European Cranberry-bush, 12 ft., white, May, yellow, sun.
	V. dilatatum—Linden, 6-10 ft., cream-white, May, red, sun/shade.
	V. dilatatum Xanthocarpum, 6-10 ft., cream-white, May, yellow, sun/shade.
	V. farreri (fragranse-Fragrant), 9 ft., pale-pink, Mar.-Apr., red/black, sun/shade.
	V. farreri alba (Fragranse alba), 9 ft., white, Mar.-Apr., yellow/black, shade.
	V. lantana—Wayfaring, 6-15 ft., cream, May, orange/black, sun.
	V. prunifolium—Black Haw, 15 ft., cream-white, May, blue/black, sun, red autumn foliage.
	V. setigerum—Tea, 12 ft., white, May, red, sun/shade.

*   *   *

The Viburnum group is large and varied and includes a number of native shrubs of varying degree of usefulness for landscape planting. The Leatherleaf is an evergreen, and Burkwood is semi-evergreen. The American Cranberrybush and the Japanese Snowball are excellent shrubs for the tall border. The latter, V. plicatum (Tomentosum sterile) is much superior to the

common snowball (V. opulus var. roseum) which is badly troubled by aphids, but is more difficult to transplant. Buy it B&B and in the spring.

Most of the viburnums are too large for the ordinary city lot. The fragrant viburnum, however, is a small grower as are the Dwarf Cranberry and Compactum. The latter has fruit, the former none. Carlcephalum is of moderate size as is Wrighti.

Most of the viburnums require moist soils that are loamy with a pH of 5.5 to 6.5. There are some, such as V. acerifolium, V. dentatum, V. lantana and V. opulus, that thrive in drier situations. Viburnum dentatum tends to form thickets in a moist situation and so is best used in a woodlands area rather than the shrub border.

V. Siebold, has an unpleasant odor and is best planted at some distance from the house. The foliage of the Leatherleaf is large and striking and should not be used in the smaller shrub border.

The viburnums are readily propagated by softwood cuttings. The V. carlesi is commercially propagated by root grafts and by budding which may be subject to "Graft Blight" and preference should be given to own root plants. Layering is used to multiply some species; root cuttings may be used on one or two species. Growing from seed is a somewhat complex process and is only used for the species.

The aphids are the principal insect pest on the viburnums and they are not serious except on the common Snowball. Diseases are not common.

WEIGELA

(Weigela species and hybrids)

Use:	Shrub border, specimen planting, cut flowers.
Plant:	Fall/spring.
Height:	4-10 feet.
Bloom:	June-September.
Fruits:	None.
Distance:	6-10 feet.
Soil:	Ordinary garden loam.
Exposure:	Sun.
Prune:	After flowering.
Varieties:	Eva Rathke—4-5 ft., crimson.
	Bristol Ruby, 6-7 ft., ruby red.
	Bristol Snowflake, 6-7 ft., June.
	Vanicek, 6-8 ft., purplish-red, June
	Boskoop Glory—4-5 ft., salmon-pink.
	W. Floribunda, 10 ft., dark crimson, May-June.
	W. florida, 6 ft., rose-pink, May-June.
	W. florida, venasta, rose-pink, May.

* * *

The weigelas are noted for their showy displays. Masses of tubular flowers are produced each spring on the wide spreading branches. The foliage is dull and the coarse dark-colored branches offer little in the way of landscape value. It is the floral effect which is outstanding.

The Weigela thrives in any good garden soil that has sufficient moisture. It is relatively untroubled by insects and diseases.

The many hybrids which have been produced differ in growth and flower habits. Eva Rathke has the longest flowering season, although the spring display is the best. It is one of the least shapely.

The Weigela is easily propagated by softwood and hardwood cuttings which root readily. Grafting may also be employed for this purpose.

CHAPTER XI

EVERGREENS FOR HOME PLANTING

The use of coniferous or narrow-leaved evergreens in the landscaping of the home grounds in the Washington area is general. They are well adapted to this purpose, although there are far too many forest trees drafted for this temporary use. Well selected evergreens of the proper size (at maturity) have excellent landscape values and give relatively permanent values.

There are a number of coniferous evergreens suitable for foundation planting such as the dwarf forms of arbor-vitae, juniper, pine, yew, and false-cypress. Note the reference to dwarf forms or varieties—there are varieties of evergreens just as there are varieties of roses. Some are good for one purpose while others have different values in the landscaping of the home grounds. For specimen plantings in the lawn or background, taller growing evergreens may well be used, but for hedges and foundation plantings the low-growing kinds and varieties are desirable, because they stay put with less effort on the part of the home owner, and for a longer period of time.

Evergreens generally are rather adaptable, although they may be expected to give the best results if planted in suitable locations. Obviously a sun-loving juniper will not do well in dense shade. On the other hand, the shade-loving yew and hemlock will do reason-ably well in full sun provided they have ample moisture. The junipers as a group will thrive in hotter, drier situations than the others. The hemlock and the yew are the most tolerant of shade. Northern adapted species, such as the spruce, balsam, and the firs, with few exceptions, do not thrive too well under local conditions.

Most evergreens do not benefit by constant stirring of the soil, a good mulch is much more to their liking. They need a soil that is reasonably well supplied with humus—compost, peatmoss—at the time of planting. This provides moisture for the roots and that is important to their health and vigor. Evergreens need a good supply of moisture during the late fall and early winter. A few evergreens, such as the hemlock and the Oriental arbor-vitae, do not thrive in wind-swept locations.

Lime is seldom beneficial to evergreens. They do best in an acid soil. Fertilizing is seldom needed if the soil is kept mulched. Lacking a good mulch some feeding may be necessary. As a rule the average commercial fertilizer is looked on as injurious to evergreens, probably because of its use in the planting hole. Small applications on the surface of the ground around an established tree may be beneficial. However, feeding for growth is seldom desirable since all but the dwarf varie-

The principal forms of evergreens are: 1. Broad or spreading, 2. pyramidal, 3. columnar, 4. globe, 5. spreading, and 6. trailer or creeping.

ties will outgrow their situation too quickly. If an evergreen seems to lack thrift and vigor, it should be examined for insect infestations or disease first. If free of them, then feeding may be needed.

Most evergreens except spruce, Deodar cedar and Douglas fir, need an annual pruning to keep them compact and youthful in appearance. This trimming is best made in March or in September, just before the new growth appears. The pruning cuts are soon covered by new growth. Clipping to a formal outline should be avoided except in a "formal" planting. If the pruning cuts are made close to a fork or to a clump of foliage, disfiguring dead stubs will not be noticeable.

The principal pest of evergreens in this area is the red spider mite. The control of this pest may be had in several ways. A strong blast of water from the hose will knock most of them to the ground except in very compact specimens. Malathion dust has been effectively used. A new systemic dimethoate is even more useful in controlling sucking insects. Dimethoate will control bagworms, mites, midges, aphids and some of the scale insects. Wet the foliage with a coarse spray, using 2 teaspoonsful per gallon of water. Apply in May.

Evergreens have other pests as well as diseases, but they are not generally encountered, unless, perhaps

it is the juniper web-worm. This pest may be controlled with DDT applied in May and June. The Malathion also will control it. Occasionally another web-worm attacks pines and needs the same control measures. It is much more easily noted because of the webbing at branch tips.

In selecting evergreens for the home grounds it is well to note three things—height at maturity, exposure, and moisture. Some variation in foliage is desirable, although off-colored evergreens which attract attention rather than provide a harmonious setting for the home, may be too freely used because they are "so different."

The following evergreens are listed according to the approximate height at maturity.

TALL GROWING EVERGREENS
(30 ft. or more)

Concolor Fir	70-80 ft.	Abies concolor
Plume cypress	25-35 ft.	Chamaecyparis plumosa
Deodor Cedar	35-50 ft.	Cedrus deodara
Virginia redcedar	35-50 ft.	Juniperus virginiana
Black Hills spruce	50-60 ft.	Picea canadensis
Norway spruce	80-100 ft.	Picea excelsa
Colorado Blue spruce	60-80 ft.	Picea pungens
Koster Blue spruce	60-80 ft.	Picea pungens kosteri
White pine	80-100 ft.	Pinus strobus
Douglas fir	70-80 ft.	Pseudotsuga douglassi
Canada hemlock	75-90 ft.	Tsuga canadensis

MEDIUM TALL EVERGREENS
(15-30 ft.)

Sawara retinospora	25-35 ft.	Chamaecyparis pisifera
Thread retinospora	15-20 ft.	Chamaecyparis filifera
Goldenplume retinospora	20-25 ft.	Chamaecyparis plumosa aurea
Hinoki cypress	10-20 ft.	Chamaesyparis obtusa gracilis
Chinese juniper	15-30 ft.	Juniperus chinensis
Column Chinese juniper	15-30 ft.	Juniperus chinensis pyramidalis
Keteleer Redcedar	15-20 ft.	Juniperus chinensis keteleeri
Cannart Redcedar	25-30 ft.	Juniperus virginiana cannarti
Schott Redcedar	25-30 ft.	Juniperus virginiana schotti
Swiss Stone pine	10-20 ft.	Pinus cembra
Hick's Yew	20-25 ft.	Taxus cuspidata hicksi
Upright Japanese yew	25-40 ft.	Taxus cuspidata capitata

MEDIUM EVERGREENS
(10-15 ft.)

Spiny Greek juniper	10-12 ft.	Juniperus excelsa stricta
Spreading Japanese yew	10-15 ft.	Taxus cuspidata
Hybrid yew	12-15 ft.	Taxus intermedia
Siberian arborvitae	12-15 ft.	Thuya occidentalis wareana

UNTRIMMED AND LOOSE SHINGLED CLIPPED

Evergreens should be regularly pruned to keep them compact and within bounds. However, the pruning should take the form of a shingling, rather than a formal clipping which destroys their natural appearance.

EVERGREENS FOR HOME PLANTING

George Peabody arborvitae	10-15 ft.	Thuya occidentalis lutea
Vervaene arborvitae	8-12 ft.	Thuya occidentalis vervaeneana
Douglas Golden arborvitae	10-15 ft.	Thuya occidentalis douglassi aurea
Oriental arborvitae	10-15 ft.	Thuya orientalis pyramidalis

LOW-GROWING EVERGREENS
(3-10 ft.)

Football cypress	4-6 ft.	Chamaecyparis obtusa compacta
Dwarf Hinoki cypress	3-10 ft.	Chamaecyparis obtusa nana
Pfitzer juniper	5-6 ft.	Juniperus chinensis pfitzeriano
Savin juniper	6-7 ft.	Juniperus sabina
Meyer juniper	3-4 ft.	Juniperus squamata meyeri
Dwarf Alberta spruce	6-8 ft.	Picea glauca conica
Mugo pine	4-8 ft.	Pinus montana mugus
Thayer's yew	6-8 ft.	Taxus cuspidata thayeri
Hatfield yew	8-10 ft.	Taxus hatfieldi
Globe arborvitae	3-4 ft.	Thuya occidentalis globosa
Hovey arborvitae	3-4 ft.	Thuya occidentalis hoveyi
Rosethal arborvitae	6-10 ft.	Thuya occidentalis rosenthalli
Goldspire arborvitae	7-8 ft.	Thuya orientalis aurea conspicus
Yellowcolumn arborvitae	7-8 ft.	Thuya orientalis elegantissima

Under 3 feet.

Spreading English yew	1½-2 ft.	Taxus baccata repandens
Dwarf Japanese yew	2-3 ft.	Taxus cuspidata nana
Parson's arborvitae	2½-4 ft.	Thuya occidentalis compacta
Little Gem arborvitae	2-3 ft.	Thuya occidentalis pumila
Berckman's Golden arborvitae	2½-3 ft.	Thuya orientalis auera nana

CREEPERS

Sargent juniper	1½ ft.	Juniperus Chinensis sargenti
Creeping juniper	1-1½ ft.	Juniperus horizontalis
Waukegan juniper	1-1½ ft.	Juniperus horizontalis douglasi
Prostrate juniper	1½ ft.	Juniperus communis depressa
Tamarix Savin juniper		
Shore juniper	1 ft.	Juniperus conferta

Cultural Notes

The firs (Abies) are attractive, tall-growing evergreens. They retain their lower branches very well, are pyramidal shaped, and are valuable in the larger landscape plantings. They thrive best in a moderately moist, though well-drained, soil containing an ample supply of humus.

The true cedars (Cedrus) are rather tall growing, although they may be restrained for a time by judicious pruning. However, they are too widespreading for the smaller lot. The colorful foliage and graceful low-hanging branches make them especially attractive. They need a rich soil and moderate moisture.

The retinosporas, sometimes called False cypress, and properly identified as Chamaecyparis, have both a juvenile and a mature foliage which is exceedingly confusing. Thus they carry a number of names. Commonly used in the foundation planting because they are inexpensive, the taller varieties are best used in the background or for windbreaks. The dwarf varieties do well in the foundation plantings where they receive sufficient sunlight and moisture. In shade and in dry soils they become open and unattractive.

The junipers constitute one of the largest evergreen groups for use in landscape plantings. While some of the junipers are hosts of the apple rust, they are so well adapted to hot dry situations and to pruning that they

Plant the evergreen in a roomy hole. Fill the space about the balled plant with a soil mixture containing compost or peatmoss. A good soaking is the last step.

are one of the most useful of the evergreen groups. The Irish juniper (J. communis hibernica) is omitted from the list because of its lack of vigor and health in this area.

Actually there are more aborvitae used in the landscaping of the home grounds than junipers, but they require a moderate supply of moisture, will not tolerate shade, and unless pruned regularly, lose their compact healthy appearance. However, they are useful and the dwarf varieties should be used where conditions are favorable.

The Washington area is in many ways too far south for the use of the spruces. Also, with but few exceptions, the spruces are too vigorous for use on the average city lot. They need a sunny situation and a moist but well drained soil.

The pines are not widely used in the planting of the home grounds, although the Mugo pine is small enough for the well-drained, rather dry bank or terrace.

The Douglas fir is a beautiful large-growing tree that merits more consideration where space permits its use. It thrives in a moist sunny situation.

The dark green, slow-growing yews are widely employed for landscaping in the Washington area. They are one of the few kinds of evergreens that are not troubled by dogs. Because they are low growing, slow growing, and have a rich foliage, they deserve full use. Actually some species and varieties are rather tall at maturity. Few people are troubled by the mature height because of the slow rate of growth and the ease by which they may be kept to desired heights through pruning. The yews thrive in shade as well as in sunny situations, provided they receive a moderate amount of moisture.

The second shade lover, the hemlock, is too strong a grower for most situations. However, it may be kept to a fairly low stature through regular pruning. The hemlocks thrive best in a moist soil. The Carolina hemlock is a bit more fussy as to growing conditions than the more commonly planted Canadian hemlock.

123

Protection From Animals

The protection of evergreens from animals, especially from dogs, is necessary if the trees or shrubs are to retain their natural shape and symmetry. Various chemical repellants are sold for this purpose, but they are volatile materials which must be regularly renewed to accomplish the purpose. Metal frames with sharp spines that protrude from the foliage constitute something of a hazard to passersby, particularly if small children play in the area, but are more or less permanent, needing only to be moved to keep pace with growth. The planting of a protective circle of barberry bushes about the evergreen also gives long-lasting protection, although they must be moved from time to time to prevent affecting the growth of the lower branches of the evergreen.

THE BOXWOOD

(Buxus sempervirens)

Boxwoods are commonly looked upon as the aristocrats of the broadleaved evergreens, especially the slow-growing or English boxwood. They give an atmosphere of grace, charm and solidity to the landscape that no other shrub can give. It might well be said that the Potomac Valley is their home for they have been grown in this area from early Colonial times. The rich green foliage and the billowy outline undoubtedly have much to do with their widespread popularity. And their freedom from serious pests is another factor, as is their tolerance to soil and exposure.

The boxwood is often used as the main feature of the landscaping in gardens of all sizes. Large specimens are to be found on the Cathedral grounds, at Mount Vernon, around the Lincoln Memorial, Woodlawn, and many other well known places of national interest. At Dumbarton Oaks there are thousands of plants of all sizes. Some are used as accent points, others for borders and dividers, while small-sized plants are used as edgings. The English boxwood is the mainstay in all of these plantings, but elsewhere the so-called American box may be seen, primarily used as a hedge plant.

Botanically the boxwood is *Buxus sempervirens*. Authorities now classify the English and the American box as the same species. The variations of foliage and growth habits are given variety (clone) names. Variety *arborescens* is the large form, probably the one commonly referred to as the American box. Variety *rotundifolia* has broadly oval leaves and is thought to be hardier than the others. Others are: *B. sempervirens var. bulata, myrtifolia, angustifolia,* as well as two varieties with variegated foliage.

In addition to the English box, there is a compact shrub from Japan, *Buxus microphylla*. This species is represented by two varieties—*japonica* and *koreana*.

The latter is believed to be the hardiest of all boxwood and is a shrub of moderate size.

The boxwood are of easiest culture, although they do resent deep planting. They are shallow-rooted and will suffer if planted one inch too deeply. Because of this shallow-root system they should not be cultivated except with extreme care.

The compact root system of the boxwood is the reason there is very little loss in transplanting. It holds the soil firmly and there is little exposure of the roots to drying sun and wind even when not balled.

Boxwood are best planted in the spring at which time it is advisable to incorporate generous quantities of compost plus a moderate amount of well-rotted cow manure in the planting hole. Do not use chemical fertilizers in the planting hole. Fertilizing after planting is best done in the very early spring so that the plants will have ample time in which to take up the plant food, to make the new growth, and that growth mature or ripen before winter. Heavy feeding should be avoided at all times. Some recommend only feeding every other year.

Pests

The boxwood are not free of pests, but the only one that is troublesome is the boxwood leaf miner. Formerly it was somewhat difficult to control, but with the advent of DDT and methoxychlor, this pest is not considered much of a problem. Another pest, probably less frequently encountered, is the boxwood psylla which causes cupping of the terminal leaves. Most gardeners ascribe the cupping to the weather or some other cause and do not attempt a control. A dimethoate spray may be used as the new growth appears and is an effective control. A combination spray of malathion and methoxychlor could be used for both pests but must be applied in mid-May to be effective.

Another problem that is sometimes prevalent in the Washington area is called, "Die-back." In most cases, it stems from the decay of leaves in the crotches of these twiggy shrubs. Nectria, a disease that is common in decaying vegetable matter, is the cause. Starting in the decaying leaves, the roots (Mycelium) of this fungus extend through the dead leaf mass and into the moist bark of the branches. Once inside the branches, the leaves show the drain and are small and pale. If allowed to go unchecked the branches may die. Cleaning out the leaves each season is the best preventative of this condition (die-back). This may be done by hand, with a whisk broom, a strong blast from the hose, or perhaps better still with a vacuum cleaner. The metal tube, should, if pushed down into the twigs, pick up most of the leaves present.

If this disease condition should exist, the best practice is to prune out all infected wood and to spray with any good fungicide.

EVERGREENS FOR HOME PLANTING

EDITOR'S NOTE: There has been very little research on boxwood culture. The above cultural notes are based upon the information available from the U. S. Department of Agriculture and other sources, primarily from the horticulturists in the area. However, in 1961 the American Boxwood Society was organized at the Orland E. White Research Arboretum (University of Virginia), Boyce, Virginia. This organization will undoubtedly foster research on all phases of this valuable broad-leaved evergreen.

The boxwood nematode has appeared in damaging numbers in some parts of the Washington area. This pest, if present, may be controlled with Nemagon. It is applied in a trench around the established plant. This method is likely to be the more practical for most gardeners. The manufacturers' directions should be followed accurately and completely if satisfactory results are to be had without injury to the boxwood.

Winter Protection

Boxwood benefit from slat coverings during the winter, although in most winters they receive no injury. In the Washington area there is the likelihood every few years of a heavy wet snow that bows the branches. Usually they spring back into shape after the snow is gone. However, there is the chance that they will be a bit mishapen.

A more serious form of winter injury, such as occurred in 1960-61, stems from the weather. Whenever there is a very mild fall followed by a sharp freeze, the boxwood can sustain serious injury and there is little that can be done to prevent it. It was noted, however, following that winter that most of the boxwood protected by slat or other coverings suffered the least injury.

Boxwood edgings around rose beds and flower borders are more likely to need protection than the larger specimens in the lawn. Those near beds receiving fertilizer and water obviously remain in a softer condition and thus are most likely to be injured. Such borders might well be covered with burlap shelters as can be made from wire and burlap.

CHAPTER XII

GARDENING IN THE SHADE

A shaded area on a part of the home grounds is both pleasant and desirable, but may present some special problems to convert it into a garden. The use or development of such an area is desirable since, if allowed to remain undeveloped, it may become an eyesore. Whether the area be large or small is not as important as it is that it be made to contribute to the family's pleasure.

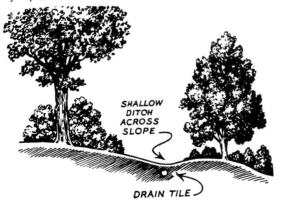

The shady garden on a slope should be protected from the "wash" from adjacent areas. A shallow ditch across the top of the slope above the garden area may suffice, but if necessary it may be supplemented with a tile drain to carry the run-off away.

Shade is a relative term, one that cannot be accurately defined. Normally, we think of shade as dense, medium or light. Shade on the north side of a building and under a low-spreading tree is likely to be dense. Under a spreading tree, such as an ash, the shade is probably medium dense. Under a dogwood, birch or apple tree the shade is light. There are plants which will thrive in each situation, although the flowering plants and shrubs adapted to dense shade are comparatively few. By removing the lower limbs of the trees, many more kinds of plants and shrubs may be grown than where the limbs are low. In other words, well trimmed trees permit more light and air and thus are more favorable to plant growth.

Shaded areas, whether on a slope or on the level, may be developed into gardens and out-of-doors recreation areas through the use of many kinds of plants provided the plants are placed in favorable growing conditions. This is the fundamental step that must be solved first. However, where there is a surface-wash problem, it should be taken care of before any effort is made to improve the soil.

Control of surface wash from surrounding areas usually involves some form of a diversion program. If a shallow ditch can be dug across the top of the bank or at the edge of the shaded area, which will carry the water to one side or the other of the garden, the job may not be difficult. If the flow of water cannot be diverted by a ditch, it may be necessary to erect a retaining wall with a tile drain to carry the water away. This involves more construction than the other, but regardless of the method of control, it is essential that no large volume of water be allowed to flow over the garden, washing away the top soil and flooding plant beds.

If the shaded area is covered with roots from shallow-rooted trees, the problem of preparing for shade loving plants is difficult and restrictive. Areas filled with tree roots are best handled by creating pockets in which plants are placed and given some protection from the greedy roots. Bulbs and other early spring-flowering plants are likely to thrive under such competition and provide most of the bloom.

Under deep rooted trees the problem is one of preparing the soil for the desired kinds of shrubs and plants. But first, it should be noted that few plants will thrive under a black walnut tree—its roots are toxic to some kinds of plants and shrubs, especially to members of the rhododendron family. Under oaks and hickory trees where roots are not a problem the soil should be enriched to a depth of 18 to 24 inches with compost, peatmoss, or other forms of humus. Normally, leaves are a problem in such a yard, but if composted they will serve this purpose very well, the only expense being the labor of putting the leaves through the compost pile and then spading the partially rotted humus into the soil.

One seldom needs to add lime to the shade areas since practically all shade-loving plants thrive in an acid soil. However, most of the soils in this area lack phosphate and because phosphate travels very slowly through the soil, it should be added in some form at time of preparation. Bone meal mixed into the soil at

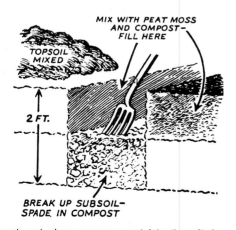

Mixing compost, and where necessary, sand into the soil, is an essential soil improvement practice for the shady garden.

the same time as the compost will provide a source of phosphate as well as some calcium.

Some variation in the preparation of the soil may be needed to take care of the requirements of special plant groups. Some may need a lighter soil and the addition of sand. Others may thrive in a moist soil, and the moisture holding capacity of peatmoss may be needed. These requirements will be noted in the discussion of groups of shade loving plants.

Planting the Shady Garden

Most of the early spring flowering bulbs thrive in a shady situation and may be depended upon for a fine floral display in the early spring. Perennials, bulbs, shrubs, and ferns will furnish most of the plant materials for the shady garden. The range in size, cultural requirements and season of bloom are considerable, and a careful selection should be made so that the shady garden will provide the color and enjoyment desired. To be effective, it should be as carefully planned as a perennial border. Height of plants, flowering season, and foliage values are important in making the plan.

The planting of the shady garden will of necessity be spread over a considerable period because not all of the plants are dormant at any one season. Many of them will die if transplanted at any time except when dormant. This is why so many collected wildflowers (usually dug while in bloom) die. However, by ordering the plants from a specialist they will be shipped at the proper season and will be of the right size, with a good compact root system to insure a good start .

Most shady gardens in this area will depend upon rhododendrons, the hollies, hollygrape, camellia, azaleas, laurel, Leucothe, andromeda, and dogwoods to provide the background. These plants will thrive in shade, although some varieties do best in a lighter shade than do the others. All need an acid soil, one that is well supplied with humus—preferably a mixture of peatmoss and oakleaf compost. These plants are normally set out in the early spring. The smaller sizes of dogwood are recommended since they suffer less shock and are thus less likely to attack by the "flatheaded apple borer."

Blueberries might be added to the list, but because the squirrels and birds love the fruit, little should be expected of them in a shady wild-flower garden, other than their foliage.

The azaleas are of value in the shady garden, coming as they do in all heights of growth and with flowering seasons from late March to mid-June. There are low-growing evergreen azaleas for beds and foreground planting. The tall deciduous species and varieties blend well with background shrubbery. Only a few azaleas will tolerate wet soils—R. viscosum (Swamp azalea) is the one most commonly grown.

Most of the hollies—American, English, Chinese, Japanese—thrive in medium to light shade, in a soil well supplied with compost. A male pollen parent is required for berry production of all except the Japanese and a few varieties of the English. They all require medium moisture and are a failure in dry soils or in soggy low spots with the exception of Winterberry (I. verticillata), which thrives in rather moist soils.

The Summersweet (Clethra alnifolia) is a summer-flowering shrub that will grow in moist soils in light shade, but reaches a height of six to eight feet and thus cannot be used in the smaller garden.

The cotoneasters thrive in shade, and their glossy foliage, neat habit of growth, and shining fruits make them desirable. The squirrels are not satisfied to harvest the berries, but cut off whole branches laden with fruit and carry them to a convenient resting place for the feast.

The Christmas rose is the earliest of spring bloomers, oftentimes holding its bloom above the snow.

Perennials for the Shady Garden

The list of perennials for the shady garden is surprisingly long and includes spring bloomers as well as a few summer-flowering kinds. Of the early spring bloomers, the primulas might well have a prominent place beside the paths; Virginia bluebells do well in the lighter soils. The wild wood phlox (P. divaricata), coral bells (Heuchera), columbine, shooting star (Dodecatheon), bleeding hearts, and violets (they are likely to become weeds) are well known early bloomers. Summer-flowering plants include the plantain lilies (Hosta), Japanese anemone, goatsbeard, snakeroot (Cimicifuga), Geum, and bellflower (Platycodon). The Christmas rose (Helleborus) often blooms in midwinter. The Eupatoriums (frostflower) will thrive in shade but are too weedy. The daylilies will thrive and flower in light shade, but will not flower in dense shade and not too well in medium shade.

Bulbs

Almost all kinds of hardy bulbs will flower in the shady garden, but tulips are least likely to be successful unless planted in beds where they may receive care. The Trilliums do unusually well as do the western troutlilies (Erythronium) in a well-drained loamy soil. Even the Turk's cap lily, sometimes called the swamp lily, may be counted upon to thrive and multiply in light shade.

Ferns

There are some 40 species of ferns native to the Washington area and many of them will be useful in the shady garden. Some are likely to be weedy and should be used with care. Others, such as the cliff brake, require a sweet soil and some sun. The delightful little walking fern is best used in a rockery. The Christmas fern, which is an evergreen, is especially useful. The showy royal fern cannot be counted upon to thrive unless its feet are close to running water.

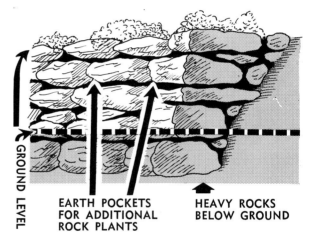

GROUND LEVEL

EARTH POCKETS FOR ADDITIONAL ROCK PLANTS

HEAVY ROCKS BELOW GROUND

Very often a rock wall is desired in the shady garden. The wall, to be stable and attractive, should be deeply laid to avoid dislocation by freezing and thawing, and should slope towards the bank.

Ground Covers

Occasionally there is a part of the shady garden that needs a carpet of evergreen to protect it from erosion and to keep weeds from becoming established. The most commonly used ground-covers are myrtle (Vinca minor), English ivy, and Japanese spurge. The myrtle is an early-spring bloomer—the others provide only foliage. The English ivy is probably the best ground cover in areas where shallow-rooted trees make the establishment of any plant material difficult.

Mazus, a tiny dwarf creeper, is good for the very small areas. The hardy begonias are both showy and effective where they have a fertile, moist, but well drained soil.

The growing of grass in a shady garden is not often attempted, but where desirable the owner has a choice of two kinds. Chewings fescue is adapted to the drier soils, provided there is little or no competition with tree roots and the shade is light. Danish bluegrass thrives in a moist soil and light to medium shade.

The omission of summer-flowering annuals is intentional. Almost without exception they are not shade lovers. A few, such as pansies, vinca, nicotiana, balsam, snapdragon, sweet alysum, and salvia will tolerate light shade provided they do not suffer from lack of moisture or plant food. The Impatiens will tolerate more shade than the others.

The following plant lists suggest the variety of plants available for the shady garden, and season of bloom as well as height at maturity.

PLANTS FOR THE SHADY GARDEN

Kind of Plant	L-M-D Shade	Height (Feet)	Space (Feet)	Blooms Mo.	Color	Soil L-M-R	Moisture	Fruit
Trees; Flowering								
Dogwood	L	15-25	15	April	White	M	Medium	Red
Fringetree	L	10-20	15	May	White	L	Dry	——
Red Bud	L	15-25	20	April	Purple	M	Medium	——
Sourwood	L	25-30	15	June	White	M	Moderate	——
American holly	M	15-40	15-20	——	——	M	Medium	Red
English holly	M	25-40	15-20	——	——	M	Medium	Red
Large shrubs:								
Mockorange	L	10-12	8-10	May	White	M	Medium	——
Firethorn	L	8-12	4-8	May	White	M	Medium	Orange-scarlet
Jetbead	L	6-10	6-8	May	White	M	Medium	Black
Cranberry bush	L	10-15	8-10	May	White	M	Medium	Red
Chinese holly	L	10-15	8-10	May	White	M	Medium	Red
Japanese holly	L	6-12	6-8	——	——	M	Medium	——
Camelia	L	6-12	3-6	Oct., Mar.-Apr.	Red/White	L	Moderate	——
Witch-hazel	M	8-10	8-10	April	Yellow	M	Moist	——
Five-Leaf Aralia	M	6-10	6-10	——	——	M	Moist	——
Rhododendron Maximus	D	10-15	10-12	June	White/Pink	M	Moist	——
Summersweet	L	8-10	6-8	July	White	M	Moist	——
Shrubs, Medium Height:								
Abelia	L	6-8	6-8	June-Oct.	Pink	M	Medium	——
Andromeda, Jap.	M	6-8	4-5	Mar.-Apr.	White	M	Medium	——
Andromeda, Mtn.	M	5-6	6	Mar.-Apr.	White	M	Dry	——
Oregon hollygrape	L	6-8	6-8	May	Yellow	M	Medium	Blue
Azalea, Flame	M	6-8	6	June	Yellow	M	Moderate	——
Barberry, Juliane	L	4-6	3	May	Yellow	M	Medium	Blue-Black
Hydrangea, oakleaf	L/M	6-8	5-6	June	White-Purple	M	Medium	——
Shrubs, Low:								
Azalea, Kurume	L	2-6	3-6	May	Various	M	Medium	——
Azalea, Mollis	L	3-6	4-6	May	Yellow	M	Medium	——
Azalea, Viscosum	M	2-3	3	June	White	M	Moist	——
Azalea, Gleen Dale hybrids	L	4-8	4-6	May-June	Various	M	Medium	——
Azalea, Gable hybirds	L	3-6	4-6	May-June	Various	M	Medium	——
Leucothoe	M	2-3	3	May	White	M	Moist	——
Mtn. Laurel	M	3-6	3	May	White	M	Moist	——
Rhododendron vars	M	2-10	4-10	May-June	Various	M	Moist	——
Boxwood	L	2-6	2-2½	——	——	M	Moderate	——
Perennials:		(inches)	(inches)					
Lily-of-the-Valley	M	8-10	10	May	White	R	Moist	——
Primroses	M	6-12	12	Apr.-June	Various	R	Moist	——
Plantain lily	M	10-30	10-30	Apr.-Aug.	White-Lavender	M	Medium	——
Columbine	L	24-30	10-15	May-June	Various	M	Medium	——
Shooting star	M	12-15	8-10	April	Lilac	R	Medium	——
Geum	L	18-24	12-15	May-June	Red/Orange	R	Medium	——
Trollius	L	12-18	8-10	Apr.-June	Yellow	R	Medium	——
Goatsbeard	M	36-60	24-36	June-July	White	R	Medium	——
Astilbe	L	24-48	18	June-July	Various	R	Medium	——
Snakeroot	M	24-48	18	Aug.	White	R	Medium	——
Lady slipper	D	12-18	12-15	May	Rose/Yellow	R	Medium	——
Bleedingheart, showy	M	18-30	18-24	May	Pink	R	Medium	——
Bleedingheart, plumy	L	10-15	10-12	May-Sept.	Rose	R	Medium	——
Christmas rose	D	10-18	12-18	Jan.-Mar.	White-Purple	R	Medium	——
Lenten rose	D	12-18	12-18	Feb.-Mar.	White-Purple	R	Medium	——
Daylilies	L	18-36	18-36	May-Aug.	Yellow	R	Medium	——
English daisy	L	6-8	6-8	Apr.-May	White-Red	R	Medium	——
Crested iris—verna	L	8-10	8-10	April	Blue	R	Dry	——
Crested iris—cristata	L	6-8	8-10	May	Lilac	R	Dry	——
Bellflower, Chinese	L	18-24	20-30	May-Oct.	White-Violet	R	Dry	——
Harebell	L	10-15	15-18	June-Sept.	Blue	M	Dry	——
Phlox, Wood's	L	10-15	6-8	May	Lavender	M	Dry	——
Bluebell, Virginia	M	12-15	10-12	May	Blue	L	Moist	——

PLANTS FOR THE SHADY GARDEN (Contd.)

Kind of Plant	Shade L-M-D	Height (Feet)	Space (Feet)	Blooms Mo.	Color	Soil L-M-R	Moisture	Fruit
Mayapple	M	15-20	10-12	May	White	M	Medium	——
Bergamot	M	30-40	15-18	June	Red/Pink	M	Medium	——
Iris, Japanese	L	24-36	24-30	June-July	Various	M	Moist	——
Anemone, Jap.	L	30-40	30-40	Sept.	White/Pink	M	Moist	——
Bulbs, Hardy:								
Daffodils	M	6-18	6-10	Apr.-May	White-Yellow	M	Dry	——
Camassia	L	15-30	10-12	May-June	White/Lavender	M	Dry	——
Troutlilies	M	8-12	6-8	May-June	White-Yellow	L	Dry	——
Scilla campanulata	M	10-15	6-8	May-June	White/Lavender	M	Medium	——
Turk'scap Lily	L	18-30	10-15	June	Orange-Red	M	Moist	——
Star-of-Bethlehem	M	10-15	10-12	June	White	M	Medium	——
Muscari	M	4-6	6	May	White/Blue	M	Medium	——
Begonia, hardy	M	10-15	8-10	May-Sept.	White/Pink	M	Medium	——
Bulbs: Tender:								
Begonia, tuberous-rooted	D-M	10-15	12-15	June-Oct.	Various	R	Moist	——

Shade: L-light; M-medium; D-dense.
Soil: L-light; M-garden loam; R-rich.

CHAPTER XIII

SHADE TREES

TEN TIPS FOR TREE PLANTING

1. Thin and shorten branches in a manner to preserve the natural form of the tree.

2. Run guy wire through discarded rubber hose to prevent damage to bark.

3. When shortening branches, cut close to lower branch or bud.

4. Entire lower limbs may be removed.

5. Wrap with burlap or crepe paper to prevent sunscald.

6. Use hardwood stakes—drive into ground at same angle as wire.

7. Work 4 inches of well-rotted manure on top of topsoil.

8. Mulch with peat moss or well-rotted sawdust.

9. Backfill around roots with topsoil mixed with peat moss or woods soil or leaf compost.

10. Place a section of field drain tile vertically into backfill and fill with stones to allow water to go deep into root area. Use four of these.

ROOT FEEDER

A safe and easy method for tree feeding. The injector may also be used for watering during drought periods.

Many a tree is found in the wood
And every tree for its use is good;
Some for the strength of the gnarled root,
Some for the sweetness of flowering fruit;
Some for a shelter against a storm,
And some to keep the hearthstone warm;
Some for the room, and some for the beam.
—Henry Van Dyke

Trees are essential to the homes of the Washington

area. The hot summer sun without the shade of trees makes the average home almost untenable. Even with air-conditioning, trees are desirable since their shade reduces the cost of operation. The same applies to the well-shaded home in winter—trees cut down the heat-drawing of winter winds and keep fuel costs down. These two practical factors account for the ever present urge to plant trees, but there is another—the sheer love of the beauty of the tree itself.

However, trees serve other purposes which add to the value and enjoyment of the home. Trees should be planted to "frame" the house, to give it an attractive setting. Trees are usually placed behind the house to give it a background. Since shade is the main function of the trees they should be so placed as to cut-off the sun's rays. Because the desirability of trees is widely recognized, it goes without saying that a home surrounded by attractive trees commands a higher price than one without them.

Because the usual practice in developing a sub-division is to remove all trees prior to building, one of the first activities of the home buyers is to purchase trees. All too often the need for shade is so great that tree quality is entirely overlooked. The major demand is for the most rapid growing trees obtainable and so many of the less desirable kinds are planted. Trees vary greatly in their qualities and because they are expected to serve the owners for many years, it is unfortunate if they have several undesirable qualities. Some may be infested with insect pests; there are a few which are attacked by many diseases; there are those whose shallow-growing roots interfere with lawn and shrubbery; and there are those that because of constantly dropping twigs and leaves are known as dirty trees.

There is no one tree that is superior on every count, consequently the home owner should seek those kinds which will serve his purpose with the minimum of undesirable characteristics. If rapid growth is of paramount importance then we must think of the Chinese elm, the Sycamore, the Silver Maple, and similar fast growers. While the Chinese elm is a brittle wooded tree and has shallow-growing roots, it does produce the much sought after shade in a comparatively few years. However, slower growing, more desirable trees might well be planted at the same time and when they have attained sufficient size the less desirable fast growers may be removed. This may be troublesome to some because they dislike removing any kind of a tree, but it is the most feasible method for both obtaining quick shade and a desirable kind of tree.

In addition to these characteristics, the buyer should also note the growth habits of the trees. Not only do they have definite outlines (shapes) (see chart), but the mature height and spread is quite variable. Some

trees have a columnar form of which the Lombardy poplar is probably best known although disease has wiped out every mature specimen in this area. Then there are those with wide-spreading branches such as the white oak. The dogwood and the hawthornes have horizontal branching habits. In addition to the form or shape, we should also be interested in the ultimate height. Especially is this important to the one story house. A hundred twenty foot tulip poplar would seem to push it into the ground. Tall houses can best use the taller growing trees. The low spreading type of building needs the lower growing trees.

There are a considerable number of kinds of trees as well as some special forms or varieties. The native trees of the area include several kinds of oaks, some maples, the tulip poplar, the sweet gum, the sour gum, and several others. Then we have a considerable number of introduced trees, such as the flowering cherries, the flowering crabapples, the magnolias, the Chinese elms, etc., as well as disease resistant European forms of our natives. The London Plane tree, for example, a counterpart of the American Sycamore, is immune to the anthracnose disease that defoliates our native trees each spring, causing the leaves and twigs to fall. The European white birch is said to be less troubled by the bronze birch borer than are the native birch trees. Many consider the European linden more desirable than our native.

With our wealth of natives why has the tree problem become so complicated? This is a sound question at this point. The oaks which have so many desirable characteristics are being attacked by the oak wilt, a disease that first appeared in the middlewest about 20 years ago. It spread rapidly for a time and many expected to see the local oak trees wiped out. For some reason the spread of the disease has greatly diminished and our tree specialists are again recommending the Willow oak which is a fairly rapid grower. Mention was made above of the Lombardy poplar. Twenty-five years ago there were a great many mature specimens in the Washington area. Today there are none. The dainty Mimosa which is really a fast growing tree of moderate size is troubled by a wilt disease although there are now immune strains available through nurseries. The lovely Sweet Gum is another tree that is rendered obsolete because of disease and is no longer recommended for planting. However, the stately American elm is the native that most people think of as having been eliminated by disease from the Eastern half of the country. The Dutch elm disease and the Phloem necrosis are two fatal diseases that take their toll of American elms each year. These are some of the factors that changed people's thinking about trees, but fortunately there are still many kinds from which to choose.

RECOMMENDED TREES FOR THE METROPOLITAN AREA:

SMALL TREES (Under 35 feet)

Shade—Flowering dogwood, Japanese dogwood, oriental cherry, flowering crabapples, saucer magnolia, sourwood, Japanese snowbell, Cornelian cherry, goldenraintree and American hornbeam.

Street—Washington hawthorn, flowering crabapples, Amur maple, sourwood.

Windbreak—Washington hawthorn, buckthorn, American holly, Babylon willow, Japanese yew, Amur maple, Hedge maple.

MEDIUM-SIZE TREES (35 to 70 feet)

Shade—Japanese pagodatree, Katsuratree, Amur corktree, American hornbeam, red, green, and white ash, Chinese elm, American yellow-wood, Schwedler maple, white pine, Chinese chestnut.

Street—Amur maple, Japanese pagodatree, American hornbeam, flowering ash, Moraine locust, American yellow-wood, Column Norway maple, Globe Norway maple, Chinese scholartree, Katsura tree, scarlet oak.

Windbreak—Siberian crabapple, Siberian elm, Canadian hemlock, American arborvitae, eastern red cedar, column Chinese juniper, American holly.

TALL TREES (over 70 feet)

Shade—Tulip poplar, red maple, scarlet oak, willow oak, ginkgo, Kentuckycoffeetree, littleleaf linden, sugar hackberry, London planetree, Black tupelo, American beech.

Street—Tulip tree, red maple, scarlet oak, willow oak, ginkgo, black tupelo, littleleaf linden, European linden, London planetree, red oak.

Windbreak—White pine, Douglas fir, American beech.

Compiled from recommendations by state horticulturists, foresters and others.

THE SMALLER TREES

Many of the more widely planted small trees are noted for their floral displays. The widely planted and much loved dogwoods are still one of the most popular trees, although few even know about the lovely late flowering Kousa dogwood. It is a bit taller growing than our native.

The flowering crabapples are receiving more attention. Not only is their height suitable for use with a rambler, but they are less troubled by insect pests than are the dogwoods and the flowering cherries. The many new varieties of the crabapple appeal to tree lovers, while the fall display of fruits is viewed with mixed reactions. Some gardeners object to the fruits which in most cases must be raked and hauled away. However, the colorful fruit display is generally considered an added dividend.

The flowering cherries of which there are a considerable number are for the most part either the double flowering Kwanzan or the weeping P. subhirtella. The Kwanzan is a small tree while the weeping cherry will in time reach to the top of a three story building. For some unknown reason the peach borer which is so destructive to the stone fruits in the orchard does not seriously trouble the flowering Japanese cherries.

In addition to the flowering cherries and the crabapples, there are others which should not be overlooked. The Silverbell (Halesia carolina), the Styrax tree (S. japonica), the Washington thorn, and Saucer and Star Magnolias (M. soulangeana, M. stellata), the Stewartia (S. ovata), and several less widely known trees should be given consideration. There are a number of the Hawthornes. The Washington Thorn is generally believed to be less troubled by rust than the others. In addition to these sun-lovers there are several small-growing flowering trees that need some shade—the Virginia Fringetree (Chionanthus virginica) and the Serviceberry or Shadbush (Amelanchier grandiflora), for example.

Both the Goldenrain tree and the Goldenchain tree are frequently planted but apparently they are on the temperamental side. The Goldenchain tree needs a cool situation and a sweet soil. The Goldenrain tree is less demanding. The Mountain ash (Sorbus americana) similarly does not do too well in the Washington area. The Redbud tree (Cercis canadensis), formerly was a dependable small flowering tree but disease has rendered it short-lived. The Mimosa (Albizzia julibrissin) should also be considered now that disease resistant varieties may be obtained from some nurseries.

An apple tree might well be considered were it not for the wormy fruit that must be disposed of. The mulberry is even worse since the soft fruits can be carried indoors on small shoes to stain the floors. Both the wild persimmon and the Gingko are dioecious so if fruit is not wanted only the males should be planted. The Sassafras is rather attractive for a small tree, but it spreads by underground stolons which must be controlled or a jungle will soon form. The Japanese beetles are quite fond of the foliage of the Sassafras tree.

The nut trees are often thought of for use as shade trees since they do not grow to huge proportions—the Chinese and hybrid chestnuts, the pecan, hickory, etc., will do well in this area. However, about the time they achieve size and the owners look forward to harvesting a crop of nuts the squirrels move in. Walnut trees have a toxic substance in their roots that is fatal to members of the rhododendron family (Rhododendrons and azaleas). Hickories are excellent trees but very slow growers.

The conifers are seldom planted in this area for shade but they do make excellent windbreaks and background plantings. The hemlock does not seem to withstand strong winds except when planted in a moist situation. The Washington area is a bit too far south for the spruce, fir (Abies), and balsam, but the cedars (Cedrus), pines, and Retinospora (Chamaecyparis) do well here. The White pine is probably the best, although the red and the black pine are occasionally planted. The Scotch pine seldom thrives for long here. The Douglas fir (Pseudotsuga) is useful both as a source of greens for holiday decorations and as a stately windbreak or accent tree.

ABOUT DOGWOOD

(Cornus florida, C. mas, C. kousa, etc.)

Uses:	Specimen, background, cutflowers
Plant:	Spring
Height:	25-60 ft.
Blooms:	Mar.-May
Fruits:	Red or scarlet
Distance:	10-15 ft.
Soil:	Enriched with leafmold, compost, peatmoss, acid
Exposure:	Sun/light shade
Prune:	As needed
Species:	C. florida—Eastern dogwood, 20-25 ft. white, red fruits
	C. kousa chinensis—Kousa dogwood, 25 ft. white, red fruits
	C. Mas—Cornelian cherry, 25 ft. yellow, scarlet fruits
	C. officinalis—Japanese cornel, 30 ft., yellow, scarlet fruits
	C. controversa—Giant dogwood, 60 ft., white, red fruits
	C. sanguinea—10 ft., inconspicuous, colored branches
	C. stolonigera—Redosier dogwood, 8 ft. colored stems, inconspicuous
Varieties:	Double-white flowered, Weeping—white flowered, Willowleaf—white flowered, Cherokee Chief—red-flowered, Cherokee Princess—pink flowered, etc.

The dogwoods are most widely planted and are counted upon to produce an excellent display of bloom in late April and May. They are small growing spring-flowering trees and are native to this area.

While the common dogwood (Eastern dogwood) is most widely planted, there are many other kinds which are adapted to this area and might be considered in selecting flowering trees. The earliest to bloom, the Cornelian cherry (C. mas) and its close relative Japanese Cornel (C. officinalis), have yellow flowers. In general they are more conspicuous than the witch-hazels which flower at the same season. The late flowering dogwood, the Kousa dogwood, closely resembles the Eastern dogwood except that the blooms appear after the leaves are out. However, the fruit display of the Kousa dogwood is more showy than that of the Eastern dogwood. The Giant dogwood, is not widely grown but may be of interest because of its size. It too has white flowers and red fruits.

In addition there are the dogwoods which are grown primarily for their bright colored stems, which make a distinct showing in the wintertime. This group, C. Sanguinea and C. stolonifera, are used mainly for background and natural-grown areas, where they may be heavily pruned in the spring to encourage strong new growth which has the more brightly colored stems.

The dogwoods are rather shallow-rooted small trees, and they delight in an acid soil well loaded with compost, leafmold, and sphagnum peatmoss. While the dogwoods seemingly like a moist soil, actually they tolerate rather dry soils in the edges of the woodlands, they will not tolerate poorly drained soils. Subsurface drainage must be good.

The dogwoods grow equally well in full sun or in light shade. In heavy shade they are sparsely twigged and thin.

The dogwood should not be planted too deeply—observe the soil-line on the trunk and allow for settling so that the root system will be at the proper level. Mulch the root area and keep it well mulched at all times both to keep the soil conditions favorable to the dogwood and also to avoid the necessity of having to mow the grass near it. Lawnmower damage to the tree trunk generally leads to canker disease.

The dogwoods are not free from insect injury or disease. The dogwood borers are probably the cause of more injury then are the diseases. A healthy, vigorous-growing dogwood is seldom troubled by the borers, but let drought or disease weaken them and the borers are highly destructive. As protection against the borers the trunks and the larger branches may be painted with a 10% solution of DDT about mid-May, mid-June and mid-July.

If diseases should appear, the trees may be sprayed in the spring as the flowers are opening with captan or some similar fungicide. Zineb is another which may be used to prevent the appearance of disease—which are most likely to appear in cool damp weather in the spring.

THE MEDIUM SIZED TREES

The medium sized trees include one of the flowering crabs as well as the stronger growing flowering cherries. They are trees of 35 to 70 feet at maturity. It is also feasible to use some of the larger growing trees by topping, thus the number of kinds is not limited as first appears.

The red or swamp maple, one of our natives, has received much attention from the arborists and now a number of varieties are available. Some of them feature desirable shapes, such as the Columnare.

Of the oaks, the Willow oak is rated rather highly by some of the nurserymen. There are some excellent specimens in the Washington area. It is a tree that should be given good care in order to develop the best type of growth. If starved, the branches are too closely spaced and growth is very slow. The shingle oak, another native, but not often seen, seems to be troubled by gall insects which disfigure it.

Of this group the Willow oak and European linden seem to be the faster growers. The Amur Cork tree is a fast grower. The Yellow-wood, the magnolias, and the Japanese Pagoda trees are noted for their bloom.

THE LARGER TREES

This group includes such well known trees as the Scarlet oak, the Sugar and the Norway maples, the American ash, and the Maidenhair tree (Ginkgo). A troublesome scale insect has appeared on some Pin oaks in this area. Perhaps the Willow and Scarlet should be given first choice. The Scarlet oak is a very rapid grower but is one of the more difficult trees to transplant. The European beech, a magnificent tree to own and to look at, is a slow grower. The Kentucky coffee tree is an attractive looking tree but some will object to the seed pods. The Japanese Zelkova resembles the American elm in many ways, including the shallow-growing root system. To the list as given by the Nurserymen we might well add the London Plane tree, Platanus acerifolia, a rapid grower.

COLUMNAR TREES FOR SCREENING

There are a considerable number of interesting columnar growing trees that may be used where space is limited. They range in mature height of from 15 to 60 feet, but more important they may be kept to a relatively narrow width with very little pruning. There are columnar forms of the flowering cherry (Amanogawa), the flowering crabapple (Pyramidal Strathmore), as well as of the shade trees. There is a columnar form of the English oak (Quercus robur fastigiata), of the Birch (Betula verrucosa fastigiata), etc. Then there are columnar forms of several of the evergreens—Chinese columnar juniper (Juniperus chinensis pyramidalis), California Inconsecedar (Libocedrus decurens), The Swiss Stone Pine (Pinus cambra), a columnar form of the white pine (Pinus strobus fastigiata), as well as of the Scotch pine (Pinus sylvestria fastigiata).

The above is not a complete listing but examples of the various kinds of columnar trees available for that narrow space.

PLANT THESE TREES IN THE SPRING

Nurserymen's practices have done much to overcome planting losses. The roots of many trees are kept in a ball of earth and this greatly reduces the shock of transplanting. Especially is this true today because the trees are root pruned every year or two, which helps to develop a compact mass of roots. But even with these modern practices there are some trees which are best transplanted in the spring. For the most part these are the ones with "fleshy" roots—the magnolias, beech, birch, dogwood, linden, elm, red and sugar maples, poplar, sweetgum, and tulip poplar. This is not to say that they must be transplanted in the spring but rather there is less likelihood of loss. But even this statement should be taken thoughtfully, since trees transplanted with their roots in a ball of soil as compared to "bare-root" trees (no soil on the roost), obviously are not likely to suffer much shock. It is essential for all trees that are not dug during the dormant season to have this ball of soil. Trees dug during the dormant season and their roots protected from drying are not less desirable. All conifers and broadleaved evergreens should be moved with a ball of soil enclosing their roots.

Trees dug from the wild or being moved about in the yard do not have compact root systems and unless handled with great care are likely to suffer considerable shock. If at all possible, such trees should be root-pruned a year before moving. Root-pruning consists of cutting the roots at a point not too far from the trunk. Following the cutting, new roots will develop, usually in a compact area close to the point of cutting. If this is done, then a larger proportion of the roots will be included in the digging.

The size of the root ball may seem out of balance with the size of the tree top. The American Association of Nurserymen have developed standards for the root balls and in most cases the individual nurserymen observe them rather closely. However, in most cases the roots are insufficient to carry the top in full growth and it is essential that the tree top be cut back to compensate for loss of roots. The more severely the top is pruned the more vigorous the new growth will be. If left unpruned the leaves will be small and weak and the recovery from the shock will be slow.

The planting of balled trees and container grown trees, as well as those with bare-roots, has much to do with the vigor of the new growth. The hole should be amply large to permit enclosing the roots in a well prepared soil mixture. The soil mixture should contain an abundance of compost or peatmoss which will hold the moisture for the roots. It should be well pulverized so that both moisture and air will penetrate to the roots. Do not add fertilizer to the soil mixture, surface application is safer. After the root ball or roots are in place and soil worked around them it is well to pour in several pails of water to settle the soil about the roots and to eliminate air pockets. After the water has soaked into the soil the balance of the hole should be filled but do not tramp or pack this top layer.

With the tree in place, the hole filled, and the soil well moistened, the last step should be to securely guy or stake the tree so that it will not whip about in the wind. Trees rocked by wind have difficulty in putting out tender feeding roots, consequently it is important that they be held in place by suitable supports.

Newly planted trees greatly benefit by having a mulch spread over the planting hole to prevent the soil from crusting. Air and moisture must penetrate into the soil if the roots are to function properly. After the tree has started into growth a certain amount of plant food should be applied to stimulate new growth. The rate of growth can be materially stepped up by proper watering and fertilizing. The plant food may be placed in holes punched into the soil, it may be spread on the surface of the soil, or it may be carried into the root area by water with an injector type of applicator. Recently, foliar feeding has received much attention. Undoubtedly it is best treated as a supplement to normal feeding procedures.

Trees transplanted from the woods or some shady situation and placed in a sunny site should have their trunks wrapped to prevent sun-burn. It only requires a light wrap (old nylons will do) and it should be left on the first season. Dogwoods might well be protected with a kraft paper wrap which helps to protect the trunk from the borers.

The transplanting seasons have been greatly extended through the use of anti-transpirant sprays which materially reduce the loss of moisture. These same sprays may be used to protect the evergreens during the winter from drying winds.

Evergreens, both conifers and the broadleaved trees, should be protected from excessive moisture loss during the winter. The smaller trees may be protected by screens which will reduce the force of winter winds, and for the more tender kinds, it may also be used to cut off the winter sun. The taller trees are best protected by one of the anti-transpirant sprays. Such protection is important, otherwise there is the real danger of the tree being materially weakened, if not defoliated by winter winds.

Most of the commonly planted trees are subject to insects and disease damage and should be given the needed protection. Some trees obviously are subject to many more diseases and insect pests than are others. Mature trees are costly to protect and so it is important in selecting trees for the yard that they be comparatively free from attack. An all-purpose spray is probably adequate for most kinds of trees. However, there are some insects, such as the gal aphids that produce unsightly bumps on the leaves, but generally are ignored because the damage is so slight. If the foliage is to be protected from them the spray must be applied early in the season before the aphids build their houses out of leaf tissue.

The pruning of shade trees is seldom practiced as it should be. It is important to guide the development of the tree top so as to avoid weak forks. The lower limbs should be removed as the tree grows to permit sunlight to reach the ground beneath the tree, otherwise it is difficult to maintain a stand of grass. Only the lower limbs of the evergreens are commonly left intact. The lower limbs of the Southern Magnolia may be allowed to remain in the larger yard, they take up too much space in the smaller yard. The same is true of the Deodar cedar, the spruce, and the firs. If space permits, the lower limbs of the beech might well be kept since because of the shallow-growing roots it is impossible to grow grass or ground cover beneath it.

Dead wood is not uncommon in a shade tree and it should be removed so as not to be a home for insects and diseases. Moreover, dead limbs constitute a hazard because they may fall without any warning.

Tree topping is a practice that is not employed as often as it should be. Many of our native trees will reach heights in excess of a hundred feet at maturity. We have little need for such huge specimens and they might well be topped when they reach a height that meets the needs of the gardener. If a tree is topped at the proper stage of growth, when the branches are still small there is little likelihood of rot entering the upper branches. Because of the height and the weaknesses of the branches this job is best left to the skilled arborist.

The changing of a grade about a tree should only be done with great care. Few trees will tolerate more than a six-inch fill over the root area. If more soil is to be placed over the root area then a well should be erected about the trunk as well as provision for aeration of the roots. Usually this latter consists of a layer of gravel, in some cases strings of tile are also laid to insure ample air circulation. The gravel is then covered with weeds or some material which will keep the soil from washing into the air spaces. If properly done there is no limit to the depth of soil which may be spread on top of the root area.

Tree bark should be protected from injury if rot is to be avoided. The lawnmower injury to dogwood trees, for example, is considered to be one of the major causes of loss of dogwoods. Whenever the bark is injured, it is important that the wound be trimmed, smoothed and coated with a prepared tree dressing. Of course, when limbs are removed in pruning the cuts should be painted with a tree dressing.

AUTUMN COLORS

One of the glories of the trees is their autumn colors. Some are a rich yellow, others a pale yellow; then there are the reds, the violets and the purples. Motorists often drive hundreds of miles to view the autumn colors of the woods.

The change in the leaf color is associated with cool weather, if an early killing frost comes before the coolness of fall weather, the leaves are killed and turn brown rather than put on an autumn show. When cool temperatures signal the end of the growing season the sugars in the leaves are changed to starches and move into the roots—it is during this process of translocation that the trees display the colors which we all enjoy so much.

SHADE TREES

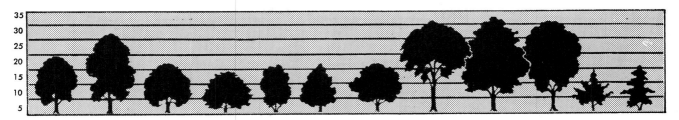

Tree growth in 10 years. Each band represents 5 feet in height. Trees in the Morton Arboretum study were 6 feet high when planted. Left to right: American ash, green ash, Amur cherry, European beech, canoe birch, buckeye, Amur cork tree, American elm, Chinese elm, Moline elm, gingko, sour gum.

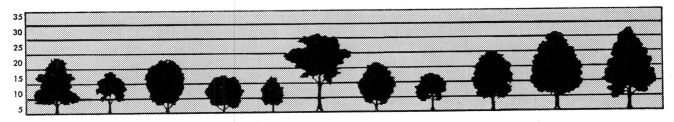

Left to right: Sweet gum, hackberry, Washington hawthorn, English hornbean, shagbark hickory, thornless honey locust, horse chestnut, Kentucky coffee tree, basswood or linden, little leaf linden, cucumber.

Left to right: Sugar maple, Norway maple, silver maple, bur oak, pin oak, red oak, white oak, sycamore, tulip, black walnut.

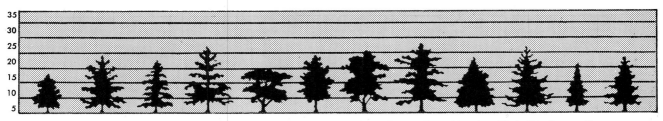

Left to right: White fir, Douglas fir, hemlock, European larch, Austrian pine, red pine, Scotch pine, white pine, Black Hills Spruce, Norway spruce, Serbian spruce, white spruce.

CHAPTER XIV

NEW & OVERLOOKED TREES & SHRUBS

Nearly every nursery handles a few kinds of woody plants that are seldom seen in local gardens. They may have been overlooked by buyers; more likely they have been passed-by because the gardener did not know about them. Usually they are not in the usual listings of plants. It would seem that they are just not known. And, of course, there are the new varieties. Certainly they are different. Sometimes they have special merits when compared to some of the older or more common-place.

It goes without saying that they will not be found in every nursery. It may take a bit of searching before they can be found. However, if it appears that they will better serve in some particular spot in the landscape planting, then they will be worth looking for.

In most cases these are not for the beginner but rather for the gardener who has the common ones and now wants something different.

It is far from a complete listing. There are scores of others. Consequently, this should be considered only as a suggestion of what can be turned up by a bit of searching.

The height and spread of some of the new kinds can only be considered as approximations. They have not been around long enough, especially the slow-growing kinds.

FLOWERING CRABAPPLE, ECKTERMEYER—OEKONOMIERAT WEEPING

(Malus)

Height:	12-15 ft.
Spread:	12-15 ft.
Exposure:	Sun
Soil:	Good garden loam
Moisture:	Moderately moist
Plant:	Mar. - Nov.
Distance:	....
Blooms:	May, light pink
Uses:	Small ornamental flowering tree

There is always a place for a small, mounding tree with attractive flowers and fruits.

DOGWOODS NEW

(Cornus florida var. Cherokee Chief—red-flowered; Cherokee Princess —blooms at early age; Weeping Dogwood—pendulous branches)

Height:	15-20 ft.
Spread:	10 to 12 ft.
Exposure:	Light shade/sun
Soil:	Enriched with humus
Moisture:	Moist
Plant:	Mar./Apr. - Nov.
Distance:	....
Blooms:	Apr. - May
Fruit:	Red berries
Uses:	Small flowering tree for the border

Three new varieties of dogwoods bring variety into the shrub border. Cherokee Chief is a good red. Cherokee Princess starts blooming at one year, is a large-flowered white dogwood. The weeping dogwood is white flowered and narrow columnar in growth. Also we may have double flowered white dogwood and a dwarf called PYGMY. The latter is also new.

TREES

Flowering—

BLACKHAW

(Viburnum prunifolium)

Height:	10-15 ft.
Exposure:	Sun/light shade
Soil:	Moist, humus
Plant:	Mar./Apr. - Nov.
Distance:	15-20 ft.
Blooms:	Mid May, large flat clusters, white
Fruit:	Blue-black, ½-in.
Uses:	Small flowering tree

The Blackhaw, which some consider a large shrub, but which can be trained as a small tree, produces a display of flowers in May and a crop of showy blue-black fruits in the fall. The summer foliage is a bright green; in the fall it turns to an orange-red. The horizontal branching is similar to that of the dogwood—not new but usually overlooked.

DOGWOOD, KOUSA

(Cornus kousa)

Height:	20 ft.
Spread:	10-12 ft.
Exposure:	Light shade/sun
Soil:	Well-drained, rich in humus
Plant:	Mar./Apr.
Distance:	15-18 ft.
Blooms:	Late May
Fruit:	Red, shaped like a raspberry
Uses:	Small ornamental

The Kousa dogwood—there are two, Japanese and Chinese—is distinct from our native dogwood in that the flowers appear after the leaves unfold. Also, the flowers lack the notch and the petals are pointed. It is an excellent small tree for the shady garden as well as in the lawn.

FRANKLINIA

(Franklinia alatamaha, Gordonia)

Height:	25-30 ft.
Spread:	10-15 ft.
Exposure:	Sun
Soil:	Sand enriched with peatmoss or leafmold
Plant:	Mar./Apr.
Blooms:	Aug. - Sept. Large, creamy-white
Fruit:	None
Uses:	Small flowering tree

An interesting late summer flowering tree that is given a historical background. However, this should not be emphasized, and more attention should be paid to the soil requirements: sandy and loaded with peatmoss or leafmold. The flowers are good sized (3-in.) and are scattered over the tree much like the Southern magnolia. The tree should not be exposed to too much wind.

PEAR, BRADFORD

(Pyrus calleryana Var. Bradford)

Height:	30 ft.
Spread:	10-15 ft.
Exposure:	Sun
Soil:	Good garden loam
Plant:	Mar./Apr. - Nov.
Distance:	20-25 ft.
Blooms:	Apr.-May—white in clusters
Fruit:	Small, inedible
Uses:	Small ornamental tree

The Bradford pear is an early spring flowering small tree for the smaller lot. They are also attractive trees for street planting. The spring bloom is especially

showy, appearing before the leaves. The fall foliage color is attractive. The Bradford pear is immune to the fire-blight disease which is so injurious to many kinds of pears.

PHOTINIA, CHRISTMAS BERRY—ORIENTAL

(Photinia villosa)

Height:	10-15 ft.
Exposure:	Sun
Soil:	Rich in humus, moist
Plant:	Mar./Apr. - Nov.
Distance:	6-8 ft.
Blooms:	May - white
Fruit:	Bright red berries
Uses:	Small ornamental tree

The Christmas berry is not as widely used as it should be. The red fruits in the fall are useful for color in the shrub border until the birds harvest them. This small tree has excellent foliage in the summer which turns to an orange-red in the fall. The tree tends to be flat-topped and should be pruned to a single trunk.

PLUM, THUNDERCLOUD PURPLE-LEAF

(Prumus cerasifera 'Thundercloud')

Height:	10-12 ft.
Spread:	10 ft.
Exposure:	Sun
Soil:	Well-drained, good garden loam
Moisture:	Moderately moist
Plant:	Mar. - Nov.
Distance:	15-20 ft.
Blooms:	May, white to pink, single
Fruit:	Few
Uses:	Specimen, small ornamental

This variety grows a bit taller than Newport, but has about the same reddish purple foliage. It does not color in shade as well as it does in sun.

STEWARTIA, KOREAN—STEWARTIA, JAPANESE

(Stewartia koreana) (S. pseudo-camellia)

Height:	30 ft.
Exposure:	Sun/light shade
Soil:	Sandy, rich in humus, moist
Plant:	Mar./Apr. - Sept.
Distance:	15-20 ft.
Blooms:	Mid-July, camellia type flowers
Fruit:	None
Uses:	Small summer-blooming shade tree

These are two small summer-flowering trees that are not often considered because they are not as showy as the spring flowering dogwoods and crabapples. However, they flower at a season when there are too few trees in bloom. They do best in a sandy soil that has been enriched with peatmoss.

Shade

BIRCH, CANOE

(Betula papyrifera—Paper Birch)

Height:	40-70 ft.
Spread:	10-15 ft.
Exposure:	Sun
Soil:	Rich in humus, moist
Plant:	Mar./Apr.
Distance:	20-25 ft.
Blooms:	None
Fruit:	None
Uses:	Shade

The Canoe or Paper birch is too often overlooked in selecting an attractive medium sized shade tree for the yard because it takes longer for the trunk to turn white than it does for the European white birch. On the other hand, once the bark has turned white it has less of the black patches which are common on the European. Also, although it is not specifically confirmed, the Canoe birch is less troubled by the Bronze birch borer which has been so destructive in recent years. The Canoe birch is most attractive when grown as a single stem tree.

SORRELTREE

(Oxydendrum arboreum—Sourwood)

Height:	30-50 ft.
Spread:	10-15 ft.
Exposure:	Sun/light shade
Soil:	Ordinary garden loam
Plant:	Mar./Apr. - Nov.
Distance:	20-25 ft.
Blooms:	Mid-July, small pendulous clusters, white
Fruit:	Dried capsules
Uses:	Small ornamental tree, distinctive for its bloom.

The sourwood or sorreltree, as it is commonly called, is a handsome medium sized flowering tree that is distinctive for its mid-summer bloom, which is fragrant, for the capsules which cover the branch tips in the fall, and for the scarlet colored fall foliage. The tree, a native, is undemanding as to soil, but will do much better in a good garden loam.

Evergreen—Conifers

CRYPTOMERIA, YOSHINO
(Cryptomeria japonica 'Yoshino')

Height:	12 ft.
Spread:	40 ft.
Exposure:	Sun/Shade
Soil:	Good garden loam, well-drained
Moisture:	Moderate
Plant:	Apr. - Sept.
Distance:	....
Blooms:	....
Fruit:	Cones
Uses:	Specimen, foundation, background

This is a dwarf form of the more or less columnar formed C. lobbi which has been dependable in this area. It is good evergreen for the narrow space.

HEMLOCK, WEEPING
(Tsuga canadensis pendula)

Height:	5-6 ft.
Spread:	10-12 ft.
Exposure:	Sun/Shade, protect from strong winter winds
Soil:	Moist
Moisture:	Well enriched with humus

Plant:	Mar./Apr. - Sept.
Distance:	....
Blooms:	....
Fruit:	Small cones
Uses:	Specimen

This hemlock is unusual because of its weeping form of growth. It is a slow grower and will not quickly out-grow its location or site, as part of the common hemlock.

HEMLOCK, SARGENT WEEPING
(Tsuga canadensis pendula 'Sargenti')

Height:	4-5 ft.
Spread:	15-20 ft.
Exposure:	Sun/Shade, protect from strong winter winds
Soil:	Enriched with humus
Moisture:	Moist
Plant:	Mar./Apr. - Sept.
Distance:	....
Blooms:	....
Fruit:	Small cones
Uses:	Specimen

Not a new weeping hemlock, but rather one that is not often seen outside of Botanic gardens.

JUNIPER, BLUE HAVEN
(Juniperus scopulorum 'Blue Haven')

Height:	20-25 ft.
Spread:	4-6 ft.
Exposure:	Sun
Soil:	Well-drained, garden loam
Moisture:	Dry
Plant:	Mar./Apr. - Sept.
Blooms:	....
Fruit:	....
Uses:	Specimen, background

An unusual, pyramidal evergreen, suitable for specimen use in the dryer sunny situation; really a columnar shaped tree.

JUNIPER, BURKI
(Juniperus virginiana 'Burki')

Height:	20-25 ft.
Spread:	4-6 ft.
Exposure:	Sun
Soil:	Dry
Plant:	Mar./Apr. - Sept.
Blooms:	....
Fruit:	....
Uses:	Specimen plant, background

A narrow pyramidal tree with steel blue foliage. It should be pruned for compactness.

JUNIPER, EMERALD GREEN

(Juniperus scopulorum 'Emerald Green')

Height:	15-18 ft.
Spread:	4-6 ft.
Exposure:	Sun
Soil:	Well drained, ordinary garden loam
Moisture:	Dry
Plant:	Mar./Apr. - Sept.
Blooms:	....
Fruit:	....
Uses:	Specimen, background

Needs to be trimmed for good dense growth.

JUNIPER, GRAY GLEAM

(Juniperus scopulorum 'Gray Gleam')

Height:	10-12 ft.
Spread:	5-6 ft.
Exposure:	Sunny
Soil:	Well-drained, ordinary garden loam
Moisture:	Dry
Plant:	Mar./Apr. - Sept.
Blooms:	....
Fruit:	....
Uses:	Specimen, background

Seldom needs pruning—dense.

JUNIPER, HOLLYWOOD

(Juniperus chinensis-torulosa—Twisted)

Height:	12-15 ft.
Spread:	4-5 ft.
Exposure:	Sun
Soil:	Well-drained, graden loam
Plant:	Mar./Apr.-Sept.
Blooms:	None
Fruit:	None
Uses:	Accent plant, tub

The Hollywood juniper has interesting twisted branches and is of primary interest for this characteristic. Like other Chinese junipers it is untroubled by those insects which trouble other species. It does very well as a tub plant.

JUNIPER, PATHFINDER

(Juniperus scopulorum 'Pathfinder')

Height:	20-25 ft.
Spread:	8-10 ft.
Exposure:	Sunny
Soil:	Well-drained, ordinary garden loam
Moisture:	Dry
Plant:	Mar./Apr. - Sept.
Blooms:	....
Fruit:	....
Uses:	Specimen, background

An unusual color in the Scopulorum junipers, it also is very compact and requires the minimum of shearing. It is slow enough growing to be useful both in the rock garden and in the perennial border.

PINE, JAPANESE UMBRELLA

(Sciadopitys verticillata)

Height:	10-15 ft.
Spread:	6-8 ft.
Exposure:	Sun
Soil:	Well-drained, good garden loam
Moisture:	Moderate
Plant:	Mar./Apr. - Sept.
Blooms:	....
Fruit:	Cones
Uses:	Specimen, background

A slow growing tree with horizontal branches and interesting foliage, it is broadly pyramidal in shape. With age the foliage becomes gray-green.

PINE, SWISS STONE

(Pinus cembra)

Height:	20-30 ft.
Spread:	6-8 ft.
Exposure:	Sun
Soil:	Well-drained, enriched with humus
Moisture:	Moderate
Plant:	Mar./Apr. - Sept.
Blooms:	....
Fruit:	Cones
Uses:	Columnar specimen

This is a slow growing, long-needle pine, that has a narrow pyramidal form of growth.

GRAY GLEAM   **HOLLYWOOD**   **JAPANESE UMBRELLA**   **SWISS STONE**

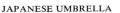

SPRUCE, HOOPS DWARF BLUE

(Picea pungens 'Hoops')

Height:	10-12 ft.
Spread:	6-8 ft.
Exposure:	Sun
Soil:	Well-drained, enriched with humus
Moisture:	Moderate
Plant:	Mar./Apr. - Sept.
Blooms:	....
Fruit:	....
Uses:	Rock garden, Specimen

A dwarf bright blue spruce for the rock garden or specimen plant, this is one of the best of the blue spruces.

Evergreens—Broad-leaved

LAURELCHERRY, PORTUGESE

(Laurocerasus lusitanica—Prunus lusitanica)

Height:	15-20 ft.
Spread:	6-10 ft.
Exposure:	Sun/shade
Soil:	Rich in humus, moist
Plant:	Mar./Apr. - Sept.
Distance:	10 ft.
Blooms:	May, white
Fruit:	Clusters similar to the choke cherries, first red then turning black.
Uses:	Suitable for foliage, also as hedge.

The Portugese laurelcherry is a rapid growing broad-leaved evergreen. It may be used as a small tree or may be used as a clipped hedge. Its foliage does not often winterburn. It is considered as hardy or hardier than the Ligustrum lucidum.

PHOTINIA, CHINESE

(Photinia serrulata)

Height:	12-15 ft.
Spread:	8 ft.
Exposure:	Sun or shade
Soil:	Rich in humus
Plant:	Mar./Apr. - Sept.
Distance:	10-15 ft.
Blooms:	May, white, flat heads
Uses:	Bright red berries

The Chinese Photinia is a rapid growing evergreen tree with luxurious foliage; the blooms are large enough to show and the fruit display is good. It needs no protection in the city but in the suburbs it should be planted near the house. The new foliage is a reddish bronze.

OAK, DARLINGTON

(Quercus-laurifolia—Laurel oak)

Height:	50-80 ft.
Spread:	30-40 ft.
Exposure:	Sun to light shade
Soil:	Good garden loam
Plant:	Mar./Apr. - Sept.
Distance:	40-50 ft.
Blooms:	....
Fruit:	Acorns
Uses:	Medium-sized shade tree

The Darlington oak is a semi-evergreen in this area, retaining its leaves in mild winters, losing a part or all of them when we have bitter blizzards. Plant where they have some protection from the north winds. They grow fairly rapidly in good soil.

OAK, SOUTHERN LIVE

(Quercus virginiana)

Height:	25-40 ft.
Spread:	40-50 ft.
Exposure:	Sun, protection from winter winds
Soil:	Rich damp soil
Plant:	Mar./Apr. - Sept.
Distance:	40-50 ft.
Blooms:	....
Fruit:	Acorns
Uses:	Wide spreading shade tree

The Southern live oak is almost evergreen in this

area, but grows slowly. Foliage and growth resembles the European olive tree.

STRANVAESIA DAVIDIANA

(Stranvaesia davidiana)

Height:	15-20 ft.
Spread:	8-10 ft.
Exposure:	Sun/light shade
Soil:	Rich in humus, moist
Plant:	Mar./Apr. - Sept.
Distance:	10-12 ft.
Blooms:	May, white, flat-topped clusters
Fruit:	Chinese red berries
Uses:	Background, espalier

The Stranvaesia is an attractive small evergreen tree with slender willow-like leaves that are dark green. The fruit display is probably its chief attraction and it is beautiful when grown against a wall. Some say it is not quite as hardy as Stranvaesia undulata.

Evergreen Shrubs

AUCUBA, DWARF

(Aucuba japonica 'Dwarf')

Height:	1½-2 ft.
Spread:	12-18 in.
Exposure:	Shade
Soil:	Enriched with humus
Moisture:	Moderately
Plant:	Apr. - Sept.
Distance:	2-3 ft.
Blooms:	....
Fruit:	Large red
Uses:	Low evergreen for specimen, massing

A shade-loving, large-leafed, tropical appearing shrub that can produce a display of red fruits. They are long lasting. The Aucuba is dioecious and a male plant must be provided if fruits are wanted. The Aucubas do not withstand strong winter winds.

BARBERRY, THREESPINE

(Berberis tricanthophoa)

Height:	2-4 ft.
Spread:	3-5 ft.
Exposure:	Sun
Soil:	Ordinary garden loam
Plant:	Mar./Apr. - Sept.
Distance:	4-5 ft.
Blooms:	May
Fruit:	Blue-black
Uses:	Planter boxes, banks, etc.

The threespine barberry is one of the hardier evergreen barberries, has attractive foliage about 2 inches long, and the spines make it a good deterrent for those who want to take short-cuts. This barberry can take our weather.

BOXWOOD, UPRIGHT (COLUMNUR)

(Buxus sempervirens fastigata)

Height:	6-8 ft.
Spread:	18-24 in.
Exposure:	Sun/light shade
Soil:	Good garden soil
Moisture:	Moist
Plant:	Mar./Apr. - Sept.
Distance:	....
Blooms:	....
Fruit:	....
Uses:	Specimen, Foundation

A really different boxwood, it has a columnar form that is compact, hardy, and does not require much in the way of pruning to keep it to a narrow upright form.

BUCKTHORN, GLOSSY 'TALLHEDGE'

(Rhamnus fragula columnaris 'Tallhedge')

Height:	10-15 ft.
Spread:	....
Exposure:	Sun/light shade
Soil:	Ordinary garden loam
Moisture:	Dry to moist
Plant:	Mar./Apr. - Nov.
Distance:	....
Blooms:	May - not showy
Fruit:	Small, cream, to pink, red to black
Uses:	Hedge

This buckthorn lacks the thorns one might expect from the name, is very columnar and stands pruning very well, and hence is a good hedge plant. It is tolerant of soil and moisture conditions.

CLEYERA

(Eurya japonica—Cleyera japonica)

Height:	8-10 ft.
Spread:	4 ft.
Exposure:	Light shade/part sun
Soil:	Rich in humus, well-drained
Plant:	Mar./Apr. - Sept.
Blooms:	Inconspicuous
Fruit:	Not significant
Uses:	Foliage

The Cleyera is grown under the same conditions as the camellia but lacks the flowers, and is of interest only for the foliage. It is not adapted to the more exposed area. It is a columnar growing broad-leaved evergreen with thick leathery foliage. The new growth is wine colored—very attractive.

COTONEASTER, BEARBERRY

(Cottoneaster dammeri 'Bearberry')

Height:	12-15 in.
Spread:	3-4 ft.
Exposure:	Light shade
Soil:	Good garden loam
Moisture:	Well-drained, moderate
Plant:	Mar./Apr. - Sept.
Distance:	....
Blooms:	Apr.-May
Fruit:	Red
Uses:	Ground cover, rock garden

A compact evergreen that may be used on the shady bank. It is one of the most prostrate growers of the cotoneasters. The tiny foliage is attractive and the small white flowers are followed by red fruits.

COTONEASTER, PYRENEES

(Cotoneaster congesta 'Pyrenees')

Height:	3 ft.
Spread:	6 ft.
Exposure:	Sun/light shade
Soil:	Good garden loam
Moisture:	Well-drained, moderate
Plant:	Mar./Apr. - Sept.
Distance:	....
Blooms:	Apr.-May
Fruit:	Bright red
Uses:	Low shrub, ground cover

This evergreen cotoneaster is both compact and low-growing. The pink to white flowers are followed by a display of red berries.

COTONEASTER, THYME ROCKSPRAY

(Cotoneaster microphylla 'Thymifolia')

Height:	2 ft.
Spread:	4 ft.
Exposure:	Sun/light shade
Soil:	Good garden loam
Moisture:	Well-drained, moderate
Plant:	Mar./Apr. - Sept.
Distance:	
Blooms:	May
Fruit:	Scarlet
Uses:	Ground cover, rock garden

The Thyme cotoneaster is noted for the tiny, dark-green shiny leaves. It is a compact grower and is evergreen.

ELAEGNUS, COMPACT THORNY

(Elaeagnus pungens 'Compact')

Height:	5-10 ft.
Spread:	8-10 ft.
Exposure:	Sun/light shade
Soil:	Ordinary garden loam
Moisture:	Moderately moist
Plant:	Mar./Apr. - Sept.
Blooms:	Fall, white, fragrant
Fruit:	Seldom
Uses:	Low-growing shrub for difficult situations

This fall bloomer with attractive foliage will tolerate smoke, dust, etc., and can be pruned into hedge form. The dwarf growth habit and the thorny branches make it an unusual shrub. It can be pruned to any height.

EUONYMUS, SIEBOLD'S

(Euonymus sieboldiana)

Height:	3½-5 ft.
Spread:	3-4 ft.
Exposure:	Sun/light shade
Soil:	Ordinary garden
Plant:	Mar./Apr. - Sept.
Blooms:	Inconspicuous
Fruit:	Typical euonymus
Uses:	Hedges, background

This euonymus is a strong grower, seems immune to the euonymus scale, and is hardier than a number of other evergreen plants. It will withstand heavy pruning during the spring season, and the height can be maintained for a long time with regularity of pruning and feeding.

HOLLY, LOW-GROWING CHINESE

(Ilex cornuta rotunda)

Height:	4-5 ft.
Spread:	5-6 ft.
Exposure:	Light shade
Soil:	Moist, enriched with humus
Plant:	Mar./Apr. - Sept.
Blooms:	Inconspicuous
Fruit:	Older strains none
Uses:	Compact holly for special uses.

The Dwarf Chinese holly resembles a large hassock with very little pruning needs. The earlier kind were lacking in fruits (berries) but a new one has been reported which does fruit, if a male is present. The leaves are sharply spined and attractive. This holly needs protection from hot sun and also from cold winter winds. A new clone has fruits.

HOLLY, DWARF CHINESE
(Ilex cornuta rotunda 'Dwarf')

Height:	2-2½ ft.
Spread:	3-4 ft.
Exposure:	Sun/light shade
Soil:	Enriched with humus, well-drained
Moisture:	Moderately
Plant:	Mar./Apr. - Sept.
Blooms:	Apr.
Fruit:	None
Uses:	Specimen, low-growing border.

A popular evergreen, now in a dwarf variety, that is slow growing, and has a low hassock-type shape. The leaves are spiny and glossy. Unfortunately this form does not fruit.

HOLLY, DARKLEAF JAPANESE
(Ilex crenata 'Darkleaf')

Height:	to 6 ft.
Spread:	2-3 ft., broader if trained
Exposure:	Sun or shade
Soil:	Well-drained, enriched with humus
Moisture:	Moderate
Plant:	Mar./Apr. - Sept.
Blooms:	....
Fruit:	Seldom seen
Uses:	Hedge, low spreader, or columnar

This is a good glossy leaved Japanese holly that can be trained to any form desired. Most of the Japanese hollies have rather dull foliage, but this one somewhat resembles the I. c. microphylla.

HOLLY, MAXWELL'S JAPANESE
(Ilex crenata maxwelli)

Height:	2-2½ ft.
Spread:	3-3½ ft.
Exposure:	Sun/light shade
Soil:	Ordinary garden loam
Plant:	Mar./Apr. - Sept.
Blooms:	Inconspicuous
Fruit:	Blue-black
Uses:	Border, facing up shrub

This is a convex-type of leaf Japanese holly similar to Ilex crenata hetzi, but slightly lower growing and with a greater spread. Its outstanding feature is its greater winter hardiness compared to the other varieties of the Japanese holly.

INKBERRY, COMPACT
(Ilex glabra compacta)

Height:	3½-4 ft.
Spread:	4-4½ ft.
Exposure:	Sun/light shade
Soil:	Rich in humus
Plant:	Mar./Apr. - Sept.
Distance:	....
Blooms:	May
	Inconspicuous
Fruit:	Black
Uses:	Mass plantings, low hedge

The Compact inkberry is a hardy disease-free holly suitable for mass plantings in sun or shade. The common inkberry is used for background plantings.

JUNIPER, DWARF JAPGARDEN
(Juniperus procumbens 'Dwarf Japgarden')

Height:	12 in.
Spread:	3 ft.
Exposure:	Sun
Soil:	Ordinary garden loam
Moisture:	Well-drained, dry
Plant:	Apr. - Sept.
Distance:	....
Blooms:	....
Fruit:	....
Uses:	Ground cover

This is a low-growing juniper with excellent blue-green foliage useful on the dry slope.

JUNIPER, OZARK COMPACT
(Juniperus chinensis 'Ozark Compact')

NEW & OVERLOOKED TREES & SHRUBS THAT ARE UNUSUAL OR DIFFERENT

Height:	3-4 ft.
Spread:	8-10 ft.
Exposure:	Sun
Soil:	Ordinary garden
Plant:	Mar./Apr. - Sept.
Distance:	10 feet
Blooms:	None
Fruit:	None
Uses:	Shrub border, bank cover

This is a new and apparently better form of the Dwarf Pfitzer. It is identical in foliage, form and color with the Pfitzer, including freedom from spider mite and juniper webworm problems.

JUNIPER, TABLETOP BLUE
(Juniperus scopulorum 'Tabletop Blue')

Height:	4 ft.
Spread:	5 ft.
Exposure:	Sun
Soil:	Well-drained, good garden loam
Moisture:	Dry
Plant:	Apr. - Sept.
Distance:	....
Blooms:	....
Uses:	Specimen, shrub border

LAUREL-CHERRY, ZABEL
(Prunus laurocerasus zabelliana)

Height:	3-4 ft.
Spread:	3-4 ft.
Exposure:	Sun/light shade
Soil:	Good garden loam
Moisture:	Moderate, well-drained
Plant:	Mar./Apr. - Sept.
Distance:	4-5 ft.
Blooms:	White, late summer
Fruit:	None
Uses:	Foreground, mass

It is a hardy form of the cherry laurel. The leaves are longer and thinner than Schipkaensis. It is also more prostrate and spreading.

LIGUSTRUM LUCIDUM CORRAECEUM

Height:	5-6 ft.
Spread:	2 ft.
Exposure:	Sun/shade
Soil:	Good garden loam
Moisture:	Well-drained, moderately moist
Plant:	Mar./Apr. - Sept.
Distance:	4 ft.
Blooms:	Small white
Fruit:	Blue-black
Uses:	Specimen, hedge

Dwarf, broadleafed evergreen with dark green, thick, crinkly leaves.

MAHONIA, CLUSTER
(Mahonia pinnata)

Height:	4-6 ft.
Spread:	2½-3 ft.
Exposure:	Light shade/sun
Soil:	Rich in humus
Plant:	Mar./Apr. - Sept.
Blooms:	Apr.-May
Flowers:	Clusters small yellow
Fruit:	Blue
Uses:	Smaller shrub border

A compact, heavily branched juniper with a silver-blue foliage. This evergreen is different in that it normally has a flat top.

This is a compact, heavily branched, upright growing shrub. It is hardy, but needs good subsurface drainage and sun. Heavy pruning in late winter or early spring is needed for best growth and appearance. The winter foliage has a distinct bluish tinge.

MAHONIA, COMPACT OREGON-GRAPE
(Mahonia aquifolium 'COMPACT')

Height:	2-3 ft.
Spread:	....
Exposure:	Light-shade, partial sun
Soil:	Enriched with humus
Moisture:	Well-drained, moderate
Plant:	Apr. - Sept.
Distance:	....
Blooms:	Apr., yellow clusters
Fruit:	Blue
Uses:	Shrub border

This is a dwarf form of the familiar mahonia and as such is useful in the shady shrub border as well as in areas where it is exposed to morning sun. Pruning improves the growth.

MAHONIA, LEATHER-LEAF

(Mahonia bealei)

Height:	4-5 ft.
Spread:	4-5 ft.
Exposure:	Light shade/partial sun
Soil:	Enriched with humus
Moisture:	Well-drained, moderate
Plant:	Apr. - Sept.
Blooms:	Apr. bright yellow clusters
Fruit:	Large, blue-black
Uses:	Shrub border

The Leatherleaf mahonia is distinct because of the bronzy-green foliage and the fruits which are much larger than those of the hollygrape.

OSMANTHUS, GULF-TIDE

(Osmanthus ilicifolius 'Gulftide')

Height:	6 ft.
Spread:	7 ft.
Exposure:	Sun/light shade
Soil:	Good garden loam, well-drained
Moisture:	Moderate
Plant:	Apr. - Sept.
Blooms:	Fall, fragrant
Fruit:	Seldom, blue-black
Uses:	Specimen

A more compact osmanthus with curly leaves, its small fragrant flowers appear in the fall, on this evergreen.

OSMANTHUS, HOLLY

(Osmanthus ilicifolius rotundifolius)

Height:	4-5 ft.
Spread:	3-4 ft.
Exposure:	Sun/shade
Soil:	Good garden loam
Moisture:	Well-drained, moderately moist
Plant:	Mar./Apr. - Sept.
Moisture:	4-6 ft.
Blooms:	Early fall, fragrant
Fruit:	None (in this area)
Uses:	Specimen, background

This is a slow-growing dwarf evergreen shrub with small, shiny, wavy-margined leaves, and a good plant for sun or shade. Like most of the osmanthus they are not hardy when small, but gain as they age.

SPRUCE, NEST

(Picea abies 'Nest')

Height:	3-4 ft.
Spread:	3-4 ft.
Exposure:	Sun
Soil:	Well-drained, moderately moist
Plant:	Apr. - Sept.
Blooms:	....
Fruit:	....
Uses:	Specimen

This is a very compact dwarf spruce that grows as a flattened globe.

PINE, SHRUBBY SWISS MOUNTAIN

(Pinus mugo pumilio)

Height:	2-3 ft.
Spread:	3 ft.
Exposure:	Sun
Soil:	Well-drained, enriched with humus
Moisture:	Moderate
Distance:	....
Plant:	Apr. - Sept.
Blooms:	....
Fruit:	Seldom produces cones
Uses:	Specimen, rock garden

This is the most dwarf of the mugho pines, but should be pruned annually (cutting the candles in half) to obtain the minimum growth.

BARBERRY, CRIMSON PYGMY

(Berberis thunbergi 'Crimson Pygmy')

Height:	18-24 in.
Spread:	18-24 in.
Exposure:	Sun
Soil:	Good garden loam
Moisture:	Moderate
Distance:	....
Plant:	Mar./Apr. - Nov.
Blooms:	....
Fruit:	....
Uses:	Low border

Here is a very dwarf red-foliaged barberry, useful for a low border.

DAPHNE, GENKWA

(DAPHNE genkwa)

Height:	2-3 ft.
Spread:	....
Exposure:	Light shade/sun
Soil:	Well-drained, rich in humus
Plant:	Mar./Apr. - Nov.
Distance:	....
Blooms:	April - lilac
Fruit:	None
Uses:	Foundation planting, shrub border

This one may be slow to become established but is worth the extra effort. The showy lilac flowers appear before the leaves unfold. Apparently it is easier to grow than the commonly planted Rose daphne. (D. Cneorum).

DEUTZIA CARNEA

(Deutzia Carnea)

Height:	2-3 ft.
Spread:	2-3 ft.
Exposure:	Light shade/sun

Soil:	Good garden loam
Moisture:	Average
Plant:	Mar./Apr. - Nov.
Distance:	2/3 ft.
Blooms:	Late May
Fruit:	None
Uses:	Cutting, display

This dwarf rounded deutzia has drooping branches compared to the more upright growth of D. gracilis. The foliage has a better landscape value, too, and is more winter hardy. The deutzias are small enough for use in the smaller shrub border and for use in front of taller growing shrubs.

ENKIANTHUS, REDVEIN

(Enkianthus campanulatus)

Height:	8-10 ft.
Spread:	6-8 ft.
Exposure:	Shade
Soil:	Rich with humus, moist
Plant:	Mar./Apr. - Nov.
Blooms:	Mid-May - Creamy-yellow, bell-shaped
Fruit:	None
Uses:	Combines well with rhododendron

The Redvein Enkianthus, a member of the rhododendron family, needs about the same growing conditions, has interesting bell shaped flowers in the spring. The foliage is good and turns to a bright red in the fall. It is a useful and attractive shrub.

QUINCE, CHINESE FLOWERING

(Chaenomele sinensis)

Height:	6-7 ft.
Spread:	5 ft.
Exposure:	Sun/light shade
Soil:	Good garden loam
Moisture:	Moderate
Plant:	Mar./Apr. - Nov.
Distance:	....
Blooms:	Mar.-Apr.
Fruit:	Large
Uses:	Cutflowers, border

This is a pink-flowered Chinese quince. There is some question as to the botanical name, but none as to the origin. Most of the others offered today are Japanese. The varieties, and there are many of them, are superior to the species. The fruits of all are good for jelly making.

VIBURNUM LANTANAPHYLLUM

(Viburnum lantana x V. rhytidophyllum)

Height:	6-8 ft.
Spread:	3-4 ft.
Exposure:	Light shade/sun
Soil:	Rich in humus, moist
Plant:	Mar./Apr. - Sept.
Blooms:	May
Fruit:	Clusters, whitish, pink, red, blue finally black Shady
Uses:	border.

This hybrid is somewhat smaller growing than the parents, has good branching, and the gray-green foliage, which does not roll in cold weather, persists into

mid-winter. The large flat clusters of white flowers are followed by clusters of fruits which first are green, turning to whitish, pink, red, blue and finally black. Several colors may be in a cluster at the same time. This shrub is hardy and may be evergreen in protected situations.

Ground Covers

ABELIA, PROSTRATE GLOSSY

(Abelia grandiflora prostrata)

Height:	18-24 in.
Spread:	3-4 ft.
Exposure:	Light shade
Soil:	Good garden loam
Moisture:	Well-drained, slightly moist
Plant:	Mar./Apr. - Sept.
Blooms:	July-Oct., white
Fruit:	None
Uses:	Ground cover, facing shrub

This is a prostrate form of the Glossy abelia that may be useful as a bank cover; or it is equally useful as a low-growing shrub in front of taller growing ones. It has small glossy leaves and season-long bloom.

COTONEASTER, CRANBERRY

(Cotoneaster adphessa praecox)

Height:	1¼-2 ft.
Spread:	3-5 ft.
Exposure:	Sun
Soil:	Good garden loam
Plant:	Mar./Apr. - Sept.
Distance:	4-6 ft.
Blooms:	Early May
Flowers:	Pinkish, small
Fruit:	Large, bright red
Uses:	Rock garden, in front of shrubbery

This cotoneaster is a slow grower and has denser growth than the commonly planted Rockspray. It is a good ground cover where space does not require a stronger grower. The fruits are larger and more showy, too. The leaves are somewhat larger.

JUNIPER, COMPACT ANDORRA

(Juniperus horizontalis plumosa 'Compacta'—Youngstown Strain)

Height:	15-18 in.
Spread:	4-5 ft.
Exposure:	Sun
Soil:	Ordinary garden
Plant:	Mar./Apr. - Sept.
Blooms:	None
Fruit:	None
Uses:	Ground cover

This is a compact slow growing form of the widely planted Andorra juniper. It also has a better habit of growth. The winter color is slightly more purplish-red than the usual bronzed purple.

JUNIPER, BLUE RUG

(Juniperus horizontalis 'Wiltoni')

Height:	4-5 in.
Spread:	6 ft.
Exposure:	Sunny
Soil:	Well-drained, ordinary garden loam
Moisture:	Dry
Plant:	Mar./Apr. - Sept.
Blooms:	Distance: 4-5 ft.
Fruit:	....
Uses:	Ground cover

A low-growing juniper with an unusual color that is useful for covering small hot dry slopes.

JUNIPER, SARGENT

(Juniperus chinensis sargenti)

Height:	18 in.
Spread:	6-8 ft.
Exposure:	Sun
Soil:	Ordinary garden
Plant:	Mar./Apr. - Sept.
Distance:	8 ft.
Blooms:	None
Fruit:	None
Uses:	Ground cover for banks, etc.

This is a low prostrate creeping evergreen usually under 18 in. with a bright steel blue color in the winter, bluish green in the summer. It seems free of the insect problems associated with J. horizontalis and other spreading junipers. Is not an especially fast grower.

SARCOCOCCA

(Sarcococca hookeriana humilis)

Height:	1-2 ft.
Spread:	12-18 in.
Exposure:	Shade
Soil:	Rich in humus
Plant:	Mar./Apr. - Sept.
Blooms:	Early spring
Flowers:	Inconspicuous
Fruit:	Black
Uses:	Ground cover, facing-up shrub

The Sarcococca is an excellent ground cover in shady situations, but is tall enough to be grown in front of taller shrubs. It does best in a soil well enriched with humus and that is moist. Winter mulching is needed in this area.

STRANVAESIA

(Stranvaesia davidiana undulata)

Height:	15-18 in.
Spread:	5-6 ft.
Exposure:	Sun/light shade
Soil:	Rich in humus, moist
Plant:	Mar./Apr. - Sept.
Distance:	6-8 ft.
Blooms:	May - white clusters
Fruit:	Showy red, persist
Uses:	Low evergreen borders

This low-growing Stranvaesia is much hardier than the taller-growing form. It will take sun or light shade; it has oval-shaped leaves 1 to 2 inches low that are green in the summer and reddish in the winter. The leaf edges are especially wavy. The white flat-topped clusters

of flowers are followed by clusters of vermillion red fruits that persist late into the winter.

Vines

HYDRANGEA, CLIMBING
(Hydrangea petiolaris)

Height:	10-20 ft.
Spread:	....
Exposure:	Shade
Soil:	Rich in humus
Moisture:	Moderate, well-drained
Plant:	Mar./Apr.
Blooms:	July, white, fragrant
Fruit:	None
Uses:	Covering a north wall

The climbing hydrangea is a bit tender when young, and slow to become established. However, it will cling to stone or brick and in time produce an excellent display of large, hydrangea like flowers, in mid-summer.

TRUMPETCREEPER—MME. GALEN
(Campsis tagliabuana 'Mme. Galen')

Height:	20-40 ft.
Spread:	....
Exposure:	Sun
Soil:	Rich with humus
Moisture:	Well-drained, moderate
Blooms:	Throughout the season—tawny-orange
Fruit:	Pods
Uses:	Screen, shade

This is a hardier form of the Trumpetcreeper, with larger flowers that are produced over a long season. This variety is considered a hybrid between the American and the Chinese, combining the best characteristics of both. It is a strong climber with aerial rootlets along the woody stems.

CHAPTER XV

ROSES FOR WASHINGTON GARDENS

Roses are almost a universal favorite among gardeners. There are few gardens, except perhaps the shady ones, which do not have one or more kinds. This would signify that roses are adaptable and quite tolerant in their requirements and also, that they may be used in many ways in the garden. This is true, but not all kinds and varieties of roses may be depended upon to thrive and flower profusely under Washington conditions. Each year many new varieties are introduced to the home gardener, however, even the varieties recommended by the All-American Rose Selections find their limitations in this area.

Uses:	Cut flowers, bedding, background, specimen
Plant:	Nov.-Dec., March
Distance:	24-36 inches
Soil:	Rich, moist but well-drained
Exposure:	Sun, very light shade
Prune:	Spring

POTOMAC ROSE SOCIETY SELECTIONS

Beginner's Dozen—
White—Ivory Fashion—MF (Flor.)
Pink—
Pink Blend—Confidence-MF, Chicago Peace-M, Tiffany-MF
Red—Avon-MF, Chrysler Imperial-MF
Yellow—Eclipse-M
Yellow Blend—Peace-M, Garden Party-M
Orange—Tropicana-MF
Pink Blend—Vogue-TF (Flor.)
Pink—Queen Elizabeth-TF (Gran.)

	Hybrid Teas	Floribundas	Climbers
White	Burnaby-M	Ivory Fashion-MF	City of York-F
	Virgo-M	White Bouquet-LF	White Dawn-F
	Sincera-MF	Shasta-MF	
Yellow	Eclipse-MF		Golden Showers-F
	Summer Sunshine-M		
Yellow Blend	Champagne-MF	Circus-L	
	Garden Party-M	Little Darling-M	
	King's Ransom-TF	All Gold-M	
	Peace-M		
Orange	Hawaii-MF	Heat Wave-MF	Spectacular-F
	San Francisco-MF	Rumba-MF	
	Tropicana-MF	Spartan-MF	
Pink	Dainty Boss-M (single)	Betty Prior-TF	Blossomtime-F
	Duet-M	Pink Chiffon-LF	Coral Dawn-F
	Margaret-MF	Polka-LF	Morning-Dawn-F
	Pink Favorite-M		New Dawn-F
	Eiffel Tower-TF		
Pink Blend	Prima Ballerina-M	Fashion-MF	
	Chicago Peace-M	Fashionette-MF	
	Confidence-MF	Pinocchio-MF	
	Tiffany-MF	Vogue-MF	
Red	New Yorker-MF	Frensham-M	Blaze
	Avon-MF	Red Pinocchio-MF	Don Juan-F
	Charlotte Armstrong-TF	Ginger-M	Gladiator-F
	Mister Lincoln-TF	Fire King-T	Red Empress-F
	Chrysler Imperial-MF		
	Crimson Glory-LF		
	Josephine Bruce-M		
	Rubaiyat-MF		
	Wendy Cussons-LF		
Red Blend	Suspense-MF	Masquerade-MF	Joseph's Coat-F

ROSES FOR WASHINGTON GARDENS

GRANDIFLORAS

White	Pink	Red and Orange-Red
Mt. Shasta-M	Queen Elizabeth-TF	Carrousel-MF
Yellow	Camelot-TF	John S. Armstrong-M
Buccaneer-TF	Pink Parfait-MF	El Capitan-TF
Golden Girl-TF		Montezuma-T
		Olé-MF

MINIATURE ROSES

Pink	White	Yellow Blend
Baby Betsy McCall	Cinderella	Baby Masquerade
Bo-Peep	Pixie	Red
Pixie Rose	Yellow	Midget
Sweet Fairy	Pixie Gold	Red Imp
Tinker Bell		Scarlet Gem

Symbols: Heights—L—under 30 inches; M—30-48 inches; T—over 48 inches; Fragrant—F

The above listed varieties are the recommendations of a committee of the Potomac Rose-Society and are considered to be the most dependable for the Washington area. Taken into consideration were vigor, quality of bloom, freedom from disease and other factors and the years of trial in local gardens.

Grandiflora Roses

The Grandiflora class of roses is the designation for a new type of rose, intermediate between Floribunda and the Hybrid Tea. Announced by the American Rose Society in the summer of 1954, several varieties have been registered for the new class: Queen Elizabeth, Buccaneer, Carrousel, Montezuma, etc.

Most gardeners think of roses in terms of the "hybrid teas," the type widely displayed by florists. There are many other kinds, some of which have a place in the rose beds. Others belong in mass color plantings, as edgings for shrub beds, drives, etc., and there are still others which belong to the shrub border. A few still are desirable as specimen plantings. Climbing roses often provide the background for flower beds.

The old "tea" roses of the South are with few exceptions too tender to be grown in this area. The hybrid teas, with few exceptions, are hardy. The cluster-flowered polyanthas and floribundas do not lack winter hardiness. The rugged June-flowering hybrid perpetuals are hardy enough, but lack in other qualities and so with few exceptions are not generally grown here. The climbers—large-flowered, monthly-blooming, and rambler—are with few exceptions suited to local climatic conditions as are most shrub roses.

With all of these types and classes of roses to choose from, the majority of gardeners buy the free-flowering hybrid-teas. Hybrid-tea roses give a long season of bloom and have a wide range of colors—white, pink, red, yellow, blends, and bi-colors. Most of the hybrid-tea varieties produce a heavy bloom in late May and early June and then flower sparsely during the heat of the summer, ending the season with a second burst of bloom in the fall. Hybrid-tea varieties vary consider-

Long-pointed rose buds are the most popular.

ably in habit and size of growth. There is a considerable variation in their susceptibility to disease. Some are almost immune to "black spot" while others are seldom free from this disease. Hybrid tea varieties vary in their freedom of bloom as well as in the form of the flowers. There are varieties with single flowers, and there are others with so many petals that the opened bloom resembles a cabbage.

Some red varieties "blue" in the summer sun. Some lack in petal substance and the flowers are not long lasting. Others are weak-necked. With such a range in characteristics, the gardener should be rather choosy and select varieties which are most desirable. Those listed above are believed comparatively free of undesirable characteristics.

Next to the hybrid-tea roses, the cluster-flower, low bushy, hardy floribundas or polyanthas, they are variously called, are most widely grown. Some floribundas are compact little plants, some are under 30 inches, and are excellent for driveway borders, along walks, and other rose plantings.

Most gardeners wish to have bloom throughout the season and the floribundas come near to meeting this requirement. Only a few are grown for use as cutflowers. They are not immune to disease, but usually are less troubled than the hybrid-teas.

The third class of roses, climbers, is best treated by types: ramblers, large-flowered (June bloomers), climbing hybrid teas, and climbers which were bred to be climbers. Each has a rather distinctive type of pruning.

The true ramblers, such as Dorothy Perkins and Crimson Rambler, are not widely planted here, although there is one variety, Chevy Chase, produced by Niels J. Hansen of Washington, D.C., which is not susceptible to mildew and consequently is of interest. The pruning of the true rambler is quite simple. Cut off all canes to the ground immediately after the flowering season. The Chevy Chase variety, however, is usually treated as a large-flowered climber and only a part of the canes are removed.

The large-flowered climbers, which are primarily June bloomers, theoretically should be pruned immediately after the flowering season. However, since few people do prune at that period, it is customary to remove from a fourth to a third of the oldest canes in the spring, cutting them off as close to the ground as possible.

The third group, the climbing hybrid teas, are pruned simply by shortening the side branches on the main canes. In other words, the framework or main canes are not disturbed as long as they are in good condition; only the side branches on them are shortened.

The other climbers, those which were bred to be climbers, are exceedingly varied in their habit of growth and the pruning needed to take care of them. For example, Gladiator is trimmed very much like a climbing hybrid tea although it is a much stronger grower. Parade is such a rampant grower that it is treated similar to the large-flowered June bloomers (canes removed) with quite a bit of shortening of the side branches on the remaining canes. This group of climbers is increasing in popularity because most of them are repeat or recurrent bloomers.

This is the basic pruning which the climbers need; however, all dead wood should be first removed and such additional pruning given as needed to fit the space allotted to them.

One cannot be specific in stating how far the canes need to be shortened since some varieties produce canes 15 to 20 ft. or more in length. The climbing hybrid teas as a group seldom exceed 10 ft. in height, and for this reason are commonly known as "Pillar" roses. Also, since the new canes begin to develop shortly after the flowering season, it is good practice to do as much pruning just ahead of this as is feasible.

Very few climbers flower the first season after they are set out. There is one exception to this rule, Clair Matin.

The climbing roses should be kept securely tied to their supports—trellises, arbors, fences, pergolas, etc. —to prevent their being whipped about by the winds. Their thorny branches not only injure other canes but also any wooden surface within their reach. These scratches are entry points for the canker diseases which in most cases are much more prevalent among the climbers than among the hybrid teas and other bush roses.

Among the shrub roses which may be used in the shrub border, as hedges and as specimen planting, are a number of worthwhile kinds and varieties. The hardy, vigorous-growing rugosas and their hybrids are admired for their distinctive foilage and large, brightly colored seed hips. Some of the more modern varieties of rugosas have a long flowering season. Most of them are large bushes, while others spread by underground runners and must be curbed to be kept within bounds. Sarah Van Fleet is considered one of the best of the rugosa hybrids. It has a more or less continuous display of flowers from spring until fall and does not spread by underground stems.

Harrison's Yellow, a disease-resistant spreading shrub, is one of the earliest to flower in the spring and is prized by many. Rosa primula (ecae) makes a large specimen shrub, has interesting bark and thorns, and is covered in the early spring with large, single, creamy yellow flowers. The Father Hugonis rose, sometimes called the Golden Rose of China, is covered, in May, with large, single, yellow roses.

In addition to the types or classes mentioned above, there are the trailing roses which may be used to cover banks. They are of questionable use because of the difficulty in controlling weeds and grass beneath the thorny canes. A new variety, Sea Foam, developed by a nearby rose hybridizer, is unique in that it grows so thickly that it is good enough for a ground cover, can be used as a broad, low hedge 2 or 3 feet wide and that tall. It can also be tied to a trellis, fence, or post, or draped over a wall. The flowers are medium size, white, fragrant, and the blooms continue throughout the summer season.

Miniature roses form another class that is frequently mentioned for use in rock gardens and window boxes. They require a proper setting to be enjoyed and are not rugged enough to take abuse and still make a showing.

The last class, which might be termed oldfashioned roses, includes many types, some of which were important in early history. The China, Bourbon, Moss, Cabbage, French, etc., are found frequently in collectors' gardens.

TREE ROSES, sometimes called Standard Roses, like Pillar Roses, can be used to good advantage among bush roses and in landscaping the home grounds. They are distinctive because of the form of the plant, with upright trunks perhaps 3 feet tall. Many of the better-known varieties of roses are available in tree form.

When to Plant Roses

In the Washington area fall planting is preferred since the work may be done rather leisurely in that season. Rose bushes keep over winter in the ground just as well as in a storage house. But most important, they are ready to start into growth in the spring much earlier than is possible with spring planting. Northern nurseries can supply this area with roses for fall planting. Southern and Western grown bushes are not available in time.

Roses are customarily planted in beds or holes that are deeply prepared through the addition of liberal quantities of compost or peat moss to a depth of 15 to 24 inches. In heavy clay soils that have little or no subsoil drainage, this may be injurious since water penetrates into a prepared soil much more easily than it does into an unprepared one. If subsurface drainage is lacking, the water must remain in the hole or bed until it evaporates. Before preparing a rose bed, the subsurface drainage should be tested. Dig a hole 18 to 24 inches deep and pour in a pail of water. If in 24 hours, the water is still in the hole and has not shown signs of penetrating into the subsoil, the rose bed should either be provided with a drain tile to carry surplus moisture away, or the incorporation of humus materials should be omitted.

In most of the Washington area there is adequate subsurface drainage and the beds should be prepared with ample supplies of humus—compost, peatmoss, well-rotted cow mature, etc. Studies show that roses benefit from additions of such materials up to 50 per cent of the volume. Bone meal and superphosphate should be mixed with the soil in the bed at time of preparation because the phosphate travels very slowly through the soil.

Lime, in the form of ground limestone, should be added to reduce the acidity of the soil to a pH reading of 6.0 to 6.5. Roses are tolerant and will grow in an acid soil, but in very acid soils certain plant foods become locked up while certain minerals that are undesirable are released. The lime should not be added without a soil test and the quantity added should be determined by the test.

The deeper the soil is worked and enriched the larger the root-run will be and the feeding area thus provided will enable the rose to make a corresponding vigorous growth. Animal manures supply some elements that are not contained in other forms of humus. To a limited extent these elements may be supplied through the addition of limited quantities of "trace elements", but very little information is available on this problem.

Planting the Rose Bush

Rose bushes normally are planted too closely together for good growth. This is an inheritance from the old theory that the foilage should shade the ground. Studies on this point indicate that wider spacing is needed for both good growth and for flowering. Where space permits, the bushes should be set 24 to 36 inches apart. Even the lower growing polyanthas need this spacing, while the strong growing hybrid perpetuals and shrub roses need three, four or even more feet of space.

The planting depth of a rose bush should be determined by the bud joint. After settling, the bud joint should be even with the surface of the ground. The depth of the hole should be determined by the size of the root system which should be spread out in a natural position. A cone of earth in the bottom of the hole aids in spreading the roots. Broken root ends should be smoothed with a sharp knife or pruning shears. Do not clip the ends of the roots "crew" style to permit planting in a "junior-sized" hole.

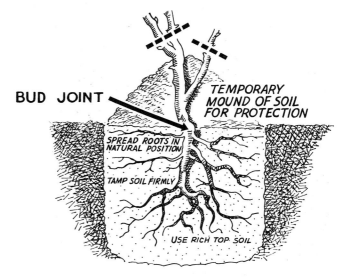

In planting the dormant rose bush spread the roots in a natural position in a hole that is large enough to accommodate them without crowding or bending.

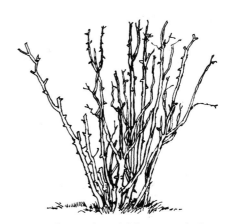

Before pruning a hybrid tea rose bush.

After the bush is in place with the roots spread out, work soil in and around the roots so as to prevent air pockets. When the hole is two thirds full, it should be thoroughly tramped to firm the soil about the roots. Then fill the hole with water and allow it to soak into the soil. When this has taken place fill the hole with soil but do not tramp or pack.

After planting, the soil should be mounded to a height of eight to ten inches, preferably with soil brought in for this purpose, rather than with that taken from the area between the bushes. The mounds are to protect the canes from drying winds during the winter. The ends of the canes protruding from the mound might well be clipped off if more than an inch or two in length.

In the spring before the new growth starts, the mound should be removed, preferably on a cloudy day to avoid sun-burning the tender bark. It is better if the removal can be extended over a week or 10 days.

Spring planted bushes except those in pots or cans, need this same protective mound, but only for a period of ten days to two weeks. By the end of that period the roots should be functioning and protection from sun and wind should no longer be necessary.

POTTED ROSE PLANTS are usually available only in the Spring. When ready to plant, prepare the site as you would for other roses. Cut the plastic or paper cover, but do not disturb the soil around the roots. Plant the bush so that the bud union, which may be high on some potted plants, shows at ground level. Fill in with good soil and use plenty of water. It is not necessary to mound soil around potted plants.

Planting Pointers

Neither manure nor fertilizer should be in contact with the roots of the newly planted bush.

If the tops or roots of the bushes were at all dry at time of receipt, the bushes should be soaked overnight in a tub of water. Do not continue the soaking for more than 24 hours. If planting is to be delayed for several days, heel the bushes in a trench, covering roots and tops with soil.

Never allow the roots to be exposed to drying wind or sun during the planting. The safest procedure is to place them in a pail of soupy mud, taking a bush out of the pail only after the hole is ready to receive it.

The canes should be shortened at planting time to a length of not more than six to eight inches. Make clean cuts with a sharp knife or pruning shears. Cover the cuts with a tree dressing or other protective material to prevent entrance of the sawfly, also called cane borer.

Discard any bush which shows signs of nematodes —usually referred to as root galls. No one wants to have his rose beds infested with these pests.

Bushes lacking an adequate root system are seldom worth planting because they do not start off with the vigor that is to be expected from a well-grown plant.

Do not plant roses in beds where they will be in competition with tree roots or heavily shaded during the major portion of the day. They will probably grow but they will give little satisfaction unless the owner is in position to give them abundant care.

Roses do better when they are protected from strong winds, both in the summer and in the winter. Such winds sap the moisture from the leaves and wood faster than it can be replaced by the roots.

Roses in a dead air pocket are more subject to disease and insect pests than those planted in a situation where air circulates freely and sunlight reaches them at least six hours a day.

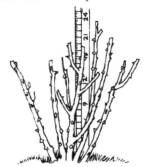

The hybrid tea rose after pruning.

Occasionally, a shoot appears beside a hybrid tea rose with seven or nine leaflets to the leaf. This is a shoot originating on the root stock, is commonly called a 'sucker', and should be removed. If allowed to grow it will deprive the budded rose of strength and the bush will gradually die, leaving only the wild root stock with its inferior bloom. This applies primarily to the multiflora rootstock. Many of the western grown roses are on Dr. Huey root stock or its progeny, and which have foilage resembling a hybrid tea. Thus, until the dark red single blooms appear, it may be difficult to know which is a sucker from the root stock and which is the budded variety on it.

Pruning

Pruning of hybrid teas, hybrid perpetuals, and poly-anthas is normally done in the early spring after danger of a killing freeze is past. This timing is to avoid further reduction in the size of the bush by freeze injury after pruning.

Prune the large-flowered climbing roses by removing from ⅓ to ¼ of the oldest canes at the ground. The older, scaly canes, which are a home for disease and insect pests, should be removed following the flowering season.

ROSES FOR WASHINGTON GARDENS

Spring pruning is confined to the removal of—1. dead wood, 2. weak and spindly growth, and 3. shortening of the remaining canes. The extent of this shortening will depend on the number of blooms desired from the first burst of bloom and the length of stems. Current practice dictates moderation in pruning because the bushes need foliage for best growth.

Treat all pruning cuts with a tree dressing or some other protective material to exclude the sawfly, which attacks only the cut ends of rose bushes.

The pruning of climbing roses should be postponed until after the spring burst of flowers. Then remove from one-fourth to one-third of the oldest canes. This is the renewal system of pruning and is designed to maintain quality of bloom as well as to keep the climber within bounds. The best quality blooms are produced on new wood of last year. Wood produced the season before will bear flowers of almost equal quality. Wood older than two years has lower quality bloom. Old canes with shaggy bark make a good winter home for insects and diseases so that a regular pruning schedule is desirable for sanitation purposes.

Climbing sports of hybrid teas should be pruned about the same as the bush forms and at the same season. Varieties of large-flowered climbers that produce bloom throughout the season are pruned in the same manner and at the same season as are the spring-bloomers.

The pruning of shrub roses is much simpler—remove the dead wood and such canes as interfere with passers-by. The rugosas and hybrid rugosas need to have their canes shortened to encourage compact growth, otherwise they grow too tall and become bare-legged.

Insect and Disease Control

The first and most important protection needed by the rose is from disease. Spraying and dusting are not cures but protective measures. The application of spray or dust after the bug has partly eaten the leaf or a disease germ has entered it is of no help to that leaf. The job of keeping the bushes healthy and free of insect injury is one of keeping the foliage covered. This is exceedingly important since a rose bush cannot thrive and bloom vigorously without its foliage. Most growers depend upon an all-purpose dust or spray, applied at weekly intervals. However, in the spring, when growth is rapid and showers are frequent, the interval between applications obviously should be shorter than during the summer when growth is slower and showers are infrequent.

The undersides of the leaves need the most protection since that is the usual point of entry of disease germs, and the hiding place for spider mites. But, the

Good spraying or dusting gives complete coverage of foliage.

rose chafer that feeds on rose buds, and the Japanese beetle that climbs into the middle of a rose to feed, are controlled only by poisons that are applied to those areas. During the height of Japanese beetle season it takes an almost daily dusting of DDT or Methoxychlor to keep the beetles under control.

The choice between a duster and a sprayer depends upon the gardener. A good job of protecting roses may be done with either one. It is not the method or the material applied but the regularity and thoroughness of the application which counts.

Winter Protection

Mention has been made of the need for protecting the rose bed from strong winds, both in summer and in winter. This may be done with an evergreen background, or even a strong climbing rose spread over a trellis or fence. In winter the bed may be covered with pine boughs or sheltered with a burlap screen.

Beyond the protection from the winter winds and sun the rose bushes do not require any special protection. A small mound of soil about the base of the bush may be desirable to prevent water collecting in the cup caused by the bush swaying about in the wind, but that is seldom needed if the bed is properly sheltered from strong winds. Covering the bed with pine boughs to keep it dormant during a mild winter has been desirable on occasion in the Washington area, but that is not often. Healthy bushes usually come through our winters without injury. It is only the bushes that are weak because of defoliation due to disease, or that are in poorly drained beds that are especially subject to winter injury.

Climbing roses should be kept well tied to their supports to prevent blowing about by winds. Allowed to blow about, the canes are scratched and bruised—points of entry for disease (canker).

Feeding the Rose

The frequency and amount of fertilizer to be given the established rose depends to a considerable extent upon what is desired from the bush. Some growers start out by giving each bush a generous handful of fertilizer (5-10-5 or a special rose food) in March, and each month thereafter to the first of August. Feeding after that date is likely to produce soft growth that might not mature before freezing weather. The use of special rose foods appeals to some and good results are obtainable through the use of such fertilizers. However, the majority of growers depend upon the commonly available general purpose mixtures.

The use of manures, applied in the winter after the bushes are dormant, is a preferred practice by some rose fanciers, but cow manure, the best animal manure for roses, is costly and difficult to obtain. Also, care must be taken to see that the manure does not come into contact with the bark. And manures do contain weed seeds.

The use of dolomitic ground limestone is desirable every few years because of its magnesium content. Only a small amount of magnesium is needed, an oversupply may be harmful.

Mulching

The mulching of the rose bed is not practiced as widely as it should be. A heavily mulched soil gives far greater returns in growth and bloom than a well cultivated bed. The kind of material used is unimportant. The important point is to apply a mulch in the spring and to keep it there until the following spring. This will serve the following functions: 1. Prevent erosion. 2. Control weeds. 3. Conserve moisture. 4. Provide better aeration of the soil. 5. Keep the soil cooler, thus permitting the roots to function during periods of high temperature, and 6. Maintain the humus content of the soil.

A mulch, to be effective, must not be a drain on the soil, which sometimes takes place when the bacteria working on the humus material are unable to obtain sufficient nitrogen. Sawdust is a good example of a mulching material that requires the addition of nitrogen to feed the bacteria. The nitrogen may be supplied in the form of sulphate of ammonia, nitrate of soda, animal manures, oilmeals (cottonseed, linseed, peanut, soybean, etc.), and slaughterhouse by-products. No rule may be given as to quantity since it will vary with the condition of the mulch when applied. Apply a given quantity and then watch the color of the rose foliage. At the first sign of yellowing add more nitrogen to the mulch.

Cutting Roses

The cutting of a bloom from a rose bush may greatly affect the subsequent growth of the bush. Normally, a new shoot may appear from each leafaxil left on the branch. Such an array of new growth is seldom desirable, but neither is the removal of all of the shoot, which would remove all foliage. The best practice is to leave one or two leaves at the base of the flowering shoot.

The removal of spent blooms generally consists of snapping off the dead flower. This leaves the maximum number of leaves on the bush, but it also leaves buds which seldom produce good bloom—i.e., the first leaf axil below the flower. Cutting back to the second or third leaf is thought to be the better practice.

Disbudding

Most varieties of hybrid-tea roses produce a cluster of buds at the terminal of each new shoot. The removal of the side buds puts the strength into the terminal bud, thus producing a larger and finer flower.

Moreover, a flower flanked by one or two unopened buds is not as attractive as blooms unburdened by side-buds. The rules of the American Rose Society disqualify from competition hybrid-tea roses that were not disbudded.

In cutting a rose, make the cut just above the second leaf at the lower end of the flowering shoot.

Disbud a portion of the roses, removing the side buds, thus putting all the plant's strength into the terminal bud.

CHAPTER XVI

PLANNING THE VEGETABLE GARDEN

Many vegetable gardens are planted without plan or previous thought. The experienced gardener has found that a plan, no matter how simple, is a useful guide. A plan prepared in advance aids in the proper selection of crops, the proper arrangement of space, and the purchase of the right amount of seed, fertilizer, dust or spray materials.

Early crops should be planted on the lightest, warmest soils. Crops that need cool, moist situations, such as celery and parsley, should be assigned to favorable locations. Tall-growing crops must not shade lower-growing crops. All of these factors are considered and taken into account when making the plan. A plan is handy in locating crops which must be rotated to avoid difficulties from diseases.

By grouping the early short-season crops in one section, the gardener is able to prepare in advance a section of the garden for early spring plantings. Fall spading is necessary, of course, but unless the garden is arranged to facilitate this it may not be done. The fall crops section should be cleared of early crops by July, so that the soil may be prepared for planting the fall crops.

The planner should take into consideration the quan-

tities needed to supply the table without waste or loss in quality. If food is to be preserved for winter use, this also must be taken into consideration both as to quantities that will be wanted and the time when the preserving is to be done. This determines the planting time.

In making the plan it is well to run the rows the long way of the plot for ease in cultivation, although it is desirable that they extend from north to south to give each row of plants the maximum sunlight. Where it is impracticable to run them in a north and south direction, the taller-growing crops should be placed on the north side of the plot, the lower-growing ones to the south.

The width of rows in the garden will vary for each kind of crop. In general, 16 inches is a good working distance for the smaller garden. Intensive cultivation permits of narrower spacing, while the use of large tillage implements requires more space. Staking sprawling and vining crops conserves space. Tomatoes and beans should not be planted so close together that the gardener cannot get through without brushing the foliage. Foliage, if disturbed while wet, is likely to "rust."

The choice of crops to be grown will depend on the size of the plot, the kinds that the family will use, those that are high in nutritive values, and those that can best be grown under the particular circumstances.

Choose only those crops that the family enjoys. There is no point in growing crops that will not be used on the family table.

Choose crops that contribute the most health-giving and protecting vitamins and minerals. The green leafy vegetables are especially important. Not necessarily all of them should be grown, but one or more from each group should be chosen to insure a continuous supply from early spring to late fall and early winter.

Avoid space-consuming crops such as corn, potatoes, squash, and cucumbers in the very small garden.

Avoid those crops whose growth and productiveness are not dependable under local conditions. It is a waste of time to give space to those which, because of disease or insect pests, or because they are not adapted to our climate and soils are not usually successful.

The plan should take into consideration the length of row to be planted each time. Avoid over-planting. It is a waste of labor, seed, and ground. Gardeners should never have to eat over-ripe vegetables from the home garden. Only vegetables at the peak of perfection are wanted. Most crops remain in this condition for a comparatively short time. A five or six-foot row of radishes will supply the average family for two weeks, and that is about as long as a planting will be in good condition.

A half-dozen hills of squash are more than ample for the average family, since squash grows rapidly and becomes hard-seeded if not used promptly. Three to six plants of parsley, if well cared for, will produce an ample supply of this flavoring herb.

All of these factors should be taken into consideration when making the plan. Several trial plans may be made before the best one is produced. When the gardener has the arrangement worked out to his satisfaction, then the dates of planting and the variety names should be marked on it. In this way all the essential information needed for actual operations will be on the one sheet. This plan should be kept for reference.

Vegetables for the Small Garden
(Under 1,000 Square Feet)

Where space is limited, a decision must be made as to the kinds of vegetables to be grown. Some kinds return much more usable food products for the space occupied than do others. Regardless of personal preference, the gardener should study this problem seriously if the garden is to be most productive for the effort put into it.

Tomatoes rank No. 1 in any garden, be it large or small. If they are well planted, given good care, staked and pruned so that they occupy relatively little space they will produce quantities of highly useful fruit throughout the season. A half-dozen well-cared-for plants should produce enough to keep the family table supplied from July until frost.

Onion sets, planted early in the season, may be counted on for a good crop of green onions as well as bulbs for boiling and slicing. If onion plants are obtainable and the gardener prefers the sweet Spanish onions, plants will yield a substantial crop in a relatively small space.

Lettuce and radishes are early-season crops that yield well for the space taken. Because they do mature so early, they are out of the way of several midseason and late-summer crops. They are cool-weather crops that cannot be depended upon beyond early spring, but may be planted again in the summer for fall harvest.

Snap beans, an excellent and popular garden vegetable which occupies a small area compared to the yield, are attacked by the Mexican bean beetle. So unless this pest is controlled they cannot be considered a productive crop for small gardens. The pole varieties are a bit slower in coming into bearing but have a long harvest period and are easier to protect from the bean beetle.

Swiss chard is one of the most productive of the "greens" and well deserves a place in any garden whose owner relishes it. It may be that the New Zealand spinach is preferred. Both produce over a long season and are excellent nutritive crops.

Carrots and beets are the two standard root crops. They are widely planted and universally used. However, they do not do well on heavy soils. One should incorporate quantities of ashes, sand, or leaf mold into the soil before planting them.

Peppers, both the sweet and the hot, are excellent for the small garden. Three or four plants of the sweet kinds and one or two of the hot will supply the average family.

Broccoli, a member of the cabbage family, yields greater return than the common cabbage and, if enjoyed, deserves a place in the small garden. A half dozen early-set plants will, in favorable seasons, produce throughout the summer and fall. Normally, however, hot summer weather checks them and a second planting is desirable for the fall and early winter crop.

Parsley is used to such a limited extent that it hardly counts in selecting crops. A half dozen plants can easily be tucked into some corner of the garden.

Turnips, kale and spinach are fall and winter crops that should be planted in most gardens to prolong the harvest season. Chinese cabbage and endive are others that tolerate frosts and cold weather.

Parsnips and salsify, root crops that must be given special care on the heavier soils, are not highly produc-

PLANNING THE VEGETABLE GARDEN

SMALL GARDEN PLAN

30 by 50 Feet, Approximately 1/30 Acre

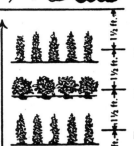

POLE SNAP BEANS—Kentucky Wonder 191, ¼ pound seed.

PEAS—Thomas Laxton, ½ pound seed. Follow August 15 with 1 row TURNIPS, Purple Top White Globe, ¼ ounce seed.

POLE SNAP BEANS—Kentucky Wonder, ¼ pound seed.

PEAS—Thomas Laxton, ½ pound seed. Follow August 15 with 1 row TURNIPS, Purple Top White Globe, ¼ ounce seed.

POLE LIMA BEANS—Burpee's Big Six, ¼ pound seed.

PEAS—Thomas Laxton, ½ pound seed. Follow August 15 with 1 row SPINACH, Virginia Savoy, ¼ ounce seed.

POLE LIMA BEANS—King of the Garden, ¼ pound seed.

TOMATOES—(Staked)—Rutgers or Chesapeake, 1 dozen plants.

BEANS—Tendercrop—½ pound of seed. Follow July 15 with 1 row COLLARDS, Vates, 1 packet seed.

CHARD—Lucullus, ½ row, ½ ounce seed.
PEPPERS—California Wonder, ¼ row, 6 plants.
EGG PLANT—Black Beauty, ¼ row, 6 plants.

BEETS—Detroit Dark Red, ½ row, ½ ounce seed.   Follow August 15 with 1 row
KOHL-RABI—White Vienna, ½ row, 1 packet seed.   PEAS, Dark Green Perfection, ½ pound seed.

CARROTS—Royal Chantenay, 1 packet seed. Follow August 1 with 1 row KALE, Dwarf Green Curled Scotch, 1 packet seed.

LETTUCE—Salad Bowl, 4 ¼ row plantings at 2-week intervals, 1 packet seed. In late July follow with 1 row CARROTS, RED Cored Chantenay, 1 packet seed.

CABBAGE—Golden Acre and Bonanza, 15 plants each, interplanted with RADISHES.

RADISHES—Scarlet Globe, 3 ¼ row planting at 10-day intervals.
ONIONS—(Yellow) 1 pint of sets. In August follow with ½ row CHINESE CABBAGE, Michihli, 1 packet seed, ½ row SPINACH, America, ¼ ounce seed.

BROCCOLI—spartan Early, 6 plants: CABBAGE, Greenback, 15 plants. Follow July 15 with 1 row ENDIVE, Broadleaved BATAVIAN, 1 packet seed.

BEANS—Topcrop, ½ pound seed. Follow with BROCCOLI, spartan Early, 10 plants.

NORTH OR WEST

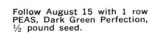

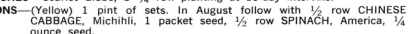

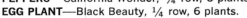

30 feet

50 feet

tive, and should only be planted in the larger gardens. They occupy the space throughout the season.

Cucumbers, like squash, are not a good crop unless safeguarded from insects and disease. Unless so protected they are not worth the space. However, if they can be given adequate care they belong in the larger gardens. Sweet potatoes and white potatoes do not belong in the smaller gardens, but if space permits they are usually grown. Sweet potatoes need a light soil for best results. They usually give a greater return than the white potato. White potatoes are most satisfactory as an early planted spring crop.

Okra, celery, Brussels sprouts and spinach are other crops that belong to the large gardens. Okra is not widely used, but for those who do like it, it is an easily grown crop. Celery is harder to handle and requires more experience for successful results. Brussels sprouts and spinach are important crops for the fall and early winter garden.

Crops for the Larger Garden
(Over 1,000 Square Feet)

Peas produce an early crop and may well be planted where tomatoes are to grow. However, they are definitely a cool-weather crop and unless planted early they may give disappointing results. Since most gardeners enjoy them and they occupy the ground for so short a time they are included in the second dozen in spite of the risks.

Cabbage was omitted from the small garden list because the plants spread out so, but if space permits it should be included. It has many uses both fresh and cooked. The average gardener should not plant more than a dozen plants each of three or four "yellow-resistant" kinds to provide a long harvest season.

Bush squash, if they can be protected from the squash borer and if they are enjoyed by the family, might well be included in this second list. It takes only a few hills to provide an ample supply. They may be protected by dusting or spraying. It may be easier to grow them under cheese cloth or screen.

Eggplants, if liked, belong in the larger gardens. They are slow to come into bearing and are killed by the first frost. Because of their relatively low production, no more space than necessary should be given to them.

Sweet corn is on the must list of many gardeners, whether their plot is large or small. Corn takes considerable space if it is to make good growth and produce satisfactorily. However, tender, freshly-gathered corn is a delicacy that cannot be obtained from the store, so many gardeners will stretch a point to have it in their gardens.

Kale is primarily a late fall and winter crop and can usually be planted after spring crops of snap beans are harvested. If handled in this way it will fit into any garden, large or small.

Edible soybeans and lima beans are other members of the bean family that are widely enjoyed, but are not quite as productive as the "snap" bean. They belong in the large garden. They must be protected from the Mexican bean beetle.

Selecting the Site

The problem of selecting a site for the vegetable plot, whether it be a part of the family lot, or a neighboring vacant lot, or in a community garden, is worthy of careful consideration. Vegetables do not grow satisfactorily in the shade. Sun is necessary for at least a half day; better if it is for three-fourths of the day or more. Poorly drained soils are cold and backward, reducing the number of crops that may be grown on them. Heavy soils are hard to work and do not produce desirable root crops.

It is admitted, however, that almost any soil may be modified so that it will grow vegetable crops reasonably well. Heavy soils may be lightened by mixing with sand, ashes, or compost. Trees that shade the plot may be cut down. However, these are costly modifications and unless the garden plot is to continue in use for vegetable growing for several years, they are hardly justified.

Gravelly soils are particularly difficult, since large quantities of humus must be worked into the soil to hold moisture and plant food. Such soils normally are so open and porous that they dry out quickly and cannot withstand drought. Plant food leaches out of them rapidly and this is costly. Soils containing large pieces of gravel and stones are difficult to cultivate. Tools do not stay sharp and stones often deflect the tools, frequently causing injury to growing plants.

Thus, unless the soil is reasonably productive or can be made so with reasonable expenditure of effort and materials, it is not apt to make a satisfactory garden. However, even the most discouraging piece of ground, if given enough care, will grow vegetables, although few of us can afford to take the time or have the strength for such plots.

The inexperienced gardener may attempt to garden too extensively. A small garden well tended will produce more and better vegetables than a larger plot poorly cared for. A 30-by-50-foot plot normally should produce enough of the smaller crops, excluding corn, cucumbers, potatoes, etc., to supply the average family and provide a surplus for canning. A 50-by-100-foot plot should provide enough for a large family and considerable quantities for preserving. The smaller plot will need at least an hour's time each day. The larger plot will need proportionately more.

PLANNING THE VEGETABLE GARDEN
VEGETABLE PLANTING GUIDE
Planting Calendar

Kinds	Seed for 100 Ft.	Distance Apart In Rows	Distance Apart In Row	Depth to Cover	Crop Matures in	When to Plant	Yield	Varieties
	Ounces	Feet	Inches	Inches	Days			
Asparagus	65*	3	18	4-6	†	March-Apr.	25 bunches	Mary Washington or Washington Strains
Beans, snap, bush, green	8	1½	4	1	50-65	April-May	72 lbs.	Tendercrop, Topcrop, Resistant Black Valentine, Harvester (fall), Tenderette
Beans, snap, bush, wax	8	1½	4	1	50-65	April-May	72 lbs.	Cherokee, Kinghorn Special
Beans, Snap, pole	8	3	4	1	65-80	April	120 lbs.	Kentucky Wonder 191
Beans, lima, bush	16	2	6	1	65-75	May	56 lbs.	Thaxter, Fordhook 242
Beans, lima, pole	16	3	6	1	75-90	May	75 lbs.	King of the Garden, Fordhook
Beets	1	1½	2	½	55-80	Mar.-Aug.	1½ bus.	Detroit Dark Red, Winter Keeper, Crosby's Egyptian, Ruby Queen
Broccoli	50*	3	24	¼	120	March	——	Waltham No. 29, Coastal, Prime
Brussels Sprouts	60*	3	18-20	¼	120	August	30 qts.	Long Island Improved, Jade Cross, Catskill
Cabbage	50*	2½	18-24	¼	60-90	March-Apr.	75-200 lbs.	Early-Golden Acre, Jersey Queen, Bonanza, Marion Market, Savoy Chieftain, Early Round Dutch, Greenback, Emerald Cross
Cantaloupe	½	6	60	½	80-90	May	50 lbs.	Hearts of Gold, Early May, Edisto, Golden Perfection
Carrot	¼	1½	2	¼	75-110	April	100-120 lbs.	Royal Chantenay, Nantes, Danvers 126
Cauliflower	50*	2½	24	¼	120-150	July	35 heads	Early Snowball, Snowball Imperial, Early Purple Head
Celery	150*	2	6	¼	100-120	May (seed)	200 stalks	Summer Pascal
Chard (Swiss)	1	2	12	½	50-60	April	50-75 lbs.	Lucullus, Fordhook Giant, Rhubarb
Chinese Cabbage	pkt.	2	12	¼	80-100	June-July	100 heads	Michihli, Wong Bok
Collards	pkt.	2-3	12-18	½	80	July-Aug.	——	Vates
Corn, sweet	4	3	15-18	1	65-120	May	120 ears	Golden Beauty, NK199, Seneca, Northern Belle, N.J. 106, Sugar King, Seneca Chief, Golden Sensation, Evergreen Hybrids, Country Gentleman Hybrids, Silver Queen
Cucumber	½	6	36	¾	60-80	May	35 lbs.	Marketer, Burpee's Hybrid, Ashley, Ohio MR 17, Polaris, FM Hybrid 51, Pixie
Eggplant	50*	3	24	⅛	100-120	May	120 fruits	Black Beauty, Florida High Bush, Black Magic
Endive	pkt.	2	12	⅛	60-80	July	100 heads	Green Curled, Batavian
Kale	pkt.	2	12	¼	50	July-Aug.	100 lbs.	Vates, Dwarf Green Curled Scotch
Kohlrabi	¼	1½	4-6	½	65	Mar. or July	80 lbs.	White Vienna, Purple Vienna
Lettuce, leaf	pkt.	1¼	10	¼	45-60	March	50 lbs.	Salad Bowl, Grand Rapids
Lettuce, head	100*	1¼	12	—	80	March	100 heads	Great Lakes, Sweetheart, Bibb
Mustard Greens	pkt.	1½	6	¼	28-40	August	50-90 lbs.	Southern Giant Curled, Green Wave, Tendergreen
Okra	1	2½	18	¼	50-60	May	90 lbs.	Clemson Spineless, Emerald, Perkins, Spineless
Onion Sets	1 qt.*	1¼	3	—	30-60	March	60 bunches	Ebenezer, Yellow Globe, White Silverstem
Onion Plants	400*	1¼	3	—	60-100	March	1½ bus.	Sweet Spanish, Aristocrat, Early Harvest
Parsley	¼	1¼	4	⅛	70-100	April		Paramount, Triple Moss Curled
Parsnips	½	1½-2	2	½	100	Mar.-April	2 bus.	Hollow Crown, Model, All-American
Peas	16	1½	1-2	½	60-100	Mar.-Aug.	30 lbs.	Dark Skin Perfection, Thomas Laxton, Alaska, Wando, Alderman
Peas, Southern	8	2½	3	1½	68-85	May	25 lbs.	Extra Early Blackeye, California Blackeye No. 5
Pepper, sweet	50-65*	2½	18		60-70	May	200 fruits	California Wonder, Yolo Wonder, Keystone Resistant Giant, Ruby King, Delaware Bell
Pepper, hot	50-65*	2½	18			May		Long Red Cayenne, Red Chili, Anaheim Chili, Hungarian Wax, Red Cherry
Potato, white	120	2½	8-10	4	110-140	March	120 lbs.	Early—Irish Cobbler, Katahdin, Bless Triumph, Late—Sebago, Pungo, Kennebec
Potato, sweet	75-100*	5	12-15	1	100-130	May	1½-2 bus.	Puerto Rico, Nemagold, Nugget, Goldrush
Pumpkin	½	6	72	1	100-120	May	75-100 fruits	Small Sugar, Cushaw, Connecticut Field, Young's Beauty
Radish	½	1	1	½	25-60	March	100 bunches	Scarlet Globe, Icicle, Cherry Belle
Rhubarb	33*	5	36	4	‡	March-Apr.	300 stalks	MacDonald, Valentine, Canada Red
Salsify	½	1½	2	½	100	May	60 lbs.	Mammoth Sandwich Island
Spinach	½	1	4	¼	40	March	50 lbs.	Fall—Virginia Savoy, Dixie Market, Early Hybrid 7, Spring—Bloomsdale Long Standing, Old Dominion, America
Spinach, New Zealand	1	2	18-24	1	70	May	45 lbs.	Zucchini, Caserta, Butternut, Early Prolific
Squash, Summer	½	4	36	½	60-80	May	120 fruits	Straightneck, Early White Bush Scallop, Cocozelle, Greyzini, Hercules
Squash, Winter	½	6	60	½	120-160	May	50 fruits	Hubbard, Table Queen, Boston Marrow
Tomato	25-50*	3	24-48	—	65-80	April-May	4-8 bus.	Rutgers, Chesapeake, Glamour, Big Boy, Roma, Sioux, Sunray, Campbell 146x, Marion, Homestead 24, Porte, Enterprise, Spring Giant
Turnip	¼	1½	2	⅛	40-60	Mar. or July	120 lbs.	Purple Top White Globe, Shogoin, Just Right, Seven Top

* Plants or sets.   † Asparagus cutting begins 2 years after planting.   ‡ Pulling stalks of rhubarb begins 2 years after planting.
(University of Maryland Leaflet 15, and Dr. R. E. Webster, U. S. Department of Agriculture.)

Succession Plantings

If the garden is to supply a continuous harvest from early summer through late fall, it will be necessary to plant a number of crops at regular intervals. This is called planting for succession, or succession plantings. Small but fairly frequent plantings will result in tender, nutritious vegetables throughout the season. Very few crops, except tomatoes, chard, and New Zealand spinach, may be depended upon for more than two or three weeks.

Cool-weather crops such as spinach and lettuce cannot be planted throughout the summer. They require cool, moist weather to produce tender, tasty crops. However, plantings made in the early spring and again after midsummer will mature during cool weather.

Hot-weather crops such as beans and sweet corn may be planted from late April until mid-July to insure continuous harvests. There is no point in continuing plantings so late in the summer that the crops will not mature before fall when the cool weather retards their growth.

Unless the fruits of such crops as cucumbers and squash are kept picked and the vines are carefully protected from disease and insect injury, they will not produce through the season.

Thinning and Spacing

In spite of our efforts to sow seed thinly, it will be noted that as the seedlings push through the surface they are too thick for good growth. Plants must have an ample area from which to draw food and moisture if they are to make strong vigorous growth—the kind of growth that produces tender, nutritious crops. Even though the space for the garden is limited and large harvests are desired, it is better to give the plants a reasonable area for root growth as well as for their tops.

Some space is required for cultivating and harvesting. Such plants as tomatoes and beans require more space so that they may be cultivated without disturbing the foliage while wet with dew or rain.

Crops for the Fall Garden

Many gardens contain only a few turnips, as early fall frosts put an end to the growth of most tender vegetable crops. This is unfortunate, for in this area there are a number of crops that may be depended upon to prolong the production of food crops into the fall and early winter months. Several of the crops withstand hard freezes while others are not injured by light frosts. To get the most out of vegetable gardens, several of these crops should be included in the planting program.

The list of fall crops is long. Turnips are widely grown. Other crops are: Chinese cabbage, endive, broc-

coli, collards, cauliflower, kale, Brussels sprouts, mustard greens, and late plantings of lettuce, radishes, peas and spinach. These are crops that are used out of the garden and are not often canned or stored.

Trampling the freshly sown seed firmly into the soil is good practice for summer sowings.

No doubt one of the reasons most gardeners do not grow these crops is that it takes more care to start seeds during the dry summer months. Or perhaps, it is because they do not know when to sow the seed and overlook the proper planting seasons for them. A garden plan should help overcome this difficulty.

In general, the problem of starting seeds in the summer is quite different from that of spring-sown crops. In the summer the soil is dryer and warmer. The seeds should be planted deeper and should be carefully firmed into the soil to obtain the moisture necessary for germination. Some gardeners, after planting their seeds, walk up and down the row pressing the seed firmly into the ground before covering with topsoil. In this way the seedlings will not have too much difficulty in pushing through the soil which is half again deeper than the covering put on in the spring.

The fall vegetable crops are predominantly greens. They are important sources of the health-protecting vitamins and minerals. They are easy to grow, have a long productive season, and should be planted in the summer at the proper time to provide for a generous supply during the fall and early winter.

Summer plantings must be carefully timed so that the weather at maturity will favor proper development and yet leave time to harvest the crop. In the outlying suburban areas frost may be expected in early October, while in the more protected sections of the city, a killing frost seldom comes before early November. Gardeners should allow for this variation when timing their plantings.

The following table indicates the approximate planting time for specific harvesting dates:

Vegetable	Sowing Seed	Setting Plants	Maturing Date
Broccoli*	June 15	July 15	Sept. 25
Brussels Sprouts†	June 1	July 1	Oct. 15
Cabbage	June 15	July 15	Oct. 1
Chinese Cabbage*	July 15		Oct. 1
Cauliflower*	July 1	Aug. 15	Oct. 15
Collards†	July 15	Aug. 20	Oct. 1
Endive*	July 15-Aug. 1		Sept. 15-Nov. 1
Kale†	July 15-Aug. 1		Oct. 15
Lettuce	Aug. 15-Sept. 1		Oct. 1
Peas, garden	Aug. 15-Sept. 1		Oct. 15
Winter radishes	Aug. 15-30		Oct. 15-30
Spinach†	Aug. 15-Sept. 15		Sept. 25
Turnips (white)	July 15-Aug. 15		Oct. 1

* Start in seed bed and transplant.
† Uninjured by freezing weather.

What To Plant

A well-diversified garden, except a very small one, should contain one or more kinds from each of the vegetable groups if it is to provide variety and a well-balanced diet. Nearly 40 vegetable crops are commonly grown in the Washington area. They may be divided into six groups. Of the root crops, nearly every garden will contain radishes, beets, carrots and onions, perhaps turnips for a fall crop. Most gardeners will select lettuce, cabbage, parsley, chard and kale from the greens. Tomatoes, in a class by themselves, should be in every garden. Beans are the only dependable member of the legume group. The vining crops are too space-consuming for the small garden. Of the "others" group, peppers, broccoli, and sweet corn are the most popular. Twelve to 18 crops will provide variety throughout the season.

If the garden is to provide the health-protecting vitamins and minerals that it should, it will contain one or more of the "greens." While two or three kinds can provide a continuous supply from early summer until late fall and winter, most gardeners will want to plant three or four kinds for variety.

Some authorities are questioning the emphasis put on spinach, chard, and beet greens because of their oxalic acid content. They urge that gardeners grow and use more broccoli, kale, collards, turnip tops, mustard, and lettuce in place of these three.

Lettuce is ordinarily planted in the early spring along with spinach, cabbage, and parsley. The lettuce and the spinach, however, may not be depended upon after hot weather arrives, and other kinds—warm-weather crops—should be planted to take their places. There are other spring crops suitable for salads and greens—cress, escarole, beet, and turnip greens. The latter are two of the most nutritious of all greens and may be grown in the spring and fall.

For summer greens—Swiss chard and New Zealand spinach are two of the most productive. Both are "cut-and-come-again" crops and so one small planting should provide the family with a liberal supply from early June until frost.

Beginning in June and July, plantings should be made of the fall crops: spinach, endive, kale, collards, and mustard greens.

Many of these crops are fairly easily grown and are troubled with few insects and diseases. Give them a fairly rich moist soil and clean culture that they may make rapid tender succulent growth. Without feeding there is danger of slow, tough growth that is neither of good flavor nor tenderness. Moisture is needed for rapid growth.

Aphids (plant lice) are sometimes troublesome on some of these crops, but they are readily controlled by spraying with nicotine sulphate and soap. A hard blast from the garden hose will knock them to the ground, perhaps killing many.

In harvesting "greens" it is well to gather them just before using. Wash well and cook immediately in very little water. Wilting and storage tend to reduce their tenderness, as well as their nutritive values.

The root crops—beets, carrots, parsnips, salsify, onions, etc.—seldom grow satisfactorily in the heavy clay soils so common to this area unless given special soil preparation. Seeds of many do not fully germinate nor do the roots develop properly in heavy soil. Often the growth is so poor that the roots are fibrous and lacking in flavor. Onion sets produce small bulbs if planted too deeply in a clay soil.

Good root crops may be grown in this area if we will make the effort to improve the texture of the soil. This may be accomplished through the addition of sifted coal ashes, sand, compost, or peat moss. These materials lighten the soil so that the seedlings can push through and they improve the rate of germination. In light soils there is room for the roots to grow and expand. Lime, an important soil conditioner, is recommended for that portion of the garden where beets and onions are to be grown.

If available, a generous quantity of peat moss, compost, sand, or ashes should be worked into the space where the seeds of root crops are to be sown; or one

To permit root expansion in heavy soils, fill a deep (4") furrow with compost before sowing seed.

may dig a narrow trench and fill it with well-rotted compost or woods soil and plant the seed in it. Lacking sufficient quantities for this, one may cover the seed with this lighter material.

Since the seedlings of carrots, beets, and other root crops have difficulty in pushing through a clay soil, radish seed may be scattered thinly in the same rows. The radish seed germinate quickly and are strong enough to push through almost any soil, thus breaking the crust and aiding the root crop seeds to come through. They also mark the row and make earlier cultivation possible.

Tomatoes

When to Plant:	Early May.
Seed:	Cover ¼ in. deep. Thin to 2 in. Time required to grow plants—6 weeks.
Plants:	Set plants 2 to 4 ft. apart in rows 4 ft. apart. Plants per 100-ft. row: 25 to 50. Yield: 4 to 8 bu.
Varieties:	Porte (70 days), Rutgers (74 days), * Sunray (85 days), * Roma (75 days), Sioux (72 days), Glamour (69 days), * Marion (71 days), * Homestead 24 (72 days), * Campbell 146 (77 days), * Enterpriser (65 days), * Spring Giant (75 days). ***Wilt Resistant**
Soil:	Rich garden loam preferably acid.
Canned:	1 bu. (60 lbs.) makes 16 to 20 qts.

The tomato, one of the most useful of all vegetable crops for the home garden, is an excellent source of vitamins and minerals. It may be used raw or cooked—as juice, stewed, baked, fried, in sauces, and as pickles. It is one of the easiest of the garden crops to grow and gives a big return for the space occupied—maturing its crop over a period of several months.

While it is commonly said that anyone can grow tomatoes, since they do not require special care, they repay good cultural conditions just as fully as any other crop. Seasoned gardeners go to considerable lengths to see that their tomato plants are well and carefully planted. The young plants put into the ground in early May should begin producing fruit in early July and continue to produce until frosts stop their growth in October. A well-handled plant should produce a half bushel or more fruit during the season.

Large planting holes filled with a mixture of compost and well-rotted manure are desirable. In such a situation, the plants should not suffer from drought and should have sufficient plant food to maintain vigorous growth and abundant fruiting. The manure needs supplementing with superphosphate or a commercial fertilizer low in nitrogen.

In selecting plants for the home garden emphasis should be placed on obtaining those that are stocky, well-developed and of a good rich, dark green color. These characteristics denote health and vigor. Insist that ample soil be left on the roots and avoid giving the plants any more of a setback than necessary. If large, well-developed plants may be obtained in individual boxes or pots, and even in bloom, it is well to buy a few

for the sake of earlier crops. For an extra early crop it may be desirable to have a few plants of such varieties as Victor, Bounty, or Break o'Day. However, early-started plants of main crop varieties such as Enterpriser will begin producing almost as early as they will.

Prune tomatoes by removing the shoots that emerge from the leaf axils to get fewer but better fruits.

Use a paper collar to protect the newly set plants from cutworms. Shade them for a few days until their roots are well established.

It is suggested that in the smaller garden the tomatoes be staked. This is to conserve space and to avoid disease. Staked tomatoes may be planted as closely as 18 inches in rows 4 feet apart. Staked tomatoes seldom suffer from rot to the same extent as those lying on wet ground. Unstaked tomatoes set 4 feet apart in rows 6 feet apart should be mulched to protect the fruit.

Staking is a simple chore. A 6 to 8 foot stake should be placed at the time the plants are set out. Drive the stake 15 to 18 inches into the ground. As the plants grow the side branches are removed but this need not cause confusion. Wait until the flower buds show plainly before removing the branch that comes out near the leaf axil. Use a soft rag or any material for tying that will not cut the bark. One stem is enough to train up, although some gardeners prune to two stems, a few to three.

The use of a strong wire cylinder, such as shown in the illustration, avoids the necessity of pruning, and, with good culture produces a great deal more fruit per plant. The wire commonly used for reinforcing concrete walks and driveways seems best adapted to this method of culture.

A large greedy worm (3-4 inches long) with a ravenous appetite occasionally attacks the plants. Locate and kill. Ordinarily there will be only one or two of them.

Tomatoes may be attacked by several leaf spot diseases and occasionally by the "late blight." The spot diseases seldom do more than cause the lower leaves to die. The "late blight," however, is a destructive disease which in favorable years destroys tomato plantings over a wide area unless the plants are protected by spray or dust. The tomato dusts and sprays containing zerlate or metallic copper are recommended. Wilt resistant varieties should be given preference where wilts are a problem, in gardens where tomatoes have been grown for several years and the soil has become infected.

Tomatoes are available in many forms and varieties. There are the small cherry, plum and pear varieties commonly grown for salads and preserving, deriving their names from their shapes. A somewhat larger size, but still smaller than the common type, is known as the early-fruiting "determinate" tomato. They are smaller growing plants which continue to grow until killed by frost. The vine growth is very slow and the foliage never heavy. While they are early fruiting, most of them have such "light" foliage that much of the fruit is sunburned by midsummer's sun. This applies to such varieties as Bounty, Victor, and Valiant.

Among the large fruited type, we have pink, red and yellow varieties as well as those that are described as meaty (thick-walled). The pink varieties are not widely grown although some of them are excellent fruit for the table. Glovel is an example. The yellow varieties are not new, but have not been especially desirable until the introduction of Sunday and Jubilee, orange-colored varieties. Sunday seems to have high vitamin content and flavor as well as being meaty—characteristics that were lacking in many of the older yellow-fruited varieties.

Advocates of this type of support for tomatoes say that yields are greatly increased, and that no pruning is necessary. If the vines are mulched at planting time, the only care needed is an occasional feeding, watering if rainfall is inadequate, and tucking stray shoots inside of the cylinder. The openings in the reinforced wire are 6 x 6 inches.

CHAPTER XVII

HERBS

During World War II when imports were greatly curtailed or cut off, the home growing of herbs was greatly increased. While imported herbs are now available, many gardeners delight in the culture of herbs and interest in this field is growing. However, not all cooks make use of herbs and most of those who do need only a few kinds. If the home gardener is interested in growing them, there are a number of kinds that are comparatively easy to grow. Many of them are annuals.

Because the list of herbs is long and many gardeners are inexperienced, it is suggested that only a few be attempted at first—those most commonly used in the home. There is no point in growing any unless they are to be used. Herb growing is a delightful hobby and may be a profitable one. Only the needs of the home garden for the more easily grown herbs which will add variety to the daily diet is considered here.

The culture of the savory herbs is not difficult. They require but a small space. Preferably this should be at one side of the garden so as not to interfere with the plowing and cultivation of the vegetable plot. If possible the herb garden should be near the house so that the plants may be watered and carefully tended and the herbs freshly gathered that are to be used in the cooking. A narrow border, 3 to 5 feet wide and 15 or 20 feet long will contain a considerable number of kinds, perhaps supply all of the herbs needed by the family for seasoning purposes.

In planning the herb garden it is well to group the annuals in one section and the biennials and perennials in another. Some of the herbs are weedy and should be pocketed away from the others.

Most of the herbs can be grown on any good, rich, well-drained soil, which in most gardens will mean a certain amount of special soil preparation. This should be undertaken at the beginning so that the plot will be productive and efficient for a period of years. Deep soil preparation—10 to 15 inches is not too much—with the liberal incorporation of manure or compost. Bone-meal and cottonseed meal are needed for enrichment and to increase the moisture-holding capacity. Coal ashes or sand should be mixed into clay soils to make them lighter and more friable. The deeper and more thorough this soil preparation the better and longer lasting will be the herb plot.

The culture of the various herbs does not differ materially except as to methods of propagation, planting distances, and moisture requirements. These will be listed under the individual kinds, together with comments on methods of harvesting. It goes without saying that the plot should be kept free from weeds, watered as needed and protected from insects and diseases.

Harvesting

The harvesting of most kinds of leaf herbs begins before the flowering season while the growing tips are young and tender. The leaves and tips should be harvested in the morning after the dew has dried, but before the heat of the day. Spread them on sheets or trays in a warm, shady situation, preferably where the air circulation is good. Turn them daily until thoroughly dried. Then crumble and store in tightly covered glass jars. Cardboard containers absorb the volatile flavors.

Seeds are harvested as they begin to change color. Clip the seed heads in the morning shortly after the dew has dried to avoid shattering. Spread them to dry on cloths. When dried rub the seeds out. The seeds need further air drying—a week or more—before storing.

BASIL

(Ocimum basilicum)

Annual—Do not transplant.
Soil:	Fertile, well-drained.
Exposure:	Sun, sheltered.
Seed:	In April, ½ in. deep, rows 15-18 in. apart.
Plants:	Thin to 12-14 in. apart.
Height:	1 foot.
Harvest:	When in bloom; flowers and the tender tips of stems with foliage.
Plants needed:	Very few.

* * *

Common basil grows to 1 foot; dwarf is much smaller. The clove-flavored leaves are used for seasoning soups, meats and sometimes in salads. Basil is especially useful for flavoring tomato dishes. Harvest when in bloom, cutting flowers and the tender tips of stems with foliage. Tie in very small bunches and dry in a shady place.

BORAGE

(Borago officinalis)

Annual—Do not transplant.
Soil:	Light, poor, dry.
Exposure:	Sun.
Seed:	Out of doors—May.
Plants:	Thin to 12 inches apart.
Height:	2 to 3 feet.
Harvest:	The young leaves may be cooked like spinach.
Plants needed:	1 dozen.

* * *

Borage is an attractive growing plant with spikes of blue flowers. It thrives in poor dry soil. It is easy to grow, the seeds germinating readily. It often self-sows, producing crops of new plants until frost.

The leaves are used for flavoring cold beverages, pickles and salads. Formerly the flowers were candied and used in confectionery.

CARAWAY

(Carum carvi)

Biennial—Do not transplant.
Soil:	Dry, light.
Exposure:	Sun.
Seed:	In April, ¼ inch deep, rows 12 inches apart.
Plants:	Thin to 12 inches.
Height:	1-2 feet.
Harvest:	Cut off seed heads when ripe, but before shattering. Young shoots and tender leaves as needed for flavor.
Plants needed:	1 dozen.

* * *

Caraway seeds are used for flavoring bread, cakes and cheese. The young shoots and leaves are sometimes used in salads. When growing for the seed crop, planting may be made in the late summer, but most gardeners sow the seed in the early spring. The seeds should be harvested before they shatter. Dry the seed heads on cheesecloth in shade. When dry rub the heads together until the seeds separate, then put them in thin cloth bags. Hang in an airy place. Before using, the seed should be washed, but not before planting.

CHERVIL

(Anthriscus cerefolium)

Annual—Do not transplant.
Soil:	Light, well-drained.
Exposure:	Partial shade.
Seed:	April.
Plants:	9 inches apart.
Height:	18-24 inches.
Harvest:	Tender leaves as wanted.
Plants needed:	6 to 12.

* * *

The parsley-like leaves of the chervil are used to flavor salads. The seeds of this annual herb may be sown in the early spring or late fall. The leaves are ready to use in from 6 to 10 weeks from spring sowings. Chervil likes shade, especially that of taller plants.

CHIVES

(Allium schoenoprasum)

Perennial—Transplanted easily.
Soil:	Ordinary garden loam.
Plants needed:	3 to 6.
Harvest:	Tender leaves as needed.
Height:	10-12 inches.
Plants:	Thin to 1 in.
Seed:	March-April, ¼ in. deep, rows 15 in. apart.
Exposure:	Sun.

Chives are little-used perennial flavoring plants that

merit wider use. They are as easy to grow as onions, and when once started, may be kept in the garden for years. By sowing a few seed in the garden and when mature transplanting to a permanent location where they will not interfere with cultural practices, this crop may be used as needed year after year.

Chives, a member of the onion family, are much milder in flavor. Ordinarily only the leaves are used as a flavoring for stews, soups, meats and salads. Their attractive blue flowers make them useful in the flower border, although if seed is allowed to form they may easily become a weed.

Chives are commonly grown from seed. Sow the seed in a well-enriched sweet soil for best results. The clumps of plants that develop from the seed should be lifted and planted in a permanent location. When once established, the clumps should be divided and the soil reworked every three or four years to keep them vigorous and productive.

Because few families can use more than a clump or two of chives, it is better to grow them in the flower border or the herb bed than in the garden. Convenience should also be considered in selecting a location, because when wanted, only a few leaves will be pinched-off.

Because chives may easily become a weed in the garden it is wise to prevent them from going to seed. Many gardeners allow them to flower—using the flowers in bouquets, but otherwise pinching off the flower heads before the seeds mature.

DILL

(Anethum graveolens)

Annual—Biennial—Do not transplant.	
Soil:	Moderately rich, sandy, well-drained.
Exposure:	Sun, protected.
Seed:	May, ¼ inch deep in rows 24 inches apart.
Plants:	Thin 12-15 inches apart.
Height:	2-3 feet.
Harvest:	Cut off heads as seeds begin to ripen.
Plants needed:	A dozen.

* * *

Dill is one of the easiest herbs to grow and has many uses. The seed heads together with an inch or so of the stem are used to flavor pickles and for this purpose are cut off just as the seeds begin to ripen. Tie in bunches. For seeds, the harvesting is delayed until the seeds ripen, after which the heads are cut off and spread to dry on sheets, the seeds threshed out and stored in cloth bags. For salads, the tender leaves are harvested as wanted.

MINT

(Mentha piperita, m. pulegium, m. spicata, etc.)

Perennials—Easily transplanted.	
Soil:	Average most garden loam.
Exposure:	Sun or shade.
Propagate:	From roots.

Plants:	5 or 6 set in a 3-foot square.
Height:	15-18 inches.
Harvest:	When plants are 6 to 8 inches high.
Plants needed:	3-foot-square plot.

* * *

There are a considerable number of the mints, although the spearmint (M. spicata, var. Viridis) is most commonly grown and used for flavoring jellies, cold drinks and tea and for sauce for meat. The leaves are ordinarily used green and for this reason a portion of the bed should be sheared off every few weeks to insure a supply of tender, aromatic, young leaves.

Propagation may be by seed, but it is normally easier to obtain a few roots which may be planted. Since the roots spread widely, sending up new plants, it is desirable to confine the mint bed with boards or masonry.

For drying, the young leaves and shoots are cut off when 6 or 8 inches tall, dried and stored in glass containers.

SAGE

(Salvia officinalis)

Perennial—Transplants readily.	
Soil:	Sweet, well-drained, rich.
Exposure:	Sun.
Propagate:	Seed, cuttings, layerings, root division.
Plants:	2-3 feet apart.
Height:	2 feet.
Harvest:	Before flowering.
Plants needed:	Two.

* * *

Sage is a popular herb for seasoning dressings, cheese, sausage, and other meats. The young leaves should be harvested before the flowering season, although it is recommended that the plants be clipped twice a year to stimulate new growth.

The plants become woody in time and should be renewed every 3 or 4 years. They are quite attractive and may be used as an ornamental low hedge.

The leaves should be thoroughly dried before storage. When completely cured, they are best stored in sealed paper bags. Some recommend that the clippings be tied in small bundles and dried over a stove, rather than the usual air drying.

Sage is commonly propagated from cuttings and layering, although it sets seed freely and under favorable conditions numerous seedlings appear.

SUMMER SAVORY

(Satureia hortensis)

Annual—Transplants.	
Soil:	Moderately rich, dry.
Exposure:	Sun.
Seed:	Indoors—March; out of doors—April.
Plants:	Transplant after May 1, 6-8 inches apart.
Height:	10-12 inches.
Harvest:	For drying—midsummer; fresh as needed.
Plants needed:	A dozen or more.

* * *

Summer savory is a fragrant annual whose leaves are

useful for flavoring soups, meats, and dressings. The leaves and tender tips of the plants are harvested in midsummer for drying, but may be used while fresh throughout the growing season.

SWEET MARJORAM

(Marjorana hortensis)

Perennial treated as an annual—May be transplanted.
Soil: Light, medium rich, average moisture.
Exposure: Sun.
Seed: April (slow to germinate). Very shallow.
Plants: Space 10 inches apart in rows 12 inches apart.
Height: 8-10 inches.
Harvest: As used, seldom cured.
Plants needed: Few.

* * *

Sweet marjoram is commonly used fresh for seasoning soup, meat pies, and for dressings. They are easily grown in pots in the house and thus supply fresh leaves throughout the year. If wanted for drying, cut the tender tips just before flowering and dry.

TARRAGON

(Artemisia dracunculus)

Perennial—Propagated by division.
Soil: Moderately rich, warm, well-drained.
Exposure: Partial shade.
Seed: Does not produce viable seed.
Plants: 12-18 inches apart.
Height: 24 inches.
Harvest: Fresh—as needed; Dried—midsummer.
Plants needed: Six.

* * *

Tarragon has a delicate flavor somewhat resembling anise. The freshly gathered leaves are extensively used for seasoning salads, vinegar, pickles, and mustard. Tarragon vinegar is a favorite for making salad dressings.

The plants are not very hardy, and it is well to cut the stems down in the late fall and to cover with litter or with leaves. The plants may be propagated by root cuttings or by division. Stem cuttings may be taken at almost any time.

NOTES

CHAPTER XVIII

BERRIES, FRUITS AND NUTS

Fruits, if space is available, are a worthwhile addition to the home garden. They do not take too much space if selected wisely. However, they must be given protection from insects and diseases if they are to produce satisfactory crops. In most cases the same equipment and materials used to protect roses will be adequate for the home fruit garden.

Some may consider fruits too slow in reaching productive size, but there are several that reach bearing age the second year. Strawberries, the "brambles," and occasionally the dwarf apples and pears bear the second season. Grapes, peaches and plums are slower.

The suburban garden may well include a few of the bush fruits to supplement the vegetable crops. Raspberries, dewberries, strawberries, etc., do well in this area and take relatively little space, but even so, with the exception of strawberries, they do not belong in the small garden plot. Blackberries are such vigorous growers that they are seldom planted in this region.

Nut trees may be grown to provide shade as well as a nut crop. Some varieties do well in this area.

Berries

BLUEBERRIES

When to Plant:	Early April or November.
Plants:	4 ft. apart, rows 6 ft. apart.
Varieties:	(In order of ripening.) Earliblue, Blueray, Berkeley, Herbert, Bluecrop.
Soil:	Rich, cool, highly acid, well drained.
Canned:	1½ qts. fresh fruit makes 1 qt. canned.

* * *

Blueberries, a bush fruit, are well adapted to this area and a number of local gardeners have planted some of the new varieties. They require an acid soil which is common throughout this area. They are low-growing, ornamental bushes that will grow in light shade. The newer varieties are much larger fruited than the native wild species. Plant at least two varieties for cross-pollination. They do best in a soil well enriched with oak-leaf compost or peat moss. Clean, shallow cultivation or heavy mulching with well-rotted compost is needed for best results. Some feeding is needed after the plants reach bearing size—3 years. Preferably the fertilizer should be an acid one, such as those sold for use on rhododendrons and azaleas. Cotton-seed meal and superphosphate mixed with compost may be used.

Jersey, a small-fruited variety, may be desirable because of its vigor.

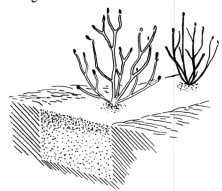

Half soil and half oak leaf compost makes good planting for blueberries. Mulch with half-rotted oak leaves in early summer and in late fall.

RASPBERRIES

When to Plant:	Late March or early April.
Plants:	Set plants 3 ft. apart, in rows 6 ft. apart.
Varieties:	Red—Latham, September; Black—Cumberland, Bristol; Purple—Sodus.
Soil:	Enrich with well-rotted compost or manure. Should be slightly moist.
Canned:	1 bushel (48 lbs.) makes 16 to 20 quarts.

* * *

A row of raspberries 50 feet long will provide fruit over a period of several weeks in late May and June. Two-year-old plants bear the first year, although it is generally agreed that it is good garden practice to remove the fruiting wood when transplanting. Commonly, the brambles are offered in 1-year-old sizes which do not bear until the second spring.

Raspberries prefer light moist soil, although clays and loams may be improved through the addition of humus so that these brambles will be both vigorous and prolific. Hot, dry situations are not suitable for raspberries nor will they thrive in heavy shade. Partial shade or shade part of the day (afternoon) seems to favor the growth and fruiting of the red, black, and purple raspberries. Dewberries need full sun.

The common practice of letting as many of the red raspberry shoots develop as nature intended is not conducive to good fruiting. Experienced growers thin out the shoots that spring up all around the crown to from 5 to 7 of the strongest. These canes should be shortened to 3 or 4 feet in height so that they will stand upright.

Many commercial growers tie the canes to a stake to insure their staying in position and to facilitate cultivation. The home gardener wanting first-quality fruit should thin the canes, mulch, and fertilize the beds. Three to four pounds of a 3-8-7, or similar mixture, should be applied to the 100 square feet of row in late March. Old canes, those that have fruited, should be removed as soon as the fruiting season is over.

Black raspberries and purple raspberries do not throw up numerous suckers as do the "redcaps," but they need to have their long, willowy canes shortened and, in small gardens, tied to stakes. However, if new plants are desired the tips of the canes should be fastened down with a peg and covered with soil. In the course of one season a new plant will develop.

Red raspberries are highly susceptible to diseases. The common wild dewberry carries some of them and for this reason the home gardener should make special efforts to keep them from his garden. Similarly, black raspberries may carry diseases which can be transmitted to the redcaps. It is recommended that plantings of red raspberries be placed at some distance—100 feet or more—from those of the black raspberries.

Because of the difficulty of controlling diseases on raspberries, it is recommended that the gardener purchase disease-free plants and avoid the chore of fighting disease. For sources of virus-free plants, contact the County Extension Services.

However, disease may be controlled by keeping the plants growing vigorously; by the use of a dormant spray, and by the application of bordeaux as needed during the growing season. The Japanese beetles are becoming a serious pest, although easily repelled by dusting or spraying with almost any material—lime, bordeaux, sulphur, etc.

STRAWBERRIES

When to Plant:	Late March or early April.
Plants:	Space plants 1 ft. apart in rows 3 ft. apart. Plants for 100-ft. row: 100-125. Yield: 30-50 qts.
Varieties:	Early to late Earlidawn, Sunrise, Pocahontas, Redstele resistant-Surecrop, Midway.
Soil:	Well-enriched, well-drained garden loam.
Canned:	1 bu. (48 lbs.) makes 14 to 16 qts.

* * *

Few fruit crops are so well adapted to the small garden as are strawberries. While they do not provide a harvest the first season, they occupy such a small area and later yield so well that they are admirably suited to the smaller gardens. The luscious, well-ripened, home-grown fruit is much superior to the commercially-grown, shipped-in fruit.

Strawberries prefer and should be planted in a well-enriched soil. This refers to the liberal incorporation of well-rotted manure or compost. A soil thus prepared provides them with ample moisture and plant food which is essential to free fruiting.

Full sun and good culture are needed, although they will grow and do fairly well with only morning sunlight.

Strawberries cannot compete with grass or weeds and so the beds need frequent cultivation. In fact, most beds cease to be profitable when foul with weeds and grass.

Strawberry plants should be set in beds or rows in the early spring—when dormant plants are available. In the home garden they are usually planted in rows 3 feet apart, the plants spaced a foot apart. Since the plants are comparatively inexpensive, they are frequently set as close as 6 or 8 inches to insure large crops, although plants usually send out "runners" and provide enough plants the first growing season. An average of 1¼ plants per square foot of bed may be expected to produce the best yields.

Twenty-five plants should produce 10 quarts or more of fruit each season. A bed will last three to five years, depending on the care given and the initial soil preparation.

Next to planting in rich soil, the most important step in planting is to see that the crowns of the newly set plants are level with the surface of the soil. Planting too deeply leads to crown rot, while shallow-set plants usually suffer from lack of moisture.

Virus-free strawberry plants of many varieties are available from commercial plant growers and should be obtained for home garden planting. Most strawberry plants formerly were infected with viruses and lacked both vigor and productiveness.

Winter care of strawberries is usually limited to seeing that water does not stand on the beds. However, a mulch of straw after the ground has frozen is desirable as a protection against "heaving." This is usually raked into the middles—between the rows—in March, just before the growth starts. The use of straw is recommended to keep the berries clean, and for this reason only a part of the straw should be raked off the plants.

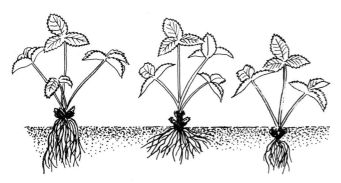

Deeply set plants are subject to crown rot; shallowly set, dry out—Place crown at soil level.

Supplemental feeding with a garden fertilizer in the fall (September) is recommended to give the plants added strength and vitality. Apply at the rate of 3 or 4 pounds per 100 square feet of bed.

In this area, the only ever-bearing variety of strawberry which has sufficient quality to justify growing it is Ozark Beauty.

Strawberries have numerous insect pests and diseases, although the home gardener will hardly notice most of them. If the soil should be infected with red stele, disease-resistant varieties such as Surecrop and Midway should be grown rather than those listed above, Rotation of beds—that is, starting each new bed at some distance from the old bed—is the best way to control most of the pests. Leaf diseases may be controlled by spraying with bordeaux just before and after flowering.

Fruits
DWARF FRUIT TREES

When to Plant:	Late fall and early spring.
Trees:	Plant in holes large enough to accommodate the out-spread roots without crowding. Set 8 to 12 ft. apart in rows 10 to 15 ft. apart.
Varieties:	APPLES—Lodi, Beacon, Stayman, Delicious, Summer Rambo, Grimes Golden, Golden Delicious, Paragon. PEARS—Seckel, Magness, Moonglow.
Soil:	Any well-drained, moderately rich garden loam. Need full sun in a not-too-windy situation.
Canned:	Apples—1 bu. (50 lbs.) makes 17 to 20 qts. Pears—1 bu. (50 lbs.) makes 22 to 25 qts.

* * *

Many gardens are too small for standard-sized fruit trees and so the gardener gives up all ideas of enjoying fruit, shade and flowers from his own tree or trees. This need not be, for today there are fruit trees growing on "dwarfing stocks"—roots that keep them growing but do not permit normal size. Nurseries using the Malling understocks offer a very dwarf (about the size of a large spirea), a medium dwarf (about the size of a large lilac) and the half-standard sizes. With three sizes to choose from it is certain that a size of apple or pear may be had that will fit the space limitations of almost any yard.

Fruit trees are as ornamental as any shrub. Their flowers, together with the fruit, make them doubly desirable. Being dwarf, there is not the difficulty in spraying and pruning that is common to the standard-size tree. Fruit from a dwarf tree is no different from that of a standard tree. Several nurseries grow dwarf apple and pear trees in a number of varieties.

Dwarf trees are as easily grown as any other tree although they do repay a little extra care in feeding and pruning with choice fruit. Planting is different to the extent that we should see that the graft (the union between the top and the root stock) is level with the surface of the ground. If covered with soil there is the danger that roots will form above the rootstock and when that occurs the rootstock gradually dies and the new roots take over. The new roots, being more vigorous, soon give the tree the stature of a standard-sized one. However, the only care needed to avoid this is to see that the graft is not covered with soil.

Dwarf trees seldom withstand drought as easily as do trees with the usual understock because of their smaller root systems. Also it is desirable to see that they are fertilized each year while small, with a handful or two of commercial fertilizer to each tree.

Dwarf fruit trees normally start to bear the second year after planting and at four or five years should be fruiting generously. This is in sharp contrast to the standard-sized trees that seldom bear until five or six years of age, some not until ten or twelve years old.

Thinning the fruit on a dwarf tree will encourage annual fruiting. If left to their own devices, there is a distinct tendency to bear every other year. Space the young fruits 3 to 6 inches apart, but do not start thinning until after the "June drop." In other words, wait until after nature thins and then complete the job.

Fruit trees generally bear better if two or three varieties are planted near each other. This is to encourage cross-pollination. Not all varieties require this, but it is considered good practice.

In pruning fruit trees—dwarf or standard—care should be taken to avoid weak forks, to remove weak spindling growth, and to keep the center of the tree open so that sunlight will reach into it. Usually the new growth on dwarf fruit trees is cut back one-half each spring.

The same diseases and insect pests attack dwarf fruit trees as the standard-sized ones. Spraying or dusting is very much the same, although much easier. Expensive equipment is not essential to their protection. The same sprayer or duster used on roses and beans will take care of them and, in most cases, the same insecticides and fungicides. However, the timing is a bit different and varies from season to season. Follow the spray charts.

GRAPES

When to Plant:	Early spring or late in the fall.
Plants:	Set roots 4 inches deep and 8 feet apart, in rows 6 ft. apart.
Varieties:	Black-Fredona, Van Buren, Concord, White—Seneca, Brocton, Niagara. Red— Dunkirk, Vergennes. White Seedless—Romulus, Himrod.
Soil:	Medium rich garden loam.
Canned:	1 bu. (48 lbs.) makes 16 to 20 quarts.

* * *

Grapes are adapted to the smaller yards better than almost any other fruit. They may be trained over an arbor or trellis, along a fence, or even fastened to the side of a building. Thus they are useful for comfort, ornament, and fruit while occupying relatively little space.

Their culture is comparatively simple, although, as with most plants, they repay good culture by producing larger and better crops. Grapes are said to do best on a medium loam, but are quite tolerant and may be found growing on nearly every kind of soil to be found in this area. They should have considerable sunlight if they are to make the most desirable growth, but they will tolerate shade part of the day.

In planting grapes, the hole should be widely dug so that the outspread roots will have plenty of space with-

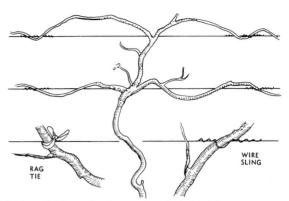

The 4-arm Kniffen system is common method of training grapes on an inexpensive support.

out crowding. Set the vines about 2 inches deeper than they grew in the nursery. Gardeners normally buy 2-year-old plants for spring planting, although good 1-year-old vines will produce just as good results and in approximately the same length of time as the larger size. After planting cut the top back to two or three strong buds.

Grapes in this area suffer from mildew and blackrot, both of which are controlled by dusting or spraying with bordeaux or lime-sulphur. A dormant spray is often sufficient protection against blackrot. A number of insects chew the foliage, but none are more destructive than the Japanese beetle. However, it may be comparatively easily controlled by dusting with hydrated lime or any other dust that discolors the foliage. DDT sprays are more effective and longer lasting than these dusts. Experienced growers enclose the fruit clusters while small in paper bags to protect them from sucking insects. This also serves to keep the fruit free from spray material.

Training grape vines is too long a subject to be discussed here. There are a number of bulletins available which give full treatment for the various methods. However, gardeners should realize that grapes bear their fruit best on new wood—wood that comes from buds on the old wood. Thus, in spring pruning there are two considerations. First—leave two or more buds on each stub; two are usually enough. A large number of buds left in pruning produces more growth and fruit than the roots can supply. Generally 40 to 60 buds are enough to leave on each vine. Secondly—prune in the early spring before the sap starts to flow. Grapes "bleed" easily and by early pruning—February and early March—this can be avoided.

The soil about the grape vines should be kept well cultivated. This serves to protect the shallow-growing roots from competition with weeds and grass and also to destroy diseases and insects that may be in mummied fruit and dead leaves. As the grape vines gain in size, a mulch of weeds, grass, or compost may be used during the summer in place of soil cultivation.

Grapes do not need to be highly fertilized. If fed—and they need a light feeding in the early spring—use fertilizers low in nitrogen. Poultry manures should not be used. Excessive quantities of nitrogen stimulate leaf and vine growth at the expense of fruit.

PEACHES

When to Plant:	Late fall or early spring.
Plants:	Plant in holes large enough to accommodate the out-spread roots. Set 15 to 18 ft. apart.
Varieties:	Earlired, Georgia Belle, Red Haven, Tri-O-Gem, Red Skin, Erly-Red-Fre, Sunhaven, Red Rose, Sun High, So Good (late).
Soil:	Any well-drained garden loam. Full sun is needed and in a situation not too exposed.
Canned:	1 bu. (60 lbs.) makes 20 to 25 qts.

* * *

Peach trees are more common to the small yard than are apple and pears. Peaches are smaller growing trees which come into bearing earlier. Next to apples, they are one of the most popular of fruits. Given a sunny, well-drained situation they will do very well over a wide area.

One-year-old trees are normally recommended; although most gardeners, buying only one or two trees, order 2-year-old and larger sizes. This is not always a desirable practice since many of the roots are lost in transplanting; the net gain, if any, may be small. The holes for planting should be large enough to permit the roots to be spread out. Compost mixed into the soil increases the moisture-holding capacity and aids root growth.

Heavy feeding is to be avoided as peaches tend to make rapid succulent growth; unless planted on poor soils, only fertilizers low in nitrogen are needed. Clean cultivation is needed. Even when planted in sod, a small area about the tree should be kept well tilled.

As soon as the new tree develops branches, select 4 to 7 which will make the framework. These should be spaced around the tree and up and down the trunk so as to avoid weak forks. Remove all others. The second spring, while the tree is still dormant, remove new branches which are not needed for the framework. This throws the vitality into the main limbs and strengthens them. As growth continues and until bearings starts, very little pruning is needed except to keep the tree in good form, to admit air and light, and to remove weak or injured growth.

Pruning after bearing starts is largely a matter of reducing the bearing surface. Fruits are borne on the old wood and unless it is reduced through heavy pruning, more fruits will develop than the roots can support. Some commercial growers delay the spring pruning of peach trees until they can determine the winter injury to the fruit buds. Where winter injury has been heavy, the spring pruning is light; but if no winter injury has been received, pruning is heavier than normal.

All fruits must be protected from insects and diseases if they are to be useable. Regular spraying or dusting is essential to protect the new foliage and the developing fruits. This protection can be afforded with one of the new all-purpose fruit dusts or sprays.

Other Fruits

There are a number of other fruits which normally are of interest to the home gardener. Currants and gooseberries are commonly thought of as desirable fruits. However, they are not generally recommended in areas where pine trees are grown. In Maryland they are prohibited by law because they are an intermediate host of the White Pine-Blister Rust. However, permits for bringing currants and gooseberry plants into Maryland may be obtained from the State Department of Agriculture (Permit Section) for areas where they are not likely to pose a problem for the pine grower. Red Lake currant and Poorman gooseberry are recommended for the heavier soils and Glenndale gooseberry for the sandier soils.

Cherries are commonly grown in this area. The sour cherry is a dependable crop, although the birds frequently do the harvesting. The sour cherry is not troubled by too many insects or diseases. It is a medium-sized tree and may be too large for most gardens.

Plums and prunes are small-growing trees and as far as size goes they are adapted to the smaller garden. However, the plum curculio and brown rot are such serious troubles that most trees are unproductive. These two pests can be controlled but few gardeners deem it wise to go to the trouble. The damson plum seems to be less troubled than the other varieties. Methley is a vigorous growing plum with good quality fruit.

Protecting Fruit Trees

The quality, yield, and usefulness of fruits depend to a very large extent upon their protection from insects and diseases. Formerly this was a rather complicated process; but now the manufacturers are offering "all-purpose" fruit sprays which enable the home gardener to do a reasonably good job without the bother of buying and mixing of chemicals.

The University of Maryland Specialists, who aided in the preparation of the Spray Calendar, now suggest that the home fruit grower use these all-purpose materials. If the gardener wishes to have full details for preparing his own mixtures, it is suggested that he obtain a copy of "Sprays for Home Fruit Plantings, Extension Service Bulletin 125 (Revised) from the University.

To prevent damage from insects and diseases, it is necessary to spray frequently, keeping a protective coat of chemicals on the trees and fruit at all times. To produce clean fruit in this area, fruit growers need to spray apples 12 to 15 times a year and peaches 10 to 12, working from early spring until the fruit is about full size.

Several reputable spray-chemical companies have one-package, general-purpose mixtures for fruit trees. These packages may not contain the exact compounds recommended by the University; however, if they are used in accordance with the recommendations on the label, control of diseases and pests for which they are recommended should be satisfactory.

To be effective, sprays must be applied thoroughly, covering all leaves and fruit. They must be timely, since disease and insect control is based upon combating the various insects and diseases in an early stage of development. To spray the tops of large trees, a spray rod or gun is necessary. A peach tree 8 feet tall with moderately heavy foliage will need about 2½ gallons of spray per application, an apple tree 12 feet tall will require about 5 gallons of spray.

Fire blight (pear blight) is a very destructive disease of pears, some apple varieties, quince, and ornamentals —such as flowering crab, firethorn, hawthorn, flowering quince and cotoneasters.

Prune and destroy the diseased twigs, cutting 5 inches or more below the visible edge of the canker. Prevention of fire blight is possible through the use of streptomycin, an antibiotic now available under trade names. Use 2 tablespoonsful (rounded) of 15% streptomycin in 5 gallons of water. Start spraying when the center bloom in a cluster is open, repeat every five days for a total of three applications.

The Peach tree borer may be controlled by spraying the trunks of the stone fruits with a 10% DDT solution three times, about July 20, August 20 and September 20. Wet the lower 2 or 3 feet of the trunk thoroughly.

Deciduous fruit trees should be given a dormant strength spray in the late fall or early spring. This spray helps to destroy the scale insects which are unaffected by the summertime control measures, also to destroy many disease spores that are overwintering on the bark. Lime-sulphur is the commonly used dormant spray. Dormant spraying may be done any time after the leaves fall and before the buds swell when temperatures are above 40 degrees F. and likely to remain above freezing for 24 hours.

Nut Trees

The idea of combining shade with nut crops has an appeal to the practical gardener. Some nut trees make excellent shade trees and where space permits they may all be used. However, two or more varieties of Chinese chestnuts, English (Persian) walnuts and filberts are necessary for cross pollination. The first two are rather large growing and eventually will require considerable space on the home grounds.

The following kinds and varieties are recommended for the Washington Area:

Chinese chestnuts—Nanking, Meiling, Orrin, Crane.
Black walnut—Ohio (the most resistant to anthracnose), Myers.
English (Persian) walnut—Broadview.
Filbert—Potomac, Buchanan, Bixby.
Pecan—Major, Indiana, Pereuque, Bixby, Sweeney, Duvall.
Hickory—Shoul, Glover.

Nut trees, as with other fruit trees, thrive best and yield good crops when given reasonably good care. This should include fertilization, watering and, if necessary, protection from insects and diseases. Since they will most frequently be used for shade little pruning will be necessary other than to avoid weak forks, perhaps to keep them symmetrical.

Filberts are hardy in this area but the early bloom is often destroyed by spring frosts. Planting on a north slope, or where they have little or no protection is not recommended.

Almond trees are hardy enough for this area but seldom produce a crop of nuts because of frost injury to the bloom. Heart nuts may also be grown on the more protected slopes and ridges but because of their susceptibility to the Bunt's disease are not recommended.

Pecan trees are notoriously hard to transplant.

Hickory nuts are so slow in reaching productive size that they are not recommended; however, for those who wish to plant them, Lingenfetler and Glover varieties are considered best. Butternuts are so susceptible to virus diseases that they are not suggested for planting in this area.

One point more should be considered. Squirrels can, and usually do, harvest the nut crops where the trees are growing near a woods.

CHAPTER XIX

WILDFLOWERS

The growing of wildflowers in the home garden is a natural desire, usually beginning during childhood. This desire persists with many gardeners all through their gardening days.

Some of this interest in wildflowers undoubtedly stems from their earliness. Others think of them because of their natural habitat in the woods. Perhaps we might add a third point of interest—they are native to this area. Also, most of them are comparatively free from insect and disease problems.

The metropolitan area's list of native flowers and ferns is very extensive. More than 50 kinds of ferns, for example, are to be found in this vicinity. Several kinds of violets, as well as the trillium, gentians, and other wildflowers, may be seen in our parks, at the nature trail at Great Falls, and in the Fern Valley section of the National Arboretum. The latter includes, of course, many wildflowers from areas distant from Washington.

Conservation Lists

Some of our native plants are being sadly thinned through thoughtless mutilation of the plants by those who want a pretty bouquet or who destroy them by careless handling. To publicize the importance of pres-

ervation, conservation groups both in Maryland and Virginia have prepared lists of those which should be protected. In addition, the garden clubs have provided lists of our wildflowers which are not permissible in flower shows or other exhibitions unless they are grown on the gardener's property.

Native Plant Protection List

For the District of Columbia and Nearby
Maryland and Virginia
Prepared by
Conrad B. Link and Russell G. Brown
University of Maryland

This list has been prepared for the National Capital Garden Club League as a guide for garden clubs and others interested in the use and preservation of native plants. It has been adapted for this area using the "Wild Flower Protection List" by P. L. Ricker, published by the Wild Flower Preservation Society, as a guide.

The preservation of our native plants is an important interest of garden clubs and others concerned with the preservation of our natural beauty and resources. One desire of such groups is the intelligent use of native plants in garden plantings, in the home, as well as in flower shows. The following list has been divided into two sections. The first part includes those native plants that are satisfactory as garden plants, many of which are propagated and sold commercially, and that are also found in this area in the wild. The second part includes those kinds that are less commonly found and are in danger of becoming extinct in this area, yet they may be abundant in other sections of the country. These native plants should not be ruthlessly destroyed and efforts should be made to protect them. Some would be adaptable for garden use whereas others are more difficult to grow because of some specialized soil or cultural condition that is necessary.

Gardeners are cautioned in the general collection of native plants. Permission should be obtained from the land owner. Certainly when fields and woods are being destroyed for construction of buildings and roads, there should be no restriction on the part of the gardeners to try and collect such plants for transplanting to a garden. Where a species grows in great profusion, with hundreds of thousands of individuals present, the taking of a plant for propagation is not likely to do serious harm. The digging of a large number of plants is to be discouraged.

Part I

These native plants are in need of protection in this area. However, since they are often propagated and grown as garden plants, they may be cut and used in flower shows. Careful picking so as not to destroy the plant is practical. In the case of woody plants, careful cutting becomes a form of pruning and not injurious.

Azalea—see Rhododendron
Bloodroot—Sanguinaria canadensis
Bittersweet—Celastrus scandens
Bluebell—Mertensia virginica
Columbine—Aquilegia canadensis
Dogwood—Cornus florida
Fringetree—Chionanthus virginicus
Holly—ilex opaca
Loosestrife—Lythrum
Lily—Lilium (native species)
Mountain Laurel—Kalmia latifolia
Phlox—native species. P. ovata
                P. maculata
                P. divaricata
                P. subulata
Shadbush—Amelanchier canadensis
Sheep Laurel (Lambskill)—Kalmia angustifolia
Stonecrop—Sedum (native species)
Rosebud—Cercis canadensis
Rhododendron—Rhododendron nudiflorum (Pixterflower)
           Rhododendron maximum—
           Rhododendron viscosum—
           Swamp Azalea

Part II

These native plants are less commonly found in this area and thus are in need of protection and preservation. Some of these are not readily adapted to garden culture. Many could be picked as cut flowers if the roots are not disturbed and if sufficient foliage and flowers are left for continued growth and reproduction.

Anemone—Anemone species
Baneberry—Actaea
Bellflower—Campanula (native species)
Bellwort—Uvularia species
Blue Cohosh—Caulophyllum thalictroides
Blue-eyed-Mary—Collinsia verna
Cardinalflower—Lobelia cardinalis
Celandine—Chelidonium majus
Checkerberry Wintergreen—Gaultheria procumbens
Clubmoss—Lycopodium
Columbine—Aquilegia canadensis (native species)
Cohosh—See Baneberry
Coralroot—Corallorrhiza
Dutchman's-Breeches—Dicentra cucullaria
False Solomonseal—Smilacina stellata; S. racemosa
Ferns—especially Walking Fern
Fetterbush—Leucothoe racemosa
Thimbleberry—Rubus odoratus
Gentians—Native species
Goldstargrass—Hypoxis hirsuta
Golden Groundsel—Senecio aureus
Groundhut—Apios americiana tuberosa
Hepatica—Hepatica amerciana; H. acutiloba
Horsegentian—Triosteum perfoliatum
Indianpipe—Monotropa uniflora
Iris, vernal—Iris verna
    crested—Iris cristata
Jackinthepulpit—Arisaema triphyllum
Jacob's Ladder—Polemonium
Ladyslipper—Cypripedium
Larkspur, wild—Delphinium tricorne
Lobelia—Lobelia siphilitica (Giant Lobelia)
    Lobelia cardinalis (Cardinal Flower)
Marshmarigold—Caltha palustris
Willowleaf spirea—Spirea salicifolia
Milkwort—Polygala paucifolia (Fringed polygala)
Mistletoe—Phoradendron
Miterwort—Mitella (Bishopscap)
Jerseytea—Ceanothus armeicanus
Orchids—all native species
Paintedcup—Castilleja
Pasqueflower—Anemone patens
Peatpink—Silene caroliniana
Phacelia—Phacelia
Phlox—Native species
Pinesap—Monotropa hypopitys
Pitcherplant—Sarracenia purpurea
Poorrobins-Plaintain—Erigeron pulchellus
Puttyroot—Aplectrum
Rosegentian—Sabatia angularis
Rue-Anemone—Anemonella thalictroides
Ruellia—Ruellia carolenensis
Saxifrage-Saxifraga—native species
Shinleaf—Pyrola elliptica
Shootingstar—Dodecatheon meadia
Solomonseal—Polygonatum biflorum: P. canaliculatum
Squirrelcorn—Dicentra canadensis
Staggerbush—Lyonia mariana
Stargrass—Aletris or Hypoxis
Sundew—Drosera species
Rosegentian—Sabatia species
Toothwort—Dentaria laciniata
Turtlehead—Chelone species
Trailing-Arbutus—Epigaea repens
Trillium (Wake Robin)—all species
Twinleaf—Jeffersonia diphylla
Violet Woodsorrel Oxalis—Oxalis violacea
Waterleaf—Hydrophyllum
Walkingfern—Camptosorus rhizophyllus
Wildbergamot—Monarda fistulosa
Wild Calla—Calla palustris
Wild Geranium (Cranesbill)—Geranium maculatum
Wildginger—Asarum canadense
Wintergreen—Pyrola species

There is an exception to the above rules. Because of the spread of real estate developments into suburban areas, it is recommended that gardeners seeking wildflowers precede the bulldozer and rescue all they can. This is in the hope that by careful handling, plants, that would otherwise be destroyed, will be saved. In this connection, it should be noted that though the bulldozer may not uproot them, the thinning of the trees and the change in the flow of soil moisture is just as fatal to our natives as is their being uprooted.

To insure success in handling our wildflowers, one should begin by noting their environment and trying to duplicate it as far as possible in the home garden. In most cases, this is a shady garden. Secondly, there are usually certain periods which are better for transplanting than are others. This, of course, cannot always be observed. Third, it is important to lift the plants with a minimum of disturbance to their root system. Next, they should be wrapped in a sheet of plastic to prevent any drying out during the trip from native habitat to garden. In planting them in the wildflower garden, it is well to incorporate generous quantities of sphagnum peat moss or leafmold into the planting area. A generous mulch of leaves to which they are accustomed is usually very beneficial, and lastly, there are some plants which are so difficult to transplant that it is seldom worth the effort. In this category, we might well include the Trailing Arbutus and the Pink Ladyslipper. The latter seems to require a layer of well-rotted leaves in which its roots will thrive. Lacking in this, it does not persist more than one or two years. The Butterfly milkweed is another example. Unless it can be dug in August when it is dormant, it is very difficult to transplant. Our beautiful Royal ferns have a very high moisture requirement, and unless this can be satisfied, they should not be disturbed.

Which of the Wildflowers Are Adapted to Our Gardens?

In the metropolitan area, we will find wildflowers growing in almost every situation—sun, shade, moist, dry, and in bogs and along stream banks. Not all these conditions can be duplicated in any one garden; therefore, it is important to select those kinds which are best adapted to the gardeners' areas. Also, it is wise to refrain from planting those which are gross spreaders. Examples of this latter point are the Common Woods Violet, the Mistflower, the Blackeyedsusan, the New England aster, and perhaps the Goldenrod. This point is particularly important where one has a mixture of the dainty small springflowering kinds and the taller more vigorous growing summer-flowering plants. The Springbeauty, for example, would soon be crowded out by the Common Woods Violet. Some kinds are more at home in a rock garden type of planting than others. In such situations, they show off to better advantage and thus give more satisfaction.

Some kinds go together effectively. The Virginia

Bluebells and the Fawnlily, for example, are good companions and thrive in the same situation.

Collect or Buy?

Whether we should go into the woods and fields to collect our wildflowers or buy them from a reputable nursery is a much debated point. In the first place, most states have a restriction or prohibition against taking plants from public lands. Most land owners resent wanton stripping of their property. Therefore, the plant collector should make certain to obtain the owner's permission before engaging in any plant collecting operations. Secondly, we should recognize that most plants move best at certain seasons of the year, and sometimes this is not at the season when most gardeners enjoy a trip through the woods or fields. Another point, usually wildflowers are growing in competition with weeds, grass and tree roots; consequently, their root systems are rather straggly and oftentimes difficult to lift intact. Thus, the securing of the desired kinds from reputable specialists has several advantages. They can provide the roots of the Butterfly milkweed at the proper season of the year. At digging time there is nothing to indicate their location unless it be a seed stalk. The showy Trilliums are nearly extinct in this area, and one should have at least a dozen of the root stocks for planting in order to have a good show of bloom. Those allergic to poison ivy might well find it to their advantage to buy rather than hunt.

Preparing the Soil

In the shady garden, it is desirable to prepare the new home as early as possible. First this involves the removing of competing tree roots and, if possible, preparing a barricade to keep them out of the planting area. The hole should be dug fairly deeply and filled with native soil whenever possible, although sphagnum peat is an excellent substitute. For the Virginia Bluebells, the soil should be made as light as possible through the addition of sand or perlite. The Fawnlily (Dogtooth violet) has a very long tuber, and the soil might well be prepared to a depth of a foot or more.

Since the wild root systems are likely to be rather straggly, it is desirable to take small plants rather than large ones. Oftentimes, the strays that are outside the patch are more likely to move successfully than are plants taken from the crowded area.

Even with small plants, it is desirable to take a fairly large ball of earth to avoid damaging the roots and to reduce the shock of transplanting. Thus, it is better to make several trips rather than try to do everything at one time. Be sure to cover the containers with plastic or some other material to prevent their drying while being transported.

Generally, the best time to take most of our wildflowers is in the early spring while they are dormant or just as new growth is starting. This is especially important of our native shrubs and trees. Of course, there are exceptions to this rule. The native azaleas can be moved when in bloom. Many others may be moved successfully if the above guides are followed. Ferns, for example, may be moved at any time, but as the new fronds begin to unroll, they are very brittle and easily broken.

It is important to plant the wildlings at the same depth as they grew in their native habitat. An exception to this rule is the hemlock and possibly the American holly. The soil should be level or slightly depressed about them so that moisture will drain into the root area rather than away from it. (This would be fatal in a soil that is lacking in subsurface drainage.) With the plant properly placed in the planting hole, the soil should be worked in and around the roots and then settled with water to eliminate air pockets. Small plants can and might well have leafmold over the planting area as a mulch. In addition, and especially for sun-loving plants, it is well to shade them for a period while they are becoming re-established. The trunks of dogwoods, redbuds, and others that are to be planted in a sunny situation should be wrapped the first season to prevent sunscald of the bark. Discarded nylons are especially well suited for this purpose.

During the first season after planting, it is important to water them whenever rainfall is inadequate. This is especially important in the shady garden since the tree leaves above oftentimes absorb a considerable portion of the rainfall.

If these plants are taken in the fall, it is well to mulch them rather heavily with leaves; however, in order to avoid the leaves matting down, it is usually desirable to first scatter brush over the area. When planted at other seasons, a fall mulch may or may not be necessary depending on whether the fallen leaves will stay in place. In a windswept situation, it is usually advisable to scatter brush to hold the leaves.

Most wildlings will suffer some root shock which is difficult to avoid unless the plants are small. If large plants are taken, a portion of the top should be removed. This practice is exceedingly important when moving woody plants such as dogwood, redbud, American holly and others. The tops of perennial plants, where they have several stems, might well be thinned.

It is seldom advisable to use commercial fertilizer or manure on any of the natives. Usually, the leaf mulch will provide enough plant food to take care of their needs. After they have once been established, an acid-forming type of fertilizer might be safely used, or perhaps dehydrated cow manure, but no inorganic fertilizer.

ALUMROOT

(Heuchera americana—perennial)

Height:	1-2 feet.
Flowers:	Slender branched spike, dull brown or bronze, June-Sept.
Exposure:	Light shade.
Soil:	Average garden loam, tolerant of acidity.
Transplant:	Any time.
Uses:	Low mounds of foliage suitable for rock garden or border in the shady garden.
Improved varieties:	Yes.
Propagate:	Seed, division in spring or fall, leaf cuttings.
Conservation list:	No.

The Alumroot, often mistakenly called Coralbells (the name properly belongs to a western species), is an attractive and easily grown wildflower. The compact mounds of evergreen foliage are surmounted by tall stems of airy flowers. The usual wildling has dull and inconspicuous blooms, but there are a number of improved varieties of Coralbells whose flowers are larger and much more showy.

The Alumroot delight in light shade and are tolerant of soil and acidity; however, they thrive best in a soil that has been enriched with leafmold, compost or peatmoss. They do not tolerate wet feet.

The excellent mounds of foliage resembling geranium leaves are useful in the shady rock garden, and along walks they give a well-defined pattern topped by spikes of bloom from June to September. They are a desirable addition to any wildflower garden.

The plants transplant easily, preferably before the tall flower spikes unfold. Propagation is mainly by division and seed, although selected specimens may be propagated by leaf cuttings.

The common species, Heuchera americana, is our native, but most of the wildflower nurseries offer the Coralbells H. sanginea, in its improved forms. The flowers are much showier. One caring only for the foliage might well use our native, but if color and show is desired, the Coralbells or its improved varieties should be ordered.

ASTER, New England

(Aster novae-angliae—perennial)

Height:	2-5 feet.
Flowers:	Violet to pink, branched flower head, late summer.
Exposure:	Sun, light shade.
Soil:	Moist, not too rich, neutral to slightly acid.
Transplant:	Spring (and in bloom).
Uses:	Informal border, background.
Improved varieties:	Yes.
Propagate:	Self-sows, divide clumps in spring.
Conservation list:	No.

The tall showy asters always command attention in the fall. They are common along our country roads, in the edges of grasslands, and in the edges of woodlands. There is considerable variation in their color. This species and other American natives were exported to Europe where the plant breeders did much to make them more attractive and useful.

The aster does well in ordinary garden soil but will repay any improvement in it with stronger growth and better blooms heads. They do need a moist soil since they are late summer bloomers.

The plants may be transplanted at any time, even while in bloom. The root system is quite fibrous and holds the soil fairly well.

Propagation is by division in the spring. Named varieties usually are lifted and divided every few years. The clumps reach large size and produce many flower stems. Normally, numerous seedlings appear, and it is well to remove them before the planting becomes unmanageable.

There are many wild asters in our fields and woodlands, some of which are fully as attractive as the New England aster. One could have quite a garden just of asters.

The flower heads of the New England aster contain a great many buds. There are always some that are about to open, some open, and some that are past. For this reason, they should be cut for indoor use just as the first flowers open. The faded flowers detract from the appearance.

In exposed situations, the tall stems should be staked before they are borne to the ground by fall rains.

BERGAMOT, SCARLET WILD

(Monarda didyma—perennial)

Height:	3-5 feet.
Flowers:	Red, shaggy flower heads, summer-fall.
Exposure:	Sun, light shade.
Soil:	Tolerant as to soil but should be moist, moderately acid.
Transplant:	Any time.
Uses:	Background, naturalizing, cutflowers.
Improved varieties:	Yes.
Propagate:	Division in spring or fall.
Conservation list:	No.

The bergamot is an oldtime favorite and has many common names such as Oswego-Tea, Bee-balm, Horse-Mint, etc. The shaggy flowers which protrude from the flower head are attractive in flower arrangements and long lasting. In the garden, they are host to the hummingbirds which add to their interest.

There are considerable variations in the flower color, and one might well have clumps of the various ones to meet the needs of color arrangements.

The bergamot is quite tolerant of soil as long as it is moist. Too rich a soil encourages or speeds the spread of a clump so that it may be too much for the location. In the fields, this is an advantage since it crowds out weaker plants and makes for a more effective show. However, this characteristic makes it useful to hold stream banks and other areas subject to erosion.

It is easily moved at almost any time. To increase the number of clumps, one may divide in the spring or in the fall. They also may be increased by saving seed.

BLACK-EYED SUSAN

(Rudbeckia hirta—annual, biennial)

Height:	2-3 feet.
Flower:	Orange-yellow with blackish-brown cone, terminal clusters, summer and fall.
Exposure:	Sun or shade.
Soil:	Poor dry to rich moist, slightly acid.
Transplant:	Easy, anytime.
Uses:	Cutflowers, mass color.
Improved varieties:	Yes.
Propagate:	Seed self-sow, division.
Conservation list:	No.

The Black-eyed susan is a hardy vigorous growing annual or biennial that thrives under varying conditions. The coarse foliage is the one feature generally criticized. The showy yellow flowers are long-lasting and the plants flower over a long period in summer and fall.

The Black-eyed susan will grow equally well in full sun or light shade and is tolerant of soil. It is normally planted in ordinary garden soil and there seems to be no especially favorable season for transplanting. It may be found growing in quite acid soils, in moist situations and in dry thin soils.

Because the flowers are long-lasting it is useful as a cutflower. It may be planted as a background for other wildflowers, in waste areas, and in fence rows.

The Black-eyed susan has been used in hybridizing and there are new kinds of varieties which make use of some of its better characteristics.

Since the Black-eyed susan is a prolific seeder, it may not be desirable to plant it in the smaller wildflower garden unless the gardener is prepared to remove the spent blooms before seed is formed. This is much easier than pulling up countless unwanted seedlings.

BLEEDINGHEART, Fringed

(Dicentra eximia—perennial)

Height:	12-18 inches.

Flower:	Reddish pink, heart-shaped on long racemes, all summer.
Exposure:	Sun or light shade.
Soil:	Tolerant but prefers moist woodsy.
Transplant:	Spring or fall.
Uses:	Ground cover, massed in border, etc.
Improved varieties:	Yes.
Propagate:	Divide clumps in early spring, self-seeds.
Conservation list:	No.

The Fringed Bleedingheart is also called Plumy Bleedingheart, Wild Bleedingheart, etc. It is not as widely planted as it might be because most gardeners do not know where to find it and lack knowledge of its attractive foliage and long season of bloom.

The Fringed Bleedingheart is tolerant but thrives best in moist woodsy soil. It will grow in full sun or in light shade. It is a compact grower topped by racemes of pink, heart-shaped blooms. It will self-seed in favorable situations and is much easier to grow than its relatives, Squirrel-corn and Dutchman's-breeches. As it remains in flower all season long, its usefulness and interest might well be called outstanding. There is an improved variety.

The Fringed Bleedingheart may be transplanted at any season although spring and fall are considered the better times.

The clumps may be divided in the early spring. It also will self-seed in favorable situations.

Mention above was given that it is sometimes called Wild Bleedingheart. This is because the Showy Bleedingheart which is so often grown in the wildflower garden is an introduced plant from Japan. We grow the Showy Bleedingheart oftentimes in the wildflower garden in rather shady situations and they do have heart-shaped flowers, but that is where the comparison ends. The Showy flowers in the spring and then dies down.

The Fringed blooms throughout the season. It has compact ferny foliage, while the Showy is a tall-grower with bold foliage.

BLOODROOT

(Sanguinaria canadensis—perennial)

Height:	6-10 inches.
Flower:	White 1 to 1½ inches, borne on solitary stems, single and double flowers to be found in wild. Early spring-flowering.
Exposure:	Light shade.
Soil:	Moist woodsy, moderately acid.
Transplant:	Early spring.
Uses:	Rock gardens, rock walls.
Improved varieties:	No.
Propagate:	Division in fall, self-seeds, seed sown as soon as ripe.
Conservation list:	On conservation list I.

The Bloodroot is an excellent plant for the wildflower garden. The showy white blooms above gray-green foliage are attractive. They are not difficult to grow, thriving in rich woodsy soil. The rhizomes spread and an appreciable clump soon develops.

The Bloodroot's showy flowers have their petals spread out wide in the morning; they are erect at noon and close at dusk. The flowers last for several days, the doubles longer.

The plant derives its common name from the juice of the stem and roots which is red.

One might well intersperse Bloodroot plants among the rhododendrons and other acid-soil loving plants in shady situations. They are quite showy in the shady rock garden and rock walls, wherever attractive foliage and bloom are desired.

Plant the thick root, about one-inch deep, in soil that has been enriched with leafmold, compost or peatmoss. The older the root the larger number of flowers a single plant will produce.

BLUEBELLS, VIRGINIA

(Mertensia virginica—perennial)

Height:	10-24 inches.
Flower:	Light blue, buds a pink, terminal clusters, early spring.
Exposure:	Semi-shade.
Soil:	Sandy, enriched with leafmold, moist, moderately acid.
Transplant:	Early spring or while dormant in summer or fall. 4-inches deep.
Uses:	Near stream banks, rock garden, companion to daffodils, primroses.
Improved varieties:	No.
Conservation list:	On conservation list I.

The Virginia Bluebell, also known as Virginia Cowslip, is an early spring bloomer, usually found near a creek bank where the soil is sandy and always moist. The bright blue of the flowers is quite showy.

The bright blue color makes them excellent companions for the daffodils and the primroses which bloom at the same season. They also make an interesting combination with the Western Fawnlily since both need the same type of soil and shade.

The Bluebells should be transplanted in the early spring or in the summer and fall while they are dor-

mant. The clumps may be divided. Once happily established, they will self-seed.

The one objection to this charming native is that it dies down in the summer leaving a bare space in the wildflower garden. For this reason it is well to have them interplanted with the Rue-anemone or other plants which retain their foliage throughout the season.

Old clumps that have become too crowded for good growth may be lifted after flowering and divided. This is about the only care needed once they are well established.

BLUETS (Quaker Ladies)

(Houstonia caerulea—perennial)

Height:	6-8 inches.
Flower:	Pale blue, star-shaped, on long stalks, early to mid-spring.
Exposure:	Sun or light shade.
Soil:	Moist, woodsy, acid.
Transplant:	Anytime.
Uses:	Ground cover.
Improved varieties:	No.
Propagate:	Self-sow, divide in early spring or fall.
Conservation list:	Not on conservation list.

The tiny Bluets do not seem to be much when viewed as a single plant, but a carpet of them over an open

space is effective. If in suitable surroundings they will self-seed and spread.

They will grow in a sunny situation provided the soil has been enriched with leafmold, compost, or peatmoss. Otherwise they seem happier in light shade, although here too they need an enriched soil.

The Bluets are easily transplanted at anytime and there is seldom need to propagate for they will quickly seed an area if it is to their liking.

If space is limited the Bluets make a better showing in a rock garden than when lost among a host of other wildlings. The flowers are tiny, averaging less than ½-inch in diameter. It is a carpet of them that produces the dainty effect. A large clump in the rock garden or in some area in the shady garden is effective.

BUTTERCUP, TALL

(Ranunculus acris—perennial)

Height:	2-3 feet.
Flower:	Bright yellow, 1 inch in diameter, on tall branched stems, spring and early summer.
Exposure:	Sun or shade.
Soil:	Rich moist soils, acid.
Transplant:	Anytime.
Uses:	Ground cover, cutflowers.
Propagate:	Seed, divisions.
Conservation list:	No.

The Buttercups are showy plants with their bright green foliage and rich yellow cup-like blooms. They make their best showing in the sun, but will grow in shade if the soil is rich and moist.

There is something symbolic about a buttercup and gardeners usually transplant them from the wild only to find that they are spreaders and will take over vacant spots in their garden if the soil is suitably prepared.

In many cases they are most useful as a ground cover in situations that are too moist for other plants. If the soil is boggy, the species R. septentrionalis, the Swamp buttercup, is probably better adapted. The Tall buttercup, for ordinary moist conditions, is a better flower for cutting and its matted growth will serve to hold a bank.

BUTTERCUP, SWAMP

(Ranunclus septentrionalis—perennial)

Height:	2-3 feet.
Flower:	Bright yellow, 1-1½ inch in dia., long stalk, late spring, and early summer.
Exposure:	Sun and light shade.
Soil:	Moist grassland, tolerant, acid.
Transplant:	Spring.
Uses:	Carpet wetlands, cutflowers.
Improved varieties:	No.
Conservation list:	No.

The Swamp buttercups are pretty much the same—they have excellent foliage, bright yellow flowers and they grow like mad. Unless one has a fairly large area to be devoted to them, they should be by-passed. They like a moist situation such as other plants will not tolerate, and that is their major contribution.

They are tolerant of exposure and soil as long as it is very moist. While they stand upright in the spring, once the flowering season is past, and it is a long one, the stems spread out over the ground and root at the nodes much the same way as crabgrass does. These rooted stems may be cut apart and a considerable number of plants obtained.

BUTTERFLY MILKWEED

(Asclepias tuberosa—perennial)

Height:	1-2 feet.
Flower:	Orange-yellow, clusters, summer-flowering.
Exposure:	Sun.
Soil:	Gravelly, moderately acid.
Transplant:	August, September.
Uses:	Cut flowers, summer color in border.
Improved varieties:	No.
Propagate:	Seed-fall, root cuttings in May.
Conservation list:	No.

The Butterfly milkweed is always attractive with its showy, orange-yellow colored bloom clusters in August. The nectar-laden blooms attract butterflies; hence its common name.

This flower thrives in hot dry situations although it does best in a gravelly soil. It is quite tolerant of acidity but seems to thrive best in a slightly acid, well-drained soil.

The plant dies down after flowering, and unless the spot is marked, is seldom located for digging while dormant. August or September is usually considered the best time to dig them. However, because the roots are large and brittle, it is usually safer to dig a small plant or to buy them from a grower.

The Butterfly milkweed may be propagated by digging a portion of the root in May, and cutting it into one- or two-inch sections which may be planted shallowly in a sandy soil. Seeds may be collected in the fall and sown in late fall, or they can be sown in the spring.

The flowers last well in arrangements. It is important to leave some of the foliage so that the root will continue to grow and develop for another season's bloom.

The Butterfly milkweed lasts for many years in a well-drained situation, and is particularly effective when placed in front of evergreens. It is not a spreader, but clumps will increase in size and a well-established one may have 10 or 12 flower stalks in bloom at a time. This is one of the reasons why it is such a desirable wildflower.

The attractive blooms are followed by beaked pods three or four inches long which are useful in flower arrangements either before or after opening.

The Butterfly milkweed is one of the most attractive of all the milkweeds. Certainly, it is much less a spreader, and for this reason is a good garden subject. However, for a moist situation, one might also wish to try the Swamp milkweed. The Purple milkweed and the Blunt-leaved milkweed are other possibilities.

CACTUS, PRICKLY PEAR

(Optunia compressa—perennial)

Height:	4-6 inches.
Flower:	Yellow, 2-3 in. dia., summer.
Exposure:	Sun, will tolerate light shade.
Soil:	Dry, poor, neutral to moderately acid.
Transplant:	Spring.
Uses:	Rock gardening, seashore gardens.
Improved varieties:	No.
Propagate:	Break off pads in spring and insert in sandy soil.
Conservation list:	No.

The Prickly-pear Cactus is a native to the eastern states, the only member of the cactus family which is. It will thrive in poor gravelly soil in full sunlight. Its habit of growth is such that it is best planted on banks. It will tolerate salt air and sandy soils.

The sprawly habit of growth requires considerable space for a wilding, and the sharp spines make it repulsive to some. Children soon learn to stay clear of it.

The fruits are edible but have tufts of bristles on them which may discourage use.

In spite of these unfavorable points, the cactus is more than an exotic plant. The wax-like texture of the flowers give them a richness of color that is unmatched by other plants.

CARDINAL FLOWER

(Lobelia cardinalis—perennial)

Height:	2-5 feet.
Flower:	Bright red on tall stalks or racemes, late summer and fall.
Exposure:	Light shade, sun if in moist situation.
Soil:	Rich humus-filled, moist, acid.
Transplant:	Spring.
Uses:	Accent near pools, along streams.
Improved varieties:	No.
Propagate:	Divide in spring, will self-seed.
Conservation list:	On list II.

The Cardinal flower is bright red and commands attention wherever it may be. The best show is provided by a clump near a pool or against a boulder.

The Cardinal flower grows best in rich, moist woodland soil, but will tolerate full sun if the soil and moisture conditions are favorable.

The late summer-flowering of this plant makes it useful in maintaining color in the wildflower garden. Some say the Cardinal flower is temperamental and will die out. This may be due to the soil becoming too dry, more likely it is not acid enough.

The flower spikes should be cut off to prevent seeding and to encourage the growth of perennial basal shoots. In this way large clumps are formed. Without this care the Cardinal flower tends to have only one or two flower stalks per plant.

COHOSH BUGBANE (FAIRYCANDLES)

(Cimicifuga racemosa—perennial)

Height:	4-6 feet.
Flower:	Tall stalks covered with tiny white flowers, summer.
Exposure:	Light shade.
Soil:	Rich, deep woodsy, moderately acid.
Transplant:	Early spring.
Uses:	Background, accent when in clumps.
Improved varieties:	No.
Propagate:	Divide crowns early spring, fall, seed.
Conservation list:	No.

The Fairycandles, so named because of their shape, are also known as Black Snakeroot, Black Cohosh, and Bugbane. They are especially noticeable in late summer in open woodlands. Under favorable conditions they will reach 6 feet in height. The tall cylindrical flower spike stands well above the attractive foliage.

It is important to plant the Fairycandles in deeply enriched soil, incorporating generous quantities of leafmold, compost, or peat moss into the soil. They like a moist soil but not wet—good drainage is important. However, they will soon fail in a poor, dry soil.

Because of the season of bloom and their height, the Fairycandles might well be included in the background of the shady flower border as well as in the wildflower garden.

A well established clump will consist of a number of crowns which may be separated in the early spring or late fall. Like other wildflowers they will self-seed in time.

COLUMBINE, WILD

(Aquilegia canadensis—perennial)

Height:	1-4 feet.
Flower:	Red and yellow, slender stalks, long-spurred, spring.
Exposure:	Sun, light shade.
Soil:	Tolerant of soil and acidity, grows on banks and along roadsides.
Transplant:	Early spring.
Uses:	Rock garden, slopes, border.
Improved varieties:	No.
Propagate:	Seed, division, self-sow.
Conservation list:	On conservation list I.

The Wild Columbine, also called American Columbine and Eastern Columbine, is a dainty grower that may be seen along the roadsides, on banks, and in moist meadows. It is colorful and attractive. However, it should not be called American Columbine since there are a number of native species.

The columbine is tolerant of soils and acidity, but responds to enriched soils that are well drained. It will grow in full sun but does best in light shade. It is excellent for the rock garden, where its foliage (if free of the miner) is attractive all season.

The clumps of Columbine are easy to divide, but generally it is easier to let them self-seed. Transplant the seedlings to new locations in the early spring.

The Wild Columbine is a dainty flower, its long-spurred blooms bob in the breeze as if to attract attention.

CRANESBILL (WILD GERANIUM)

(Geranium maculatum—perennial)

Height:	1-2 feet.
Flower:	Magenta to lavender pink, terminal clusters, spring and summer.

Exposure:	Light shade.
Soil:	Dry to moist, not too rich, tolerant of acidity.
Transplant:	Anytime.
Uses:	For extensive areas, among ferns, etc.
Improved varieties:	No.
Propagate:	Free seeder, clumps may be divided spring and fall.
Conservation list:	On list II.

The Wild Geranium makes a colorful display in the shady garden, but it is a free seeder and may become weedy under favorable conditions. The flowers are showy and produce over a long season, but wilt quickly if cut.

The seed pod is shaped like the crane's bill, hence one of the common names. However, it is a true geranium and thus is always of interest although lacking in some desirable features.

The plants may be transplanted at any time, and desirable clumps may be divided in spring or fall.

The Wild Geranium is useful among ferns, where it provides color, and in wooded areas that are not devoted to dainty wildings.

DAISY, FIELD

(Chrysanthemum leucanthemum—perennial)

Height:	1-2 feet.
Flower:	White daisy-like on long stems, summer.
Exposure:	Sun.
Soil:	Tolerant of soils, meadowlands, neutral to moderately acid.
Transplant:	Anytime.
Uses:	Border, cutflowers.
Improved varieties:	No.
Propagate:	Seed, division in spring, fall.
Conservation list:	No.

The Field Daisy, or Ox-eye Daisy as it is often called, is an introduced plant that has made itself at home. It is to be found along the roadsides, in meadows, and in gardens where its vigor and tolerance make it adaptable.

Because of its free seeding it can be weedy, and unwanted seedlings should be promptly removed.

The Field Daisy is a productive bloomer and is well worth cultivating as a cutflower. The individual blooms range from 1 to 2 in. in diameter.

EASTERN PENSTEMON (BEARD-TONGUE)

(Penstemon hirsutus—perennial)

Height:	1-2 feet.

Flower:	Purple or violet with lighter colored lip, panicles, spring.
Exposure:	Sun, light shade.
Soil:	Well-drained, gravelly or sandy, moderately acid.
Transplant:	Anytime.
Uses:	Sunny border, rock garden, cutting.
Improved varieties:	Yes.
Propagate:	Division early spring, seed.
Conservation list:	Not on list.

The Beard-Tongues are easily grown, useful plants. The flowers, which are borne in panicles, are small but numerous. However, the foliage is attractive throughout the season.

The Eastern Beard-Tongue may be transplanted at any time, but if to be divided this is best done in the early spring. The Beard-Tongues seed freely and this may not be desirable in a rock garden.

The Mid-Land Penstemon, also called the Foxglove Penstemon (P. barbatus), has spread into the eastern states and this may cause some confusion. However, its flowers are large, white with purple lines, and it is a taller grower. It may be more attractive to some than the Eastern Penstemon.

The Penstemons are easily raised from seed. However, the Western Penstemons, which are more showy than those mentioned above, are often available but unfortunately do not always like our climate.

FAIRYBELLS

(Disporum lanuginosum—perennial)

Height:	1-2 feet.
Flower:	Creamy bells, red fruited, solitary/pairs at tip of stems, spring.
Exposure:	Light shade.
Soil:	Enriched woodland, moist, acid.
Transplant:	Spring, fall.
Uses:	Background, filler plants.
Improved varieties:	No.
Propagate:	Division early spring, fall; seed (depulp before sowing).
Conservation list:	Not on list.

The Fairybells are dainty little flowers that thrive in light shade in a woodsy soil that is not too dry. They are tolerant of acidity and will thrive among azaleas and rhododendrons. The fruits turn red in the fall and are long lasting.

The Fairybells are often mistaken for a Solomon-plume (False Solomonseal) to which they are related—as well as to the true Solomonseal, Twisted Stalk and Bead Lily. It is well to note the difference in the flowers if the other characteristics are not known. The name Fairybells is descriptive and they appear either singly or in pairs at the tip of each stem.

The plants transplant best in early spring or fall. Large clumps may be divided, and they are easy to raise from seed. Seeds should be depulped before sowing in the fall.

The Fairybells with their creamy white or green-tinged flowers which hang down may not be showy enough for some. However, they are easy to establish and are attractive both in flower and fruit.

FAWNLILY

(Erythronium Spps.—perennial)

Height:	8-12 inches.
Flower:	Lily-like of various colors—spring.
Exposure:	Light shade.
Soil:	Sandy, enriched with peatmoss, leafmold, acid, well-drained.
Transplant:	Difficult, best buy bulbs in fall.
Uses:	In wildflower border, rock garden.
Improved varieties:	No.
Propagate:	By offsets.
Conservation list:	Not on lists.

The Fawnlily is its accepted common name, but in this area they are known as the Dogtooth Violet, Adder's-Tongue, etc. In the west, where they are common, they are called Troutlily, Fawnlily, Glacierlily, etc.

The common Eastern Fawnlily usually grows so thickly in our woods that it seldom flowers freely. Also, the stems are short and the flowers not too showy. The Western Fawnlilies are taller growing, have larger flowers, and are more dependable.

The corm or bulb of the Fawnlily is long and slender, and is very brittle. Consequently it must be well packed to prevent damage in shipping and in planting. Because of its form the digging of the corms in the wild is seldom satisfactory except in sandy soils.

The Fawnlilies make a very pleasing combination with the Virginia Bluebells in the wildflower garden, blooming at the same season and requiring about the same kind of soil and moisture. Both disappear in early summer and the space might well be used for the planting of summer-flowering annuals.

The Glacierlily of the northwest has bright yellow flowers; the Fawnlily (E. californicum) has creamy white flowers E. hendersoni of Southern Oregon has pale lavender flowers with purple throats. These are only a few of the many kinds of Fawnlilies.

FERN, CHRISTMAS

(Polystichum acrostichoides—perennial)

Height:	2-3 feet.
Flower:	——————.
Exposure:	Light shade.
Soil:	Deep gravelly, enriched, moist, acid.
Transplant:	Early spring.
Uses:	Ground cover, border, background for small wild-flower bed.
Improved varieties:	Good named forms available.
Propagate:	Division in early spring.
Conservation list:	On list II.

The Christmas Fern is a popular evergreen for shady gardens in this area. It is tolerant of soils, although thriving in a gravelly well-drained one. However, the soil should be enriched with leafmold, compost, or peat moss to insure moisture.

This fern transplants best in the early spring but care should be taken not to injure the brittle fronds which are unfurling. It should be planted in a shady situation, will thrive even on the north side of a building.

The Christmasfern may be grown among evergreen shrubs such as azaleas and rhododendrons as it is not a rampant spreader.

This fern is somewhat variable in color and growth and consequently there are a number of named forms offered by wildflower nurseries. They may be preferable to collected specimens for the more personal wildflower garden or shady border. The common collected specimens should be adequate for a ground cover in a woodsy garden.

Established clumps may be divided in the early spring.

Like most of our native ferns, they are on the recommended conservation list. This means that collectors might well clean out woods that are being staked for bull-dozer action. Otherwise it is well to remember that the wildflower nurseries have desirable forms.

FERN, COMMON POLYPODY

(Polypodium vulgar virginianum—perennial)

Height:	10-12 inches.
Flower:	—————
Exposure:	Light shade.
Soil:	Loose woodland, moist.
Transplant:	Spring, early fall, space 2 feet.
Uses:	Evergreen ground cover.
Improved varieties:	None.
Propagate:	Division early spring.
Conservation list:	On list II.

The Common Polypody is an attractive evergreen fern with neat growth habits. The fronds are about 2 inches in width and 10 to 12 inches in length.

The fern grows in light shade in a moist woodland soil, but will tolerate short dry periods. The clumps should be spaced about 2 feet apart for good cover.

The Common Polypody is a hardy fern and like the rhododendron curls its fronds in cold weather.

It is a slow spreader and thus is considered one of the better ferns for use in the shady garden.

This fern may be moved at anytime, but like all ferns, it is not easy to handle without damage to the fronds when they are beginning to uncurl.

FERN, MAIDENHAIR

(Adiantum pedatum—perennial)

Height:	12-14 inches.
Flower:	—————.
Exposure:	Light shade.
Soil:	Rich with humus, well drained but moist at all times, acid.
Transplant:	Early fall best, but anytime.
Uses:	Delicate ground cover, for foliage in arrangements.
Improved varieties:	No.
Propagate:	Division.
Conservation list:	On list II.

The dainty Maidenhair fern is considered one of the best for the shady garden. It is delicate and a slow spreader.

It will thrive in a deep woodsy soil that is always moist. Hence it is most commonly found along stream banks and near springs. However, it will not tolerate wet feet, thus, there is a desirable balance between soil moisture and drainage.

The Maidenhair fern is a slow spreader and will not usurp a large area in the garden. In the wild it is commonly found in isolated patches. In the wildflower garden it is often used to hide areas left bare by dying foliage of such plants as the Virginia Bluebells. They may be grown among the Rhododendrons and other broadleaved evergreens.

Propagation is by division in the early spring. However, it takes keen observation to note the slowly rising croziers which are earth-colored. The best time to divide is just as they begin to show.

FERN, ROYAL

(Osmunda regalis var. spectablis—perennial)

Height:	1-5 feet.
Flower:	—————.
Exposure:	Light shade.
Soil:	Deep, rich, moist but not wet feet, acid.
Transplant:	Early spring before the fronds begin to unfurl.
Uses:	Ideal for along stream banks.
Improved varieties:	No.
Propagate:	Division in early spring or fall.
Conservation list:	On list II.

The Royal fern is looked upon as one of the most stately of ferns. It is especially attractive when growing along some small stream where its roots are always moist but not in wet soil. In other words, the roots can adjust to their moisture needs. This fern cannot take dry soils.

It is only suited to the larger garden where streams, springs, or pools provide suitable growing conditions. Also, because of its tall growth under favorable conditions, it is likely to be too tall for many situations.

This fern is deciduous—it dies down in the fall as does the Maidenhair; the other two included are evergreen. It is best divided in the early spring before the fronds begin to unfurl or in the fall. If divided in the fall the newly planted divisions should be well mulched to prevent heaving.

GINGER, WILD

(Asarum canadense—perennial)

Height:	8-10 inches.
Flower:	Small jug like, brown-purple, very early in spring.
Exposure:	Shady.
Soil:	Rich with humus, well drained, moderately acid.
Transplant:	Spring, fall.
Uses:	Ground cover, under rhododendrons, etc.
Improved varieties:	No.
Propagate:	Division spring, fall.
Conservation list:	On list II.

There are many areas along the Eastern seaboard

where the Wild Gingers may be found. They thrive in any woodland where there is moderate moisture and a deep rich soil. They may be found on loamy slopes in soils that are neutral to moderately acid.

In the garden the Wild Ginger is useful as a low-growing ground cover and it is at home beneath a Rhododendron or similar tall growing shrub.

This native should be handled in the early spring or fall to avoid checking its growth.

The Wild Ginger is a slow spreader and thus is adapted to the smaller wildflower garden.

The small jug-like flower is hidden by the large round leaves and is seldom noticed. Its color is a brownish purple and is roughly an inch in diameter.

GOLDENROD, PLUME

(Solidago juncea—perennial)

Height:	1-5 feet.
Flower:	Large fluffy flower masses, curving at the top, golden-yellow June to November.
Exposure:	Sun.
Soil:	Tolerant, moderately enriched with compost, leaf-mold; moderate to strongly acid, medium moist.
Transplant:	Spring.
Uses:	Mass effect, cutflowers.
Improved varieties:	Yes.
Propagate:	Divide, self-seed freely.
Conservation list:	Not on list.

There are a large number of native goldenrods in the U.S., and the east is not without its share of these late-summer and fall-bloomers. They range from small flat-topped species to tall willowy kinds with interesting curves to the racemes. Some have dainty foliage, other coarse, rough leaves that may be too large for good appearance. Thus it is important in selecting a native to choose plants which have the more desirable characteristics.

The Plume Goldenrod is considered by many to be one of the best in this area. It thrives in open sun and in dappled shade in meadowlands, and along the road-sides. Its height and flower display will be affected by the soil and moisture where growing. It may be recognized by the smooth reddish stems. Also, in this species there are small leaves growing in the axils of the larger leaves.

Most goldenrods are too strong growing for the smaller garden, but there are some that grow only a foot in height that may be used if the spent blooms are removed before they drop their seeds.

A desirable plant may be increased through division of the root mat in the spring. Thus, it is best to choose carefully and take only a suitable plant and do the propagation the next spring.

Goldenrods are quite tolerant of soil and moisture but should have full sun if they are to give the display wanted. The richer the soil, the taller and the larger they will grow. But of course, the foliage will be larger and coarser too.

HEPATICA, LIVERLEAF

(Hepatica acutiloba—perennial)

Height:	6-8 inches.
Flower:	White to pink, single on stems, early spring.
Exposure:	Light shade.
Soil:	Moist rich woodland soil, moderately acid.
Transplant:	Anytime, even while in flower.
Uses:	Rock gardens, rock walls.
Improved varieties:	No.
Propagate:	Division after flowering or in fall, self-sow.
Conservation list:	On list II.

The dainty little Hepaticas, in spite of their common name, Liverleaf, are considered very choice wildflowers for the shady garden. While small and shown to best advantage in a rock garden, they may be used in other spaces. The flowers are borne on willowy stems above the foliage and show to advantage.

There are two native Hepaticas, the Sharplobe and the Roundlobe. The Sharplobe is more commonly found in this area, and is not as demanding for high acidity as the Roundlobe.

They are easily transplanted, even while in flower. Propagation, if desired, consists of pulling the crown apart after flowering or in the fall. Usually, in favorable situations they self-sow freely and division is not necessary. This is preferable since the older and larger plants make the best displays.

In planting the Liverleafs, it is well to use generous quantities of woods soil in the planting hole, lacking this use compost or peatmoss.

They should not be allowed to dry out during droughts. They are evergreen and the bronzy foliage is attractive during the winter. A mulch of leaves is help-ful but do not cover the foliage.

IRIS, CRESTED

(Iris cristata—perennial)

Height:	4-6 inches.
Flower:	Pale lavender blue, short stalks, spring.
Exposure:	Shade.
Soil:	Well-drained and enriched with leafmold, compost, moderately acid.
Transplant:	Anytime, best after flowering.
Uses:	Rock garden and in wildflower garden where low growth may be seen.

Improved varieties:	Yes.
Propagate:	Divide after flowering.
Conservation list:	On list II.

The dainty little Crested Iris are considered one of the better wildflowers for the shady garden. They do not withstand competition with weeds and coarse growing wildflowers, hence are more likely to thrive in the rock garden. However, a bed of them near the pathway can be equally interesting.

They may be moved at anytime, but in the spring before flowering it is well to lift them with a ball of earth on the roots. After flowering they may be moved bare-root without injury. After flowering is the time to divide the rhizomes and to replant in soil that has been enriched with leafmold, compost or peatmoss. Do not attempt to cover the rhizomes with more than a half inch of soil. They will work to the top of this once the roots have become established.

The Crested Iris is a shade lover and will not thrive in full sun.

Protect the planting from injury; they are so small that many may not notice them. Walking upon the Crested Iris is not considered beneficial, nor should animals be allowed to romp over them.

IRIS, VERNAL

(Iris verna—perennial)

Height:	6-8 inches.
Flower:	Lavender-blue to white, on short stalks, spring.
Exposure:	Light shade.
Soil:	Rich in humus, moist, sandy, acid.
Transplant:	Anytime.
Uses:	Rock garden, small beds.
Improved varieties:	No.
Propagate:	Division after flowering.
Conservation list:	On list II.

The dainty little Vernal Iris is a bit larger grower than the Crested Iris. They are sometimes found in the same general area, but usually in different localities. Both are shade lovers and need a soil that has been enriched with leafmold, compost or peatmoss. Both need a moist situation but will not tolerate wet feet.

The Vernal Iris may be moved at any time, but if moved before flowering should be lifted with the roots in a ball of soil. After flowering they may be moved bare-root.

The rhizomes should be separated after flowering. Plant in a slightly raised bed and barely cover the rhizomes. Once the divisions are established the rhizomes will be on top of the soil.

The Vernal Iris like the Crested, makes a pleasing show in the shady rock garden, or on top of a rock wall. Beds beside the walk in the wildflower garden are showy but may be in danger of being stepped upon unless protected.

JACK-IN-THE-PULPIT, WOODLAND

(Arisaema triphyllum—perennial)

Height:	1-2 feet.
Flower:	The white Jack is beneath a green canopy stripped purple-brown, green or white. In late summer the Jack may become a cluster of red berries.
Exposure:	Light shade.
Soil:	Tolerant, but thrives best in deep rich soil that is moist, acid.
Transplant:	Anytime, spring, fall, dig deep enough to include the "indian turnip."
Uses:	Accent plant in the wildflower garden.
Improved varieties:	No.
Propagate:	Division, seed.
Conservation list:	On list II.

The stately Jack-in-the-pulpit is an accent plant in any wildflower garden. While related to the Skunk Cabbage, they are much easier to grow and are more

interesting. The Jack-in-the-pulpit will attain good size and foliage if planted in a soil that is moist and has been deeply enriched with woods soil, compost, or peatmoss.

The Jack-in-the-pulpit may be transplanted at anytime but this is best done in the early spring or in the fall. Since the Indian Turnip, the corm from which the plant grows, is deep down it is well to dig deeply so as not to disturb the roots below the turnip.

The Indian Turnip, as the corm is called, is supposed to be edible but actually is bitter and not at all pleasant to eat. The leaves and the turnip are poisonous only to the extent that they may cause skin irritation (dermatitis) to those who are susceptible.

The Jack-in-the-pulpit will tolerate boggy conditions but cannot withstand poor, dry soils or sun.

JACOB'S-LADDER

(Polemonium reptans—perennial)

Height:	9-12 inches.
Flower:	Light violet, bell shaped, terminal clusters, spring.
Exposure:	Sun, light shade.
Soil:	Woodsy, rich humus, moist, neutral to moderately acid.
Transplant:	Spring, fall.
Uses:	Rock garden, among azaleas, front of shady border.
Improved varieties:	No.
Propagate:	Divide after flowering, self-sow.
Conservation list:	On list II.

There is some confusion as to the botanical species of the Jacob's-Ladder. Our native is Polemonium reptans. There is an introduced species, P. caeruleum, which is quite similar. Collected plants are likely to be the P. reptans, while the purchased ones may be P. caeruleum. The latter has undoubtedly escaped in some areas since it has found conditions here to its liking.

The other common names for the Jacob's-Ladder are Greek Valerian and Spring Polemonium. The name Jacob's-Ladder undoubtedly derives from the alternate arrangement of the leaves, ladder-like in appearance.

An attractive plant with lacy leaves and pleasing clusters of flowers at the tips of the upper branches, it needs only a rich woodsy soil to thrive in a rock garden, or along the paths in the wildflower garden. It will take either sun or light shade; the latter gives better results in this area except where both soil and moisture are adequate. The Jacob's-Ladder does not persist for long in a droughty soil either in sun or shade.

This plant should take away some of the bareness of the Rhododendron planting with its lacy foliage.

It is best transplanted in the early spring or in the fall. Divide old clumps after they have flowered. However, in a suitable situation they will self-seed freely.

LILY, TURKSCAP

(Lilium superbum—perennial)

Height:	2-8 feet.
Flower:	Orange-red spotted purple, recurved petals, late summer.
Exposure:	Light shade, sun.
Soil:	Moist, sandy-peat, meadow—enriched.
Transplant:	Early spring, late fall.
Uses:	Shady flower border.
Improved varieties:	No.
Propagate:	Seed, division, scales.
Conservation list:	On list I.

The Turkscap lily is a native of this area and is to be found in moist woodland soils near creeks; also in meadows near a stream bank. It thrives in a sandy soil that has been enriched with leafmold, peatmoss, or compost. The soil should be acid. In a suitable soil it will thrive in full sun and attain a height of 6 to 8 feet.

The bulbs should be lifted in the early spring or in late fall.

Propagation is from seed, separation of the bulbs which are on a long angular rhizome, or a special form might well be propagated by the scaling method.

The flowers are so fully recurved that this lily may well be viewed from any angle. It adds color to the border in late summer.

It is on the Conservation list I, hence unless being rescued from a development area, might well be obtained from a lily grower or from a wild-flower specialist. It is easy to grow. Its height suggests planting among shrubs.

This lily is base-rooting, hence does not require deep planting. In the wild the bulbs may be found with only a couple of inches of soil over them. However, 4 to 5 inches is the recommended depth in a well enriched sandy soil.

MAYAPPLE

(Podophyllum peltatum—perennial)

Height:	12-15 inches.
Flower:	Hidden by foliage, 1½-2 inches, fragrant, white, spring.
Exposure:	Light shade.
Soil:	Enriched, moist, acid.
Transplant:	Anytime, early spring best.
Uses:	Carpets open woodlands, is a spreader.
Improved varieties:	No.
Propagate:	Division.
Conservation list:	No.

The Mayapple is a familiar spring-flowering plant in open woodlands. The wide-spreading, umbrella form of foliage usually hides the fragrant white flower below. There is only one flower on a plant and appears in the

axle of the two leaf stems. It may be 1½ to 2 inches wide.

The Mayapple may be transplanted at any time, but early spring is less of a shock to the plant.

A moist soil well enriched with leafmold, peatmoss

or compost is suitable for this flower. However, it is a spreader and should not be planted in the smaller wildflower garden. Certainly, an ideal soil favors the rapid growth of the spreading rhizomes.

The fruit, when ripe, is edible, but green fruit, roots and foliage are poisonous. They contain a bitter resinous substance that is sometimes used as a purgative. The rootstock may cause severe dermatitis on some.

The Mayapple is also known as Mandrake which alludes to its flowering season, but the name properly belongs to a European plant.

MEADOWRUE, TALL

(Thalictrum polygamum—perennial)

Height:	3-6 feet.
Flower:	White, large feathery clusters, summer and early fall.
Exposure:	Sun, light shade.
Soil:	Soil should be moist and rich.
Transplant:	Spring or fall.
Uses:	Background for lower-growing plants in light shade.
Improved varieties:	No.
Propagate:	Division early spring or after flowering.
Conservation list:	No.

There are a number of the Meadowrues in this area. This species is known both as tall and as fall Meadowrue. The foliage somewhat resembles that of the Columbine.

It is an easy plant to grow, but prefers a moist, rich soil. It will grow fully as well in sun as in light shade if the soil is favorable.

The early Meadowrue (T. dioicum) is a lower grower (2 ft.), flowering in the spring. The flowers are a green-yellow and borne in panicles.

The Purple Meadowrue (T. dasycarpum) differs from the tall in that its stems are purple and the flowers are both white and purple. The showy clusters appearing in summer.

MISTFLOWER, HARDY AGERATUM

(Eupatorium coelestinum—perennial)

Height:	1-2 feet.
Flower:	Azure blue, fluffy terminal clusters, Aug.-Oct.
Exposure:	Sun, light shade.
Soil:	Rich, moist, moderately acid.
Transplant:	Anytime, spring preferred.
Uses:	Sunny border, cutflower.
Improved varieties:	No.
Propagate:	Division, in spring, seed.
Conservation list:	No.

The Hardy Ageratum, Mistflower, or Eupatorium as it is variously called is a showy fall bloomer. The blue flowers are fully as attractive as the true ageratum. It is of easy culture.

The one bad fault, and it is a bad one, is that it spreads rapidly both by underground stolons and by seed. It is almost impossible to eradicate once it gets into a rock garden. The foliage is rather coarse for the smaller wildflower garden.

The flowers are much sought after for flower arrangements in the fall. It might be useful to prevent erosion on a moist sunny slope.

PHLOX, SWEETWILLIAM

(Phlox divaricata—perennial)

Height:	8-12 inches.
Flower:	Lilac to lavender, showy terminal clusters, early to mid-spring.
Exposure:	Light shade.
Soil:	Rich leafmold, moist, acid.
Transplant:	Anytime, early spring best.
Uses:	Cultivated borders, naturalize in wildflower garden.
Improved varieties:	Yes—alba, laphami.
Propagate:	Division, root cuttings, seed.
Conservation list:	On list I.

The Sweetwilliam Phlox, also called Wild Wood's phlox, Blue phlox, etc., is of the easiest culture and will spread by seed. However, it dies down early in the summer and thus this habit can hardly be called a fault. The color display in the wildflower garden or in an open woodland is excellent.

The Sweetwilliam is easily divided if a special form is desired. It also may be propagated by root-cuttings. However, most gardeners will enjoy the ordinary form and let it spread naturally.

Give the Blue Phlox a soil that has been enriched with leafmold, sphagnum moss or compost. This will make the soil acid and hold the moisture.

There are many other kinds of phlox native to this area. The P. maculata, which is also called Sweetwilliam, is also desirable. It has about the same size of plant and flowers, but the flowers are pink or purple. The stems are purple-spotted.

Another native is the Wild Pink Phlox, P. ovata, which has larger flowers, and are rose-pink. The stems are a bit shorter. It flowers in late spring. Creeping Phlox, P. stolonifera, usually grows about 6 inches high, has mauve-pink flowers and is useful as a ground cover in woodland areas.

The Mountain Pink, Moss Phlox, or Moss-Pink, P.

subulata, which is so commonly sold by merchants in the early spring, is also native in this area. Unlike the others it is a sun-lover. However, all want a soil that has been generously enriched with peatmoss. The Moss Phlox will tolerate a drier soil and loves to sprawl over a large rock.

QUEEN-ANNE'S LACE

(Daucus carota—biennial)

Height:	2-4 feet.
Flower:	White in large flat umbels, summer.
Exposure:	Sun.
Soil:	Grasslands.
Transplant:	Spring (small roots).
Uses:	Cutflowers, dried flowers.
Improved varieties:	No.
Propagate:	Seeds.
Conservation list:	Not on list.

The Queen-Anne's Lace is so widespread and often considered a weed, that it is a surprise to many that it is an introduced plant. Also, it is the wild species from which our common vegetable, carrots, have been developed.

The Queen-Anne's Lace is useful both as a cut-flower and for dried flower arrangements. The plants are so commonly available in roadside and meadow that it is doubtful one would want to raise them. Especially so since the seed have to be sown one season, live over winter as small plants (roots) and then produce the flower stalk the next season. If plants are grown the gardener should prevent the formation of seed. For drying the flowers are cut just as they open and before seed formation begins.

To transplant Queen-Anne's Lace it is well to dig the small roots in the early spring. They may also be dug in the late fall.

Queen-Anne's Lace flourishes in any good garden soil in full sun.

RATTLESNAKE-PLANTAIN, DOWNY

(Goodyear pubescens—perennial)

Height:	Plants 3-6 inches, flower stalk 12-16 inches.
Flower:	White, helmet shaped, many on stalk, late spring, summer.
Exposure:	Light shade, sun.
Soil:	Woodsy, acid, moist but well-drained.
Transplant:	Anytime.
Uses:	Rock gardens, terrariums.
Improved varieties:	No.
Propagate:	Division spring and fall by separating rhizomes.
Conservation list:	Not on list.

The curious little Downy Rattlesnake plantain, a member of the orchid family, is of most interest for use in terrariums, although it is also useful in the rock garden. The main interest seems to be in the curiously marked leaves, which some believe to resemble snake-skin.

The plant may be lifted at anytime, but this should be with a minimum disturbance to the roots.

The Rattlesnake-plantain thrives in woodsy, acid soil. It should be moist but well drained.

The mat of rhizomes may be divided if additional plants are needed. This is best done in the spring or fall.

The flowers of the Rattlesnake-plantain are not showy, and many would not recognize it by them. It is the white veined green leaves that are of interest.

ROSEMALLOW

(Hibiscus palustris—perennial)

Height:	3-5 feet.
Flower:	White, pink, some have a red eye, summer.
Exposure:	Sun, light shade.
Soil:	Deep, rich, moist—tolerant of moisture and will grow in usual garden soil.
Transplant:	Early spring.
Uses:	Background, mass color.
Improved varieties:	Yes, many hybrids offered.
Propagate:	Seed.
Conservation list:	No.

The Rosemallow, Swamp Mallow, and sometimes called Hibiscus, is normally found along streams and moist situations. The huge flowers are most showy.

The large fleshy roots are difficult to handle except while dormant. Since the plants are easily grown from seed, there is little point in trying to dig them except for some special color or form. However, most flower seed merchants unually offer selections or hybrids and for this reason it may not even be advisable to collect seed in the wild.

The Rosemallow is supposed to thrive in deep moist soils but apparently will do almost as well in the usual garden soil. It will grow in full sun but the colors and flowers seem brighter in light shade.

During the height of the Japanese beetle invasion the flowers were badly damaged since the Rosemallows were in bloom when the beetles were flying. Since the beetles are seldom troublesome now, the Rosemallow may be worth growing for its mass color effects.

RUE ANEMONE

(Anemonella thalictroides—perennial)

Height:	6-9 inches.
Flower:	Clusters of 1-inch flowers at tips of stems, mid-spring.
Exposure:	Light to dense shade.
Soil:	Rich, humusy, moist, acid.
Transplant:	Late spring.
Improved varieties:	No.
Propagate:	Divide late spring (tubers), fall.
Conservation list:	In list II.

The dainty little Rue-anemone is considered excellent for the shady wildflower garden, although its small stature would indicate it might be lost among taller growing plants. Perhaps it is best used in the rock garden.

The gray-green leaves are quite similar to those of the Meadowrue and the Columbine.

This wildflower seems to thrive in shade in a deep woodsy soil that is moist but well-drained.

Each clump has many tiny tubers which may be divided in late spring. The plant is completely dormant by early summer. While this plant may seem to be delicate, actually it is a sturdy wildflower and is easily established in a shady garden.

SOLOMONPLUME, FALSE SOLOMONSEAL

(Smilacina racemosa—perennial)

Height:	2-3 feet.
Flower:	Feathery white panicles at the tip of the branches, late spring.
Exposure:	Light shade.
Soil:	Woodsy, moderately acid, moist.
Transplant:	Spring or fall.
Uses:	Companion plant for Solomonseal, ferns, etc.
Improved varieties:	No.
Propagate:	Division, seeds.
Conservation list:	On list II.

The False Solomonseal is a showy wildflower both in the spring and in the fall when the dark-red fruits appear. However, the birds seem to favor the berries and once ripe they quickly disappear.

This wildflower is a good companion for the ferns. In the wild it is frequently to be found among them. It does well in light to moderate shade.

Propagation is by dividing the rhizome, this is best done in the fall, although it may also be done after flowering.

The soil needs to be enriched by the addition of peatmoss, compost or leafmold. It should be moderately acid and moist.

The foliage of the False Solomonseal resembles that of Solomonseal in quality as well as in veining.

Some consider the False Solomonseal to be a spreader because of the rhizome root, but this is slow and not objectionable.

SOLOMONSEAL

(Polygonatum biflorum—perennial)

Height:	2-3 feet.
Flower:	Bell-like yellow-green hanging from each node, late spring.
Exposure:	Light shade, sun.
Soil:	Rich, moist, acid.
Transplant:	Early spring.
Uses:	Shady wildflower garden.
Improved varieties:	No.
Propagate:	Seeds.
Conservation list:	On list II.

The Solomonseal is a popular plant for the wildflower garden. The many bell-like flowers hanging from the leafnodes are followed by green berry-like fruits which turn dark blue in the fall. The foliage is attractive and may be useful in the background of the smaller wildflower border.

The Solomonseal will thrive either in sun or shade if planted in a soil that has been enriched by the addition of peatmoss, compost, or leafmold. It should be moist and acid.

This plant is not easily divided and so propagation is usually by seed.

The Solomonseal makes a good companion plant for Rhododendrons and other broad-leaved evergreens in shady situations.

SPRINGBEAUTY, CAROLINA

(Claytonia caroliniana—perennial)

Height:	5-10 inches.
Flower:	White or rose tinted, deeper rose veins, clusters, spring.
Exposure:	Light shade, sun.
Soil:	Moist, rich woodsy, acid.
Transplant:	Spring, fall, or after flowering.
Uses:	With Virginia Bluebells, carpet woodland.
Improved varieties:	No.
Propagate:	Division spring or fall, seed.
Conservation list:	No.

The Carolina Springbeauty is a dainty little flower that will carpet the ground under favorable conditions. Its early spring display is always desirable. When picked,

the flowers soon wilt, but they are so attractive that every child wants to pick them.

This wildflower thrives in light shade in a moist soil that has been enriched with peatmoss or other humus. In such a situation it soon spreads by seed to carpet the area.

It is not difficult to transplant. The tubers should be covered with about 2 inches of soil. The plants disappear by mid-summer.

The Springbeauty may be planted in special soil pockets in the rock garden, it is also attractive when planted among the Virginia Bluebells. They may also be potted up for forcing.

The Carolina Springbeauty is smaller flowered than the Common Springbeauty (C. virginica) which is also native to this area. The latter is also called Mayflower, Grass-Flower, and Good-Morning-Spring.

STAR-OF-BETHLEHEM

(Ornithogalum umbellatum—perennial)

Height:	5-10 inches.
Flower:	White in flat-topped clusters—spring.
Exposure:	Sun, light shade.
Soil:	Rich, woodsy, moist but well drained.
Transplant:	Anytime.
Uses:	Rock garden, border for woodland paths.
Improved varieties:	Yes.
Propagate:	Division of bulbs in late fall.
Conservation list:	No.

The Star-of-Bethlehem is a dainty little bulbous flower that has found eastern North America a suitable home and has become widely naturalized. In the areas where naturalized many of the clumps have so impoverished the soil that they are poor bloomers. However, if lifted and separated, they should soon regain their normal flower display.

The Star-of-Bethlehem thrives in a rich woodsy soil, one that has been enriched by the addition of peatmoss, leafmold or compost. It does best in light shade.

The bulbs may be lifted in the late summer or early fall, divided and reset in enriched soil.

This plant which dies down in the summer leaving a bare spot in the wildflower garden or rock garden may be followed with summer-flowering plants.

The flowers are showy. There may be 15 or 20 on 10- to 12-inch stems. Dainty and star-shaped, but more especially happy in our climate, as well as tough and enduring they should not be overlooked for the wildflower garden.

TRILLIUM

(Trilliuam grandiflorum—perennial)

Height:	10-15 inches.
Flower:	2-3 inch white blossoms.
Exposure:	Light shade.
Soil:	Enriched with peatmoss, leafmold or compost, moderately acid.
Transplant:	Anytime, preferably in the fall after the bulbs have matured.
Uses:	In moist shaded woodlands, moist situation in rock garden.
Improved varieties:	No.
Conservation list:	On list II.

The Trilliums are widespread. There are few sections where one or more do not exist. The White Trillium, also called Showy Trillium and Wake-Robin is one of the least demanding of all Trilliums. It blooms very early in the spring, hence the name Wake-Robin.

The Trilliums need a rich soil that is always moist. They do not tolerate a bone-dry soil for very long. They may be found in heavy shade, but generally they do best in light shade.

The bulbs should be planted in the fall, preferably in clumps of ten or a dozen since they do not multiply rapidly. They may me lifted after flowering and the bulbs replanted then or stored until fall.

The Trillium bulbs need protection from rodents which may be supplied by surrounding them with hardware cloth. A covering is also desirable since the bulbs are given only a 2-inch covering with soil.

The White Trillium is the most showy and easiest to grow, but there is also the Nodding Trillium, the Red Trillium, the Painted Trillium, etc. The latter is usually considered more demanding and requires an acid soil, considerable moisture, a cool situation in summer, and a soil that is generously enriched with some form of humus.

VIOLET, BIRDSFOOT

(Viola pedata—perennial)

Height:	5-10 inches.
Flower:	Upper petals lilac, lower ones dark purple-black, spring.
Exposure:	Sun, light shade.
Soil:	Well-drained, rich in humus, acid.
Transplant:	Anytime.
Uses:	Sunny rock garden, border.
Improved varieties:	No.
Propagate:	No.
Conservation list:	No.

The Birdsfoot Violet is one of the better violets to grow. It may be short-lived in a soil that is lacking in acidity. It is often to be found along the roadside, sometimes on high banks.

There are many forms of the Birdsfoot Violet to be found in most parts of the United States. Some seem to be thriving in soils that are lacking in the acidity of the Eastern States. This has been interpreted by some to indicate that in time these violets build up a toxicity from which they eventually perish. To demonstrate this theory, they dig up the plants every few years and re-plant in fresh soil.

The Birdsfoot Violet gets its name from the deeply divided leaves which are thought to resemble a bird's foot, having 3 or more segments. The flowers are quite large and showy when grown under favorable conditions.

The Birdsfoot Violet is not aggressive and hence is not objectionable in the wildflower garden while the common woods violet soon becomes a weed crowding out other plants.

The foliage dies down in the summer leaving a bare area where summer-flowering annuals might well be planted.

Under favorable conditions this violet self-seeds and hence division is seldom practiced. It may be safely transplanted at anytime if kept moist during transportation. The flowers are fragrant and long-lasting.

YUCCA

(Yucca filamentosa—perennial)

Height:	4-6 feet.
Flower:	On tall stalks with a large cluster of waxy-white blooms—summer.
Exposure:	Sun.
Soil:	Dry, tolerant of acidity.
Transplant:	Early spring taking small rosettes.
Uses:	In dry, sunny border.
Improved varieties:	No.
Propagate:	Divide taking smaller rosettes, self-seeds.
Conservation list:	Not on list.

The stately Yucca makes an appreciable showing in the sunny border in mid-summer. The tall spikes with many flowers, which may be 2 inches in length and almost as much in diameter, bloom in June or July.

This plant, which is normally associated with the West, actually is a native from south Delaware and one of the few Yuccas that will tolerate the wet soils of the east.

The Yucca thrives best in full sun in a poor gravelly soil. The hotter and drier, the better. It is tolerant of soil acidity but most gardeners avoid the use of peatmoss or other acidifying materials.

The tall flower stalks should be removed after flowering and before the seeds fall. Otherwise the gardener may find many seedlings to be removed or transplanted.

The Yucca is a long-lasting perennial that produces many rosettes which may be dug and new plants established. Seed may take 4 or 5 years to attain flowering size, the rosettes usually in 2 or 3 years.

The Yucca is often called Spanish Bayonet and Adam's Needle. These names derive from the long sharp pointed leaves that grow from the main root in rosette form.

The Other Wildlings

Mention above of a number of other wildflowers and plants has been omitted for several reasons. For example, the Trailing-Arbutus is only happy when it can be planted on a slope. It is not often easily transplanted. The Chelone is a native that is better bought from a nursery than collected, largely because it moves best when dormant or very early in the spring. The commercial nurseries ship it in the spring or fall. The wild orchids, such as the Pink Ladyslipper and the Yellow Ladyslipper, are not easily transplanted because of their stringy root system. The pink is particularly difficult to move. The same is to be said of the ground cover commonly called Crowfoot to Ground Pine. It prefers the area beneath pine trees if it is not to die. The Teasel is an interesting prickly, tall growing biennial that is popular in flower arrangements. Undoubtedly some will want to grow it. Interestingly enough, it is an introduced plant that likes our climate and soils and is to be found growing wild in many places.

Another well-known wildflower, Chickory, is such an invasive weed that although we love its chickory-blue flowers we should not plant it in the garden unless we can build a retaining wall around it. Another common wildflower, sometimes called Butter-and-Eggs and Yellow Bedstraw, is so fragile and transitory that most people lose interest. The Pitcher Plant is adapted to bog conditions which are seldom feasible in the garden. It is no more than a curiosity.

Collecting Seeds

Most of these wildflowers seed rather freely, and if the seed is collected when mature and sown immediately in a suitable bed, it is quite possible to produce new plants. Oftentimes, they will seed naturally, and these seedings should be lifted and transplanted to a suitable area until large enough to be incorporated in the planting. Such plants, of course, are of interest to other gardeners, and the surplus is usually easily disposed of.

Propagation

Many of these wildflowers may be propagated by division, a few by root cuttings, and a very few by rooting of stems in suitable propagating media. Generally, however, this is the work of the specialist, although many gardeners find it an interesting and rewarding practice. Certainly those who have sizable shady gardens will have need for many plants of each kind. Specific mention of methods was made above in the case of plants which I have grown.

CHAPTER XX

GARDEN GLOSSARY

Acid (soil)—Soils may be acid, alkaline or neutral. There are plants which require acid soils, some that need a sweet (alkaline) soil, and many that prefer a neutral or near neutral soil. The degree of acidity or sweetness of the soil affects the availability of some of the minerals which the plants need for their growth.

Aeration—Most plants must have air through their roots. When soils are compacted or are water-logged, plants cannot breathe. If planting is too deep, too much soil piled over the roots, then the roots cannot obtain sufficient air and the plants suffer. Waterlogged soils must be drained or the plants will suffocate for lack of air.

Air-Layering—There are several methods for developing roots on the stem of a plant that are used on those plants which do not root readily when slips (cuttings) are placed in the usual sand, or sand and peatmoss mixture. The newest method consists of cutting a slit in the stem and covering with slightly dampened sphagnum moss and wrapping the moss with a plastic.

Alkaline Soil—This is the opposite of acid soil. Desert plants usually thrive in an alkaline or sweet soil. However, it may contain too many of the alkali salts and very few plants can thrive under such conditions.

Alternate—A term used to describe the position of leaves on the stem of a plant when they are not opposite, but alternate, that is, first on one side and then on the other.

Amendment, Soil—Any material, other than fertilizer which may be added to the soil to improve it. Lime is added to reduce the acidity. Sulphur is added to increase the acidity. Peatmoss, salt, boron and other materials are other soil amendments.

Ammonium Sulphate or Sulphate of Ammonia—A nitrogenous fertilizer commonly used to add nitrogen to the soil as a plant food, used where acid conditions are desired.

Annuals—Plants which grow from seed, flower, set seed and then die within the year. Many perennials are treated as annuals. Zinnias are a popular annual.

Ants—Common garden insects which are objectionable because they tend to cultivate aphids. Also they make unsightly patches in the lawn and garden. Their tunnels drain the soil and make it too dry for good plant growth. They are noted for biting the gardener.

Aphids—Small sucking insects that attack most kinds of garden plants. They are controlled to some extent by other insects that feed upon them. They are best kept out of the garden by regular applications of sprays. Aphids are particularly destructive by spreading diseases from one plant to another.

Aquatic Plants—Those plants which live in water or in water-logged soils. A water lily is an aquatic that lives in water, cat-tails live in water-logged soils.

Arbor—A shelter composed of vines trained over a framework.

Arboretum—A collection of trees and woody plants arranged for educational and scientific purposes.

Arsenate of Lead—An arsenical material commonly employed as a stomach poison for the control of chewing insects.

Asexual Reproduction—The propagation of plants by slips or cuttings, by budding, by layering, and by division.

Ashes, Wood—Wood ashes contain potassium carbonate and calcium carbonate (lime). Wood ashes may contain from 5 to 7 percent potash, 1 to 1.5 percent phosphoric acid and up to 25 or 30 percent lime. If allowed to leach (wash out) they will lose most of their potash. Apply to the garden at the rate of 5 to 10 pounds per 100 square feet. They should not be used on lawns or near acid loving plants.
Coal ashes may be used to lighten heavy soils. They contain very little of the major plant foods, but do contain small amounts of sulphur, copper and other of the minor elements.

Ball—The rounded mass of roots and soil that fill a pot; the roots and soil attached to a tree or shrub after digging.

Balled and Burlapped (B & B)—The term applied to wrapping a root ball in burlap and tying with a stout cord. The burlap need only to be loosened at planting time.

Banding, Tree—A stripe treated with a sticky compound that will catch and hold insects as they try to crawl up a tree. The bands are placed a few feet above ground so that the sticky strip will not be fouled by dust.

Basal Rot—A serious disease attacking the bottom (base) of narcissus, hyacinths and crocus.

Bedding Plants—Planting in beds to obtain mass effects, usually a combination of low growing and taller growing plants. Ordinarily bedding plants are greenhouse grown to attain a uniformity of growth and to permit setting the beds early in the summer.

Biennial—A plant that must go through a rest period before it will flower, i.e., the seed are planted one season and the plants wintered over before they will flower and fruit, and then die. Sweet William is an example.

Bonemeal—A slow-acting fertilizer made from animal bones. High in phosphorus, it is a safe fertilizer to use around plants. Normally containing 1 to 3 percent nitrogen, 23 to 25 percent phosphorus. To be useful, the soil must contain humus to support the bacteria which cause the bonemeal to decompose and become plant food. This process may take from 6 months to 3 years.

Border—The plantings around the perimeter of the yard or along the driveway or walks are commonly referred to as borders. Shrub border, flower border, etc.

Borer—Insects that bore into the wood of trees, shrubs and plants. They do serious injury to peach and dogwood trees, but may also attack many other plants—lilacs, rhododendrons, etc. Best control is to prevent entry by spraying tree and shrub trunks and limbs with DDT about the time the eggs hatch and the larvae (worms) crawl to a suitable place for boring into the trunk or branch.

Boron—A minor element that is often deficient in local soils. It is important to the successful growing of beets, lima beans, occasionally other plants. Twenty-Mule Team borax is the usual form obtained for garden use. One, maximum two, tablespoonsful to the sprinkling can full of water applied to 100 square feet of area. An overdose can be injurious to plants.

Broad-Leaved Evergreens—Shrubs and trees that retain their foliage during the winter and that are not conifers (needle leaved). Rhododendrons, evergreen azaleas, Southern magnolia, Leucothoe, etc., are examples. The California privet is considered to be a broad-leaved although defoliated occasionally during the winter.

Bud-Joint—The point of union between the budded or grafted top and the root stock. Usually the bud-joint is near the surface of the ground on roses and most dwarf fruit trees. It is conspicuous and usually represents a slight bend in the trunk or stem.

Columnar—A tree or shrub that has a narrow or column type of growth. Usually there is not much difference in the diameter at the base and near the top. The Irish juniper is a good example to this type of growth. The Lombardy poplar was popular for this reason.

Coldframe—An enclosed and covered frame, the top covered with glass or plastic and so situated that it catches the rays of the sun. Useful in starting plants or keeping young plants growing in the early spring. Seldom safe to use before mid-March for hardy plants; April for very tender ones.

Chewing Insects—Those insects which eat the leaves of plants, such as the Japanese beetle and the tomato hornworm, as distinguished from sucking insects that suck the juices from a plant. Chewing insects are controlled with stomach poisons and with synthetic materials such as DDT that affect their nervous systems.

Conifers—Needled trees and shrubs that with few exceptions retain their needles over several years. The pines, yews, arbor-vitae, hemlock, and spruce are examples.

Corm—A bulbous underground fleshy stem that is solid. Gladiolus and crocus have corms. True bulbs are made up of scales or layers.

Compost—Decayed leaves and vegetable matter usually mixed with soil and fertilizer. A loose material high in vegetable material content. Valuable in improving soils for gardens, potting mixtures, etc. Lime may be added in the preparation to reduce the acid content for use on lawns and in soils where plants do not tolerate high acidity are to be grown. Compost is usually made without the use of lime so that it will be useful around azaleas and other acid-soil-loving plants.

Drain-Tile—A cylinder made by baking clay. Usually laid without covering the joints so the excess moisture may seep into the drain tile. Primary use is to remove the excess moisture from the soil. It should be laid with a slope of 6 inches in 100 feet. The primary benefit is to avoid having open ditches which interfere with the use of the land.

Deciduous—Plants that go into a dormant stage during the winter and drop their leaves. Maple, dogwood, some azaleas and magnolias are deciduous.

Deep-Rooted—A term used to denote that type of root growth which is several feet below the surface of the ground. Oaks and hickories are deep rooted trees in contrast with maple trees whose roots are on the surface or close to it.

Dormant—Plants that have ceased active growth and are in a resting stage. Usually this refers to the winter resting period, but some plants have a dormant period during the summer such as the oriental poppies.

Duster—A device used to blow finely divided insecticides and fungicides onto the foliage of plants. Some kinds operate like a bellows, others by plunger action. A quick way to apply pesticides to plants, but it is most successful when there is some dampness on the foliage. Properly used, a duster gives as effective coverage as a sprayer.

Egg Masses—Most insects lay their eggs in clusters, commonly referred to as egg masses. The cluster of eggs deposited on a twig by the Praying Mantis is an example.

Evergreens—Trees and shrubs and plants that retain their foliage all year long, conifers and broad-leaved. Vinca minor and Pachysandra are evergreen plants.

Fibrous-Rooted—Plants that have much branched root systems such as the azalea, boxwood and barberry.

Fastigate—Erect, narrow or columnar type of growth, usually having slightly greater width at the base than at the top.

Fall—Term applied to the three outer segments of the iris flower. Originally the falls hung down, but modern iris form is to have the falls extend outward at right angles from the base of the flower.

Fertilization—Two meanings: 1. the union of pollen with the female reproductive body (eggs) to prduce off-spring (seeds). And, 2. the application of plant food to the soil.

Fertilizer—Any material added to the soil which aids plant growth or increases the quality of yield of the plants. Organic fertilizers are composed of natural products, such as cottonseed meal, raw rock phosphate, etc. Inorganic or chemical fertilizers contain, in part or wholly, material derived from chemical action such as nitrate of soda, superphosphate, etc. Organic materials formerly were considered safe to use about plants at any time and in any way. Much of the injury by inorganic fertilizers was due to the very active forms of nitrogen which they contained. Today there are inorganic fertilizers containing forms of nitrogen which do not injure the plants regardless of how they are applied.

Fire—A name given to the botrytis blight of tulip.

Fire-Blight—The name of a serious disease of pear trees, some varieties of apples, quinces, cotoneaster, haw-thorn and a number of others. The disease blackens the new growth and shrivels the stems. Controlled with the antibiotic, Terramycin.

Flagstone—Rocks that may be split into layers with fairly smooth surfaces and used for walks and patio floors.

Flat—The name of a shallow box in which seed may be sown or seedlings planted. Usually 16 by 22½ inches in length and width and from 2 to 4 inches deep.

Floribunda—The name given to a type of rose produced by crossing hardy hybrid tea roses with polyantha or rambler rose. Flowers are larger. Sometimes the bush is larger than that of the polyanthas.

Flower Pot—A clay or plastic container for the growing of plants. It may or may not have a drainage hole in the bottom (they all should). Shallow pots are called bulb pans, ¾ pots are usually referred to as azalea pots. Temporary pots made of pressed peat or other such materials have recently come into general use. Some of the materials contain fertilizers.

Foliage Plants—Plants that are grown for their leaves or foliage only, although all of them have some form of flower under favorable conditions. The Philodendron, Dracaena, Coleus are examples of foliage plants.

Forcing—This term refers to growing plants so that they grow and flower at a season other than is normal. Bulbs may be forced into bloom in the winter months by bringing them into warmth and light after they have developed a suitable root system. Many other kinds of plants such as we see at the big spring flower shows may be forced under suitable conditions.

Foundation Planting—The plants which are grown near the foundation of a building. Generally a foundation planting includes shrubs, but occasionally perennials, even annuals may be included.

Frost—A freezing condition. Frost in the ground refers to a layer either on the surface or below the surface that is frozen.

Frost Injury—Damage done to plants that have started growth in the spring or before they have matured in the fall, as distinct from damage done during the winter by below freezing temperatures.

Fumigation—The control of insects by gases applied usually within an enclosed area such as a tank, tent, or even under a plastic cover.

Fungicide—A material used to destroy or control diseases. A fungicide applied to the foliage of a plant is to prevent the entry of disease.
Very few materials will destroy a disease once it has penetrated the tissues of a plant, thus the standard procedure is to try to kill the disease before it enters the plant tissue by covering the foliage, fruit, or even bark with a protective material.

Germination—The beginning of plant growth in a seed. The percentage of the seeds that sprout is the rate of germination.

Grafting—The inserting of a piece of one plant upon a compatible or related plant. The one into which it is inserted is usually referred to as the root-stock but grafts may be made on any part of another plant. A graft is a piece of the twig or branch as distinguished from just the bud that is taken out of the twig for budding.

Grafted Plant—One that has grown from a graft inserted in another plant. A practice common to the propagation of desirable trees and many plants.

Globe-Shaped—A round or globular shape of the top of a plant, either natural as in a Globe Arbor-vitae or artificially created by pruning.

Gravelly Soil—Soil that contains a considerable proportion of gravel or small stones.

Greenhouse—A glass or plastic covered structure for the growing of plants, usually heated to keep temperatures favorable to plant growth.

Green Manure—Certain crops that are grown to be plowed or spaded into the soil to improve it through increased humus and/or the addition of nitrogen such as is supplied by clover, vetches, etc.

Greens, Edible—Young plant stems and/or leaves that may be consumed either raw or cooked. Spinach, kale, dandelions, nasturtiums, etc., are considered edible greens.

Greens, Ornamental—Any green branches or foliage that may be grown for enhancing the garden or for decorative purposes indoors.

Ground Cover—Plant material, such as ivy, myrtle, etc., that is used to cover the ground, sometimes between shrubs or trees, sometimes an entire area. Grass is seldom included in the meaning of this phrase.

Hardening-Off—The growing of plants under conditions which will enable them to take out-of-door temperatures after being grown under controlled conditions in a cold-frame, hotbed or greenhouse. Usually done by steps, each one a little colder than the previous one.

Hardy—Plants that are adapted to the winter temperatures of an area. Half-hardy indicates that they may be able to take some or partial normal winter conditions: for others it means they need some protection: and for some annuals that they can be started out-of-doors even though the cold has not passed for the season.

Hardwood Cutting—Pieces of dormant wood taken in the fall that will develop into a new plant under suitable conditions. Rose cuttings taken during the winter are a common method of propagating new roses on their own roots.

Heart-Rot—The destruction of the heartwood of a tree. Diseases that work in the center of a limb or trunk of a tree. Usually weaken and may destroy the tree.

Heaving—The pushing of plants or other materials out of the soil by the alternate freezing and thawing of the soil. Plant injury may come from the breaking of the roots or by exposing the roots to the drying action of the air. Usually prevented by covering the soil with a mulch after it has once frozen.

Hedge—The growing of any kind of plant in a row and keeping it trimmed to more or less straight lines. Many kinds of trees and shrubs may be trained into a hedge. The narrower a hedge is kept the more trimming is required.

Heel—The small piece of old wood that is attached to the new growth when it is pulled from a branch. Some believe it necessary to have a heel to improve the rooting of such a cutting. However, the heel can prevent firming the soil about the end of the cutting and the air pocket thus created can have the opposite effect.

Heeling-In—The storing of dormant plants in a trench, the roots covered with soil until they can be put in their permanent location. The usual practice in heeling-in plants is to dig a ditch a foot or two in width but not deep with the dirt placed on one side to more or less support the tops. Dirt is spread over the roots and, if possible, worked in among them so that there are no air-pockets. Plants may be stored under such conditions for several months if necessary.

Heater Cable—An insulated electric cable used to heat hotbeds or to provide heat to the under side of a propagating bench. The use of an electric heater cable has practically eliminated the use of stable manure as a means of heating a hot bed.

Herbaceous Border—A bed planted with non-woody plants along the side of an open space or at the border of the garden. It is not uncommon to have a herbaceous border in front of a shrub planting.

Herbicide—Materials applied to weeds to kill them. Tendency today is to develop materials which are specific for one kind of plants. Some herbicides work only on broad-leaved weeds as distinguished from the grasses. Some herbicides may be applied to keep seeds from germinating, others to prevent the growth of plants between crops already growing.

Hill—A term used to describe raising the soil to a slight mound for planting, or refers to setting plants some distance apart. In the case of the winter protection of roses, the soil is hilled up around the crown of the bush.

Hoe—A flat bladed tool used in cultivating the soil and removing weeds. It also refers to the act of doing this type of work.

Hormone—A substance which affects the functions of various parts of a plant. Some hormones stimulate the formation of roots, others the setting of fruits. Within the plants certain hormones are produced which stimulate growth, etc.

Hose, Garden—A flexible rubber or plastic tubing used to convey water from a hydrant to a flower bed or where needed.

Hose in Hose—Term used to describe a semi-double flower in which the rows of petals are arranged in a circle within a circle.

Hotbed—A heated enclosure usually covered with glass or plastic to permit the entry of light. Used to grow plants or seedlings when out of door temperatures are too low. The hotbed may be heated by electric cable, by hot air flues, or as formerly by decaying stable manure. Enables the growing of plants in late winter without a major structure and equipment.

Hot-House—Common term applied to greenhouses.

House Plants—Plants that may be grown indoors under normal household conditions of light, heat and humidity.

Humus—Partially decayed plant material that is produced by bacteria action or decay. The finer the decayed plant particles are the better the distribution through the soil. Humus holds moisture, separates soil particles and in many other ways improves the condition of the soil. Without humus there would be no bacteria action in the soil.

GARDEN GLOSSARY

Hybrid—The product from cross breeding of two or more species. It can be either a natural cross or an artificially made cross. Hybrids usually are more vigorous and productive than inbreds.

Immune—Free or unaffected by a disease. Resistant means partially susceptible, immune means unaffected under any conditions.

Inoculation—May be beneficial or injurious. The placing of beneficial bacteria on the seed of a legume is a common meaning of the term.

Inorganic—Not living is the strict meaning. Gardenwise, it refers to fertilizers produced chemically.

Insecticide—A material, either chemical or organic, which will cause the death of an insect. Some insecticides kill when eaten, others suffocate the insect, and a third class destroys the insects' nervous system. Occasionally repellants are referred to as insecticides. Because of the different methods of functioning, which are necessitated by the habits of the insects, insecticides are grouped—1. Stomach poisons, those that poison the insect when eaten. 2. Contact poisons that kill upon coming in contact with the insect, 3. those that suffocate such as gases or oils, and 4. DDT and similar ones that destroy some part of the insects' functioning parts.

Internode—The space between the nodes of a plant's stem or branches. Is especially noticeable on plants with hollow stems such as bamboo, alder, hydrangeas. At varying distances the stem is closed by a form of growth known as the node (the point where leaves arise, buds form, etc.)

Iron—One of the minor mineral elements that is essential to plant growth. The lack of iron in azaleas produces a yellowing of the leaves although the veins retain their green color. This is called chlorosis. Iron is unavailable to many plants in a sweet soil, hence the higher the acidity the more available iron is to certain groups of plants.

Japonica—A name often applied to the Japanese quince, but incorrectly. It should be used to refer to Japan as an area of origin, as Camellia japonica, etc.

Larva—The first stage of growth of an insect after hatching from an egg. Usually this is a soft bodied worm-like insect.

Lath-House—A structure covered with slats to let air and light through the plants. It reduces the intensity of light and helps to increase the humidity by reducing the air circulation.

Lath-shade—Slats spaced a short ways apart on a frame without side walls used to cover plants without touching them.

Lawn—The area planted to grass about the residence or in the garden. The grass in a lawn is kept cut at an appropriate height as distinguished from a field or pasture where it is allowed to grow and is used for a different purpose. The lawn provides a portion of the setting for the residence.

Lawn-mower—A mechanical device for cutting the grass. There are reel-type lawnmowers that have curved blades which press the grass against a cutter bar in cutting the grass. The rotary lawnmower consists of a blade rotating at a very high speed that severs the grass blades by impact. The third type of lawnmower, the sickle bar, has a reciprocating blade that cuts the grass as the blades push it against guards.
Many of today's lawnmowers are operated by gasoline or electric motors and many of them are propelled by these power units.

Lawn-broom—A series of long bamboo or wire fingers mounted on a long handle and used to sweep the leaves, grass or other material, as contrasted with a rake which is used to pull these materials. A light and flexible tool that is necessary to the satisfactory maintenance of the lawn.

Layering—The method of propogating plants vegetatively by covering a portion of the stem or branches with soil. A notch should be cut at the point where rooting is desired. It is advisable to keep the cut open to prevent healing. A layer of dirt is then put over the point to keep it moist and to prevent the roots from drying during the early stages of growth. Once the roots have formed and begun to function the branch may be severed from the parent. It is a new plant complete with its own root system.
There are air-layering and mound layering, as well as the branch layering described above.

Leader—The central trunk of a tree or shrub from which the side branches develop. Some conifers will not grow in a normal shape once the leader has been destroyed.

Leaf-miner—A tiny insect that lives between the surfaces of a leaf. Particularly injurious to the boxwood, but disfiguring to the holly and the columbine. May be controlled by a surface application of DDT or Methoxychlor just before the period of emergence.

Leafmold—The decayed leaves usually covering a forest floor—the decayed leaves lying below the more recent and undecayed top layer and the soil.

Leaf-spot—Any one of several plant diseases that kill a portion of the leaf as they develop. Some are known by this or similar names—Blackspot of roses, etc.

Legume—Any plant that takes nitrogen from the air through nitrifying bacteria that live upon its roots. Clover, lespedeza, garden beans and peas, locust and many other plants belong to the leguminosae family.

Lifting—A term referring to the digging of plants, bulbs, etc., not necessarily connected with harvesting.

Light—Light is of importance to plants in their normal functioning. They cannot live without it. Many of their important developments are controlled by the amount of light, or the light rays which they receive. Chrysanthemums do not begin to form flower buds until the days get shorter. The poinsettia will not develop color in its bracts until the nights are 12 to 13 hours in length.

Lime—A compound, usually natural, containing a large portion of calcium in such a form that it will neutralize the soil acids. Ground or pulverized limestone, a natural rock, is commonly used to treat soils to reduce the acidity and make them more favorable for plant growth. Wood ashes and other materials contain lime and may be used for this purposes. Lime, more properly the term calcium, refers to a mineral which is used in the plant structural growth.
Lime is also supplied in the form of pulverized oystershells and other lime bearing materials.

Lime-loving plants—This refers to that group of plants which grow best in soils that are well supplied with calcium—conversely low in acidity.

Lime-sulphur—A compound of lime and sulphur used to control scale insects and plant diseases. It cannot be used upon many plants when air temperatures are about 85°F. Dormant strength lime sulphur is applied to deciduous plants while they are dormant. Summer strength lime-sulphur is used on plants that are growing.

Liquid manure—A term formerly associated with the soaking of fresh animal manures in a container of water. A portion of the plant nutrients were dissolved from the manure so that the liquid contained considerable of the plant foods. Today the term is commonly applied to chemical (inorganic) fertilizers that are dissolved in water and applied to the plants.

Loam—A grade of soil that is in between a clay and a muck or sandy soil. It has a moderate humus content as well as some sand. Loams are much easier to prepare and till than a clay soil.

Leaf, entire—A simple leaf such as on the forsythia.

Compound leaf—Leaflets attached to a stem such as the walnut and rose. A double compound leaf—leaflets attached to a branch of the stem such as a mimosa.

Leaf Mulcher—A mechanical device for pulverizing or breaking fallen leaves into small pieces.

Maggots—The soft, legless larvae of flies. They are especially troublesome in apples, cabbage, etc.

Magnesium—One of the minor mineral elements essential to the growth of plants. Magnesium deficiency is usually displayed by a narrow brown edging of the leaves, also by the lowering of the sugar content of some fruits. It is commonly supplied in the form of Epsom salts. A heaping tablespoonful of the Epsom salts to a sprinkling can full of water will adequately treat 100 square feet of area. An over-dose can be injurious to plant growth.

Manure—Animal and vegetable matter used to enrich the soil. A product from cattle and dairy farms. Usually low in plant food, but rich in bacteria, amino acids, and other elements necessary to good plant growth. Old or rotted manure normally has lost a considerable portion of the major plant foods (nitrogen). Fresh animal manure may be, and usually is, too strong to be applied to growing plants. Horse manure is much stronger than cow manure. Poultry manure cannot be safely used around plants until it has aged.

Mattock—A grub-hoe—A pick axe type of head on a handle. Used to dig in hard soils, or root-filled soils.

Mature—To describe the stage of growth of fruit or a plant. Ripe has the same meaning when applied to fruits. The wood of a plant is manure when the seasonal growth has stopped and the starches have been converted to sugar. In this condition it is not subject to winter injury.

Metaldehyde baits—Poisonous baits effective in killing slugs and snails. Metaldehyde attracts these pests. Place small quantities under pots, boards, rocks where pets and children will not have access to it, but leave a crack for the slugs and snails to get to the poison.

Methyl Bromide—Colorless volatile liquid used to disinfect soil, grain and dormant plants as a means of destroying insects, including nematodes.

Mildew—Common name for several fungi that attack garden plants when days are warm and nights are cool. Gives the plants a downy covering which later turns them black and wrinkled. Controlled through the use of sulphur, Karathane and Phaltan. Sulphur cannot be used when air temperatures are above 85°F.

Miner, leaf—Tiny worms that live between the surfaces of leaves. Boxwood leaf miner weakens plants; miners in holly and columbine disfigure the foliage. DDT or Methoxychlor applied to the foliage prior to emergence effective in controlling miners.

Miscible oils—Oils that will mix with water. Used to control scale insects on evergreens. Best applied with a sprayer equipped with a mechanical agitator.

Mites—Name applied to the tiny sucking insects that infest house and garden plants. Red spider mite, cyclamen mite, etc., are among the most troublesome. Number of materials available commercially for their control. Malathion, Dimite, Aramite, Kilmite, etc., sold for this purpose. Materials should be applied three times at 3 to 8 day intervals, depending upon air temperatures. At the higher temperatures the interval should be short as the life cycle of these pests is much shorter than when the weather is cooler.

GARDEN GLOSSARY

Mosaic—A virus disease that weakens and kills plants. Usually evident by a yellowish streaking of the green leaves. In flowers sometimes produces streaking of the colors in the blooms (tulips). All infected plants should be removed and destroyed to prevent spread of disease by sucking insects, the chief carriers of the virus diseases.

Mulch—Name applied to various kinds of materials used to keep the soil cool, reduce evaporation, control weeds, etc. Peatmoss, vermiculite, sawdust, compost, salt hay, peanut hulls, ground corncobs, etc., used for this purpose.

Mulching—The spreading of a mulch material over the soil. The depth of a mulch will vary with the nature of the material. An inch of peatmoss, two inches of sawdust, three inches of corncobs, four inches of pine needles, indicate the variations in depth of materials commonly used to control weeds. A nitrogen material, organic or inorganic, should be applied with the material to supply the needs of the bacteria which feed on the mulch. Without this supplemental application of nitrogen the bacteria will rob the soil.

Naphthalene—Active ingredient in moth balls and flakes used to repel moths. Also used to destroy thrips and mites on stored bulbs. Apply in paper bags or other closures to confine the fumes for a few days. About a tablespoonful of the flakes to 50 gladiolus corms. After a week's time remove excess flakes and allow free air circulation.

Nematodes—Tiny worm-like animals that infest the soil. Many kinds, some beneficial, some injurious to plants. Several kinds infest roots of roses, boxwood and other ornamentals, robbing the plants of food and reducing the functioning of the root systems. Certain chemicals are useful for killing Nematodes. Some can be used around living plants, majority of chemicals will kill all living plants.

Nicotine—An extract from tobacco used in killing by contact, sucking insects such as thrips and aphids. A poison that should be handled with care.

Nitrogen—One of the major plant foods applied to crops. Available in many forms, both organic and inorganic. Essential to leaf growth. Lack of nitrogen usually evident by paleness of green color of leaves. Poor color may be due to other causes such as lack of air, disease, etc. Percentage of nitrogen in fertilizer is the first figure of three given on the tag 5-10-5 means 5 percent nitrogen.

Nutrient solution—A solution containing all of the foods needed for plant growth, as used in water culture (hydroponics).

Oil Sprays—Compounds of mineral and vegetable oils used to control scale insects on trees and shrubs. Oils to be safe must be thoroughly emulsifiable in water. When diluted the solution should be kept thoroughly agitated especially if it is to be used on evergreens.

Organic—Plant or animal material. Organic fertilizers are those composed of pulverized or ground plant materials such as cottonseed meal, or animal products such as bloodmeal, tankage, bone meal, etc.

Pan—A name given to shallow flower pots used for germinating seeds and forcing bulbs.

Paper mulch—Paper or plastic materials used between plants to control weeds and prevent the loss of moisture from the soil through evaporation. Widely used in certain areas on special crops, such as pineapple in Hawaii.

Parasite—Plant or insect that attaches itself to a plant and obtains food from the host. Dodder is a common parasite of some kinds of plants in this area. Dogticks obtain their food supply from animals.

Peat—Partially decayed deposits of plant materials from ancient lake beds and similar situations. Two kinds in common commerce—sedge peat and sphagnum peat. The former is a black material that breaks down fairly quickly when mixed with soil. The sphagnum peat is a brownish material, often called German peat, that is widely used for mulching and soil improvement. Both of these are to be found in the U. S.

Perennials—Plants which under suitable conditions live for two or more years. Many tropical perennials which flower from seed in one year may be treated as annuals. Peonies, daylilies, and a large number of other garden plants are perennials.

Perianth—The name given to part of a flower when the calyx and the petals form a unit as a whole—such as in the lily.

Persistent—Blooms or parts that last much longer than usual. Also refers to plants that remain in bloom a long time.

Petal—One of the usually colored segments of the flower. Together they form the coralla.

Phosphate—A general term used for compounds of phosphorus, one of the three essential major elements needed for plant growth. In many soils phosphates are so lacking that an application of just phosphate produces visible results in growth—sometimes referred to as the "poor man's fertilizer". Formerly sold as "acid phosphate", which was somewhat of a misnomer since the acid referred to the manufacturing process and not to its effect upon the soil. Today, commonly sold as, superphosphate.

Photoperiodism—Refers to the effect of differences in length of day upon the plants functioning. Some plants are called short-day plants; some are known as long-day plants, and then there are those which do not seem to be affected and those that are intermediate. Very important to many common plants such as chrysanthemums, poinsettias, sweetcorn, etc.

Photosynthesis—The process that takes place in the leaves which in the presence of sunlight converts carbon dioxide, water and air into starches and sugars.

Physiological diseases—Diseases that are not due to fungi or bacteria, but are due to lack of certain materials such as iron, magnesium, potash and in the case of tomatoes, an imbalance, usually due to excess nitrogen, or to too much water or too little water.

Pinching—The cutting or pinching off of terminal growth to stimulate branching. Most widely used on annual plants, but important also for potted plants, some shrubs, dahlias, and chrysanthemums.

Plant breeding—The placing of the pollen of one flower on the pistil of another. This is commonly done by insects, but also by people interested in producing better flowers, plants, or crops.

Plant foods—Usually refers to the three elements nitrogen, potash and phosphate. Sometimes includes the minor elements. Most soils in this area are deficient in nitrogen and phosphate. The common fertilizers usually contain 20 percent, in various proportions such as the familiar 5-10-5 or the 10-6-4. The value of a fertilizer not only depends upon the quantity of plant food contained but also the form in which the materials are contained. Each can be supplied in many forms. There are highly soluble plant foods, some which may be absorbed through the leaves. Others are very slow acting and will not injure tender roots. Raw bone meal may be used to supply some of the potash but it is very slow acting.

Planting—Sometimes refers to the arrangement of plants within a garden or border. Commonly means to place the plant, bulb or seed in the soil.

Plant lice—Tiny soft-bodied sucking insects that are most commonplace in the garden. Spread diseases by sucking the sap from one plant and then moving to another. Usually killed by a contact insecticide such as lictotine sulphate, and various other materials, including Malathion.

Plunge—To sink a pot up to its rim in soil, peatmoss or some other material.

Pollen—The dusty material borne on the anthers of a plant. It is the male cells of a plant and must be transferred to the stigma or pistil of the flower. Some plants are known as pollen bearing—male plants, such as the holly.

Polyethylene—Plastic material sold under various trade names which has many uses in the garden. Covers for cold frames and green houses in place of glass, wrapping plants and their roots to prevent drying out, covering seed pots and flats to prevent seed from drying. It is clear, light in weight, and tough. It does not permit the passage of moisture but does allow some inter-change of gases.

Potash—One of the three major elements in plant food. A mineral mined from the soil, also obtained from wood ashes. Potash is commonly believed important to the stem and fruit of a growing plant. Some plants, such as tobacco require a great deal of potash for desirable growth.

Potting—Usually means to put plants in pots such as young rooted cuttings, but also includes putting bulbs in pots for forcing, as well as seedlings that when grown are to be sold as potted plants.

Pricking-out—The operation of lifting tiny seedlings and planting them in flats or beds. Usually done with a small wooden stick with a sharp point or two points so as to keep some moss or soil on the young roots.

Propagating, Propagation—The growing of more plants either from seed, from cuttings, by budding, grafting, or layering. Grandmother grew many plants from slips. We do it today but call the slips, cuttings.

Pruning—The cutting of branches or twigs to shape a plant, the removal of dead wood, strengthening of a plant, and other modifications is often referred to as pruning. It should be done with sharp tools. The cuts made in pruning should be sealed with a tree dressing to prevent rot organisms from entering the heartwood. Stubs do not heal over and a good workman makes his cuts in such a way as to facilitate healing.

Puddle—Is a mixture of clay and water used to coat the roots of plants to prevent their drying. Also refers to the working of wet soils so that the structure is completely destroyed. This converts clay soils into "adobe-like" condition which excludes air and moisture."

Pulverize—Finely ground material such as lime, sulphur, etc. Pulverized sphagnum moss is chopped up in a mill.

Pyramidal—Cone shaped. The base is spreading and the outline from the edge of the base to the top is more or less straight-sided.

Quicklime—Commonly referes to limestone that has been burned to drive out moisture. It is very quick acting and will injure plants that come in contact with it.

Raceme—Term used to describe flower clusters in which the florets are borne on a stem as contrasted with a spike in which the florets are attached to the central stem. Lilacs are a good example of a raceme. There are drooping racemes, loose racemes, and compact racemes.

Rake—A tool for the pulverizing and leveling of the soil, for the bringing together of leaves, etc. There are wooden rakes, iron rakes, bamboo rakes, and those made from steel strips, all with long handles.

GARDEN GLOSSARY

Red Spider—Name commonly applied to the tiny mite that is a universal pest, sucking the sap from a great many kinds of plants. Since the Red Spider works on the undersides of the leaves his presence is seldom noted until the plant leaves have been greatly weakened. Presence usually indicated by blotched appearance of leaves and by deposits on their undersides.

Repellents—Are various substances which drive insects and animals away either because of color, physical characteristics, or by volatile odors. They do not kill but repel. Any light colored material on the foliage usually repels Japanese beetles.

Resistance—Refers to a plant's ability to resist diseases or to withstand unfavorable weather of one kind or another. Cold resistance refers to ability to escape injury, depending upon degree of cold resistance. Resistance refers to ability in varying degrees, whereas immunity means 100 percent resistance.

Rest-period—A season of inactivity in plant growth usually due to internal factors and not to external, such as cold weather. Many plants must have a rest period, but there are some that continue in full activity throughout the year.

Rhizome—An underground stem thickened in some kinds of plants such as the iris, but root-like in the case of the Sheep Sorrell and Bermuda grass. New plants and roots come from the joints.

Ridging—Consists of pulling the soil into a low ridge, also to the pulling of soil up to the base of plants. Potatoes are usually ridged or hilled.

Ringing—The practice of removing a narrow strip of bark from around a limb to shock the tree into fruiting. The bark only is removed and the ring does not extend into the cambium (sap carrying) layer beneath.

Rogue—The name applied to a plant that is off-type in some way from the others in the row or field. The elimination of rogues in seed production fields helps to fix or develop plants of uniformity in one or more characteristics.

Root-aphids—Sucking insects that work on the roots of some kind of plants. They are more prevalent in the lighter soils.

Root-forming substances—Also called root hormones . . . Materials that stimulate or aid in the formation of roots. Such materials are commonly applied to cuttings.

Rooting media—Materials in which the cuttings are placed during the development of roots, Pulverized sphagnum moss, sand, vermiculite, and various other materials are used for this purpose. They are usually sterile so as to avoid rot.

Root knot—Growths on the roots of plants produced by nematodes. The principal causal agent, the Root knot nematode. Serious on roses, azaleas and other garden plants.

Root-stock—A strong growing species or kind used as an understock for a less vigorous variety. Roses are commonly grown on Rosa multiflora understock.

Root pruning—The cutting of the roots to stimulate a more compact type of growth; to keep them within bounds; to stunt the top growth, and in the case of cabbage to prevent the heads from splitting.

Rotation of crops—A practice involving the change of location in a regular schedule to avoid building up disease organisms, insects, or toxic substances in the soil for certain crops. Common practice among tomato growers, but other crops benefit from this practice.

Runner—A long trailing stem which may take root and develop a new plant. Strawberry runners are a good example of this type of growth.

Sand—A silica form of rock that has no plant food. Its usefulness consists of, when mixed with clay, making the soil more porous and workable, Two kinds of sand, the river sand with smooth edges that will compact, and the sharp bank sand which is much better for garden purposes. Especially is it the more useful form for rooting cuttings.

Sand Culture—The growing of plants in sand, feeding them with nutrient solutions.

Sanitation—The removal of all materials capable of harboring disease and insect pests. Commonly referred to in connection with putting the garden in readiness for winter. However, it should always be a consideration in the problems of keeping the garden free from insects and pests. For example the removal of pokeweed, which is a host of a number of viruses, is always good practice.

Scald—A bleaching of the skin of plants due to too much exposure to the sun, especially in winter.

Scale—Sucking insects that usually are found beneath a hard shell. Some scales are under a fluffy mass. Many kinds are prevalent in the Washington area. Very few Euonymus escape the Euonymus scale for long. Scale insects multiply rapidly and greatly weaken the plants. Many of them can be controlled on deciduous plants effectively by spraying during the winter with lime-sulphur or some other scalicide. Scale insects on evergreen plants are harder to control. Malathion will control many, especially if the spraying is done while the scale insects are in the crawler stage. Emulsifiable oils are effective but should be used with care.

Scion—A piece of a plant (bud or graft) that is to be inserted in the already established rootstock. One of the major methods of propagating the improved varieties of fruits and nuts.

Screens—A planting of tall growing plants (perennials, annuals, shrubs and trees). So named as they are commonly used to screen-off unsightly views, to provide privacy, and as a protection against strong winds.

Selection—The process of choosing those plants which have certain desirable characteristics. If continued over a period of years these characteristics will become fixed and persist. Formerly one of the major steps in plant improvement. Today more emphasis is placed upon crossing.

Self, Selfing—Means using the flower's own pollen upon its stigma. If continued for several years it tends to produce stable characteristics in a plant. Even after hybridization selfing is practiced in order to obtain greater uniformity among the progeny.

Seedless Set—The use of certain hormones on flowers which tend to produce fruit with few seeds. Of more interest than practical value.

Shade, Shading—Is a relative term and consists of using a lath screen or some other material to reduce the intensity of sunlight. Usually most important during the summer months, but also important during the winter to protect plants from the heat of the sun.

Shears—A cutting tool consisting of a sharp blade that presses against a flat surface or of two sharp blades that cut from each direction. Used in pruning, cutting flowers, taking cuttings and in other ways. The small pruner is most commonly used, but there are hedge shears, lopping shears and pole pruners. Good shears are long-lasting useful tools.

Sheath—A term used to describe any part of a plant that encloses another. The buds of the paper-white narcissus are enclosed in a paperthin sheath.

Shifting—Moving plants from pot to pot is the usual meaning.

Shrubs—Refers to woody plants of low to moderate size. Generally with more than one stem, whereas trees are usually restricted to one stem.

Shallow-rooted—Plants whose roots are close to the surface of the ground. They are in sharp contrast with deep-rooted plants, suffer more from drought and are difficult to cultivate around without injury to the roots.

Shade-loving—Those plants which thrive under varying degrees of protection from the sun. Usually refers to those plants that grow under the shade of a tree. Sun-loving is the opposite and refers to those plants which need full sunlight in order to thrive. A sun-loving plant in the north may benefit from some shade or partial shade in the south.

Silt—A type of soil resulting from the deposits of streams. Usually fine and comparatively lacking in sand. Usually considered to be easily worked.

Slugs, Snails—Crawling type of insect that feeds at night on many kinds of plants. Usually leaves a visible trail. Slugs lack the shell of a snail but otherwise they resemble each other. Control through the use of metaldehyde baits which attract them.

Slips—Another name for a cutting. Hardwood cuttings are taken during the dormant season. Softwood cuttings are taken from the new growth just as it begins to become firm. Popular method of propagating shrubs.

Soaker hose—Cotton or plastic hose with either a weave that permits water to slowly soak through onto the ground, or one that has minute holes that permit tiny streams of water to pass through. Very useful in thoroughly wetting the soil without wetting the foliage.

Snow-mold—A disease of lawn grasses in the north, characterized by a cottony growth of the fungus as the snow melts in the spring.

Sod—A name given to a thin layer of grass, roots and soil. Much used in covering a newly graded area, producing a grass cover in a comparatively short time. Varies greatly according to the care given as well as the original seed mixture planted. Sod should be put upon a prepared soil if the roots are to penetrate and become established.

Soil—The name given the earth surface that is composed of clay particles, humus and sand. Generally, it is applied to that earth which is capable of plant growth, although forests may be seen growing among the rocks where there is very little soil.

Soilless Culture—The growing of plants in tanks or supporting material and which receive their food from a nutrient solution.

Soil Testing—The use of chemicals and other devices to measure the acidity, plant food content and humus in the soil. Soil testing kits can be very simple or very elaborate depending upon the need for accuracy in testing. Testing for the minor elements is seldom practical with a testing kit.

Soot—The fine particles deposited in chimneys from coal furnaces. Is sometimes used to propagate cuttings in. Has some nutritive values.

Sootymold—A mold that forms on the honeydew, produced by aphids. Seldom injurious but repulsive in appearance.

Spade, Spading—The spade is a common tool used for digging holes, for turning the soil and for other garden work. The term spading refers to the use of the spade in turning the soil—burying any trash or manure present and for pulverizing the soil so that air and moisture may reach the roots of the crops to be planted. The soil should not be spaded while wet, to do so is to destroy its physical character.

GARDEN GLOSSARY

Spading Fork—A spadelike tool with tines instead of a wide flat blade.

Sphagnum—A name given to moss like plants which thrive in water. The decayed or partially decayed material from these plants is also called sphagnum.

Spike—An elongated spire-like flower cluster. The florets are attached to the stem rather than on individual stalks.

Spine—The sharp pointed growth from stem or leaf, as on a holly leaf.

Sport—A change from type or form of flower or fruit that is markedly different from the rest of the plant, due to some unknown factor. Usually found on a branch rather than the whole plant.

Sprayer, Spraying—A device for applying the solution under pressure to the plant. Widely used for applying insecticides and fungicides, also used for applying herbicides and for other purposes. Most sprayers depend upon a pump action to compress the air in the tank. They are most effective when the spray is finely divided, mistlike, and applied under sufficient pressure to blow the leaves, thus coating both sides.

Spray Injury—Injury to the foliage because the material was not suited to the plant, or was too strong, or applied under unfavorable conditions. Spray injury often resembles disease symptoms.

Spreaders and Stickers—Materials added to the spray mixture to make the spray adhere to the foliage. Detergents are frequently used to remove surface tension so as to give good coverage. The sticker is a chemical material usually sold as a sticker that holds the spray to even glossy or waxy foliage.

Spray Residue—The spray material still adhering to the foliage at time of harvest. This may be a serious problem if one of the non-water soluble materials was used. Ordinarily most of the spray materials disintegrate within a few weeks and the foliage is safe to use as food or feed.

Sprinkler—A device for spraying water on lawns and flower borders. There are many such devises on the market with all manner of adjustments and uses. Most of them have a rotating arm to throw the water to great distances. Nozzles permit regulating the spray from fine, mist-like, to coarse streams.

Spur—One or more of the petals of a flower forming a tube-like structure as in a columbine. The tube is often filled with nectar to attract insects. A fruit spur is a short shoot, usually two years old, that bears the flowers and fruits of apples and pears.

Staking—The practice of fastening stems or flowers to sticks to hold them erect. Common practice both in the greenhouse and in the garden to protect the flower shoots.

Standard—Name applied to the more or less erect petals of a flower. The standard of an iris bloom are the three petals that form the hood over the heart of the flower.

Standards—The rules or forms prescribed for the evaluation of flowers, plants, and fruits as set down by the major group interested in the plant.

Stem—The ascending trunk or stem of the plant from which the leaves emerge or that bears the flowers. Most stems have some stiffness and can support the branches, foliage, flowers and fruit, but there are others with trailing or drooping stems.

Stomach Poisons—Materials which will kill insects if taken into their stomachs. Many such materials are used in controlling the eating and chewing types of insects.

Sterilization—The killing of insects, diseases, and in some cases the weed seeds in soil or plant material through the use of chemicals, stem or heat. Sterilization is important in greenhouse culture to protect plants from diseases under conditions which are very favorable for the development of diseases.

Stolon—A branch or shoot emerging from the crown. It may grow either above or below ground. Rooting may take place at the tip or at the joints. Many grass plants spread by means of the stolons.

Stone Fruit—Plants whose fruits contain a pit or stone. Cherries, peaches, plums, apricots, etc. are stone fruits.

Stool, Stooling—Stems that arise from the crown of a plant, sometimes referred to as suckers. The latter is more appropriate to those stems that arise from the roots rather than from the crown. Oftentimes propagation consists of taking the suckers after they have rooted sufficiently to support the stem.

Stopping—The practice of pinching the tip shoots to prevent further growth. Common practice in raspberries to keep the canes from becoming too long. should be applied to the strong new growths of forsythia.

Stratification—The storing of large seeds in alternate layers of sand, peatmoss, or other materials that retain moisture and keep the seeds from drying out. Stratified seeds are usually stored under low temperatures, but oftentimes under alternating temperatures. This practice greatly improves the germination of seeds— mostly woody seeds such as those of the hollies.

Stunt—A name applied to certain virus diseases that dwarf plants and render them unproductive. Also caused by infestations of nematodes.

Sub-Irrigation—The watering of crops by some underground device. In a few cases where there is an impervious layer somewhat below the surface of the ground it is possible to let water soak down to the layer and thus wet the soil. Usually means applying water through tile, or perforated pipes.

Subsoil—This term refers to the layers of the soil below the top-soil, usually below the six-inch level. Generally, however, refers to the deeper soil, a foot or more below the surface.

Succulents—Plants which have thick fleshy stems and leaves, usually from arid or semi-arid areas. The plants store moisture in these fleshy tissues to take care of their needs between rainy seasons, and in some cases store dew. These plants usually require neutral to alkaline soils for good growth.

Sucker—Unusually refers to a stem that rises from a root such as a lilac; also may come from a bud along the stem of the plant. Usually grows very rapidly, oftentimes is unproductive, and may cause crowding of branches. Some suckers arising from a limb may in a short time become larger than the parent limb.

Sulphur—An element that has many uses. Some plants require sulphur in their growth processes. Sulphur is used as an insecticide and as a scalicide, and is useful to increase the acidity of the soil.

Sun-scald—Injury caused by too much sunlight, or sunlight when the plants are wet—the droplets act as magnifying lens and burn the tender tissues.

Superphosphate—see phosphate.

Syringe—A rubber bulb device for wetting the foliage. The water is forced through small openings and gives a mist-like spray.

Sweet-Soil—A soil that is neutral or above, as contrasted with an acid soil that is below neutral on the pH scale.

Tankage—A mixture of slaughter-house refuse that has been sterilized and pulverized for use as a fertilizer. Usually considered to be a quick-acting material.

Tendril—A slender flexible growth on certain plants which entwines or wraps around objects and supports the vine. Some tendrils actually have disk-like ends that adhere to smooth surfaces.

Thrips—Tiny winged insects that suck the sap from plants. The gladiolus thrip ruins the bloom, causing it to hang limp. The rose thrip prevents the flower from opening. Usually best controlled by spraying with a good contact mixture before the buds begin to show color. Thrips are most troublesome when showers are infrequent.

Top-dressing—Applying compost, fertilizer and other materials to the top of the soil. The food must be carried into the soil by rain. Some fertilizers that are applied as a top dressing are lightly cultivated into the soil, although this is not strictly top-dressing.

Topiary—The training and pruning of plants into images of animals, etc., or into some other unnatural form, such as pillars, chains, arbors, etc.

Top-working—To graft another variety onto the branches of a tree so that when completed the productivity will be entirely of the scions which have been placed on each branch or limb. Only the roots and the trunk remain of the original variety.

Trace Elements—Minor soil elements—minerals that form some part of the life processes or act as catalyses in the plant functions. They occur only in minute quantities in the soil but in their absence the plants are unable to function properly. Boron, manganese, cobalt, copper, zinc are some of these elements. Oftentimes an excess may prove toxic to the plants. Some manufacturers offer combinations of trace elements, or minor elements as they are also called, for garden use.

Transpiration—The process by which water is given off by the leaves of a plant. Tremendous quantities of water are taken up by the roots, flow through the tubes to the leaves and pass out of the leaves through openings called stomata.

Transplanting—The lifting of a plant with its root system intact and moving it to another location. Usually a portion of the roots is lost in the shift, hence the top should be correspondingly reduced to compensate for the root loss. Many plants must be lifted with a ball of earth enclosing the root-system. Deciduous trees and shrubs may be transplanted during the dormant season without a ball of earth but at no time should the roots be allowed to dry out.
Plants often benefit by shading following transplanting. This reduces transpiration and allows the plant to recover from the shock of transplanting.

Tree-dressing—A paste or paint used to cover the wounds of a tree following an injury or pruning. The material to be effective should adhere tightly to the wood. It should not crack or permit entry of disease organisms or in any way inhibit or retard the growth of the callus layer which is to cover the wound.

Trenching—A method of deep digging. Usually the first layer of soil is laid to one side of the trench or taken to the opposite end of the garden. The second spade depth is also removed. The top of the second width is then deposited in the bottom of the first furrow. American gardeners seldom double dig or trench in their soil preparation.

Trowel—A wide blade tool with a short handle used in lifting small plants, in transplanting, or in digging holes for bulbs or for any other use that does not involve the moving of much soil.

Tuber—A swollen underground stem or root that stores food. The potato is a tuber, as is the dahlia root. In same cases the eyes for new growths are on the tuber, in others at the point of attachment to the stem.

INDEX

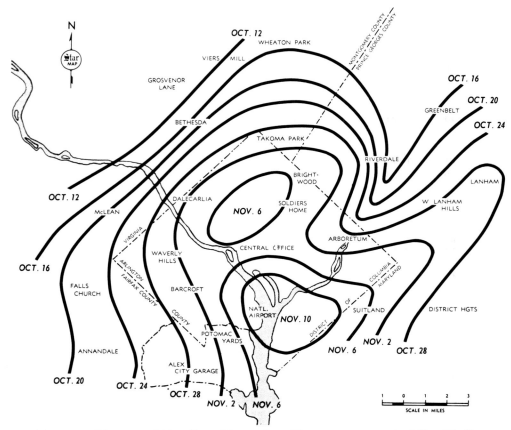

Average Dates of Earliest Freezing Temperatures in The Fall
Based on Observations for Period 1946-60

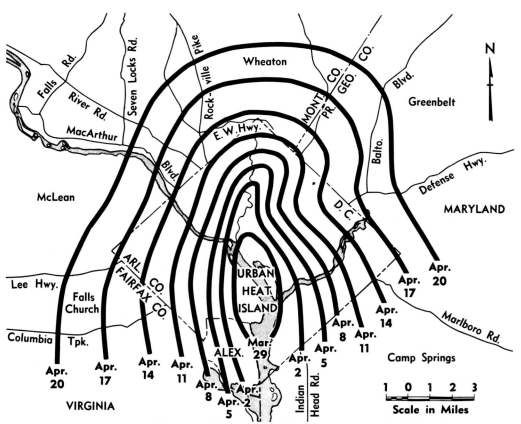

Average Dates of Latest Freezing Temperatures in The Spring
Based on Observations for Period 1946-60

Data prepared by—C. A. Woollum U.S.W.B.

CONVERSION TABLE

For Converting Tons or Pounds Per Acre Into Pints, Cups, Tablespoons, or Teaspoons Per Row or Plant.

From Agriculture Department Tables

Weights of various fertilizing materials per acre, per 1,000 square feet, and per 100 square feet and the approximate equivalent-volume measures for 100 square feet, grouped according to weight in comparison with that of water.

Materials	Weights specified per—			Volume measure
	Acre	1,000 Sq. ft.	100 Sq. ft.	for 100 Sq. ft.
	Pounds	Units	Units	Units
Weight about the same as that of water	1,300	30 Pounds	3 Pounds	3 Pints
	870	20 "	2 "	2 "
(Ex. Cal-Nitro, A-N-L)	435	10 "	1 "	1 "
	220	5 "	½ "	1 Cup
	110	2½ "	¼ "	½ "
Weight about 1.3 that of water	5,660	130 "	13 "	10 Pints
	3,485	80 "	8 "	6 "
(Ex. Ground limestone, ground dolomitic limestone, granular sodium	870	20 "	2 "	1½ "
nitrate potassium sulfate.)	565	13 "	21 Ounces	1 "
	280	6½ "	11 "	1 Cup
Weight about 9/10 that of water.	1,960	45 "	4½ Pounds	5 Pints
	1,650	38 "	3¾ "	4 "
(Ex. ammonium phosphate, super-phosphate, 5-10-5, 4-8-4, etc.	1,220	28 "	2¾ "	3 "
muriate of potash.)	1,000	23 "	2¼ "	2½ "
	785	18 "	30 Ounces	2 "
	610	14 "	21 "	1½ "
	390	9 "	15 "	1 "
	300	7 "	11 "	1½ Cups
	200	4⅝ "	7½ "	1 "
	100	2¼ "	3½ "	¼ "
	50	18 Ounces	2 "	4 Tbs.
	11	5 "	½ "	1 "
Weight about 8/10 that of water.	1,740	40 Pounds	4 Pounds	5 Pints
	650	15 "	1½ "	2 "
(Ex. Epsom salts, bonemeal.)	175	4 "	6½ Ounces	1 Cup
	44	1 "	1½ "	4 Tbs.
Weight about 7/10 that of water.	1,740	40 Pounds	4 Pounds	6 Pints
	1,525	35 "	3½ "	5 "
(Ex. Sewage sludge, Uramon, Ammonium sulfate, granular ammonium	650	15 "	1½ "	2 "
nitrate, aluminum sulfate, granular borax.)	300	7 "	11 Ounces	1 "
	150	3½ "	5½ "	1 Cup
	44	1 "	1½ "	4 Tbs.
	11	5 Ounces	½ "	1 "
Weight about 6/10 that of water.	1,300	30 Pounds	3 Pounds	5 Pints
	545	12½ "	1¼ "	2 "
(Ex. Cottonseed meal, sulfur, fish scrap.)	260	6 "	10 Ounces	1 "
	130	3 "	5 "	1 Cup
Weight about 5/10 that of water.	1,100	25 "	2½ Pounds	5 Pints
	435	10 "	1 "	2 "
(Ex. Hydrated lime.)	220	5 "	8 Ounces	1 "
	110	2½ "	4 "	1 Cup
Manure (moist):				
Loose	13 Tons	600 Pounds	60 Pounds	2 Bushels
Packed	13 "	600 "	60 "	1 "
Dry straw or leaves packed tightly with hands.	5 "	250 "	25 "	2 "

...oximate Equivalent-Volume Measures of Materials to Use in the Row and Per Plant at Various Rates Per 100 Square Feet.

per 100 Sq. Ft.	Rates per 10 feet, rows Spaced—			Rates per Plant, Spaced—		
	3 ft.	2 ft.	1 ft.	5x5 ft.	2¼x2¼ ft.	2x1½ ft.
Pints	3 Pints	2 Pints	1 Pint	2½ Pts.	1 Cup	½ Cup
"	3½ Cups	2½ Cups	1¼ Cups	3 Cups	½ " (h)	¼ " (h)
"	3 "	2 "	1 "	2½ "	½ "	¼ "
"	2½ "	1½ "	¾ "	2 "	6½ Tbs.	3 Tbs. (h)
"	1¾ "	1¼ "	½ " (h)	1½ "	5 "	2½ "
2½ "	1½ "	1 "	½ "	1¼ "	4 "	2 "
2 "	1¼ "	¾ "	6½ Tbs.	1 "	3¼ "	1½ "
1½ "	¾ " (h)	½ " (h)	5 "	¾ "	2½ "	1 " (h)
1 "	½ "	6 Tbs.	3¼ "	½ "	1½ "	2½ Tsp.
1½ Cups	½ "	5 "	2½ "	6 Tbs.	1 "	1½ "
1 "	5 Tbs.	3¼ "	1½ "	4 "	2½ Tsp.	¾ "
½ "	2½ "	1½ "	¾ "	2 "	1¼ "	½ "
4 Tablespoons	1¼ "	2½ Tsp.	1¼ Tsp.	1 "	½ "	¼ "
1 "	1 Tsp.	½ " (h)	⅓ "	¼ "	1/6 "	1/12 "
2 Bushels	½ Bus. (h)	1½ Peck	6 Qts.	½ Bush.	3 Qts.	1½ Qts.
1 "	1 Peck (h)	1 " (s)	3 "	1 Peck	1½ "	¾ "

Tbs.—tablespoon; Tsp—teaspoon; (h) heaping; (s) scant.

Note: Pint of water weighs 1.046 pounds; Acre contains 43,560 sq. ft.; Pint=2 cups=32 tablespoons=96 teaspoons. Measures given are level-full except as noted.